Conversational Repair

Humans are imperfect, and problems of speaking, hearing and understanding are pervasive in ordinary interaction. This book examines the way we "repair" and correct such problems as they arise in conversation and other forms of human interaction. The first book-length study of this topic, it brings together a team of scholars from the fields of anthropology, communication, linguistics and sociology to explore how speakers address problems in their own talk and that of others, and how the practices of repair are interwoven with non-verbal aspects of communication such as gaze and gesture, across a variety of languages. Specific chapters highlight intersections between repair and epistemics, repair and turn construction, and repair and action formation. Aimed at researchers and students in sociolinguistics, speech communication, conversation analysis and the broader human and social sciences to which they contribute – anthropology, linguistics, psychology and sociology – this book provides a state-of-the-art review of conversational repair, while charting new directions for future study.

MAKOTO HAYASHI is Associate Professor in the Department of East Asian Languages and Cultures at the University of Illinois at Urbana-Champaign.

GEOFFREY RAYMOND is Associate Professor of Sociology at the University of California, Santa Barbara.

JACK SIDNELL is Associate Professor of Anthropology at the University of Toronto.

Studies in Interactional Sociolinguistics

Editors

Paul Drew, Marjorie Harness Goodwin, John J. Gumperz, Deborah Schiffrin

1 *Discourse Strategies* John J. Gumperz
2 *Language and Social Identity* edited by John J. Gumperz
3 *The Social Construction of Literacy* Jenny Cook-Gumperz
4 *Politeness: Some Universals in Language Usage* Penelope Brown and Stephen C. Levinson
5 *Discourse Markers* Deborah Schiffrin
6 *Talking Voices: Repetition, Dialogue, and Imagery in Conversational Discourse* Deborah Tannen
7 *Conducting Interaction: Patterns of Behaviour in Focused Encounters* Adam Kendon
8 *Talk at Work: Interaction in Institutional Settings* edited by Paul Drew and John Heritage
9 *Grammar in Interaction: Adverbial Clauses in American English Conversations* Cecilia E. Ford
10 *Crosstalk and Culture in Sino-American Communication* Linda W. L. Young (with foreword by John J. Gumperz)
11 *AIDS Counselling: Institutional Interaction and Clinical Practice* Anssi Perakyla
12 *Prosody in Conversation: Interactional Studies* edited by Elizabeth Couper-Kuhlen and Margret Selting
13 *Interaction and Grammar* edited by Elinor Ochs, Emanuel A. Schegloff and Sandra A. Thompson
14 *Credibility in Court: Communicative Practices in the Camorra Trials* Marco Jacquemet
15 *Interaction and the Development of Mind* A. J. Wootton
16 *The News Interview: Journalists and Public Figures on the Air* Steven Clayman and John Heritage
17 *Gender and Politeness* Sara Mills
18 *Laughter in Interaction* Philip Glenn
19 *Matters of Opinion: Talking about Public Issues* Greg Myers
20 *Communication in Medical Care: Interaction between Primary Care Physicians and Patients* edited by John Heritage and Douglas Maynard
21 *In Other Words: Variation in Reference and Narrative* Deborah Schiffrin
22 *Language in Late Modernity: Interaction in an Urban School* Ben Rampton
23 *Discourse and Identity* edited by Anna De Fina, Deborah Schiffrin and Michael Bamberg
24 *ReportingTalk: Reported Speech in Interaction* edited by Elizabeth Holt and Rebecca Clift
25 *The Social Construction of Literacy*, 2nd Edition edited by Jenny Cook-Gumperz

26 *Talking Voices*, 2nd Edition by Deborah Tannen
27 *Conversation Analysis* edited by Jack Sidnell
28 *Impoliteness: Using Language to Cause Offence* Jonathan Culpeper
29 *The Morality of Knowledge in Conversation* edited by Tanya Stivers, Lorenza Mondada and Jakob Steensig
30 *Conversational Repair and Human Understanding* edited by Makoto Hayashi, Geoffrey Raymond and Jack Sidnell

Conversational Repair and Human Understanding

Edited by

Makoto Hayashi

University of Illinois at Urbana-Champaign

Geoffrey Raymond

University of California, Santa Barbara

Jack Sidnell

University of Toronto

CAMBRIDGE
UNIVERSITY PRESS

University Printing House, Cambridge CB2 8BS, United Kingdom

One Liberty Plaza, 20th Floor, New York, NY 10006, USA

477 Williamstown Road, Port Melbourne, VIC 3207, Australia

314-321, 3rd Floor, Plot 3, Splendor Forum, Jasola District Centre, New Delhi-110025, India

79 Anson Road, #06-04/06, Singapore 079906

Cambridge University Press is part of the University of Cambridge.

It furthers the University's mission by disseminating knowledge in the pursuit of education, learning and research at the highest international levels of excellence.

www.cambridge.org
Information on this title: www.cambridge.org/9781108460156

First published 2013
Reprinted 2013
First paperback edition 2018

A catalogue record for this publication is available from the British Library

Library of Congress Cataloging in Publication data
Conversational repair and human understanding / edited by Makoto Hayashi, Geoffrey Raymond, [and] Jack Sidnell.
p. cm. – (Studies in interactional sociolinguistics ; 30)
ISBN 978-1-107-00279-1 (Hardback)
1. Conversation analysis. 2. Speech acts (Linguistics) 3. Sociolinguistics. 4. Social interaction. I. Hayashi, Makoto. II. Raymond, Geoffrey. III. Sidnell, Jack.
P95.45C6685 2013
306.3´46–dc23

2012024321

ISBN 978-1-107-00279-1 Hardback
ISBN 978-1-108-46015-6 Paperback

Contents

Figures

Tables

Contributors

JULIJA BARANOVA, Language and Cognition, Max Planck Institute for Psycholinguistics

REBECCA BARNES, School of Social and Community Medicine, University of Bristol

JOE BLYTHE, Language and Cognition, Max Planck Institute for Psycholinguistics

PENELOPE BROWN, Language and Cognition, Max Planck Institute for Psycholinguistics

MARK DINGEMANSE, Language and Cognition, Max Planck Institute for Psycholinguistics

TYKO DIRKSMEYER, Language and Cognition, Max Planck Institute for Psycholinguistics

PAUL DREW, Sociology, University of York

SUSAN EHRLICH, Languages, Literatures and Linguistics, York University

N. J. ENFIELD, Language and Cognition, Max Planck Institute for Psycholinguistics

SIMEON FLOYD, Language and Cognition, Max Planck Institute for Psycholinguistics

SONJA GIPPER, General Linguistics, University of Cologne

RÓSA S. GÍSLADÓTTIR, Language and Cognition, Max Planck Institute for Psycholinguistics

KAORU HAYANO, Center for Foreign Language Education, Ochanomizu University

MAKOTO HAYASHI, East Asian Languages and Cultures, University of Illinois at Urbana-Champaign

JOHN HERITAGE, Sociology, University of California, Los Angeles

GERTIE HOYMANN, Language and Cognition, Max Planck Institute for Psycholinguistics

KOBIN H. KENDRICK, Language and Cognition, Max Planck Institute for Psycholinguistics

MARDI KIDWELL, Communication, University of New Hampshire

GENE H. LERNER, Sociology, University of California, Santa Barbara

STEPHEN C. LEVINSON, Language and Cognition, Max Planck Institute for Psycholinguistics

LILLA MAGYARI, Language and Cognition, Max Planck Institute for Psycholinguistics

ELIZABETH MANRIQUE, Language and Cognition, Max Planck Institute for Psycholinguistics

DOUGLAS W. MAYNARD, Sociology, University of Wisconsin

RICHARD OGDEN, Language & Linguistic Science, University of York

GEOFFREY RAYMOND, Sociology, University of California, Santa Barbara

JEFFREY D. ROBINSON, Communication, Portland State University

TANYA ROMANIUK, Linguistics and Applied Linguistics, York University

GIOVANNI ROSSI, Language and Cognition, Max Planck Institute for Psycholinguistics

LILA SAN ROQUE, Language and Cognition, Max Planck Institute for Psycholinguistics

EMANUEL A. SCHEGLOFF, Sociology and Applied Linguistics, University of California, Los Angeles

JACK SIDNELL, Anthropology and Linguistics, University of Toronto

FRANCISCO TORREIRA, Language and Cognition, Max Planck Institute for Psycholinguistics

TRACI WALKER, Language and Linguistic Science, University of York

1 Conversational repair and human understanding: an introduction

Makoto Hayashi, Geoffrey Raymond, and Jack Sidnell

1.1 Introduction

Any serious effort to contend with the real time production and understanding of human actions in everyday interaction can scarcely avoid noting that they are characterized by the routine occurrence of troubles, "hitches," misunderstandings, "errors," and other infelicities. Indeed, these phenomena – and participants' efforts to contend with them – are so ubiquitous that very few approaches within the human and social sciences have avoided commenting on, or contending with them, in some way. In many approaches within the social sciences, researchers looked past these phenomena altogether, treating them as epiphenomenal to the proper object of study (however that is defined) or as matters to be reduced, remedied, or otherwise overcome. More recently approaches from various disciplines have recognized their import in different ways, thereby raising the more nettlesome issue of just what is to be done with them or what can be done with them. Here, approaches vary considerably: some have simply incorporated these phenomena into the larger domain of human conduct being investigated (whether it is the psyche in psychology, ritual and culture in anthropology, or social structure in sociology), conflating a range of matters that are more profitably treated as distinct from one another. In many such cases, however, scholars interested in learning about the mind, self, language, society, and culture have treated these phenomena as special – as even more informative than other types of conduct. For these approaches the ubiquity of such troubles (and their management) makes them especially attractive since their occurrence in the stream of conduct impacts on virtually every aspect of it. The perception that such troubles are special derives from a belief that they entail (or reveal) an authenticity obscured by more "practiced" behavior, or that they offer a window into the mind, or the depths of personhood, identity, and social relations, otherwise obscured by socialization, experience, or politeness. In these respects we might say that such approaches "exploit" such troubles insofar as they are not interested in them as such, but for how the apparently "unpracticed" character of such hitches, or the apparently revealing character of errors and the like, has seemed to promise a special opening through which analysts could empirically investigate the human phenomenon of "real" interest to their respective disciplines but which remain "hidden" because of the reflexive character of human consciousness, experience, and action.

From the point of view of the contributors to this edited volume, these infelicities, hitches, and other troubles are now recognized as belonging to a broader domain of human conduct referred to as "the organization of repair" (Schegloff, Jefferson, and Sacks, 1977). In contrast to the apparent appeal of hitches and misunderstandings as "unpracticed" behavior that reveals something more "real" and "enduring" than other forms of human conduct (as indicated above, and in many of the approaches we go on to describe), conversation analysis (or CA) has shown that the organization of repair consists of a broad array of systematically organized, party-administered practices through which a conversation's participants manage troubles in speaking, hearing, and understanding – as they arise – lest those troubles make continued action, or continued intersubjective understanding, problematic or even impossible. In this respect, the organization of repair can be appreciated as one among a set of basic practices *of* interaction – what Schegloff (1992: 1338) calls part of the "procedural infrastructure of interaction" – insofar as it furnishes participants with resources for organizing social life *at the point of its production*. This appreciation of repair depends on viewing such hitches, errors, and other problems in their own terms, however, and not primarily as a "window" into other domains or areas of interest. This perspective is by no means exclusionary. As we shall see, an approach that treats repair as a domain of conduct worthy of study in its own right does not preclude the use of repair, its organization, or even naturally occurring instances of it, as a source of analytic insight into other domains of human life; in fact, as we shall argue, the approach adopted by conversation analysis actually deepens and enriches such investigations. To help situate the emergence of this view, and the advances enabled by it, we begin by surveying the most prominent approaches to the study of infelicities, hitches, and other forms of trouble in the production and appreciation of action that predated it (and to which it was, in part, responsive).

In the first portion of this chapter we briefly consider some of the ways in which errors and related phenomena have been investigated in a range of different fields in the human and social sciences. In discussing these matters we will also consider some of the limitations that stem from the particularistic interests that appear to drive these approaches. In the second section we review the essentials of a CA approach to the organization of repair. The aim is not to delimit interest in the phenomenon of troubles – or repair – but rather to establish how a more grounded, technical appreciation of the underlying phenomena and their organization – in their own terms – actually enhances such investigations by enabling scholars to make more precise inferences regarding conduct, and the way in which it might be informative in light of their own interests. In the third section we return to the question of how a focus on repair, error, correction, and so on can inform the analysis of other domains of human conduct.

1.2 From "slips of the tongue" to "remedial interchanges": trouble and repair in the human sciences

Perhaps the most well-known approaches to (so-called) "speech errors"[1] (a very common form of trouble) developed in psychology, where errors made in the course of speech production have been regarded as providing a window into the unconscious and the human mind more generally. Undoubtedly the most prominent figure in this treatment of speech errors is Sigmund Freud (1914 [1901]; 1929 [1916–1917]). Freud begins his *Introductory Lectures on Psycho-analysis* with a fairly extensive discussion of what he calls "parapraxis," which includes slips of the tongue and other speech errors. Notably for Freud, every slip of the tongue is a consequence of deeper unconscious motivations that are allowed expression through such errors. Slips, according to Freud, are not accidental hitches in speech production, but rather are outward manifestations of repressed subconscious thoughts.

Freud also suggests that the mechanisms involved in slips of the tongue may reveal the "probable laws of formation of speech" (1914 [1901]: 75). The possibility that speech errors may allow us to see the "laws" of speech production at work has been pursued more rigorously by subsequent generations of (psycho-)linguists. For these linguists, speech errors provide a valuable means to test a variety of hypotheses regarding otherwise unobservable processes of utterance generation (i.e., models of "linguistic performance") as well as hypotheses regarding speakers' tacit knowledge of language structure (i.e., models of "linguistic competence"). Thus, there has been a line of psycho-/neuro-linguistic inquiry that investigated speech errors in attempts to model the actual mechanisms of speech production process (e.g., Lashley, 1951; Hockett, 1967; Boomer and Laver, 1968; Fromkin, 1968, 1971; MacKay, 1969, 1970; Levelt, 1983, 1989; van Wijk and Kempen, 1987; Blackmer and Mitton, 1991; Bredart, 1991).[2] Another, closely related, line of inquiry has undertaken to show how speech errors provide evidence for the psychological reality of theoretical linguistic concepts such as distinctive features in phonology, morpheme structure constraints, syntactic and semantic features in representations of underlying linguistic structure, and so on (e.g., Fromkin, 1968, 1971; Fry, 1969; Green, 1969).[3] More recently, those working in the field of natural language processing have started to pay serious analytic attention to speech errors and their corrections in spontaneous speech (e.g., Hindle, 1983; Bear, Dowding, and Shriberg, 1992; Nakatani and Hirschberg, 1993; Heeman and Allen, 1994). In these studies, efforts have been made to construct computational algorithms that detect and correct speech errors in processing spontaneous spoken language data. As these developments in the psychological study of speech errors suggest, what began as something of a curiosity on the margins of the discipline now occupies an important, if not central, place within this approach.

In much the same way, anthropologists have (occasionally) acknowledged troubles encountered in the prosecution of action, though primarily in the service of other interests and concerns. Nevertheless, in his *Crime and Custom in Savage Society*, Malinowski (1926) complained that the very methods of anthropology produced accounts that were highly idealized and gave little sense of the give and take of everyday life. Although also engaged in so-called "participant-observation," anthropologists rely crucially on native testimony – anthropologists ask what a ritual is called, why it is performed, what it means, and so on and receive in return answers in which natives attempt to clarify the significance of the phenomena asked about. The problem, as Malinowski saw it, is that the resulting accounts are "normative" idealizations that typically bear more on what *should* happen than on what does happen in any given case. Of course one of the things that tends to drop out here are the infelicities, errors, troubles, and so on that inevitably attend any bit of human conduct.

However, occasionally the descriptions of anthropologists have included discussion of errors and related matters in their studies. For the ethnographer, such phenomena sometimes provide a means to gain insight into how the people being described make sense of events in the world that surrounds them; in other cases, accounts of trouble and its management are woven into the analysts' descriptions of the ceremonies and rituals. In his classic account of witchcraft and sorcery beliefs among the Azande in Central Africa, Evans-Pritchard takes the first of these tacks, describing how "embodied trouble" (i.e., injury) experienced by Azande in the course of everyday activity is understood and explained. He writes:

> I found it strange at first to live among Azande and listen to naive explanations of misfortunes which, to our minds, have apparent causes, but after a while I learnt the idiom of their thought and applied notions of witchcraft as spontaneously as themselves in situations where the concept was relevant. A boy knocked his foot against a small stump of wood in the centre of a bush path, a frequent happening in Africa, and suffered pain and inconvenience in consequence. Owing to its position on his toe it was impossible to keep the cut free from dirt and it began to fester. He declared that witchcraft had made him knock his foot against the stump. I always argued with Azande and criticized their statements, and I did so on this occasion. I told the boy that he had knocked his foot against the stump of wood because he had been careless, and that witchcraft had not placed it in the path, for it had grown there naturally. He agreed

that witchcraft had nothing to do with the stump of wood being in his path but added that he had kept his eyes open for stumps, as indeed every Zande does most carefully, and that if he had not been bewitched he would have seen the stump. As a conclusive argument for his view he remarked that all cuts do not take days to heal but, on the contrary, close quickly, for that is the nature of cuts. Why, then, had his sore festered and remained open if there were no witchcraft behind it? This, as I discovered before long, was to be regarded as the Zande explanation of sickness. (Evans-Pritchard, 1976: 20–21)

Like Freud, the Azande seek an explanation for troubles that afflict human conduct. Whereas Freud located that source of errors in the recesses of the human mind, the Azande treat it as utterly obvious that troubles of the kind experienced by the boy in this example result from witchcraft. Thus, it would seem that they locate the source of error not in the human mind but in the world of social relations with known others – a witch can only affect someone personally known to them. But in fact the situation is more complex and the contrast with Freud only partial. For, as Evans-Pritchard explains, the witch is often unaware of his own true nature and power – i.e., that s/he is in fact a witch. As such witchcraft – a capacity for which is understood to be inherited from a parent – is often an *unintended* expression of bad feelings. So, returning to the comparison, we can say that, whereas Freud locates the source of troubles in the unconscious of self, the Azande locate it in the unconscious (or subconscious) of others. The more general point here is that, in the classic anthropological study, a people's way of accounting for troubles encountered in the normal course of events in everyday life is used as a way to understand their belief system.

By contrast, Elinor Ochs Keenan (1973) emphasizes the significance "error" and its management as a central element of Malagasy oratory during the event of "public marriage request." According to Keenan the central goal of the event – securing an alliance between the families of the bride and groom – requires a delicate balancing of the subsidiary elements necessary for it: efforts to honor the bride's family and build confidence in the groom's family. In this event, each family is represented by a speechmaker, who engages in a dialogic performance in traditional ceremonial speech called *kabary*. However, conceptions of the ground rules of proper *kabary* are not always shared among different families and therefore what constitutes an "error" is open to dispute. For this reason, *kabary* performances are characteristically argumentative, with disputes emerging regarding what counts as "speaking according to tradition." Thus, Keenan writes:

It takes no great stretch of the imagination to realize that *kabary* performances serve … [the] personal ends of the speechmakers. They are platforms for exhibiting knowledge of traditional oratory. In the marriage request *kabary*, the speechmakers are concerned not only with the matter at hand, the marriage contract. They are greatly concerned with maintaining or enhancing their status as *tena ray aman-dreny* ["true (wise) elder" – MH/GR/JS]. The making and breaking of 'traps' must be seen in this light. The speechmaker for the girl's family may display his knowledge by indicating errors or gaps in the oratory of his adversary by making traps. The boy's speechmaker, on the other hand, shows his skill by successfully freeing himself from these traps and by generally proceeding with as few errors as possible. The speechmaker for the boy is, then in a bind. He needs to admit a few errors to be a successful 'requestor', to show honor to the girl's family. But, as a speechmaker and elder, he does not wish to be trapped too often lest his status suffer. A consequence of this is that a *kabary* performance may break into heated debate over the point of what constitutes speaking *ana-dalana* ["according to tradition" – MH/GR/JS]. (Keenan, 1973: 229)

Here, then, the way in which the notion of an "error" is debated is examined as part of the practices that *kabary* performers use to negotiate one's reputation as a skillful orator while attending to the successful accomplishment of the event at hand.

Repair-like phenomena also figure in the trance behavior among the Malagasy speakers of Mayotte (a small island off the northwest coast of Madagascar) as described by Michael Lambek (1981). In his account, Lambek notes that the process through which a new spirit comes into being is organized and accomplished through repair-like challenges and questions that people pose to the newly emerging spirit. Among Malagasy speakers, a spirit that possesses a person constructs a personal identity through the possessed person's behavior during trance (most notably, by the announcement of its name). When an unexpected identity of a new spirit emerges, that is, when an unexpected name is announced, people ask the spirit to repeat the name, question its validity, negotiate among themselves, and eventually agree to accept the identity of the new spirit. Here, trouble and its solution during the emergence of a new spirit are described as part and parcel of the phenomenon of possession and trance as a social activity.

Much as in anthropology, key figures in the different intellectual tributaries that gave rise to contemporary sociology took up a range of positions regarding the study of errors, infelicities, and other troubles. On the one hand (contra Malinowski's interest in the give and take of everyday life) Weber's emphasis on the "ideal/typical" as the central problematic for social science virtually excludes a focus on repair, and the forms of routine trouble to which it is addressed. As Weber (1968 [1956]: 6) writes, "it is convenient to treat all irrational, affectually determined elements of behavior as factors of deviation from a conceptually pure type of rational action." The resulting persistent opposition of rational and non-rational forms of action dominated the social sciences through the first half of the twentieth century, resulting in what critics came to call a "sociology of error" that was primarily concerned with explaining the "tendency for actors to persist in invalid or erroneous views of the world (and in non-rational courses of action) despite the fact that they would be more successful in their projects by correcting them" (Heritage, 1984: 26).[4] However, in the *Rules of Sociological Method*, Durkheim (1982 [1895]) recognized the methodological relevance of error, deviation, and trouble as central features of human affairs rather than as phenomena observers should either overlook or seek to eradicate altogether. In Durkheim's view trouble could make visible the normative structures – the social facts that are constitutive of society. Goffman and Garfinkel, both of whom were followers of Durkheim in their own way, would later cash out this promise in studies of interaction.

In his discussion of "remedial interchanges" in *Relations in Public* (1971), Erving Goffman describes a range of social practices that are relevant to what conversation analysts would later come to analyze as repair. In this work, Goffman examines the process of social control whereby infractions of social norms are discouraged, and argues that "in the realm of public order it is not obedience and disobedience that are central, but occasions that give rise to remedial work of various kinds" (p. 108). He writes:

> In major crimes the fuss and bother created by apprehension and trial is of less concern to everyone than the crime and its proper attribution; or at least (it is felt) it ought to be. But in interactional matters things are different. Since the guilt is small and the punishment smaller, there often will be less concern – and admittedly so – to achieve proper attribution than to get traffic moving again. When a robbery is committed, no innocent party is likely to volunteer himself as the culprit; when an interactional offense occurs, everyone directly involved may be ready to assume guilt and to offer reparation. The adversary theme that marks negotiations at court is here not strong; rather a tacit collaboration is likely to be sustained even though the participants may be unaware of their coalition. (Goffman, 1971: 107–108)

Common types of "reparation" offered by those who commit an interactional offense, according to Goffman, are accounts, apologies, and requests. These practices are used by the offender to transform what could be seen as offensive into what can be seen as acceptable by "striking in some way at the moral responsibility otherwise imputed to the offender" (p. 109).

Though Goffman does not discuss cases of repairing trouble in speaking, hearing, and understanding specifically, his description of remedial work is relevant to some of the practices used for conversational repair. For instance, when there is trouble in hearing, an apology expression ("I'm sorry?") may be used to initiate repair. Its use, according to Robinson (2006), conveys that the recipient of the trouble source turn (i.e., the *I'm sorry*-producer) assumes responsibility for disrupting the progress of the talk, rather than imputing responsibility to the trouble-source speaker (see also Schegloff, 2005).[5] Also, instead of, or in addition to, an apology expression, an account may be used to justify a request for repetition – e.g., "(Sorry,) I couldn't hear you." When a

›n of what another person has just said becomes relevant, an outright ›n – an interactionally offensive move – is typically avoided; rather, a for confirmation would be used instead (e.g., A: "Single beds are awfully thin to sleep on." B: "You mean, narrow?" A: "They are awfully narrow, yeah."; Schegloff et al., 1977).

With his famous "breaching experiments" (Garfinkel 1963, 1967), Garfinkel attempted to destabilize normally stable features of the organization of everyday activities in order to empirically demonstrate how a society's members establish and sustain a "world in common" through the maintenance of what Schutz (1962) called the "reciprocity of perspectives." Garfinkel writes:

> In accounting for the persistence and continuity of the features of concerted actions, sociologists commonly select some set of stable features of an organization of activities and ask for the variables that contribute to their stability. An alternative procedure would appear to be more economical: to start with a system with stable features and ask what can be done to make for trouble. The operations that one would have to perform in order to produce and sustain anomic features of perceived environments and disorganized interaction should tell us something about how social structures are ordinarily and routinely being maintained. (Garfinkel 1963: 187)

An example of these destabilizing operations is an experiment in which Garfinkel instructed his students to "engage an acquaintance or friend in an ordinary conversation and, without indicating that what the experimenter was saying was in any way out of the ordinary, to insist that the person clarify the sense of his commonplace remarks" (Garfinkel, 1963: 221). For example:

> On Friday night my husband and I were watching television. My husband remarked that he was tired. I asked, 'How are you tired? Physically, mentally, or just bored?'

S: I don't know, I guess physically, mainly.
E: You mean that your muscles ache, or your bones?
S: I guess so. Don't be so technical.
(After more watching)
S: All these old movies have the same kind of old iron bedstead in them.
E: What do you mean? Do you mean all old movies, or some of them, or just the ones you have seen?
S: What's the matter with you? You know what I mean.
E: I wish you would be more specific.
S: You know what I mean! Drop dead!

(Garfinkel, 1963: 222)

Here, the practice that conversation analysts later describe as "other-initiated repair" is used as a crucial component of the breaching experiment. By insistently asking for clarification of what the subject has said, the experimenter succeeded in breaching one of the most basic, taken-for-granted assumptions of social life – i.e., that one's interlocutor will draw on background knowledge of "what everyone knows" and supply whatever unstated understandings may be required in order to make sense of what one says. Other-initiated repair thus provides a tool to uncover the "seen but unnoticed" process whereby "social actors come to know, and know in common, what they are doing and the circumstances in which they are doing it" (Heritage, 1984: 76). We can further notice that breaching these assumptions has a deep moral significance for these participants. So E is first reprimanded for being overly "technical" and subsequently for being obtuse (i.e., "you know what I mean"). With "drop dead," S conveys that he believes E is not only responsible for the trouble but moreover has produced it intentionally.

This section has provided a brief overview of the ways in which repair-related phenomena have been investigated in various disciplines in the human and social sciences. The next section describes the interactionally grounded specification of the organization of repair by conversation analysts.

1.3 Repair as interactional infrastructure – the conversation analytic approach

The broad array of practices through which action-in-interaction is organized constitutes a natural interactive system – that is, a system where the coordination of action and the mutual understanding that underpins it "is locally organized, recipient designed and subject to local, sequential, contextual, environmental and organizational contingencies moment by moment" (Raymond and Lerner, forthcoming). In such a system, there must be some way for members to manage troubles in speaking, hearing and understanding as they arise lest those troubles make continued action – or continued intersubjective understanding – problematic or even impossible. The organization of repair refers to a set of systematically organized, party-administered practices through which a conversation's participants manage such inescapable contingencies.

Though now recognized as central to the organization of interaction as such, prior to the 1970s scholars rarely treated practices of repair as worthy of investigation in their own right. A key turning point was a seminal article by Schegloff et al. (1977). This article proved fateful in carving out an empirically specifiable domain of conduct for investigation and in establishing a basic approach to it. The article began by re-specifying three key aspects of what they deemed "repair."

First and perhaps most crucially, Schegloff et al. offered a "typological amplification" that re-specified how to conceive of the basic domain of phenomena to be investigated. To the extent that analysts even addressed problems in speaking (or hearing and understanding) prior to 1977, most were preoccupied with "correction." For example, Bolinger lamented his fellow linguist's *lack* of interest in correction, observing that:

> Up to now, Linguistic scientists have ignored it because they could see in it nothing more than the hankerings of pedants after a standard that is arbitrary, prejudiced and personal. But it goes deeper. Its motive is intelligibility, and in spite of the occasional aberrations that have distracted investigators from the central facts, it is systematic enough to be scientifically described. (Bolinger, 1965 [1953])

Still, by approaching these phenomena in terms of "correction," analysts such as Bolinger evidently connected them to language and usage rather than to "action" and "interaction." For example, as Bolinger evocatively noted in the same paper: "Correction, the border beyond which we say 'no' to an expression is to *language* what a seacoast is to a map" (Bolinger, 1965 [1953]: 248, emphasis added).[6]

The "typological amplification" proposed by Schegloff et al. involved replacing this concern with correction with a focus on what they describe as "repair." This was more than a mere change in terminology since, as an empirical matter, not all errors are corrected (recipients often overlook mistakes and other infelicities if they can grasp the basic import of what is being said), and not all matters that are subject to repair involve errors (as when ambient noise makes hearing a remark impossible). In this respect a focus on correction was both misleading and unnecessarily limiting precisely because a concern with "correction" tends to focus analysis on "mistakes." As Schegloff et al. observe:

> The term correction is commonly understood to refer to the replacement of an 'error' or 'mistake' by what is 'correct.' The phenomenon we are addressing, however, are neither contingent upon error, not limited to replacement … Accordingly we will refer to 'repair' rather than correction in order to capture the more general domain of occurrences. (Schegloff et al., 1977: 363)

This critical distinction established a solid basis for further inquiry into a domain of phenomena grounded in the conduct of participants in interaction with one another (as opposed to one grounded in the various disciplinary interests of analysts). Moreover, in establishing the independence of repair from the phenomenon of error, Schegloff et al. vastly expanded the domain of potentially relevant conduct; since any aspect of conduct can be a source of trouble "nothing is, in principle, excludable from the class 'repairable'" (ibid: 363).

The second major re-specification offered by Schegloff et al. was addressed to the distinction between "self-" and "other-" initiated repair. Calling whatever comes to be treated as "trouble" the "trouble source," Schegloff et al. (1977: 363–364) observe that repair can be initiated by "self" – that is the *speaker of a trouble source*, or by "other" – any party *other than speaker of the trouble source*. A concern with *both* self- *and* other-initiated repair was important for two reasons. First, in prior work analysts used the distinction between "self" and "other" primarily to justify a disciplinary division of labor, with "self-correction being occasionally discussed by Linguists ... and other-correction by psychologists" (Schegloff et al., 1977: 361 footnote 1). By observing that self- and other-correction/repair were systematically related to one another, Schegloff et al. made a convincing case that both should be addressed as part of a single over-arching domain of human conduct. Second, Schegloff et al. further proposed that since self- and other-initiated repair constituted alternatives within a single over-arching organization, analysts should investigate *the relationship between them*, thereby enabling a key set of observations regarding what came to be called the "preference for self-correction" – a matter to which we return below.

Third, Schegloff et al. (1977: 365) proposed an "organizational amplification," observing that across almost every instance of repair, "one can distinguish between the *initiation* of reparative segments from their *completion* (whether with success or failure)." Most immediately this organizational amplification focused analysis on (at least) two distinct *sets* of practices:

(1) Practices for initiating repair: methods for indicating trouble and making its management the focal activity within the interaction until either the trouble is resolved or efforts to do so are abandoned;
(2) Practices for "repairing" trouble: that is, practices for resolving whatever trouble of speaking, hearing or understanding has arisen or been indicated.

If we combine this organizational amplification with the focus on self- vs. other-repair, we can further note that a range of possible forms emerges: self-repair can issue from either self-initiation or other-initiation, and other-repair can issue from self-initiation or other-initiation (see Schegloff et al., 1977: 364–365 for exemplars of each). Though each of these forms is empirically possible, their actual occurrence and distribution within conversation is very heavily skewed, with self-repair the most common outcome, even when others initiate repair.

The practices through which participants initiate and manage repair are organized by reference to the trouble source turn within what Schegloff et al. (1977: 375) call the "repair opportunity space" (see also Schegloff, 1992). This opportunity space is structured via the turn-taking system for conversation (Sacks et al., 1974) into a set of sequentially organized positions that extend forward in time, alternating between self- and other-. Within this "opportunity space," practices for initiating and managing repair are sensitive to (1) the sequential position from which repair is initiated, and (2) the speaker's relation to the trouble source (i.e., self- or other-). Thus, because these opportunities unfold in time with the trouble source speaker having the first, and the most, opportunities for both indicating *and* managing troubles, the procedural machinery of repair is systematically biased in favor of having speakers manage their own troubles – or, as Schegloff et al. describe it, the organization of repair embodies a preference for self-correction.

This preference can be illustrated by considering the opportunities that self- and other- have for indicating and managing repair. The first two opportunities for locating trouble occur within, or directly adjacent to, the trouble source turn. Because the turn-taking system confers on a current speaker a right to produce a complete TCU, a current speaker has the first opportunity to deal with whatever troubles arise within his or her own turn. A great many troubles occur, and are managed within, a current turn – before a speaker reaches its first possible completion. For example, in the following, taken from a call between two young women directly following the opening of the call, Ava encounters trouble completing the query she is posing, briefly halting the forward progress of her turn to initiate what turns out to be a word-search (line 5) (see Schegloff, this volume; Lerner, this volume).

(01) TG1

Bee: hHowuh you:?
Ava: Oka:::y?hh=
Bee: =Good. =Yihs⌈ou:nd ⌉ hh
Ava: ⌊<I wan⌋ 'dih know if yih got a–uh:m
wutchimicallit. A:: pah(hh)khing place °th's
mornin'. ˙hh

In this case Ava initiates repair with a cut-off (or glottal stop) on "a," thereby indicating some trouble with the ongoing production of her turn. That Ava has initiated a word search is foreshadowed by the delay token she produces ("uh:m"), and confirmed by the "dummy term" "whatchimicallit" that she produces in place of the "missing" word. As soon as she locates the word, "parking place," she replaces the dummy term with it, reproducing the "a" to indicate where in the turn she was starting over.

Several observations can be registered from this instance of repair. First, repair – even when conducted by a single speaker within a single turn – is accomplished through a series of phases or operations: Ava uses a cut-off to indicate trouble with the ongoing production of her turn, thereby alerting the recipient that what follows may not be more of the same turn that she had been producing up to that point. Indeed, what immediately follows the cut-off "a" is not a projected next element of her turn: "uh:m" does not advance the turn's progressive realization and the dummy term "whatchimicallit" is produced as a temporary stand-in (see Enfield, 2003). Thus, the initiation of repair, and the search itself (which, in some cases, can become quite extended, see Goodwin and Goodwin, 1986), are both distinct from the repair proper, which is accomplished via restarting of the noun phrase and the production of the located word, "parking place," after which Ava resumes her turn bringing it to a possible completion at "this morning." Second, because the producer of the trouble source (the current speaker) both initiates repair and manages its completion before the in-progress turn reaches its first possible completion, she manages her own "correction." Third, in this and other cases we will examine below, a spate of talk can be characterized as involving "repair" when the (1) *forward progress of an in progress unit* (in this case a TCU) *comes to be momentarily suspended* and (2) *the focal activity of the interaction becomes removing whatever barrier to that unit's progress is the current source of trouble.* That is, when the ongoing production of whatever else was in progress is suspended so that managing troubles in speaking, hearing, and understanding comes to be the focal activity of the interaction, we will call that "repair."[7]

A second position within the repair opportunity space occurs at the completion of a TCU (or turn), but before a next speaker starts. Two such transition space repairs occur in the following stretch of talk.

(02) From Schegloff et al., 1977: 366

J: He's actually the first assistant but – he's calling
the show.
J: -> They take turns=
J: -> =he and the production manager take turns calling the
show.

As J's telling comes to a possible completion at "show" in line 2, he adds a next component that disambiguates an element of the prior turn: "they take turns." As it happens, the collective reference "they" is itself a source of trouble; thus after the completion of "turns" in line 3, J initiates a second transition space repair to disambiguate the referent, and redoes the entire telling over. Although it is not true in this case, a great many of such "transition space repairs" come to be in this position precisely because the trouble source is the last item in the TCU. We can note, however, that the potential for a next speaker to begin a next turn at a transition relevance place disciplines current speakers to manage possible troubles before that happens. Schegloff (1997b) describes a variant of transition space repair – third turn repair – which occurs when a next speaker begins early following a possible completion, producing a simple TCU which does not reveal a problematic understanding of the prior turn (e.g., a continuer such as "uh huh," etc.), after which the speaker of the trouble source initiates and deals with a trouble in their prior turn. As Schegloff notes, these are only contingently after a next speaker's talk, and therefore have a different character and composition than third position repair, which we describe below.

Of course not all troubles come to be recognized by a current speaker within her own turn; others may initiate repair in the next turn. Indeed, while it is possible for others to initiate repair from other positions (as we shall see below) the vast majority of instances of other initiated repair occur in the turn following the trouble source (Schegloff, 2000). If we return to the call from which example 1 was taken we can note that the very item that posed trouble for Ava – parking place – is a source of trouble for her recipient as well.

(03) TG 1

```
01  Bee:       hHowuh you:?
02  Ava:       Oka:::y?hh=
03  Bee:       =Good.=Yihs[ou:nd ] hh
04  Ava:                  [<I wan]'dih know if yih got a–uh:m
05             wutchimicallit. A:: pah(hh)khing place °th's
06             mornin'.˙hh
07  Bee:  ->   A pa:rking place,
08  Ava:       Mm hm,
09             (0.4)
10  Bee:       Whe:re.
11  Ava:       t! Oh: just anypla(h)ce? I wz jus' kidding yuh.
```

In line 7 Bee initiates repair, indicating trouble with "parking place" by repeating it, evidently seeking to confirm that she has heard Ava correctly (see Robinson, this volume). We can note, then, that by repeating "parking place," Bee indicates that what should relevantly come next – an answer to Ava's query – cannot be produced until the barrier to progress that she has indicated is removed. We can further note that, unlike the previous cases (in which the same speaker initiates and manages the repair) in cases of other initiated repair, the "other" speaker leaves it to the speaker of the trouble source to actually effect the repair itself. This appears to hold even in a number of cases in which the other "knows" the repair or correction – and so could provide it on his or her own (see Schegloff et al., 1977: 377–378).

Taken together, these first three opportunities for indicating trouble – by initiating repair – catch the vast majority of troubles in speaking and hearing, as well as many problems in understanding. In some cases, however, problems in understanding only become apparent in a next speaker's conduct, which, in revealing an analysis of what sort of course of action is underway, may make apparent a trouble in understanding that had yet to be detected. Thus, there are two further opportunities for managing trouble in the "repair opportunity space": third position repair (which deals with a problematic analysis displayed by "other" in next turn) and fourth position repair (which deals with a problematic analysis/understanding by "other" in next turn that is revealed in the trouble source speaker's next turn premised on a third position treatment of it). Though difficult to grasp in the abstract, these can be illustrated and grasped with concrete examples easily enough. For example, if we follow the sequence regarding the "parking place" through one more turn we can see that it involves a third position repair:

(04) TG 1

	Bee:		hHowuh you:?
	Ava:		Oka:::y?hh=
	Bee:		=Good.=Yihs [ou:nd] hh
p1	Ava:		[<I wan] 'dih know if yih got a–uh:m
p1			wutchimicawllit. A:: pah(hh)khing place °th's
			mornin'. ˙hh
NTRI	Bee:		A pa:rking place,
	Ava:		Mm hm,
			(0.4)
p2	Bee:	->	Whe:re.
p3	Ava:	->	t! Oh: just anypla(h)ce? I wz jus' kidding yuh.

After Ava confirms that she was asking (in first position at line 4–5) about a parking place, Bee begins to attempt to answer the question (thus producing a "second position" action – one premised on the initial query posed by Ava). By indicating that she will require further information before she can respond in this next turn ("where") Bee displays a specific analysis of the query posed by Ava: namely, that she is taking it seriously (on joke/serious, see Sacks, 1972, 1975; Schegloff, 1987b, 2001, 2009). In her next turn, then, Ava first begins to respond ("oh just anyplace") before "confessing" to the joke (such as it is) that is underway: "I was just kidding yuh" – thereby making explicit that the understanding Bee's response had displayed of Ava's prior turn had been problematic (see Schegloff, 1992: 1312–1313).

Instances of fourth position repair are even more rare; they are for "other" the mirror version of what third position repair is for "self." The following contains a particularly comical instance. In this call, Linda calls her husband at work to release him from a request she had made earlier, namely to bring some paper plates for the party. Linda responds to Jerry's institutional identification (line 1) with a greeting plus identification that makes his reciprocal identification of her relevant (Schegloff, 1979, 1986, 2007a). In a first sign of trouble, however, Jerry passes on this opportunity and simply confirms his identity (line 5). Apparently undaunted, Linda presses ahead offering a "familiar" greeting (a stressed, slightly high-pitch and stretched "hi") thereby making clear that she had called for him and providing him with a second opportunity to recognize her (or claim recognition) or indicate some trouble. As we can see, however, Jerry responds with a similarly familiar greeting, thereby claiming he has recognized the caller and forwarding the call to a next sequence premised on the claimed identification and recognition achieved in the opening.

(05) TC_I(b):_#13_RC_68_Side_1_TC-650_1017–1047

((phone rings))
01 Jer: (W'chuhrdihbluepri:nt)
02 Lin: Hey Jerry?
03 (.)
04 Lin: .h[h
05 Jer: [Ye:[s.
06 Lin: [hHi:..h[h
07 Jer: [HI: [:.
08 Lin: [He:y:- you don'haftuh bring'ny
09 paper plates I think ah'll jus:t use the plates ah'v
10 go::t,hh
11 Jer: Who's thi:s.
12 Lin: Linda.ehh[hhhkhhh
13 Jer: [↑OH(h):.
14 Lin: °henh°
15 Jer: H[i::.
16 Lin: [Wuhdihyou mean uwho(h)'s[this,
17 Jer: [heh heh .hh

In overlap with Jerry's returned greeting Linda moves to first topic (produced as the reason for the call), "Hey you don't have to bring any paper plates ..." (lines 8–10); evidently this action (releasing Jerry from a previous obligation and accounting for this change in plans) depends on both Jerry's relationship to his wife and a shared understanding of the plans to which she is referring. Put simply, this next action is premised on the claimed recognition embodied in Jerry's reciprocal greeting in line 7. Moreover, it makes a next action relevant by Jerry that depends on his grasping what that action is, which depends in part on who is producing it. Insofar as Jerry cannot make sense of either, he deals with a trouble missed in his turn in line 7, revealing that the greeting he produced was premised on a problematic understanding (of who was calling, or perhaps, that he would be able to figure out who was calling once he heard what she wanted). In response, Jerry learns what Linda has known all along: it's his wife. Note, then the heavily marked "oh" in line 13 (which indicates a "change of state"), and the redoing of the earlier, problematic action – "hi" – which he now directs to his wife (see Drew, 2002, for a more extended analysis of this case).

Insofar as third and fourth position repair constitute the last structurally provided opportunities for managing such trouble in interaction – any troubles that slip past such instances may be missed altogether, or excavated and managed in ways other than through the operation of repair (see Schegloff, 1992; Jefferson 1988).

1.4 Repair as interactional resource: making mental processes "visible"

From the perspective of the psychological sciences (psychoanalysis, psychology, and psycholinguistics) phenomena such as slips of the tongue and word-searches provide a window into the human mind: access to mental processes that is relatively more direct than provided by the *content* of speech. According to this view, the content of speech can never provide a direct window to mental processes due to the very fact of human consciousness, which of course introduces the possibility of secondary rationalizations and dissembling. In this, the psychological disciplines echo more obviously commonsense, folk notions of, for instance, a "Freudian slip" – "an unintentional error regarded as revealing subconscious feelings," as one dictionary puts it.

The conversation analytic framework we have described allows for a re-specification of this popular understanding. Specifically, we can ask, if self-repairs are regularly understood as revealing "just what the speaker was thinking" what can speakers use them to accomplish in interaction? This line of analysis was first suggested in a paper by Gail Jefferson (1974) titled "Error correction as an interactional resource."[8] Clearly writing against the grain of then-current generative linguistics in which errors and so on were dismissed to the wastebasket of "performance," Jefferson (1974: 181) writes: "This paper considers some small errors which occur in natural talk, treating them as matters of competence, both in the production of coherent speech and the conduct of meaningful interaction." Jefferson goes on to describe an "error correction format" exemplified by instances such as the following:

(06) PTC Materials: I : 41
Wiggens: I wz– made my left, uh my right signal ...

(07) SFD Materials: IV : 7I
Desk: He was here lay– uh earlier, but 'e left.

(08) GTS Materials: I : I : 43
Louise: A twelve–year–old guy comes over I say whose y– older brother is he?

As Jefferson notes, in each case the repair takes the following form [WORD_1 + HESITATION + WORD_2]. However there are differences in what she describes as "degree of error" (i.e., the degree to which the error is exposed). Thus in example 6 the entire error word is produced: "left," in example 7 the first syllable of "later" is produced and in example 8 only the first sound of "younger" is produced. Obviously, as the degree of error diminishes, recipients (and thus analysts) may be proportionally less certain about the initial word replaced by the speaker. Jefferson shows, however, that recipients do have resources – beyond the evidence provided by whatever phonetic material remains – for retrieving even partially articulated words. For example, participants operate on the assumption that the partially produced word is a "co-class" member, and often the other member of "contrast pair," of the one produced.

Jefferson further shows that in some cases the "degree of error" may be so diminished that only its "projection" remains – like the smile of the Cheshire cat which momentarily lingers after the cat has himself disappeared:

(09) PTC Materials: I : 41
Wiggens: ... so, and, uh, I turned, onto THUH–uh left lane.

Here the only evidence of an error word is a cut-off in the word "the"/THUH and the fact that it precedes the vowel-begun "uh." Given that, as Jefferson shows, the definite determiner takes the form "THEE" before vowels (rather than THUH), a hearer/recipient can infer an initial projection of the other member of the contrast pair, "right" (e.g., onto THUH right lane), the actual production of which has been arrested just before it was to begin (i.e., after "THUH") and replaced by "left." Thus the form of the definite article distinguishes the error-correction format in which a projected "right" is replaced by "left" from a possible word search in which the speaker delays in the production of "left" with the vowel-begun item "uh" (which would take the form "THEE uh left lane.").[9]

Jefferson goes on to argue that this can serve as an interactional resource in so far as by means of the error correction format a speaker can show that what s/he is saying is not what s/he would normally or usually say but has been selected in response to some current formulation of the situation or the relationship between speaker and hearer. Jefferson's key cases, which come from a traffic court, involve the speaker cutting off the production of THUH and thereby projecting a next word beginning with a consonant. The speaker then produces the word "officer," thereby showing the word withheld by the error correction format was "cop."

(10) From Jefferson, 1974
Parnelli: I told that to thuh– uh– officer.

(11) From Jefferson, 1974
Barrows: Well? according to thuh– – thee officer...

Jefferson writes,

> '... thuh- uh- officer' can convey not merely that someone happened to be on the verge of saying 'cop' and replaced it with 'officer,' but that this is the sort of person who habitually uses the term 'cop' and replaced it with 'officer' out of deference to the courtroom surround; someone who is to be recognized as operating in unfamiliar territory, e.g., a regular guy talking to a Judge in a courtroom ... one can propose 'I am not like this but am talking by reference to the fact that you are' by finding ways to show that the terms one produces are not the terms which first come to mind.

Jefferson describes the examples in 10 and 11 as "one step down the degree of error continuum." By simply projecting the error-word while nevertheless avoiding it Parnelli and Barrows "can acknowledge the courtroom surround without prejudice to their identity as regular guys by recognizing the relevance of the courtroom to their talk no sooner than 'just in time.'"

So here the idea that self-repair provides a window into the speaker's mind has been "respecified" (see Button, 1991). The "window" is provided in the first place not to the analyst but rather to the recipient for whom it may be relevant that the speaker initially arrived at some word other than the one eventually produced. This can then be turned to interactional purposes – to show that the speaker is not "of" the context in which she finds herself speaking for instance. The error avoidance format, like the error correction format, "can be used to invoke alternatives to some current formulation of self and other(s), situation and relationship, and thereby serve as a resource for negotiating and perhaps reformulating a current set of identities" (Jefferson, 1974: 181).

Following a line similar to Jefferson's, Goodwin investigates word searches with an eye to what interactive and social work they accomplish. "Forgetting a name" is, of course, another of the phenomena Freud grouped under the heading "parapraxes." As we have already noted, forgetting a name or any other word (e.g., parking place) is a source of trouble in interaction that can engender a specific repair practice – a word search. Goodwin (1987: 115–116) writes: "displays of forgetfulness and uncertainty not only enable a speaker to display to others some of the information processing, or other 'backstage' work involved in producing an utterance, but also provide participants with resources for shaping their emerging interaction." Through the way in which a speaker performs the display of uncertainty, he or she can make a variety of proposals about his or her relation to the others present. Thus, a speaker can signal that another participant shares with him or her access to the material marked as problematic, and invite that participant to aid in the search for it. (Lerner, this volume, explores these and related issues.)

In a detailed analysis, Goodwin shows that by virtue of their differential participation in the activity of searching for a word or name, participants make visible to one another particular social relationships. He considers the following case:

(12) G 86 : 490

Mik: I was watching Johnny Carson one night
en there was a guy by the na– What was
that guy's name. = [Blake?
Cur: [The Critic.

Just as he reaches "the na-" Mike shifts his gaze from Curt, who has been the primary addressed recipient up until this point, to Phyllis (his wife). By thus addressing the request for help in the word search specifically at Phyllis he introduces a categorization of the participants that has not been relevant to the interaction up until this point – specifically, on the one hand, there is the possibly "knowing recipient," Phyllis with whom, it turns out he watched the television show in question, and, on the other, there are several "unknowing recipients." Goodwin (1987: 116) writes:

> signaling that a particular recipient shares with the speaker access to a specific type of information can mark those participants as a couple, and in so doing make an identity relationship such as "husband-wife" relevant to the organization of the talk of the moment.

So again we see that, by considering them within their sequential and turn-constructional home of talk-in-interaction, the potential of these kinds of phenomena to provide a window into what is happening in the mind is re-specified. Specifically, it is possible to see that the "mental processes" so revealed are consequential for the unfolding course of talk by virtue of the way the participants themselves take them into account in designing their own talk.

We can see then that the conversation analytic framework for the analysis of repair allows for a re-specification of the phenomena Freud (and others) understood in strictly individual and psychological terms.[10]

1.5 Repair as interactional resource: disclaiming understanding

As we discussed in the previous section, conversation analysts have shown that the sequential architecture of talk-in-interaction enables and underwrites a most basic form of intersubjectivity. Insofar as each utterance provides a "here and now" definition of the situation to which subsequent utterances are oriented (cf. Sacks et al., 1974; Heritage, 1984), the organization of interaction through sequentially related turns at talk provides participants with a "proof procedure" for establishing how (and whether) they have been understood by other speakers. For any next turn, its design, content and placement (anything from "uh-huh" to an elaborate denial or second story) provides a first speaker with resources for seeing if and, if so, how she has been understood. Where a recipient finds that she does not or cannot understand what a speaker has said she can initiate repair in an attempt to have it clarified. Where a response reveals a misunderstanding of what the speaker has said, that speaker can initiate repair and correct that understanding in third position and so on. Clearly this organization is foundational to the organization of conversation and as such to the organization of human social life. As Schegloff (1992: 1296) puts it: "without systematic provision for a world known and held in common by some collectivity of persons, one has not a misunderstood world, but no conjoint reality at all."

Given this situation, it is not hard to understand why participants take challenges to intersubjectivity so seriously. Problems of intersubjectivity exposed by the practices of repair initiation reveal constant challenges to the world we work at sharing in common. Consider then the prevalence of other-initiated repair in moments of disagreement and disaffiliation. For instance, in the following case, Jon and Guy are discussing where they might be able to play golf later in the afternoon.

(13) NB 1.1

Jon: Well I'm s : ↑ure we c'get on et San Juan ↑Hi:lls ↑that's
ni:ce course ah only played it ↑o:nce.
Guy: ° Uh huh? °
(0.6)
Guy: a–> .hhh °↑It's not↑ too bad,°
(0.4)
Jon: b–> Hu : h?
Guy: c–> 'S not too ba:d,
(.)
Jon: No : .

Although repair can target an apparent problem of hearing – an orientation to which is revealed, in part, through the use of repetition to repair the problem in line 8 – it is involved, at the same time, in the larger course of action being pursued. That is, at lines 1–2 Jon has offered up San Juan Hills as a place they might play golf and has recommended it on the basis that it is a "nice course" and that he's "only played it once." Guy's "It's not too bad" responds specifically to the assessment "nice course" (and not, for instance the number of times he or Jon have played it), refusing to endorse it with an equivalent or upgraded evaluation (e.g., "yeah, real nice," etc.). It is within this context of emergent disalignment that Jon initiates repair. In doing so he provides Guy with an opportunity to revise, modify, or withdraw his non-aligning assessment. And notice that, when Guy does not do this, Jon treats it as if it were a positive assessment agreeing with "no:." So while repair is often used to fix problems of hearing, speaking, and understanding – that is, in the maintenance of intersubjectivity – it is also a vehicle for social action.

More dramatic examples are provided by instances in which repair is initiated by "what-do-ya-mean?" (see Schegloff, 1997a). This phrase can be used as a stand-alone form as a practice used by "others" to initiate repair (as in examples 14 and 15) or it can be used to accomplish other actions when speakers append materials to it (as in examples 16–18). The connection between these practices and the very different outcomes accomplished through them provide materials for a brief discussion regarding the boundary between repair and other domains of action, returning us to some of the conceptual and definitional issues raised at the beginning of the chapter.

In example 14 (below) Priscilla uses "what do you mean" to target an apparent problem with Marjorie's opening of the call, and the query she poses as the reason for it, which suggest that Priscilla owes her – or at least can provide – a report regarding an as-yet-unnamed, though presumed-to-be-known-in-common, state of affairs. Several features converge in conveying this understanding: (i) Marjorie cuts the opening of the call short to pose a question directly after identifying Priscilla (i.e., where Priscilla's reciprocal recognition/identification of her would otherwise be relevant, and an exchange of "how are yous" might have occurred), thereby conveying an orientation to "pending" (or urgent) business (cf. Schegloff, 1986). (ii) The question she poses in place of these activities, "what happened today," proposes that the parties share a basic knowledge of a specific state of affairs as well as an orientation to its mutual significance that makes naming it superfluous (indeed Marjorie can use such an empty formulation of events as a sort of clue to convey to Priscilla just what she is referring to). And (iii) by directing the query to Priscilla, Marjorie positions herself as the party to be informed about the matter (rather than vice-versa, e.g., since she placed the call and raised the matter). In these ways, Marjorie conducts the opening of the call as if Priscilla was (or should have been) *already* inclined to tell her about a specific state of affairs, and Marjorie's placement of the call has simply provided the occasion for her to do so.

(14) Trio 2 (Repair)

01 Pri: H'llo::.
02 (.)
03 Mar: Priscilla?
04 (.)
05 Pri: Ye:a:h.
06 (0.2)
07 Mar: What happen'tuhda:y.
08 (0.6)
09 Pri: Whaddiyuh mea::n.
10 (.)
11 Mar: What happened et (_) wo:rk. Et Bullock's this evening.
12 Pri: ˙hhhh Wul I don' kno:::w::.
13 Mar: My–Loretta jus ca:lled'n she wz goin:g went by: there
14 et five thirdy you know on'er way ho::me…

Such an opening provides Priscilla with the opportunity to convey a strong understanding of what is "on Marjorie's mind": if Priscilla responds substantively to the query (by providing a report), she both confirms Marjorie's suppositions regarding what she knows and conveys that she shares her orientation to the events in question. As we can see, however, Priscilla's response, "what do you mean," initiates repair instead, suspending the forward progress of the sequence until what, precisely, Marjorie is referring to can be clarified. Marjorie attempts to resolve the matter by adding a location (naming a store where Priscilla works) and more precisely specifying the time frame, but as Priscilla's response (line 12, "I don't know") suggests, these additions only confirm that Priscilla cannot provide the report Marjorie anticipated. We can note, then, that once the parties have resolved just what they do – and do not – share as a basic understanding of events, Marjorie embarks on a different project (than the one she initiated the call to pursue) by beginning to inform Priscilla about a set of events that she treats as having a special relevance for her (beginning on line 13) by virtue of her connection to them (as a person who works at the store where they occurred).

A similarly compressed opening – and a related use of "what do you mean?" – can be observed in example 15. In this case, directly after the parties mutually identify one another (lines 2–3), Debbie poses a comparably presumptuous query (line 4): "what is the deal." As in 14, the foreshortened opening conveys urgent or pending business. The features of this opening – and the design of the question Debbie poses (in line 4) – combine to suggest that the pending business in this call entails Shelley's response to a presumed-to-be-known-in-common accusation or complaint regarding her conduct. Beyond the compression of the opening, two elements are most critical in conveying this understanding. First, Debbie uses marked prosody in naming

Shelley, deploying a prosodic contour perhaps most recognizable as one parents use to summon children when they are in trouble (which Shelley orients to by mimicking, and thereby mocking, in response, line 5).[11] Second, the orientation tacitly embodied in the prosody of Debbie's turn in line 2 becomes explicit in her question in line 4: by asking, "what is the deal" Debbie makes relevant Shelley's provision of an explanation regarding a presumed-to-be-known-in-common transgression. Much as in example 14, then, Debbie organizes the opening of this call as if Shelley was *already* inclined to produce a specific action – in this case, an apology for, or explanation of, some aspect of her conduct – and Debbie's placement of the call has simply provided the occasion for her to do so.

(15) Debbie and Shelley

01	She:		distric attorneys office.
02	Deb:		Shelley:¿
03	She:		Debbie¿=
04	Deb:	->	↑what is tha dea::l.
05	She:		whadayou↑mean.
06	Deb:		yuh not gonna go::?
07	Bee:		(0.2)
08	She:		well –hh now: my boss wants me to go: an: uhm finish
09			this >stupid< trial thing,u[hm

Following Debbie's query, Shelley confronts a choice between (a) displaying her shared knowledge of, and orientation to, what is an evidently prominent state of affairs for Debbie – and acquiescing to the accusation/complaint adumbrated by her prior turn in the process – or (b) disappointing Debbie's expectation that Shelley would know what she is talking about, and thereby (tacitly) asserting her innocence. In this context, Shelley's use of "what do you mean" resists the assumption that she owes Debbie an explanation, but her production of it actually goes further: In using markedly high pitch to produce her turn, Shelley more strongly indexes a claim of innocence, thereby foreshadowing a disagreement with the basic implication of Debbie's query, and indeed the very project on behalf of which the call was made in the first place (i.e., that Shelley has already committed a transgression of some kind; see Schegloff, 2007b: 100–105 on the use of repair to foreshadow disagreement). As is apparent in Debbie's next turn, Shelley succeeds in prompting Debbie to back away from a key element of her trouble source turn. Evidently, Debbie's "you're not going to go" makes explicit her understanding that Shelley has decided to withdraw from a trip planned with a group of friends, and thereby forwards the complaint (cf. Schegloff, 2005, on the use of negative formulations and complainables). By inviting Shelley to confirm this understanding, however, Debbie also opens the door for Shelley to challenge it. And, indeed, in her next turn and its sequelae, Shelley asserts that her change of heart has been more modest: namely, although she had previously committed to going on the trip, now she is questioning her participation in it. As she is uncertain, however, any apology by her would be premature. Nevertheless, over the course of this exchange, Debbie successfully resolves the (or at least one) problem with her prior turn (i.e., the state of affairs indexed by it) and thereby enables Shelley to produce a next turn that moves the (now significantly modified) sequence forward. As it happens, the progress made here only brings additional substantive differences in understanding to light – differences that the parties spend the rest of the call attempting to resolve.

In the most basic sense, speakers use "what do you mean" in example 14 and 15 to target what a prior speaker's action treats as common knowledge. As the foregoing analysis suggests, speakers' use of this practice to temporarily suspend the progressive production of an in-progress unit (in this case a sequence) until the problem blocking a next item in it (in this case a next turn) is removed, confirms its status as an instance of repair initiation (cf. Schegloff et al., 1977; Schegloff, 1997a). As we have also noted, however, the removal of such a barrier is not a mere neutral operation pursued outside of the courses of action engaged in by the parties; rather, in each case the outcome of the repair operation significantly re-shapes just what was in progress. In both cases, managing the problematic presumptions in a trouble source turn reveals other problems and differences central to each call's basic aims (and the participants' varying orientations to it), for example that the called party owed – or could even provide – a telling (in example 14) or an explanation (in example 15). In this respect, speaker's usage of "what do you mean" in 15 (and to a lesser extent in 14) targets a prior turn as a trouble source and, in the process, foreshadows a possible disagreement or dispute with it. As with virtually any other practice, such an outcome, however, depends both on the specific form the practice takes, and the specific sequential environment in which it is used.

As our next cases illustrate, when a modified version of this practice is used to target a more distal prior turn, its status as a method for disputing prior claims becomes more apparent, while its use as a method for initiating repair becomes less so. For example, in at least some cases, "what do you mean" can be used in conjunction with a partial repeat of some earlier talk to challenge or dispute a prior speaker's claim. Consider then the following, in which the parties discuss a weaving that Kathy has just completed. Following Kathy's (suitably downgraded) participation in a sequence appreciating her own weaving (lines 1–3), she further distances herself from responsibility for the weaving by claiming "it wove itself once it was set up" (line 4).

(16) KC–4, 16

Fre:	That is beautiful
Kat:	’n that nice
Rub:	Yah. It really is
Kat:	It wove itself once it was set up.=
Fre:	=It’s woo:l?
Kat:	It’s wool.
	(0.8)
Rub:	Whaddyou mean it wove itself once it w’s set up.=
	=[What d’s that] mean.=
Kat:	=[O h i –]
Kat:	=Well I mean it’s ve:ry ‘simple, (˙hhh) it’s
	exactly the same=

Although Freda and Kathy both move on (in lines 5 and 6), suggesting that for them the utterance poses no problem, Rubin challenges this (now distal) self-deprecating comment (in line 8). Several features of the sequence Rubin initiates with this utterance are notable. First, his use of an expanded version of the basic practice (“what do you mean” *plus* a repeat of Kathy’s turn in 4) is clearly sensitive to the distal location from which he launches the turn (since a basic version of the practice would otherwise target the immediately prior turn in line 6). Second, Rubin immediately continues his turn (in overlap with Kathy’s initial attempt to respond in line 10), revising the terms of the question he poses for her – “what does that mean” (in line 9). This alteration “depersonalizes” the query (i.e., in replacing “you” with “that”), and thus more clearly *challenges* the claim embodied in her prior utterance rather than indicating a basic problem understanding it. Third, in response, Kathy does not explicate the reference (as in the prior cases); instead, she offers a more moderate version of her claim (“it’s very simple”) as a basis for beginning a longer recitation of just what producing the weaving entailed. Thus, although both Rubin’s and Kathy’s contributions to this sequence contain repair-like features (e.g., “what do you mean” in line 8, “what does that mean” in 9, and “I mean” in line 11) it’s not clear that Rubin confronts an actual problem that prevents *his* next contribution to the sequence (as was the case for speakers initiating repair in examples 14 and 15), or that Kathy ever entertains the possibility that any problem of understanding needs to be addressed. Rather, the ensuing sequence suggests that Rubin used a *claimed* problem in understanding as a method for reviving the relevance of, and challenging, Kathy’s claim that the weaving required no effort. Kathy treats this other-attentive challenge (insofar as it is in the service of praising her), as an invitation to elaborate just what she did (contra her claim that the weaving “wove itself”).

Our analysis of example 16 suggests a quite different usage for “what do you mean” prefaced utterances (including repeated utterances) than what we documented in examples 14 and 15. If speakers can use this form to challenge or dispute the appropriateness of a prior utterance, however, one would like to see cases where it is used when the speaker's understanding of the turn it targets *cannot* be a barrier to the continued realization of the in-progress unit. And so consider again the following case, which we discussed earlier:

(17) TC_I(b):_#13_RC_68_Side_1_TC-650_1017–1047

((phone rings))

01	Jer:	(W'chuhrdihbluepri:nt)
02	Lin:	Hey Jerry?
03		(.)
04	Lin:	.h[h
05	Jer:	[Ye:[s.
06	Lin:	[hHi:..h[h
07	Jer:	[HI:[:.
08	Lin:	[He:y:– you don'haftuh bring'ny
09		paper plates I think ah'll jus:t use the plates ah'v
10		go::t,hh
11	Jer:	Who's thi:s.
12	Lin:	Linda.ehh[hhhkhhh
13	Jer:	[↑OH(h):.
14	Jer:	°henh°
15	Jer:	H[i::.
16	Lin:	[Wuhdihyou mean uwho(h)'s[this,
17	Jer:	[heh heh .hh
18		(.)
19	Lin:	[.hhhhhhhhhhh
20	Jer:	[Hm::. huh hu-eh .hu::[:h.
21	Lin:	[khh[hh
22	Jer:	[Oh::: yeah fine?en you?

In this case, Linda has responded to Jerry's "Who's this." in line 11 with a self-identification thereby displaying an, apparently correct (see lines 12 and 14), understanding of what Jerry intended. As in the prior case, Linda's use of the expanded form clearly makes its distal production all the more critical here since she has already responded to the utterance she is now treating as a problem. Indeed, in this respect, Linda's "What do you mean who's this," at line 16 is somewhat gratuitous – i.e., it does not address an unresolved problem of understanding but rather challenges Jerry's question as inapposite or unwarranted, presumably on the assumption that he should be able to recognize his own wife (especially after she has given substantial, if indirect, evidence as to her identity at lines 8–10!). And this is how Jerry hears it too: he first laughs (uncomfortably) and then attempts to resume the call's opening by producing a response to a "how are you" Linda never actually produced (thereby making it appear as if he is going along with her continuation). Given Linda's use of "what do you mean + repeat" following her (ratified) response to the targeted utterance, an analysis of it as a practice for initiating repair is difficult to sustain in this excerpt; instead, her sequential positioning of, and modifications to, this practice suggest that she is using it to accomplish some other kind of action — namely complaining.

And finally consider the case given below, in example 18, in which Curt and Mike are talking about a local car racing circuit. Talking about a driver known to the participants as "Al," Curt remarks: "He- he's about the only regular <he's about the only go[od regular out there'z, Keegan still go out?" (See Schegloff, 1987a). With the insertion of "good" (see Schegloff, this volume) Curt is apparently acknowledging Mike's superior knowledge about who "goes out" but in doing so he has implied that the others are not good. It is this suggestion that Gary challenges at line 17 and 18 saying "Wuhyih mean my:, My brother in law's out there," Gary treating Curt's talk as an insult to him by formulating the person indirectly (and perhaps inadvertently) characterized as "not good" as "my brother in law." That this is not the only way in which this person might be formulated is revealed in lines 22 and 24, where Gary now refers to him as "Hawkins" (thereby withdrawing the claim to have been personally insulted).

(18) Auto Discussion

01	Mik:		Generally evry Satur[dee.
02	Gar:		[Un[derneath th'table,
03	Car:		[( )
04	Phy:		He wins js[about evry Saturday too.
05	Car:		[(Y'doin(hh)hi:de?)
06	Rya:		Bo [:Bo!
07	Cur:	->	[He– he's about the only regular <he's about the
08		->	only go[od regular out there'z, Keegan still go out?
09	Car:		[°(Help me up.)
10	Mik:		[Keegan's,
11	Car:		[(gently,)
12	Mik:		out there(,) (he's,)/(each)
13	Car:		[Oghh!
14	Mik:		[He run,
15			(0.5)
16	Mik:		E:[r h e' s u h::]
17	Gar:	->	[Wuhyih mean my:,]
18	Gar:	->	My [brother in law's out there,]
19	Mik:		[doin real good this year'n] M'Gilton's doin real
20			good thi [s year,
21	Cur:		[M'Gilton still there?=
22	Gar:		=hhHawki[ns,
23	Cur:		[Oxfrey runnin? I heard Oxfrey gotta new
24			ca:r.*
25	Gar:		Hawkins is ru[nnin,

As in example 17, Gary's "what do you mean" query attracts no response, suggesting that the participants did not hear it as indicating a problem of understanding – or any other type of issue that made forward progress in the sequence problematic. As such, we have argued that these cases should not be counted as involving repair operations, thereby helping us to define the boundary between the domain of repair and other phenomena that are related, or adjacent, to it.

Beyond the connections in practice these examples share, we can also note the recurrent connection between problems in shared understanding and moral assessments of actions or the understanding of the world on which they are premised. So far we've considered the way other-initiations of repair (and a closely related practice) may be heard, by recipients, as questioning the tacit assumption that participants know and share a world in common – a relation of "intersubjectivity." In so far as they can be heard to challenge such assumptions they become the vehicles for other actions. In conveying that she does not understand what the prior speaker has said, the recipient can challenge its obviousness, accuracy, relevance and so on ... the very tacit assumptions upon which intersubjectivity in talk rests. As Schegloff (1997a) notes, the potential problems exposed by such claims may partly account for the findings registered in one of Garfinkel's breaching experiments (discussed above on pp. 8–9). The rapidity, and hostility, with which subjects responded to "what do you mean" prefaced utterances in that experiment may reflect the degree to which that form is associated with challenges, disputes and disagreements.

As the preceding review and our examination of varying exemplars of types of repair demonstrate, analyses that explicate the social organization of repair as a basic constituent of interaction, per se, have provided scholars with an immensely powerful tool for understanding the social lives of humans. In part, the power of this approach derives from the ubiquity of repair in social phenomena. As Schegloff (1992) observes, the range of conduct subject to repair not only includes everything that happens in interaction, but even extends to conduct that participants have merely *imagined* when in the co-presence of others (as when one party says "huh" in response to talk they imagine the other party to have produced). In this respect, few organizations match the reach of repair. But the analytic purchase understanding these phenomena provides also emerges from the basic problems of social organization and coordination to which practices of repair are addressed: as we have noted above, instances of repair are oriented to the acceptability of action, matters of agreement (and its alternatives), intersubjectivity of, and in, actions and occasions, and thus the very possibility of a world known in common that transcends the views of individual actors. Opening these aspects of the social world for analysis, however, depends in no small part on our ability to differentiate what is part of repair as a form of social organization and what isn't – a distinction that is impossible without a clear understanding of the organization of repair in its own terms.

1.6 Repair in interaction: an overview of the present volume

In this introduction we have attempted to sketch the contours of our current understanding of repair as a set up for the contributions of the current volume. Drawing on Schegloff et al.'s (1977) distinction between self- and other-initiated repair, we have informally divided these contributions into two sections: in part 1, chapters by Schegloff, Drew et al., Lerner, Raymond and Heritage, Romaniuk and Ehrlich, and Maynard describe practices of same-turn, self-initiated repair, or phenomena that instances of it help us to better understand. The data for these chapters are drawn from conversational and institutional occasions of interaction (conducted in English) that have been collected in the US, Canada and the UK. In part 2, chapters by Kidwell, Robinson, Hayashi and Hayano, Sidnell and Barnes, and Enfield et al. examine practices of *other*-initiated repair in next and subsequent turns. Most of the chapters in the second half of the book focus more directly on practices of repair, as such (or on the boundary between repair as a method for dealing with trouble and alternatives to it). In these chapters, the opportunity for comparative analyses afforded by formal specifications of the sequential positioning of actions (i.e., that across languages and cultures, next turn is the first place for recipients of a stretch of talk to indicate trouble with it if they wish to do so), and the range of basic social contingencies that practices of repair can be used to address in them enables authors to develop context-free/context-sensitive analyses of repair operations across languages (Hayashi and Hayano, and Enfield et al.), or categories of personhood (such as stage of life in the case of Kidwell's analysis of troubles in encounters with very young children).

Though the chapters cover a diverse array of issues, forms of trouble, and languages, three main themes emerge across the volume as a whole.

First, and perhaps most easily overlooked, these chapters reveal just how much more there is to learn about the organization of repair, the range of practices that are constitutive of it, and the ways in which specific deployments of these forms can be consequential for current and subsequent actions. In the first chapter, Schegloff focuses on same-turn, self-initiated repair, delineating and illustrating ten operations that speakers can perform: Replacing, Inserting, Deleting, Searching, Parenthesizing, Aborting, Sequence-jumping, Recycling, Reformatting, and Reordering. In formulating his approach to these phenomena Schegloff emphasizes that, "only the repair *operations* are to be taken up, and not other facets of these repairs, such as the *components* of the repair segments through which the operations are prosecuted, the *techniques* employed in accomplishing those operations, and the *systemic or interactional import* that may be understood to inform the doing of a same-turn repair in any given instance." In this way, Schegloff's chapter both expands our current understanding of same-turn, self-initiated repair while simultaneously providing a specification of what a full account of a practice of repair might include – and thus how little we actually know! Hayashi and Hayano also focus on practices of repair, per se, though their approach differs in two ways: they consider other-initiated repair (OIR), and focus on a specific practice – proffering an insertable element – thereby enabling the authors to produce an account with the elements Schegloff describes in the first chapter. In focusing on practices of OIR in Japanese, Hayashi and Hayano also contribute to a growing body of studies that explores commonalities and differences in OIR practices across languages (see, e.g., Egbert, 1996; Wu, 2006). The specific practice they examine – proffering an insertable element – involves a next speaker suggesting "an 'add-on' element" that is "structurally dependent on the design of the prior speaker's turn," thus enabling the next speaker to manage the potential tension between achieving intersubjectivity and "minimizing the disruption to [the] progressivity" of the unfolding stretch of talk (Heritage, 2007). This paper exemplifies the advantages of pursuing a detailed analysis of a single practice, and contrasts (in this respect) with the paper by Enfield et al. that exemplifies just what can be gained by a very broad cross-linguistic comparative approach. In their chapter, Enfield et al. examine two basic practices for open-class other-initiation of repair in twenty languages from around the world, revealing what they share, and how they vary. As they note, "speakers of all of the spoken languages in the sample make use of a primary interjection strategy (in English it is *Huh?*), where the phonetic form of the interjection is strikingly similar across the languages"; however, they also discover that "most of the languages have another possible strategy for open-class other-initiation of repair, namely the use of a question word (usually 'what')" that involves "significantly more variation across the languages." By beginning to draw the basic boundaries around an evidently generic problem of interaction – that is, indicating that there is some (possibly global) trouble with a prior turn (such as with "huh?" or "what" in English) – the authors provide useful insights into ways that such cross-linguistic comparisons can advance Schegloff et al.'s (1977) claims regarding the context-free, context-sensitive character of repair. Despite the advances scholars have made in further specifying repair in recent years (e.g., see Wilkinson and Weatherall, 2011), these contributions remind us that we still have only the barest outline of this domain – and that a much deeper understanding of its organization and import will have to wait for researchers to take up the many challenges Schegloff (this volume) sets for them.

A second major theme that emerges in these chapters concerns connections between repair and concerns with aptness or propriety, on the one hand, and disagreement, conflict, or defensiveness, on the other. In the chapter by Drew et al., the authors take up the significant methodological advantages that instances of same-turn, self-initiated repair offer where the repair targets something other than "factual error." In those cases, one can compare the "original version, the repairable – that is the version that the speaker begins, though sometimes does not complete … with the eventual version, the repair, to identify in what ways the speaker has modified, altered, or adjusted their turn." As Drew et al. demonstrate, such instances of repair seem to be best understood as efforts by the speaker to design their unfolding turn to accomplish a specific action or outcome. Thus, "in comparing the initial (repairable) version with the subsequent (repair) version, we see exposed the *work that it takes to design a turn in the way the speaker treats as best suited to its interactional placement and needs*." By identifying and explicating the methodological advantages of such an approach, this chapter provides grounding for approaches taken by several subsequent chapters, including those by Raymond and Heritage, and Romaniuk and Ehrlich. In their chapter, Romaniuk and Ehrlich address how participants can use similar practices to demonstrate their orientation to institutional requirements particular to talk in courtrooms. Drawing on Jefferson's (1974) article, "Error correction as an interactional resource," Romaniuk and Ehrlich show that participants in the courtroom can convey their orientation to their institutional roles as witnesses and lawyers by halting an emerging utterance, and then recasting it in "ways that serve other kinds of interactional contingencies, namely: (1) presenting a preferred version of events; (2) restricting the epistemic status of claims; and (3) conforming to constraints on asking questions."

For their part, Raymond and Heritage consider instances of same-turn, self-repair in which one question is posed (directly) after another. As the authors show, the modifications via repair here are responsive to at least two broad sets of contingencies. On the one hand, questioners are attuned to the epistemic claims that attend a question and may modify them where these are revealed to be possibly problematic. On the other hand, and simultaneously, questioners may modify a question in order to adjust the particular constraints it sets for a next positioned response. Thus, with a second question, a speaker may back down from the epistemic claim a first question makes even while ratcheting up the pressure exerted on a recipient to respond within a narrow range of alternatives. The authors show how these and other contingencies involved in the asking and subsequent self-repair of questions are linked to broader socio-relational concerns of the participants – what they describe as the "distance-involvement dilemma."

In his chapter, Lerner takes up some basic methods participants use to manage the appropriateness of some aspect of a turn at talk (or other conduct), particularly when it is potentially delicate or indiscreet in some way. Lerner describes "an infrastructure for collaborative indiscretion" by explicating various ways in which the design and production of delicate matters within turns can implicate recipients (directly or indirectly) in their production (or interpretation), thus distributing responsibility for them. As he notes, a basic aim of the chapter is to "show how the texture of interpersonal relations shaped by an orientation to matters of social propriety and impropriety can rest upon – and thereby be contoured by – a formal infrastructure of speech exchange in talk-in-interaction."

If we move from a concern with aptness and appropriateness to ways in which speakers address, contend with, or anticipate disagreement or conflict, we can see a similar connection to practices of repair. For example, although Kidwell does not focus on practices of repair, per se, she uses her chapter to take on one very basic kind of trouble to which they can be oriented. By examining the ways that workers in a day-care setting monitor/police – and in some cases intervene in – ongoing interactions between children, Kidwell explicates how such day-care workers orient to, and manage, very basic problems of interactional coordination, which she argues can "generally be subsumed under the term, *troubles with availability*." Maynard's chapter also explores the boundaries of repair, showing that the formatting and sequential placement of "I mean" prefaced utterances (or IMPUs) reflect a kind of defensiveness on the part of speakers. Maynard's characterization of the practices as "defensive" – which he explicitly connects to, and contrasts with, Freud's conception of "defense mechanisms" – derives from two main sources: First, speakers typically modify complaints via an "IMPU" transition space repair. And second, speakers use this practice preemptively to "solve troubles where so far none has been overtly exhibited except that a speaker may have launched a risky type of action. In that respect, they may anticipate trouble with recipiency, and engage a repair form ("I mean") suggesting that some clarification or explication is in order."

Third, and finally, a number of chapters explicate the connection between repair and issues of understanding, intersubjectivity, and epistemics. Sidnell and Barnes, for example, take up a key analytic insight of Sacks, Schegloff and others: namely, that any person or state of affairs can be described in multiple ways, and thus the selection of any particular way of describing someone or something reflects participants' orientations to matters of action, relevance, and the like. By analyzing cases in which participants "orient to the availability of alternate possible descriptions and, further, suggest that an initial description is in some way insufficient, inaccurate or otherwise problematic," Sidnell and Barnes show that "[w]here a description concerns matters in the initial speaker's domain the second speaker merely identifies the problem, where the description concerns matters in the second speaker's domain the second speaker replaces the problematic description." As they note, this finding complicates the conception of "self" and "other" at the heart of repair. Specifically, these findings suggest that "the preference for self-correction is modulated by epistemic relations such that a participant is entitled to produce a replacement/correction where the matter described falls within his/her epistemic domain."[12]

Robinson's chapter takes up what Schegloff (2007b) articulated as the analytic *problem of action formation*, i.e., members' socially organized methods for designing recognizable social action, and argues that a necessary part of the description of such methods involves *epistemics*, or what interactants know about each other's knowledge (see Heritage, 2012, for a similar line of argument). To understand the *particular* repair-related action being accomplished by a partial questioning repeat, the recipient must determine how much the producer knows about the repeated item in context, that is, how thoroughly, accurately, and/or authoritatively the producer understands the meaning of the repeated item in the context of the unit of talk that contains the putative trouble. On the one hand, if the recipient figures that the producer *has* knowledge of the repeated item, then the recipient will be more likely to recognize the partial questioning repeat as implementing a [K+] repair-initiation action. [K+] actions index their producers' "disagreement" with the repeated item. On the other hand, if the recipient figures that the producer of the partial questioning repeat does *not* have knowledge of the repeated item, then the recipient will be more likely to recognize it as implementing a [K–] action, or one that indexes either the producer's lack of understanding of the repeated item, or a lack of adequate hearing of the repeated item.

REFERENCES

Bear, John, Dowding, John and Shriberg, Elizabeth (1992). Integrating multiple knowledge sources for detection and correction of repairs in human-computer dialog. In *Proceedings of the 30th Annual Meeting of the Association for Computational Linguistics*, pp. 56–63.

Blackmer, Elizabeth R. and Mitton, Janet L. (1991). Theories of monitoring and the timing of repairs in spontaneous speech. *Cognition* 39: 173–194.

Bolinger Dwight. (1965[1953]) The life and death of words. *American Scholar* 22, 323–335. Reprinted in Isamu Abe and Tetsuya Kanekiyo, eds., *Forms of English: Accent, Morpheme, Order*. Cambridge, MA: Harvard University Press; Tokyo: Hokuou.

Boomer, D. S. and Laver, J. D. M. (1968). Slips of the tongue. *British Journal of Disorders of Communication* 3: 2–12.

Bredart, Serge. (1991). Word interruption in self-repairing. *Journal of Psycholinguistic Research* 20: 123–138.

Button, G. (1991). Introduction: ethnomethodology and foundational respecification of the human sciences. In G. Button, ed., *Ethnomethodology and the Human Sciences*, pp. 1–9. Cambridge University Press.

Drew, Paul. (2002). Out of context: an intersection between domestic life and the workplace, as contexts for (business) talk. *Language and Communication*, 22(4): 477–494.

Durkheim, E. (1982 [1895]). *Rules of Sociological Method*, trans. W. D. Halls. New York: The Free Press.

Edwards, D. (2006). Discourse, cognition and social practices: The rich surface of language and social interaction. *Discourse Studies* 8(1): 41–49.

Egbert, M. M. (1996). Context sensitivity in conversation analysis: eye gaze and the German repair initiator 'bitte'. *Language in Society* 25(4): 587–612.

Enfield, N. J. (2003). The definition of what-d'you-call-it: Semantics and pragmatics of recognitional deixis. *Journal of Pragmatics* 35: 101–117.

Evans-Pritchard, E. E. (1976). *Witchcraft, Oracles, and Magic among the Azande*. Oxford: Clarendon Press.

Freud, Sigmund. (1914 [1901]). *The Psychopathology of Everyday Life*. Transl. A. A. Brill. New York: Macmillan.

(1929 [1916–1917]). *Introductory Lectures on Psycho-Analysis*. Transl. J. Riviere. London: Allen and Unwin.

Fromkin, Victoria. (1968). Speculations on performance models. *Journal of Linguistics* 4: 47–68.

(1971). The non-anomalous nature of anomalous utterances. *Language* 47: 27–52.

Fry, Dennis B. (1969). The linguistic evidence for speech errors. *Brno Studies in English* 8: 70–74.

Garfinkel, Harold. (1963). A conception of, and experiments with, "trust" as a condition of stable concerted actions. In O. J. Harvey, ed., *Motivation and Social Interaction*, pp. 187–238. New York: Ronald Press.

(1967). *Studies in Ethnomethodology*. Englewood Cliff, NJ: Prentice-Hall.

Goffman, E. (1971). *Relations in Public: Microstudies of the Public Order*. New York: Harper and Row.

Goodwin, C. (1987). Forgetfulness as an interactive resource. *Social Psychology Quarterly* 50(2): 115–130.

Goodwin, M. H. and Goodwin, C. (1986). Gesture and coparticipation in the activity of searching for a word. *Semiotica* 62(1/2): 51–75.

Green, Eugene. (1969). Phonological and grammatical aspects of jargon in an aphasic patient: a case study. *Language and Speech* 12: 103–118.

Heeman, Peter and Allen, James (1994). Detecting and correcting speech repairs. In *Proceedings of the 32nd Annual Meeting of the Association for Computational Linguistics*, pp. 295–302.

Heritage, John. (1984). *Garfinkel and Ethnomethodology*. Cambridge: Polity Press.

(2007). Intersubjectivity and progressivity in references to persons (and places). In Tanya Stivers and N. J. Enfield, eds., *Person Reference in Interaction:*

Linguistic, Cultural and Social Perspectives, pp. 255–280. Cambridge University Press.

(2012). Epistemics in action: action formation and territories of knowledge. *Research on Language and Social Interaction* 45: 1–29.

Hindle, Donald. (1983). Deterministic parsing of syntactic non-fluencies. In *Proceedings of the 21st Annual Meeting of the Association for Computational Linguistics*, pp. 123–128.

Hockett, Charles F. (1967). Where the tongue slips, there slip I. In *To Honor Roman Jakobson: Essays on the Occasion of His Seventieth Birthday, 11 October 1966*, vol. II, pp. 910–936. The Hague: Mouton.

Jefferson, Gail. (1974). Error correction as an interactional resource. *Language in Society*, 3(2): 181–199.

(1987). On exposed and embedded correction in conversation. In G. Button and J. R. E. Lee, eds., *Talk and Social Organisation*, pp. 86–100. Clevedon: Multilingual Matters.

(1988). Remarks on "Non-correction" in Conversation. Presented at the Department of Finnish Language, University of Helsinki. Unpublished manuscript.

Jespersen, Otto. (1922). *Language: Its Nature, Development, and Origin*. London: Allen and Unwin.

Keenan, Elinor Och. (1973). A sliding sense of obligatoriness: the polystructure of Malagasy oratory. *Language in Society* 2: 225–243.

Lambek, Michael. (1981). *Human Spirits: A Cultural Account of Trance in Mayotte*. Cambridge University Press.

Lashley, Karl S. (1951). The problem of serial order in behavior. In L. A. Jeffress, ed., *Cerebral Mechanisms in Behavior*, pp. 112–146. New York: Wiley.

Levelt, Willem. (1983). Monitoring and self-repair in speech. *Cognition* 14: 41–104.

(1989). *Speaking: From Intention to Articulation*. Cambridge, MA: The MIT Press.

MacBeth, D. (2004). The relevance of repair for classroom correction. *Language in Society* 33(5), 703–736.

MacKay, Donald G. (1969). Forward and backward masking in motor systems. *Kybernetik* 6: 57–64.

(1970). Spoonerisms: the structure of errors in the serial order of speech. *Neuropsychologia* 8: 323–350.

Malinowski, B. (1926). *Crime and Custom in Savage Society*. London: Routledge and Kegan Paul.

Nakatani, Christine and Hirschberg, Julia (1993). A speech-first model for repair detection and correction. In *Proceedings of the 31st Annual Meeting of the Association for Computational Linguistics*, pp. 46–53.

Paul, Hermann. (1889). *Principles of the History of Language*, trans. H. A. Strong. New York: Macmillan.

Raymond, Geoffrey and Gene H. Lerner (forthcoming). *Towards a Sociology of the Body in Action: The Body and its Multiple Involvements.*

Robinson, J. D. (2006). Managing trouble responsibility and relationships during conversational repair. *Communication Monographs* 73(2), 137–161.

Sacks, H. (1972). An initial investigation of the usability of conversational materials for doing sociology. In D. N. Sudnow, ed., *Studies in Social Interaction*, pp. 31–74. New York: Free Press.

(1975). Everyone has to lie. In M. Sanches and B. G. Blount, eds., *Sociocultural Dimensions of Language Use*, pp. 57–80. New York: Academic Press.

Sacks, H., Schegloff, E. A. and Jefferson, G. (1974). A simplest systematics for the organization of turn-taking for conversation. *Language* 50(4), 696–735.

Schegloff, E. A. (1979). Identification and recognition in telephone openings. In G. Psathas, ed., *Everyday Language: Studies in Ethnomethodology*, pp. 23–78. New York: Lawrence Erlbaum.

(1986). The routine as achievement. *Human Studies* 9: 111–151.

(1987a). Analyzing single episodes of interaction: an exercise in conversation analysis. *Social Psychology Quarterly* 50(2), 101–114.

(1987b). Some sources of misunderstanding in talk-in-interaction. *Linguistics* 25: 201–218.

(1992). Repair after next turn: the last structurally provided defense of intersubjectivity in conversation. *American Journal of Sociology* 97(5), 1295–1345.

(1997a). Practices and actions: boundary cases of other-initiated repair. *Discourse Processes* 23(3), 499–545.

(1997b). Third turn repair. In G. R. Guy, C. Feagin, D. Schiffrin and J. Baugh, eds., *Towards a Social Science of Language: Papers in Honour of William Labov*, vol. II: *Social Interaction and Discourse Structures*, pp. 31–40. Amsterdam: John Benjamins.

(2000). When "others" initiate repair. *Applied Linguistics* 21(2): 205–243.

(2001) Getting *Serious*: *Joke -> serious* "no". *Journal of Pragmatics* 33(12): 1947–1955.

(2005). On complainability. *Social Problems* 52(3), 449–476.

(2007a). Conveying who you are: the presentation of self, strictly speaking. In N. J. Enfield and T. Stivers, eds., *Person Reference in Interaction: Linguistic, Cultural, and Social Perspectives*, pp. 123–148. Cambridge University Press.

(2007b). *Sequence Organization in Interaction: A Primer in Conversation Analysis*. Cambridge University Press.

(2009). *Prolegomena to the Analysis of Action(s) in Talk-in-interaction*. Paper presented at the LISO, University of California, Santa Barbara.

Schegloff, E. A., Jefferson, G. and Sacks, H. (1977). The preference for self-correction in the organization of repair in conversation. *Language* 53(2): 361–382.

Schutz, Alfred. (1962). *Collected Papers*, vol. I. The Hague: Martinus Nijhoff.

Sidnell, J. (2010). *Conversation Analysis: An Introduction*. Oxford: Wiley-Blackwell.

Sturtevant, Edgar H. (1917). *Linguistic Change: An Introduction to the Historical Study of Language*. The University of Chicago Press.

(1947). *An Introduction to Linguistic Science*. New Haven: Yale University Press.

van Wijk, Carel, and Kempen, Gerard. (1987). A dual system for producing self-repairs in spontaneous speech: evidence from experimentally elicited corrections. *Cognitive Psychology* 19: 403–440.

Weber, M. (1968 [1956]) *Economy and Society*, ed. Guenther Roth and Claus Wittich Berkeley: University of California Press.

Wilkinson, Sue and Weatherall, Ann (2011). Insertion repair. *Research on Language and Social Interaction* 44(1): 65–91.

Wu, R. R. (2006). Initiating repair and beyond: the use of two repeat-formatted repair initiations in Mandarin conversation. *Discourse Processes* 41(1), 67–109.

NOTES

1 We've bracketed the term "speech errors" following the observation in Schegloff et al. (1977) that infelicities in speech production include phenomena that cannot be characterized as "errors" in any usual sense of that term. Schegloff and his colleagues developed the term "repair" (to describe the practices participants use to locate and manage troubles in speaking, hearing and understanding) precisely to avoid the potential confusion terms like "error" seem to invite. Nevertheless, we use the term "error" in this section of the chapter because the notion was central to psychologically grounded approaches to these phenomena.

2 Levelt's work (1983, 1989) and the research inspired by it (van Wijk and Kempen 1987; Bredart 1991; Blackmer and Mitton 1991) differ from the earlier psycholinguistic studies on speech errors in that Levelt and others examine not only speech errors per se, but also the process of correcting them (i.e., repair) in their attempt to model the mechanisms of speech production.

3 Some linguists studied speech errors as a source of historical linguistic change (e.g., Paul, 1889; Sturtevant, 1917, 1947; Jespersen, 1922). These linguists suggest that common speech errors might reveal a natural cause of certain types of linguistic change.

4 Of course, Weber did address – however briefly – routine forms of trouble in some of his later works. For example, in *Economy and Society*, after proposing a definition of social action, he subsequently illustrates the matter with the following contrast: "a mere collision of two cyclists may be compared to a natural event. On the other hand, their attempt to avoid hitting each others, or whatever insults, blows or friendly discussions might follow the collision, would constitute social actions" (Weber 1968 [1956]: 23).

5 "Sorry" can also be used by a trouble-source speaker as a way to initiate self-correction (e.g., "I put it in the trunk … sorry, I mean closet"), which conveys the sense of assuming responsibility for the trouble, i.e., mis-speaking.

6 According to Bolinger, the dynamic character of language structure is a result of a dialectic between purist practices of "correction" and anti-purist practices of "error."

7 In this respect, instances of repair can be differentiated from other ways of managing potential troubles that do not make that management the current focus of the interaction. For example, one recurrent outcome aimed for by same-turn, self-initiated repair is replacement. Instances of what Jefferson called "embedded correction" result in a similar outcome – the introduction of one word to replace another – but that outcome is accomplished in such a way that progress in the unfolding activity is *sustained* with the replacement done in a by-the-way fashion, as opposed to halting the activity itself to make managing the trouble the focal activity in its place (see Jefferson, 1987). In an exchange at a hardware store, a customer who had requested help from a salesperson regarding a wood screw rejects the candidate replacement offered by the salesperson on the grounds that the "wales" on the one she is replacing are "wider apart."

From Jefferson, 1987: 93

```
01  Cust:  MM, the wales are wider apart than that
02  Sale : Okay let me see if I can find one with wider threads
03         ((Looks through stock)
04  Sale : how's this?
05  Cust:  Nope the threads are even wider than that.
```

We can note that after the salesperson uses "threads" instead of "wales" the customer picks up on this usage and adopts it in her next turn. As these contrasting cases suggest, participants have a wide range of methods for dealing with troubles and infelicities in speaking, hearing and understanding. When participants encounter some barrier to what should go next – whether a word, turn or continuation of a course of action altogether – that makes continued progress problematic they may stop that course of action to make dealing with the trouble the focal action of the interaction. In such cases we can say that the participants are engaged in "repair." In such situations we can inspect the various practices through which forward progress of a focal action is suspended on behalf of dealing with the trouble, who initiates the suspension, who effects the repair and how, as part of the systematic organization of repair (see also MacBeth, 2004).

8 More recently Derek Edwards has noted that repair is potentially "a domain of public accountability in which psychological states are made relevant" (Edwards, 2006: 41) by participants in their everyday interactions with one another. See note 10 below.

9 Jefferson (1974: 185) writes: "Suppose that the latter collection captures a specific feature of speech, a form of error correction in which the correction is made after the occurrence of the article and before its projected, partially stated, consonant-begun subject. That is, the words which actually occur (in the first place 'UH', and secondly 'left' ...) are not the ones which were initially projected. So ... Wiggens was about to say 'I turned onto thuh right lane' and corrected it to '... left lane', ... In each case, the wrong or inappropriate word is cancelled just prior to delivery, resulting in 'THUH-UH'."

10 In a set of related studies, discursive psychologists (who have adopted many of the methodological practices and theoretical precepts of both ethnomethodology and conversation analysis) have focused on the connection between interactional conduct and (apparently) mental – or psychological – processes. As Derek Edwards notes, discursive psychology

> approaches the topics of cognition, mental states and psychological characteristics as matters under active management in talk and text. The start point is everyday discourse considered as a domain of social practice. Mostly, it is talk-in-interaction (Schegloff, 1987), but written text is analyzed too. The key to DP is that it is primarily a way of analyzing talk and text. It does not start with psychological questions, and does not offer a rival theory of mind. Not does it deny the reality and importance of subjective experience. Rather, DP rejects the assumption that discourse is the product or expression of thoughts or intentional states lying beneath it. Instead, mental states, knowledge, thoughts, feelings, and the nature of the external world, figure as talk's topics, assumptions and concerns (Edwards, 2006: 41).

11 Shelley's re-use of the same prosody to name Debbie hearably mocks her by virtue of the different sequential position in which she produces her turn. As the caller, Debbie's naming of Shelley (using marked prosody) anticipates the pending business the opening of her call is designed to project. By contrast, as the called party, and the recipient of Debbie's prior turn, Shelley cannot claim to have pending business in the same way. Thus, her use of precisely the same prosody accomplishes a very different action – mocking Debbie for the chastising tone she has adopted in her initial utterance in the call's opening. (On addressing the recipient by name with marked prosody see Sidnell, 2010: 258–270.)

12 In their analysis of the preference for self-correction, Schegloff et al. (1977) implicitly suggest that rights (and obligations) to talk about something attach specifically to the role of speaker *qua* speaker. Some recent work on epistemics (e.g., Heritage, 2012, for an overview) which Sidnell and Barnes draw upon, suggests that a presumed distribution of knowledge (i.e., epistemic status) inflects or perhaps even underwrites such rights.

2 Ten operations in self-initiated, same-turn repair

Emanuel A. Schegloff

As part of a larger-scale effort to provide an analytic and descriptive account of the organization of repair in conversational talk-in-interaction,[1] this installment is addressed to a sharply demarcated, albeit substantial, domain, and one facet of the repair undertaken there. The domain is "self-initiated, same-turn repair"; the facet is the sorts of *operations* that get implemented there. What this leaves out is even more substantial: first, *other* loci of *self-initiated* repair (i.e., transition-place, third turn and third position) and the domains of *other-initiated repair*; second, within the self-imposed domain to be treated here, only the repair *operations* are to be taken up, and not other facets of these repairs, such as the *components* of the repair segments through which the operations are prosecuted, the *techniques* employed in accomplishing those operations, and the *systemic or interactional import* that may be understood to inform the doing of a same-turn repair in any given instance. These will be addressed in the larger work of which this contribution is but a part. Given the focus on "same-turn" repair, it may be useful to say a bit about what is meant by that phrase here.

2.1 The setting

It's a virtually automatic reflex to refer to the setting of our target phenomenon as "same turn" and to figure that we know what we mean by that. But I'd like to take a few paragraphs to sketch some of the main features it would be useful to have made explicit.

In common with many of the types of units employed by parties to talk-in-interaction, turns at talk have an *overall structural* organization and a *local* organization. In past writing on conversation analysis, the term "the overall structural organization" has ordinarily been followed by the phrase "of the unit 'a single conversation,'" but little has been said of other units to which "overall structural organization" might apply, which made it relevant to specify "a single conversation" as one such unit. The turn at talk is, I think, another such unit.

The most commonly realized overall structural organization for the turn in ordinary talk-in-interaction is a single turn-constructional unit (or TCU). This is so in large measure because of the way the turn-taking organization is made to work by the parties to the talk – in particular, because of the transition-relevance of possible turn completion which is encountered as the first TCU is coming to possible completion. But we know that transition does not *always* occur there, that both the current speaker and potential next speakers can contribute to the outcome (whether actual transition or not), and that those contributions to the outcome can occur at various places in the developing course of that first TCU. We also know that the several TCUs that can come to occupy a multi-unit turn can be related to each other in various ways: they can constitute a story-telling, a list, an argument, an extended description, components of distinct sequences, and many others. And we know that which of these multi-unit, intra-turn relationships a current turn is the site of can be projected from its outset, can develop over its course, or both. These are instances of what I am calling the overall structural organization of the unit "a single turn," but so is the single TCU turn an instance of a turn's overall structural organization, and it too can be signaled or projected from its outset, at least in English.

The analytical contrast with "overall structural organization" is "local organization," which can apply at various levels of granularity in the composition of a turn. Applied to traditional, familiar, almost vernacular units like words, phrases, and clauses, or to other construction types that appear to set the terms for speakers' production and recipients' on-line analysis, grammar is one local organization of TCUs, whatever form that grammar takes – whether Asian, Indo-European, Romance, Semitic, Slavic, etc. Applied to sub-lexical units, local organization can relate syllables, components sounds, components of those components, and so forth. This is not simply a *pro forma* recognition of different specializations in a sister discipline; it will bear directly on the understanding of same turn repair in the text to follow.

So, to sum up, a turn at talk can in principle have an *overall structural organization*, expandable to include a number of TCUs of various sorts or limited to a single TCU, and a *local organization* that operates from sub-unit to sub-unit as the TCU or the turn progresses. Speakers and recipients are closely oriented to both of these orders of organization, and continuously project from what has transpired so far to what the alternatives are for what might be coming up next. That is to say, the talk implicates for its participants both *macro*-projection and *micro*-projection:

- macro-projection concerns what sort of TCU this is and where in it we now are; and, if a multi-unit turn, what sort of multi-unit turn this is, what shape or trajectory such a project takes, and where in that shape or trajectory we now are;
- micro-projection concerns what kind of construction this is, and what it makes relevant next; what kind of word and what that projects for next word; what kind of sound and what that projects for what might follow.

I do not mean to suggest that local organization is exclusively grammatical, phonological, or in other ways linguistic-y; it can include how places or persons should be referred to or re-referred to, how story-tellings should be constructed, and all the other things that get done in TCUs and their turns.

As I understand it, the basic dynamic of talk and other conduct in talk-in-interaction is directional and progressional toward possible completion of whatever units compose the several orders of organization in play at any given moment. What is due next is some possibly relevant next sound, next syllable, next word, next action, etc., and the parties' orientation to progressivity is organized by reference both to macro-projection of the overall structural organization of the turn and any given TCU in it and at the same time by reference to the local organizations that move the talk and other conduct forward bit by bit by reference to their order of granularity. The macro-projections are always realized by progress at the local, bit-by-bit organization; the local organizations and micro-projections are tailored, shaped and interpreted by reference to the developing project of the overall structural organization currently in the works.

This is how I understand the TCUs and turns that are the environment for same-turn repair. The first thing to be said about same-turn repairs is that they are overwhelmingly (but not exclusively) same-*TCU* repairs. The second thing to be said is that, in one way or another, they intervene to *interrupt the progressivity of the talk*. And now on to the limited focal topic on the agenda of this chapter: same-turn repair *operations*, where these assertions can be grounded in some data.

2.2 Operations

As far as I can now make out, there are ten main types of operation which speakers employ to deal with some putative trouble-source in an ongoing turn-at-talk in conversation or to alter it in some interactionally consequential way. Instead of the conventional use of nouns like "replacement," "insertion," and the like, I have opted for action terms like "replacing," "inserting" and the like to emphasize that these are *operations* that speakers carry through – that they *do*, not pre-packaged products that they select. The downside is awkward neologisms when referring to more than one instance of such an operation – "replacings," "insertings," and the like, for which I beg your tolerance and forgiveness. Here they are, with a few exemplars of each:

2.2.1 Replacing

The term "replacing" is meant to refer to a speaker's substituting for a wholly or partially articulated element of a TCU-in-progress another, different element, while retaining the sense that "this is the same utterance," as in examples 1–3:[2]

(01) TG, 7

Bee: .hh Yihknow buh when we walk outta the cla:ss.=
Ava: =nobuddy knows wh't [wen' on,]
Bee: [Wid– .hh] h=
Bee: =Li (hh) ke wu– .hh Didju n– Didju know what he wz=
talking about didju know wh't [structural paralysis=
Ava: [dahhhhhh !
Bee: =was I sid no I sid but we're supposetuh know what it
–> is (*fuh* **Weh–**) .hh yihknow *fuh* ***tihday's*** [class. 'n,
Ava: [.hhh Mmm.
Bee: He nevuh wen' o:ver it 'n, t! .hhhh

(02) TG, 3

Bee: Becuz they're gonna do the operation on the teeuh
duct. f[fi: rs]t. Before they c'n do=
Ava: [Mm–hm,]
Bee: =t [he cata] ract]s.
Ava: [Right.]Yeah,]
Bee: .hhh So I don'know I haven:'t yihknow, she wasn' home
–> **by the t–** yihknow ***when*** I lef'fer school tihday.=
Ava: =Mm hm,
Bee: Tch! .hh So uh I don't kno:w,

(03) Debbie and Shelley, 3

Deb: =you go,becu:z »I mean« that's what Jay Tee told me
you told hi:m¿
Shl: w'll that's what– when I called him I told him that I
didn't have the money ar that ((he–/kee–)) Mark can't
go becu:z o:f work.
Deb: mmh[m
Shl: [that's why he can't go: , . hh an I said b–to be
real honest with you: I have to decide do I wanna
spend this money becuz if Mark was goin .hh he was
–> gonna pay fer- fer **m–** ***alot of it***, cause he won money
playing footba:ll.
Deb: uhuh
Shl: So: it w's like awright fi:ne, I'll let you: buy my–
my plane ticket, that's not a problem

So in example 1 at line 8, what was starting to be "We[dnesday's] class" is replaced by "today's class"; in example 2 at line 7, what was well on the way to "by the t[ime]" is replaced by "when;" and in example 3 at line 10, what was on the way to "for m[e]" (or "for m[ost of it") is replaced by "for a lot of it."

Let me use these three exemplars to make several points:

(1) Replacings need not be the same sort of linguistic or grammatical object as the trouble-source being replaced, but they *can* be. In example 1, incipient "Wednesday" is replaced by "today" – word for word; in example 2, an incipient phrase is replaced by a word; in example 3, an incipient word is replaced by a phrase.
(2) The replacing may repeat elements of the turn-so-far just preceding the trouble-source (as with the "for" in example 1) or not, as examples 2 and 3; it may also repeat elements *following* the trouble-source (if any). Such repeats can serve recipients as one sort of resource for locating what is being treated as a trouble-source or alterable by "framing" it.
(3) Another such resource for locating the trouble-source is the "sort of thing" the replacement is, which can indicate "that sort of thing" as what is being replaced. So in example 1, where we already have a frame to serve as resource, we have one term for naming a day replacing another; in example 2 we have one temporal reference replacing another; in example 3 ... we *do not*! Here, the replacement is a quite different object than what it is replacing; it is also not framed by preceding or following elements of the turn-so-far.
(4) Finally, we can note that in each of these exemplars, the trouble-source or alterable (or some part of it) has been prematurely terminated – in each case by a cut-off, that is, some version of a stop.

With these initial four observations, we have temporarily abandoned the topic of this chapter – *operations* of same-turn repair, in order to register (however informally) at least a sense of other, equally important aspects, to be addressed elsewhere. These include several components of the *technology* for doing same-turn repair – the cut-off as one way of initiating repair, and "framing" as a component of the repair segment usable to locate the trouble-source or alterable; and we have alluded to some *systemic or interactional issues* which the repair can be understood to deal with – in example 1 that one refers to "the day one is in" not by its name but as "today" (this is one sort of "systemic" issue – a word-selectional one), and in example 3 mitigating the potential crassness of the economic motivation of Shelley's withdrawing from the outing because the boy friend, in not going, was the loss of her meal ticket (this is one sort of interactional issue).

So now we return to the other nine operations, with only occasional excursions from that commitment.

2.2.2 *Inserting*

A second operation is as straightforwardly named as the first: a speaker inserts one or more new elements into the turn-so-far, recognizable as other than what was on tap to be said next, as in examples 4–6:

(04) Joyce & Stan, 4

Sta: And fer the ha:t, I'm lookin fer somethi:ng uh a
-> little different. Na– uh:f: *not f : :* ***exactly*** funky but
not (.) a r-regular type'a .hhh >well yihknow I I<
have that other hat I wear. yihknow?
Joy: Yeah,

(05) TG, 10

(0.5)
Bee : -> °(I 'unno)/° (So anyway) .hh Hey do you see *v*– (0.3)
-> ***fat ol'*** Vivian anymouh?
Ava: No, hardly, en if we do:, y'know, I jus' say hello
quick'n,

(06) Virginia, 31

Wes: (Momma) / (Mom ha') you been readin' her mail ag'in?
(0.2)
Wes: hhhhhhh! [huh huh] huh (huh [huh)
Pr?: [e h hh!] huh hah [(hah)
Mom: [^We:sley?
(0.5)
Mom: -> What is *thuh* [*m*:– ***in thuh wo:rlds****'s 'uh* matter with=
???: [((sniff))
Mom: =[you?I don't read her ma:il¿
???: [mt
Wes: Oh you don't?
(.)

In example 4, Stan inserts "exactly" before "funky"; in example 5, Bee inserts "fat ol'" before "Vivian"; and in example 6, Mom inserts "in the world" before "is the matter." In each case the speaker has articulated the first sound of the element before which the insert is to be inserted, and has then initiated repair – by a cut-off on that sound as in example 5, by a sound stretch on it as in example 4, or both as in example 6.

Excursus: The domain to which this volume and its several chapters are addressed is, as the title announces, "repair." In vernacular English, something in need of (or the object of) "repair" is defective – broken, inadequate, ill-suited, the source of trouble (hence "trouble-source"), or, most generally, "repairable," that is, subject to being fixed.

On the whole, this terminology has served us well. But in undertaking an overview of work in this area, the terminology seemed to me to under-represent a whole domain of objects and operations of repair. If I may invoke an analogy from the craft of tailoring clothing, a suit that someone tries on may be torn at the underarm; this is a trouble-source and is in need of repair.

But it happens as well that there is nothing "wrong" with the outfit, but the tailor remarks that it would be more flattering to the wearer if the lapel was a tad narrower. If agreed, the undertaking would be termed an "alteration"; it is not that something was wrong and had to be fixed, but it could be better realized by an "alteration."

And so it is in talk-in-interaction: a speaker may find that saying the thing they are in the course of saying could be better realized by this-or-that change, and when they undertake it, they are not so much "repairing" as they are "altering." The operation of "inserting" is one environment in which "altering" is found (as is the operation of "parenthesizing" taken up below): a speaker stops the TCU-in-progress and repeats it or part of it, but incorporates an additional word or phrase. To be sure, it is possible that the added word was in fact "missing," and the turn was on the way to being defective. But not always. Consider, for example, the exchange in example 5 just examined (and reproduced below) between two college young women who live in the same neighborhood but have apparently drifted apart. At one point, Bee asks Ava about another girl whom they both knew in the past:

(05) TG, 10

(0.5)
Bee: –> °(I 'unno)/°(So anyway) .hh Hey do you *see v–* (0.3)
–> ***fat ol'*** *V*ivian anymouh?
Ava: No, hardly, en if we do: , y'know, I jus' say hello
quick'n,

Here, Bee is on the way to asking "Hey do you see Vivian anymore?" – a perfectly well-formed inquiry of the sort she uses in other inquiries. In stopping to insert "fat old," Bee is not necessarily addressing a trouble with her turn-in-progress – a "repairable." She could well be incorporating the reference form that she and Ava always used to refer to Vivian in days gone by, and thereby be invoking – and inviting Ava to participate in reviving – the camaraderie of the past. Not then a tear in the underarm, but a narrowing of the lapel; not fixing a trouble, but using the turn to invoke a past intimacy; not a repairing of a trouble-source, but an enhancing with an alteration. In the text that follows, where appropriate, I will gradually incorporate the terms "alteration" and "altering" for what some "repairs" are being addressed to.

2.2.3 Deleting

A third operation is as straightforwardly named as the first two: a speaker deletes one or more elements already articulated in part or fully in the turn-so-far. Deletings are far less common than most of the repair operations we have so far encountered. All of the ones that I have collected involve deleting one word (if "it's" is treated as one word), as in examples 7–9:

(07) TG, 9

01	Bee:		Ih wz, I don'know what I'm gunnuh do. hEn all the
02			reading is from this one book so f(h)ar the(h)t I
03			haven' go(h)t!
04	Ava:		hhhhhhhh!
05	Bee:		˙hhhh So she tol' me of a place on Madison Avenue 'n
06			Sevendy Ninth Street.=
07	Ava:		=M[mm.
08	Bee:	->	[tuh go en try the:re. *Because I* **als–** *I tried* Barnes
09			'n Nobles 'n, (0.6) they didn' have any'ing they don'
10			have any art books she tol' me,
11	Ava:		Mmm

(08) Auto Discussion, 25

01	Cur:		[No in a little snowmobile that's
02			a little bit too fast.
03	Gar:		No well that's nothin. They're duhposetuh go a hunnerd
04			'n twunny a hunnerd'n[twunny five miles'n hour. ( ),
05	Car:		[°(Scuze me),
06	Cur :	->	*That's* **still** *That's* too fas[t.
07	Gar :		[That[’s too fast.
08	Mik :		[Ain' no way I'd get
09			inna snowmobile going that fast.

(09) Coffee Chat, 8

01	Ric:		This lady's been in ruh– –real –estate– (0.3) uh she's
02			been a teacher– (1.1) an' what else?
03			(.)
04	Ric:		You've been a number uh things,
05			(0.2)
06	Bet:		°.p° Insurance agent,
07	Ric:		Insurance?
08			(0.3)
09	Bet:		Store manager,
10			(.)
11	Bet:	->	[Name anything I've done it, I *can* **even** *run*=
12	Tom:		[Kuh–
13	Bet:	->	=thee:: ˙hhh/(1.1)
14	Bet:	->	I *can run* thuh– –elevator. hh heh heh [heh heh
15	Tom:		[Hav–
16	Tom:		[Ever been in newspaper business?=
17	Bet :		[heh heh

In example 7 an almost completed "also" is deleted; in example 8, it is "still" that is deleted.[3] And in example 9, the "even" is deleted, perhaps because it treats the activity being named as of lesser standing.

2.2.4 *Searching*

Then there is searching. Past CA literature referred to "word searches," but that turns out to be too restrictive. Sacks noticed that a great many searchings fell into two types, which he termed "precises" and "delicates," both of which Gene Lerner has been collecting and working on as an offshoot of his work on joint production (Lerner, 1991, 1996, 2004). Names are particularly common targets of "precise"-type searches, however transient – names of people (even close relatives, even ones sitting at the same table), places, businesses, and the like, as in example 10's search for the name of the Plaza Theater.

(10) Joyce & Stan, 5

Joy: Why don'tchoo: go into Westwoo:d, (0.4) and go to
Bullocks.
(1.2)
Stn: -> Bullocks? ya mean that one ***right u:m (1.1) tch! (.)***
-> ***right by thee: u:m (.) whazit the Plaza? theatre::=***
Joy: =Uh huh,
(0.4)
Stn: °(memf::)o
Joy: °Yeah,

But the characteristic features of searching – its technology – may be employed when the source of the problem is quite unclear, as in example 11, where the search is for the very thing which has prompted its speaker to preempt first topic from the caller.

(11) TG, 01

Ava: H'llo:?
Bee: hHi:,
Ava: Hi:?
Bee: hHowuh you:?
Ava: Oka:::y?hh=
Bee: =Good.=Yihs[ou:nd] hh
Ava: -> [<I wan]'dih know if yih got ***a–uh:m***
-> ***wutchimicawllit. A:: pah(hh)khing place*** °th's
mornin'.˙hh
Bee: A pa:rking place,
Ava: Mm hm,
(0.4)
Bee: Whe:re.
Ava: t! Oh: just anypla (h) ce? I wz jus' kidding yuh.
Bee: Nno...

More often than not, if the target is not a recognizable "precise," it is a "delicate," as it is shown to be in example 11 when the searcher eventually allows that she was "just kidding."

And there are searches that follow interruptions or side-tracking – what I will call "resumption searches, or searchings," as in example 12, which allows us to see and hear how precise can be the retrieval of exactly where the side-tracking had intervened.

(12) TG, 17-18

Ava: [Maybe you wanna come downtuh school] see what the
new place looks like,
(0.5)
Bee: Yih may:be. (N)a::[h, b't I hadn'–]
Ava: –>> [*You c'n come innoo*] *a cla:ss with*
–>> *m[e.*
Bee: [I haven' thought about that la(h)tely hh huh eh–
[huh!
Ava: [Why donch[a I mean you won' haftuh do any]thing,
Bee: [.hh You know I wu-u-u] I wonder
if Do:nna went back tuh school, i'z=
=[I wz curious tuh know,]
Ava: [I n– Y'know– Fridays is] a funny day. mMost a' the
people in schoo:l, ˙hh that's why I only have classes
on Tuesday en Fri:day ˙hh (0.3) °u– one cla:ss, because
most a' them have o:ff those days. Yih kno[w like if=
Bee : [Ye::h,
Ava: =yih kuh work yer schedule out that [way=I cuutn't.
Bee : [Right.
(0.7)
Ava: Tch! But if you wanna-uh:m (0.2) come in en see.
Bee : Tch! I wouldn' know wheretuh look fuh her(hh) hnhh–
hnh [h!˙hh
Ava: –> [Well you know, you know, come along with me,
(0.7)
Ava: –> A:nd uh:m,
(0.7)
Ava: –> °Wuhwz I gonnuh say.
(0.7)
Ava: –>> *You c'n come in the class with me,* it's a logic class=
=I think yih gonna see a pitcher o:n on something good
tomorruh in that class anyway so it's n[o ha:ssle,
Bee : [°Nnh,
Ava: ˙hh 'T's only f'f'fty minutes anyway,
(0.6)

Here we can see that Bee can access at least roughly (line 24) the last thing she said (line 5) before the diversion of the talk (lines 10–23), but cannot then resume what that earlier utterance was leading up to, yielding the overt "searching" utterances (lines 26 and 28), then retrieves what preceded the diversion more precisely (line 30, redoing the earlier line 24).

2.2.5 *Parenthesizing*

Not all parentheticals are engaged in dealing with possible trouble in the talk, but they *can* be deployed for such use (Mazeland, 2007). Like insertings, they add to the turn-in-progress something other than a next-due element; *unlike* insertings, they are ordinarily composed of clausal TCUs, and are implemented by different practices – by a different "technology" – than is found with insertings. Parenthesizing can be interpolated into a turn-constructional unit and be contained there, as in example 13, where Shelley registers her awareness that she may be telling something she has already told to her interlocutor, and resumes the telling directly after having done so (by returning to the pre-parenthetical talk).

(13) Debbie and Shelley, 1

Deb: <it's not causeuh:m (0.5) Mark's
no*t going*.
Shl: no– well that wuz initially and then I'm like no:
I'll just go and then uhm yaknow this- this tow
bandit (•) thing that I have, that were doing,
-> [*he w*]*a:nts me:* **I– >I don't know if I tol' you this, <**
Deb: [mmhm]
Shl: -> *he wants us* to come out to his house and do:, ˙hh like
spend a whole day o:n putting everything together
cause we don't get the shit done while were at work=

Or it can invite – or at least make room for – uptake or response by the recipient, as in example 14, in which Kathy explains to friends Rubin and Frieda what she meant by saying of a weaving of hers that it "wove itself once it was set up."

(14) KC–4, 16

Rub: Whaddyou mean it wove itself once it w's set up.=
=[What d's that] mean.=
Kat: =[O h i –]
Kat: =Well I mean it's ve:ry simple, (˙hhh)
(0.8)
Kat: -> It's exac[tly the same in the we]:ft as it is in the=
Dav: [She also means th't–]
Kat: -> =warp.

09			(0.2)
10	Kat:	–>	That is if the warp has sixteen greens an two blacks
11			an two light blues and two blacks an sixteen greens
12		–>	an: sixteen blacks on sixteen blues an so on, ˙***hh***
13		–>	***y'know the warp are the long pieces.***
14			(0.5)
15	Fri:	–>	***Mhhm***
16	Kat:		The weft has exactly tha:t.
17	Fri:		Yah.
18			(0.5)

Having used the technical weaving term "warp" (at lines 6/8 and 10), she stops before completing her account to anticipate and preempt a possible trouble in understanding by explaining what the term means, and waits for them to register their understanding before continuing and completing her account.

And in example 15, the teller of the story, Mike, figures his interlocutors already know about the character in the story he is telling (or, at least, treats them as already knowing it), and uses a parenthetical (at lines 4–5) to articulate it as a point that will heighten the impact of the episode he is describing.

(15) Auto Discussion, 7

01	Mik:		[But in ne meantime it'd cost Keegan three spo:ts'nnuh
02			feature.
03	Cur:		Yeah¿
04	Mik:	–>	So, boy when Keeg'n come in *he–* **yihknow how he's gotta**
05		–>	**temper anyway**, *he* js::: °wa::::h sc[reamed iz damn
06			e:ngine yihknow, [
07	Cur:		[Mm
08			(0.5)
09	Mik:		settin there en'e takes iz helmet off'n clunk it goes
10			on top a' the car he gets out'n goes up t'the trailer…

2.2.6 *Aborting*

I use this term in its contemporary senses, which I quote from the Encarta World English Dictionary: "to bring something to an end at an early stage; to end a space flight or similar mission before it is completed; to abandon a computer program, command, or operation before it has finished." There are two different orientations to a TCU which is left uncompleted: one takes the form of abandoning what was being said altogether, at least for the time being; the other takes the form of abandoning the way in which the TCU-so-far was saying or doing the turn's project in favor of another way of getting the same undertaking done. Examples 16 and 17 provide instances of the second of these practices; examples 18 and 19 provide instances of the first.

In example 16, Sherrie has asked Mark (at line 1) about the identity of a girl she had seen in their dormitory, and Mark's first try (at line 4) is a canonical recognitional reference form, recipient-designed for someone taken to already know *about* this person who simply did not recognize her (Sacks and Schegloff, 1979; Schegloff, 1996). Sherrie's response (at line 6) disclaims such knowledge, or, at least, the adequacy of that reference form in activating it.

(16) SN-4, 08

Shr: Who w's the girl that was outside
 (his door¿)/(the store¿)
 (0.8)
Mrk: Debbie.
 (0.8)
Shr: Who's Debbie.
Mrk: °(Katz.)
 (0.7)
Mrk: ->a_1 ***She's jus' that girl thet: uh:, (0.2)***
 ->a_2 ***·hh I met her through uh:m::, (1.0)***
 I met 'er in Westwood.=I (caught that–) (•)
 'Member I wenttuh see the premie:r of (0.3)
 Lost Horizon¿ [( )
Shr: [I DID'N KNOW YOU did,=

So at line 9, Mark launches another try, still a recognitional – on the way to being a recognitional descriptor (Schegloff, 1996), but part of the way into it, he thinks the better of that mode of approach as well, and he *abandons* it, aborting that TCU-in-progress, marked as "a_1" in the transcript. Then he launches another try, one which gives up on a recognitional reference to the target person, but tries to link her to someone Sherrie knows, still trying to incorporate an element of recognitiality in the person reference; but as he arrives at the moment for delivering that intervening person reference, he again thinks the better of it, and again *abandons* the effort, again aborting the TCU-so-far at "a_2" in the margin, and launches yet another effort, this time apparently not a recognitional reference.

In example 17, ten-year-old Kalin calls to his mother (who is engaged with her daughter Beth on something else) about a splinter he has been trying to remove, with no success.

(17) Fish Dinner, 29

01	Kal:	Hey mo::m, ((from the stairs))
02		(.)
03	Mom:	Aloe an' [vitamin E an' whatever.
04	Kal:	[I (uh) splinter (in)
05	Bet:	Which one [should I have.
06	Kal:	[but .hh
07	Kal:	when I used thuh tweezers, I even did it really ha:rd¿
08	Mom:	What [happened.
09	Kal: ->	[It's- It's just (.) too:, It's just (.) too:
10	->	uhm (buh [it's) barely op[en skin.
11	Be:	[Kalin. [Kalin.

At line 9, he tries several times to explain the problem but apparently cannot find the right word(s) to describe it (perhaps "deeply embedded"?), abandons that way of describing it and launches a new TCU – clearly different, but, as clearly, addressing the same undertaking in a different way.

On the other hand, there is example 18, previously examined for another issue as example 14.

(18) KC–4, 16

01	Kat:	It wove itself once it was set up.=
02	Fre:	=It's woo:l?
03	Kat:	It's wool.
04		(0.8)
05	Rub:	Whaddyou mean it wove itself once it w's set up.=
06		=[What d's that] mean.=
07	Kat:	=[O h i –]
08	Kat:	=Well I mean it's ve:ry simple, (˙hhh)
09		(0.8)
10	Kat:	It's exac[tly the same in the we]:ft as it is in the=
11	Dav: ->	[***She also means th't–***]
12	Kat:	=warp.
13		(0.2)
14	Kat:	That is if the warp has sixteen greens an two blacks
15		an two light blues and two blacks an sixteen greens
16		an: sixteen blacks on sixteen blues an so on, ˙hh
17		y'know the warp are the long pieces.
18		(0.5)
19	Fre:	Mhhm
20	Kat:	The weft has exactly tha:t.
21	Fre:	Yah.

Now we are focused on lines 8–12. Rubin, you will recall, had asked Kathy what she meant by saying of her weaving that "it wove itself once it was set up." At line 8, Kathy delivers what will turn out to be a "topic sentence," to be unpacked in what follows, but a long silence of (0.8) at line 9 ensues at what is a possible completion point of a TCU and, therefore, transition-relevant. Her husband Dave appears to have been waiting for the silence to reach the (1.0) second mark that Gail Jefferson (1989) found to be the "standard maximum silence" in conversation before starting to add to Kathy's account, but Kathy had just started (0.2) of a second earlier, and so they find themselves in overlap. Kathy is multiply entitled to this turn position because (1) the question being responded to was addressed to her, so she is the selected next speaker, (2) she is the authority on the matter at hand, and (3) she was the first starter. Still, Dave persists for five syllables, and then yields by *abandoning* the utterance he had begun, aborting the turn-so-far before possible completion. Here, then, the TCU is simply abandoned, with no effort to try it again or try it differently.

Example 19 should, by now, be recognizable as yet another installment of this exchange – just after Kathy has completed her explanation in lines 1–2.

(19) KC–4, 17

Kat: =˙hhh So once I'd set up the wa:rp, (0.8) it was very
simple to jus keep– jis to weave it.
(1.0)
Kat: You know,=
=[( )]
Dav: -> ***[B u t– (•) b u t] listen tuh how long it]***
Rub: [In other words,] you gotta string up thee:–]
you gotta string up thee: colors, is that it?=
Kat: =Ri[ght.]
Rub: [I n][thee:] in thee: [warp.]
Dav: [°yeh°] [ ]
Kat: [Right.] Right.
(0.2)
Dav: -> ***Buh listen tuh [how lo:ng it took to put in the–]=***
Kat: [A n d th e n e a c h w e f t–]
Dav: -> ***=the:– the wa:rps. [(though)]***
Kat: [A n d] then each we:ft, y'know
then I did– I s– my warp was strung up. so that [I had
(each colors.)

When Rubin (who had requested the explanation) is slow to register it at line 3, Kathy (after the one-second silence) starts up again, once again trailed by Dave at line 6, but now Dave's competition is not so much Kathy as it is Rubin, the asker of the question who now wants to check his understanding of the answer (at line 7), and once again Dave yields to the protagonists of the sequence, *abandoning* the line he is taking and aborting the turn before reaching possible completion. (We return to this exchange following example 23 below.)

2.2.7 *Sequence-jumping*

Although similar in several respects to aborting, sequence-jumping invites separate treatment. As we have seen, in aborting, the abandonings are followed by a different effort or tack to achieve the same result, and may pause before doing so, or give up the production of the turn with no further ado. By contrast, the specimens examined here follow abandonment of the TCU-so-far by turning sharply to something unrelated to the turn and sequence in progress, and do so with either no break or hardly any break at all. In fact, the shift to an altogether different matter marks this repair practice as quite distinctive; although the repair is initiated and carried through in a single turn by its speaker, what is getting repaired is the sequence to which the turn is contributing. The TCU which is cut-off by the repair-initiator belonged to the sequence in progress at the turn's start; the repair that follows the initiator either launches a new sequence (as in examples 20 and 21) or addresses something said by an interlocutor in the just prior turn which is thereby treated as the start of a new sequence (as in example 22).

Example 20 is drawn from the KC-4 materials drawn upon previously. Rubin and Frieda who are dinner guests at Kathy and Dave's (the women are long-time friends) have in the past given Kathy and Dave access to their country home outside the city; Frieda has just been explaining that they have recently also given access to the home to other friends with an invalid mother, but hastens to reassure them that they (Kathy and Dave) can still use the house.

(20) KC–4, 14

01	Rub:		They don mind honey they're jus not gonna talk to us
02			ever again.=
03	Dav:		=(hehem)/(ri:(h)ight)
04			(0.8)
05	Kat:		We don mind <[we jus ne:ver gonna talk to you e:ver=
06	Dav:		[(No, b't)
07	Kat:		=(hh heh)
08	Rub:		heheheheh
09	Kat:		[No::] that's awright
10	Fre:		[So ::]
11	Dav:		[( )]
12	Fre:		[You know what we're gonna–] in fact I'm– she I
13		–>	haven't seen her since I spoke to you but I'm going to
14		–>	talk to=***what a you making¿***
15			(0.2)
16	Kat:		It's a –bla:nket.
17	Fre:		Did yu weave tha[t yourse:lf]
18	Kat:		[I wo ::]ve this myself.=

A longish silence sets in, broken by Rubin's intendedly ironic (we must assume) turn at lines 1–2, addressed to his wife Frieda but meant for Kathy and Dave. Kathy registers the joking/ironic intent by repeating Rubin's utterance with an upgrade (from "not … ever" to "never … ever"), and then (at line 9), with a joke-to-serious "no" (Schegloff, 2001), offers an unconvincing assurance, "That's all right." So here they are in this uncomfortably sticky situation, with Frieda finding herself extending it further still at lines 13–14, when she notices a piece of woven goods. And then, she escapes by running the TCU-in-progress from "but I'm going to talk to" (with the next words most likely projectable as "her" or "them") directly into "What are you making," thereby shifting from one sequence to an altogether different one.

In example 21, Arthur and Rebecca are two twenty–thirty-year-olds looking to "make it" in Hollywood; Arthur has called to record a conversation for his friend at UCLA who is taking this course on conversation. Once they get past that, they talk respective careers. Arthur has tentatively accepted a job offer from the entertainment company and TV network ABC and is looking it over to make a final decision, and has been describing what he has seen at ABC.

(21) Arthur and Rebecca, 3

01 Art: =A:nd uhm: .hhh an then there's all these editing
02 ro:oms for (.) thirty-five millimeter an' seventy
03 millimeter stuff?
04 Reb: °Hmm
05 (0.8)
06 Art: s– big (0.2) you know w– (0.6) all these ro:oms,
07 (0.6) and um so: it's jus kinda interesting.
08 (1.0)
09 Art: Um:: (0.4) so I c'n certainly lea:rn from it.
10 (0.3)
11 Reb: Eh::ye:ah,
12 Art: A:nd um: it's not a bad place to be (0.5) becuz
13 -> it's real– (.) ***ya know I got humming birds no:w?***
14 (0.2)
15 Reb: What?
16 Art: I(h) .hh I have hu:mming birds.
17 Reb: Oh::: gre:at, [You should get a fee:der.
18 Art: [°Yeah,

The uptake from Rebecca has been desultory at best, and ironic when not at its best. Arthur has made a number of tries to show he's done, but Rebecca does not pick up the clues, and keeps on feeding him continuers (for example, at lines 4, 11), not to mention the silences in between them. And then, at line 13, the *escaping* here (as in the previous instance) via doing a noticing where otherwise the next element of a TCU-in-progress was due, but was aborted.

Finally, in example 22, after about thirteen minutes of conversation about school, and mutual acquaintances, Bee launches what could be an invitation or arrangements-making sequence with the query, "So yih gonna be arou:n this weeken'?" (it is a long "Presidents' Day" four-day weekend – at least for Bee). To this possible pre-invitation Ava replies with a problematic response – almost a minute full of commitments and possible involvements, and hardly encouraging a pursuit of a get-together, though not precluding it. On its completion, Bee responds (lines 1–2) by mentioning the possibility of "seeing" Ava if she's around:

(22) TG, 16

01	Bee:		[Well if yer arou:nd
02			I'll probably see y(hh)ou hn[hh! ˙hh
03	Ava:		[Why, whuts (Bob doing)
04	Bee:		Uh–u–uh:: goin o:ff::
05	Ava:		Where's he goin.
06	Bee:		To Wa:shin'ton,
07	Ava:		Oh.
08			(0.7)
09	Bee:		He asn' been there sih-since Christmas [so:. hHe's
10	Ava:		[Mm.
11	Bee:		going.
12			(0.5)
13	Ava:		Yeh w'l I'll give you a call then tomorrow.when I get
14			in 'r sumn.
15			(0.5)
16	Bee:		Wha:t,
17	Ava:		<I'll give yih call tomo[rrow.]
18	Bee:		[Yeh:]
19	Bee:		'n [I'll be ho:me t'mor]row.
20	Ava:		[When I–I get home.]
21	Ava:		I don't kno–w– I could be home by–˙hh three, I c'd be
22			home by two [I don't] know.]
23	Bee:		[Well] when]ever. I'll poh I-I might
24			go t'the city in the mo:rning any[way,
25	Ava:		[It depends on how
26		–>	(tough the)=***So what time y'leaving f'the city,***

After hearing that Bee's boyfriend will be away, Ava makes a responsive gesture to the prospect of getting together, offering to call Bee when she gets back from school, and alerting her to the indeterminacy of that call (lines 13–14), and then again at 20–22, with an incipient account for the indeterminacy due (very likely) to the traffic, at line 25 when her hearing/parsing of what Bee has just said about going into "the city" (New York) in the morning registers, and she jumps from the sequence she was adding to (about when she would call Bee upon returning from school) to a new possibility that has just materialized for meeting with Bee in the morning, and at lines 25–26 Ava jumps from the one sequence to pursue the other.

2.2.8 Recycling

The term "recycling" refers to a speaker's saying again some stretch of talk – almost always less than a full TCU – that they have previously said, ordinarily *just* previously said. Recycling has various uses, of which I'm sure I understand only a few.

One that we have already encountered is the use of recycling to frame a repair: a replacing framed by a recycled "for" in example 01; an inserting framed by a recycled "is the" in example 06; a deleting framed by a recycled "I" in example 07, and another framed by a recycled "That's" in example 08; a solution to a search framed by a recycled "a" in example 10, and so on. In these instances, the recycled element(s) *figure* in the repair segment but *not* as the repair *itself*; they are resources, but not the product, and there are other such applications.

But recycling can be a repair operation in its own right. One site in which recycling regularly serves as the repair operation itself is at the emergence of a "surviving turn" from overlap with another, as in example 23.

(23) KC–4, 07

Rbn: Well thee uhm (•) (a paz) they must have grown a
culture.
(0.5)
Rbn: You know, (•) they must've I mean how lo– he's been
in the hospital for a few day:s, right?
{(1.0)/'hhh}
Rbn: Takes a[bout a week to grow a culture,]
Kay: -> [I don think they grow a] ***I don think***
-> ***they –grow a culture to do a biopsy.***
Rbn: No::. (•) They did the biopsy while he was on the
–table.
Kay: Nononono. They did a frozen section. when he
[was on the tab[le.
Rbn: [Right, [( )
Kay: But they didn't do the– it takes a while to do a
complete biopsy.
(0.8)

Here Kathy and Rubin are talking in overlap, and just as Rubin comes to the possible completion of his turn (at "culture"), Kathy withholds production of the next element due in *her* turn-so-far, and instead recycles the turn-so-far from its beginning. Getting it said "in the clear" is designed to deal with whatever trouble in hearing or understanding accompanied its involvement with simultaneous, and potentially competing, talk by another, including in particular trouble in hearing or understanding *by that other* (cf. Schegloff, 1987 [1973]).

But how is this different from the exchange in example 19, where Dave says "But listen to how long it" at line 6 in overlap with Rubin, and then a moment later, at lines 14–16 recycles it and brings it to possible completion (this time in overlap with Kathy)? It was offered in our earlier discussion as an instance of *abandoning*; why not of *recycling*? Or why is the first saying here in example 23 *not* said to be an instance of abandoning? Timing is all! When Dave withdraws from the competition in example 19, it is without any assurance that he will get a chance to say it again; who knows what direction the talk will take in the aftermath of the turn to which he is yielding? At that point, he is abandoning that saying. When the opportunity presents itself later to try again, he does so, and his doing so can be heard by the other parties to the interaction as his recycling of something that he had abandoned earlier. But in example 23, Kathy can be heard to be stopping the advancement of her TCU *by virtue of* the ending of the competing talk, and so she can be heard, *not* as *abandoning* that talk, but as gearing up to get it said in the clear. It is, then, a *recycling* from the get-go, and the recycling is here the *star* of the repair show, not a secondary supporting role.

When previously articulated talk is recycled, the second saying may diverge from the first in various respects. Note, for example, that in example 23, "grow" is produced at markedly higher pitch in the recycle that in the first saying. It is a judgment call whether such variance is the designed point of the resaying or not – a judgment call in the first instance for the recipient(s), and in the second instance for the external analyst. In including this data extract in the set of exemplars for recycling, I reveal, and rely on, my judgment that the variance is not the point of the repeat; if it were, it should be included in the data set for replacings. I will return to this point in a moment.

Before that, I want to register the resistance of many occurrences of recyclings to analysis – at least so far, at least for me.[4] I've included some instances below to share my frustration with readers ("rcl" indicates "recycling;" "rpl" indicates "replacing").

(24) TG, 09

```
Bee:    B't I still have one more book tuh buy I can't
        get it,
        (0.8)
Bee:    °So uh,
        (0.6)
```

06 Bee: -> rcl I don'know.The **school**– ***school*** uh, (1.0) bookstore
07 doesn' carry anything anymo (h) uh,
08 Ava: Mno?hh
09 Bee: No, I don'know I guess (inna) spring term they don'
10 -> rcl order ez– y'know many books ez **they**–***they***– really are
11 suppo:se to.

(25) Concert Tickets, 5

01 Al: -> rcl Okay. **I'll**– ***I'll*** find out: what I can tomorrow when
02 -> rpl I go to **the**– (.) ***thee uh*** (.) office et UCLA:: and
03 I'll give you a call if I:– know anything mo:re.

(26) Automobile Discussion, 21

01 Cur: -> Well? see I don't know any, I wouldn'know **what**–
02 -> rcl (0.4) ***what*** dimensions t'even start tuh give'em.
03 (0.4)
04 Cur: Wouldn'know what t'hell eed want.
05 Gar: Go down nere'n measure hi:s. ˙hh
06 (1.0)
07 Mik: -> **They use to u[h : ,]**
08 ???: [(C'mmere.)]/((clears throat))
09 (3.0)
10 Mik: -> rcl ***They use to uh,*** (0.4) ˙hh make'm any way y'know they
11 -> rcl use to go up'n get'em **fer the** (0.5) ***fer the*** stock
12 cars out there.
13 (0.4)

So, in example 24 I have nothing cogent to say about the recycling of "school" at line 6 or of "they" at line 10, and the same for the recycling of "I'll" in line 1 of example 25, or of "what" at lines 1–2 in example 26, of "They use to uh" at lines 7 and 10 in example 26 (including the "uh"!), or of the "fer the" at line 11.

On the other hand, we have example 27. Notice that at line 01 there are virtually identical productions of "he's," followed by a recycling of the entire run-up to that word issuing in a heavy stress of "he's."

(27) Debbie & Shelley, 4

01 Shl: -> rcl So: I mean it's not becuz ***he's***– ***he's***– I mean it's
02 -> rpl not becuz ***he:'s*** not going, it's becuz (0.5) his
03 money's not: (0.5) funding me.
04 Deb: okay,

This is no passing variance; this has been an effortful, and initially failed, commitment to give "he's" the heightened stress that will make of it the point of reference for a subsequent contrast ("not HIM, his money!"). So this re-production is *not* a recycling; it is a *replacing* – no less so because it is in the *prosody* rather than in the *lexicon* that the replacing is to be found.

With this explication in hand, we might return to example 25, where we previously registered the recycling of "I'll" in line 1, and focus for a moment on line 2. Here we have the article "the" recycled, or *do* we? The second saying is not "the," it is "thee"; and we can recall the beginning of Jefferson's "Error correction" paper of 1974, and wonder what was going to be the consonant-initial next word after "the," that got replaced by the vowel-initial "office," and the vowel-initial "uh" before it (perhaps nothing more than "box-office"!). Is this, then, an opaque recycling, or a potentially consequential (and mostly hidden) replacement?

2.2.9 *Reformatting*

The starting point for the operation of reformatting is grammatical. In example 28 at line 12, what starts out as a declarative ("Well Beth [got to work ...]" or "Well Beth [didn't have to wait ...]") is reformatted as a negative interrogative ("Didn't Beth get to work ..."), the shift being accomplished by using "didn't" as a pivot – the next word of the initially started TCU, the first word of the reformatted TCU.

(28) Virginia, 5

01 Vir: ˙hh Beth gets all the clo:thes.
02 (.)
03 Mom: Well: –Beth (.) spends her own money on her clothes.
04 (0.7)
05 Vir: <Well if I got more money °I could spend my own
06 mon[ey.
07 Mom: [But Beth works.
08 Vir: Wull why can't I::?
09 Mom: Beh– oh:, Vuhginia, we've been through this. When
10 you're old enough you ca:n work in the store.
11 (0.2)
12 Vir: –> ˙hh **Well Beth *didn'*** *Beth get tih work b'fore she was*
13 *sixteen?=*
14 Mom: =No::! I'd– (0.2) I would let her wrap presents an'
15 packages et Christmus an:'– °times we needed
16 somebady.° ˙hh >But people just don't want< (0.4)
17 chu:ldren (0.2) waiting on[('um).

In example 29 at lines 5–6, what starts as a WH-question is reformatted as a Y/N question done as an assertion plus tag.

(29) TG, 04

01 Bee: So, <I got some lousy cou(h)rses th(hh)is te(h)e(h)rm
02 too.
03 Ava: Kehh huh!
04 Bee: ˙hhh[h m–]

05 Ava: -> [W–whe]n's yer uh, weh– *you have one day y'only*
06 -> *have one course uh?*
07 Bee: mMo[nday en Wednesday:[s right.] That's] my=
08 Ava: [ˑhhhh [O h.] that's–]
09 Bee: =linguistics course [hh

And in example 30, at lines 9–12, a simple declarative ("I hope X") is reformatted into a cleft- or pseudo-cleft construction ("What I hope happens is …"), a reformatting that is promptly reversed by reformatting back to the simple declarative – "I hope that they announce …"

(30) Concert tickets, 3

01 Jim: Well I dunno: –I¯ ordered two: sea:ts.
02 Al: You did,
03 Jim: Ye:s.
04 Al: Did you order rese:rved seats?
05 Jim: I just said give me two seats plea:se and he said
06 ¯well the computer will pick them out for you
07 si:r– ((mimicking voice)) ['n (heh heh)
08 Al: [And it'll mail it to you
09 and even if it–
10 Jim: -> Right. Now see– .hhh **I– I** ***wwhut I ho:pe happens is***
11 -> ***that*** [I hope=
12 Al: [( )
13 Jim: =that they announce another sho:w like at (.) the
14 universal amphitheater or something,

The reversal does not blunt the relevance of addressing as an issue what such a reformatting can be understood to have been about in the first place.

But there are other forms of reformatting that are not grammatical, and may appear to be some other form of repair. Example 31 comes after a fair amount of bickering at the dinner table about Virginia's insistent request for an increase in her allowance, parried by Mom's insistent queries about what she needs it for, as in line 1 of the extract.

(31) Virginia, 22

01 Mom: If I could see what you did with your money,
02 (0.3)
03 Vir: You want me to write you a: a little list¿every
04 w[eek(?)
05 Mom: -> **[I: would–** (.) ***that would be*** great.
06 (0.5)

This elicits from Virginia an offer to keep written track of how she spends her money – an offer that exceeds Mom's wildest dreams. She can barely contain herself as she begins to respond, "I would …" almost certainly on the way to "I would LOVE THAT!" But she stops and initiates what could be taken for a replacement of "I" by "that," framed by the recycle of "would." Might we entertain the possibility that this too is a reformatting, not grammatical but *perspectival* – making the focus not "Mom's pleasure" but "Virginia's suggestion"?

Whatever we make of that particular possibility, it is the tip of a larger issue, and that is the need to distinguish between what I will call *first- and second-order operations*.

First-order operations are the basic operations a speaker may bring to bear on the TCU-in-production at any moment in its development: There are, as far as I can make out, seven of them: replacing, inserting, deleting, searching, parenthesizing, aborting, and recycling. These are what I am calling "first-order" operations: they name the basic, *prima facie* job being done on the TCU-or-turn-in-progress.

By "second-order operations," I mean repairs which *could* be understood in the terminology of the first-order operations, but whose analysis would have missed the point if left at that. Even without getting into the interactional import of the repair, we need to see (as the *co-participants* need to see in the first instance) that the basic or first-order repair operations are being used to bring off a *different* repair operation altogether. Sometimes the interactional import is grounded in the first-order repair operation; sometimes we (and the recipient, in the first instance) will miss the point without grasping the second-order operation, which is the proximate source of the interactional upshot. Reformatting is one such second-order operation, and taking the repair in example 30 to be nothing other than the replacement apparent on the surface would miss the perspectival reformatting that is being implemented by it.

In example 30, we could see only that there has been an inserting of "what" before the "I," and there has. But here the inserted object serves to reformat the turn from what had started as a straightforward statement of hope – "I [hope that they announce another show …]" to the "cleft" or "pseudo-cleft" construction – "What I hope happens is …" To stop at seeing it as an *inserting* will miss the point, as would treating the repair in example 31 as a simple replacement: the replacement is the vehicle for another, second-order operation. The tenth and final operation that I am aware of – which I am calling "reordering" – also gets used both as a first-order and as a *second-order* operation.

2.2.10 *Reordering*

Reordering is an operation speakers can use when trying to work out the order in which elements of a turn-in-progress should be arrayed.

As a first-order operation, it serves to re-order elements of a TCU-in-progress. In example 32, at line 8, Bea is on her way to saying "you just never saw such devotion" when she hears coming out of her mouth "you never just"; what follows is a resaying with the out-of-order elements reordered.

(32) SBL 1:1:10:R

Rse: An'it– (0.3) An'it left'er (0.4) quite permanently
damaged °I s[uppose°
Bea: [˙tk
Bea: Uh:pparently,
(•)
Bea: Uh –he is still hopeful
Rse: The husb'n.
Bea: –> Ah hah end yih **never jus'** (•) eh yih ***js' never*** saw
such devotion in your li:fe …

And in example 33, at line 4, an interviewer talking on the telephone to a "guest" on a radio talk show asks the guest, "But do you get alway-," catches the problem and redoes the TCU with the elements reordered.

(33) Sidnell, 2006: 8

Ans: if you: w:–watch any of the briefings
you'll see that:– ahm: usually one of
the la:st people to get called on,
Que: –> But do you **get alway**– d'you ***always get***
called on?
Ans: not always, no.

But the second-order operation of reordering operates not on words in a TCU, but on TCUs in a turn, and the first-order operation by which it is brought off is not reordering but replacing.

In example 34, Vic, who is a janitor in an apartment building in New York, is recounting his confrontation with a tenant who has admitted that his son broke a window in a neighboring building, the glass of which Vic has cleaned up for his friend, James – the janitor of that building. Vic has just finished reporting the confession and his (Vic's) asking whether the kid got hurt.

(34) Upholstery Shop, 1

Vic: ˙hh I caught the gu::y, I said wo:w the son'vabitch
who did this=So dih gu:y says tuh me, – –th' guy says
tuh me–˙hh my son [didid.
Ric: [Wuh/(jeh)/(de) do:.=
Vic: =I said did, he, get, hurtch. He said no, only a li'l
bid'v a cut. ˙hh So I sez, ˙hh wa:l whuddiyou goin do
about this 'e sez oh dih soopuh ul clean it up,
(0.3)
???: hhheh
Vic: –> So I sez. ***I zez***–˙hh ***he sez***– ˙hh ***I sez*** well haddidih
happen.
He says tuh me:, …

Inspection of the talk on line 10 of example 34 might suggest that we have here two replacings – "I" replaced by "he" and then "he" replaced by "I" – both replacings being framed by the recycling of "sez." But the issue here is not who said the utterance about to be reported; it is, rather, what should be the next thing told in the recounting – what the tenant/perpetrator said or what Vic said. The repair operation is, then, concerned not with replacing one word with another, or one TCU with another, but with the optimum ordering of the TCUs that compose the telling. Although the first-order operation is replacement, it is there to implement the second-order operation – reordering the tellables that compose the storytelling.

Example 35 offers another case in point. At line 1 we find Bee apparently doing two consecutive replacements.

(35) TG, 07

Bee: –> =Oh he–he's too much.**He doesn't**– en he put– ***they put***
–> ***us in this gigantic lectchuh hall.***
Ava: Mmm.
Bee: –> Tch! An::! (0.2) **He doesn't** speak- (0.2) very lou:d
anyway.=
Ava: =Mm hm,
Bee: Tch! An:', bo:y oh boy hhhhihhhnh! ˙hhhh!

First, she cuts off the turn-so-far "He doesn't-" and apparently replaces the "doesn't" with "put," framing the replacement by recycling the "he." Second, she cuts off the "put" and apparently replaces the subject of the predicate "he" with "they," framing the replacement with a recycling of the "put." Now it appears she figures that she's got it right, and runs the TCU-as-now-reconstituted to possible completion.

The account I have given so far is meant to approximate what a recipient could make of this in real time. The initial "he doesn't" has been buried under two rounds of replacings – first targeting the verb, then targeting the subject or agent. But then, at line 4, the "He doesn't" re-appears, and the TCU that starts that way now goes to possible completion.

Here again what appear at first to be replacings end up being what I am calling reorderings, and what is getting re-ordered are the TCUs that compose the turn. Bee finds that making her point will be well served if her account of the instructor's soft voice is delivered into an already-characterized very large lecture hall, and her repair is designed to re-order the several TCUs that will have composed her turn. The payoff is the "anyway," which serves to underscore the total upshot of what is now a gestalt.

And in example 36, what might appear initially to be the inserting of a "This" before the "is" that had started to be said after the initial "hello" also turns out to be a *reordering* – in this case of sequences and sequence types.

(36) ID, Openings, 233

Irn: Hello:
JM: -> Hello. **Ih–** ***This is Jan's mother.***
Irn: Oh yes.
JM: -> **Is** Jan there by any chance?

Irene is the mother of a fourteen-year-old daughter whose friend Jan is visiting in their home. The caller is Jan's mother, who was apparently starting to ask to speak to her daughter; I take the "Ih-"in line 2 to be the start of the "Is" at line 4. Jan's Mom has decided to first identify herself so as to ground the legitimacy of her request before making it, and the consequence is a *reordering* of the two sequences.

A final observation on re-ordering: as noted earlier, unlike most of the other operations we have examined, reordering can be a repair operation on the *turn*, not the TCU. It is, of course, initiated within a TCU, but, by the time it is done, what has been repaired is not the TCU in which it was launched, but the ordering of the several TCUs that compose the turn. And, once registered explicitly with respect to *reordering*, we can be alerted to the possible relevance of other of the operations to repair of a *turn*, as well as repair on a *TCU*. For example, searching can also be a repair operation on the turn, as is the case for the "resumption searches," as in example 12.

And a final observation on first- and second-order operations: having been introduced in the context of the last two operations discussed here (reformatting and reordering), it is worth making explicit that it applies to more than these two operations. Whatever gets done by some repair operation addressed as a first-order operation, the result invites inspection (by co-participants, and therefore by us as analysts) for what second-order operation it may implicate. One exemplar will have to suffice.

Mark has dropped in on fellow students Sherrie, Ruthie and Karen in their dormitory room. Some question has been raised about his contact with reality in light of recent drinking binges – in the turn just before example 37 concerning what day of the week it is; Sherrie has just pointed out that it is Monday.

(37) SN-4, 15

Shr: As in we had cla:sses tuhday?
(0.2)
Mrk: Oh well I was si:ck.
(0.2)
Shr: [Oh.]
Mrk: [Y'kn]ow.
(•)
Mrk: (t's) whu I told the lady thet I work– (0.2) yihknow
up on campus.

10 (0.8)
11 Mrk: -> *Called 'er 'n I t– **well a:ckshilly I*** **told 'er thet– my**
12 **best friend hed gotten: the measles.**
13 (0.4)
14 Mrk: Sh' s'd– "Oh that's TE:rrible. (•) W'l you better stay
15 in an' re:st." So I said "Yeah I [sure better,"
16 (?): [hhh
17 (•)
18 Mrk: I didn't tell'er I wz sick I jus' said my best friend
19 [had the mea:sles.=
20 (?): [hunh
21 Shr: =˙HHH Djiju tell'er you 'ad symph athih– sympathy
22 pai[ns for'm?
23 (?): [(°heh)
24 Mrk: h(h)h No. I din' tell'er anyth(h)ing. ˙hhh
25 (0.8)
26 Mrk: S'I got outta w:orking anyway. hhh
27 (1.4)

At line 11, Mark appears to be doing an inserting of "actually" before the incipient "I t-[old her ...]" which was destined to be "I was sick," as is shown at line 18. But "actually" has, among its diverse usages (Clift, 2001, 2003), an alert that a replacement is possibly upcoming, and this is in fact what it is being used to do here. So, in this case, the cut-off is used to launch an inserting, and the insert is being used to launch (and announce the launching of) a replacement of what had been about to be said (and is later reported) by what was in fact the case.

The upshot, then, is that the second-order operation being implemented by a first-order repair operation need not be either reformatting or reordering; it can itself be one of the operations introduced earlier as first-order operation.

2.3 Closure (for now)

These, then, are ten recognizable and recurrent repair operations initiated in the same turn, and almost always in the same TCU, as the talk they show themselves to be addressed to. There may well be others awaiting recognition and inviting description. But the account provided in these pages addresses but one aspect of same-turn, self-initiated repair – the operation(s) being performed. It is incomplete without an account of the resources that bring these operations into recognizable form – what speakers do to provide for recipients the recognizability of a repair operation of type X. And it is incomplete without an account of the interactional work any given instance of any of these repair operations can be understood to be doing in context. The first of these is striking for how a very few practices of talking make possible such a range of operations. The second of these is striking for how diverse are the environments and interactional outcomes which these very few operations achieve. Both of these missing parts will have to be found elsewhere.[5]

REFERENCES

Clark, H. H. and Fox Tree, J. E. (2002). Using *uh* and *um* in spontaneous speaking. *Cognition* 84: 73–111.

Clift, R. (2001). Meaning in interaction: the case of "actually." *Language*, 77(2), 245–291.

(2003). Synonyms in action: a case study. *International Journal of English Studies* 3(1), 167–187.

Drew, P., Walker, T. and Ogden, R. (this volume). Self-repair and action construction.

Fox, B., Wouk, F., Hayashi, M., Fincke, S., Tao, L., Sorjonen, M. -L., Laakso, M. and Hernandez, W. F. (2009). A cross-linguistic investigation of the site of initiation in same-turn self-repair. In J. Sidnell, ed., *Conversation Analysis: Comparative Perspectives*, pp. 60–103. Cambridge University Press.

Jefferson, G. (1974). Error correction as an interactional resource. *Language in Society* 2: 181–199.

(1989). Preliminary notes on a possible metric which provides for a "standard maximum" silences of approximately one second in conversation. In D. Roger and P. Bull, eds., *Conversation: An Interdisciplinary Perspective*, pp. 166–196. Clevedon: Multilingual Matters.

Lerner, G. H. (1991). On the syntax of sentences-in-progress. *Language in Society* 20: 441–458.

(1996). On the 'semi-permeable' character of grammatical units in conversation: conditional entry into the turn space of another speaker. In E. Ochs, E. A. Schegloff and S. A. Thompson, eds., *Interaction and Grammar*, pp. 238–276. Cambridge University Press.

(2004). The collaborative turn sequence. In G. H. Lerner, eds., *Conversation Analysis: Studies from the First Generation*, pp. 225–256. Washington, DC: University Press of America.

Mazeland, H. (2007). Parenthetical sequences. *Journal of Pragmatics* 39: 1816–1869.

Raymond, G. and Heritage, J. (this volume). One question after another: same-turn repair in the formation of yes/no type initiating actions.

Sacks, H. and Schegloff, E. A. (1979). Two preferences in the organization of reference to persons and their interaction. In G. Psathas, ed., *Everyday Language: Studies in Ethnomethodology*, pp. 15–21. New York: Irvington Publishers.

Schegloff, E. A. (1987[1973]). Recycled turn beginnings: a precise repair mechanism in conversation's turn-taking organisation. In G. Button and J. R. E. Lee, eds., *Talk and Social Organisation*, pp. 70–85. Clevedon: Multilingual Matters.

(1996). Some practices for referring to persons in talk-in-interaction: a partial sketch of a systematics. In B. A. Fox, ed., *Studies in Anaphora*, pp. 437–485. Amsterdam: John Benjamins.

(2001). Getting serious: joke -> serious "no" *Journal of Pragmatics* 33:12, 1947–1955.

(2009). One perspective on *Conversation Analysis: Comparative perspectives.* In J. Sidnell, ed., *Conversation Analysis: Comparative perspectives*, pp. 357–406. Cambridge University Press.

(2010). Some other "uh(m)"s. *Discourse Processes* 47: 130–174.

Sidnell, Jack (2006). Repair. In Jan-Ola Ostman and Jef Verschueren, eds., *Handbook of Pragmatics 2006*, Amsterdam/Philadelphia: John Benjamins.

Wilkinson, S. and Weatherall, A. (2011). Insertion repair. *Research on Language and Social Interaction* 44(1): 65–91.

NOTES

1 A volume in preparation to be published by Cambridge University Press with the title *Repair Organization in Interaction: A Primer in Conversation Analysis II*, to appear. A version of the material included in the document you are reading was presented at a conference on repair organized by Jack Sidnell at the University of Toronto, March 2008; I am grateful to its participants for their comments, questions, and suggestions, as I am, as well, to Geoff Raymond and Tanya Romaniuk for helpful suggestions for greater clarity in the penultimate version of the text.

2 The arrows point to the relevant lines in the extracts, where italics and bold face will take over. The thirty-seven data extracts that appear in the text are drawn from sixteen different sources, including both audio and video recordings and involving forty-one different participants. Digitized files of audio and/or video data can be accessed at: www.sscnet.ucla.edu/soc/faculty/schegloff/sound-clips.html.

3 For good reason – it makes no sense. Having said about a snowmobile going 80 mph that it's "a little bit too fast" (lines 1–2), he's then told it can go 125 mph, so *of course* that will be too fast; it would only be "*still* too fast" if the second number was *lower* than the first! Here again, then, we can take note of the interactional job being done.

4 Fox et al. (2009) propose that recycling may serve to provide a beat of delay in coping with some production problem, a proposal which I call into question in the same volume (Schegloff, 2009) on various grounds, among them: a) the failure to differentiate recycling as a frame for another type of repair operation and recycling as itself the repair operation, and b) the absence of any account of the difference between recycling and other practices of delaying such as silence and "uh(m)" which regularly occur in the same environments (Clark and Fox Tree, 2002; Schegloff, 2010), as can be seen in examples 24–26.

5 See, for example, Wilkinson and Weatherall (2011), Drew, Walker and Ogden (this volume), Raymond and Heritage (this volume) and perhaps others in this volume, as well as the volume promised in note 1.

3 Self-repair and action construction

Paul Drew, Traci Walker, and Richard Ogden

3.1 Introduction

One of the cornerstones of conversation analytic research into social interaction is our close exploration of *turn design* – the ways in which speakers design their turns with respect to *where* in a sequence a turn is being taken, *what* is being done in that turn and to *whom* the turn is addressed; in short, in constructing their turns at talk speakers orient to *sequence*, *action* and their *recipient(s)* (Drew, forthcoming). Moreover, speakers construct their turns in such a way as to be understood in a certain way, to be doing the action the turn is designed to accomplish (which is the accountability of a turn's construction). Turn design is consequential insofar as sequences of interaction proceed according to what action a turn is designed to do, and how that action has been constructed; the design of a turn creates the context out of which the recipient's next turn/action is shaped and understood (Heritage, 1984a: 242).

Methodologically, our approach to investigating turn design is broadly comparative. When, usually in the earlier stages of analysis, we are trying to get a handle on the work done through the way in which a particular turn was designed, we consider how else the speaker might have designed that turn – how else they might have designed that action, or what other action they might have designed the turn to do. As our inquiries develop, we may compare the (different) design of the 'same' action. For instance, we can compare rather directly how the same inquiry is constructed, when made to different recipients; in the examples below Leslie is telephoning around members of the local branch of an organisation, to find out who is coming that evening to a meeting for which she evidently is responsible.

This report arises from our project on *Affiliation and disaffiliation in interaction: language and social cohesion*, ESRC grant 00023–0035. We gratefully acknowledge the ESRC's support for this project.

(01) Field C85:3 (Telephone call)

01 Myr: … two eight?
02 (0.2)
03 Les: Oh hello:, uhm hh Leslie ↑Field ↓he:re?
04 (0.6)
05 Myr: Sorry?
06 (.)
07 Les: Leslie[Fie:ld?
08 Myr: [↑Oh hell↓o hell↓o[: °Leslie yes sorry°
09 Les: [Hello,
10 (.)
11 Les: ↑Are you **thinkin:g of comin:g** t'the meeting
12 t'↓night

(02) Field C85:4 (Telephone call)

01 Joy: °(Eight four eight seven: six oh five)°
02 Les: Oh ↑hello Joyce are ↑you **going**↑ t'the mee↓ting
03 t'ni:ght,

These two enquiries (lines 11 and 2, respectively) are identical except for the bolded components; where Leslie asks Myra whether she's *thinking of coming*, she asks Joyce whether she's *going* to the meeting. There's no need here to go into the interactional particularities and significance of the difference in *social* deixis from *coming* and *going* (they live in approximately the same area/place and in a similar configuration to one another) (Fillmore, 1997), nor the difference that constructing the verb as *thinking of* coming might make (though these differences in turn construction might orient to the different relationships Leslie has with Myra and with Joyce, relationships that are somewhat evident in the different openings). For present purposes, note only that we can compare rather directly these two instances of the 'same' enquiry, in order to investigate how Leslie might have come to select different verbs in the two cases.

There is a range of other comparative methods or techniques for investigating how particular aspects of turn design 'work' interactionally, one of which has been somewhat overlooked in the research literature – and that is *self-repair*. From time to time, speakers may correct something they have said, or be in the course of saying, as in these examples.

(03) Field:J86:1:4:168/69 (Telephone call)

01 Les: And em (0.6) .tch (0.5) Well now we've got t'try'n
02 reply 'n **our En:g our French** isn't up to it,hhh

(04) Field: SO88(II):2:8 (Telephone call)

Mum: Oh ↓yes. .hh Eh-m:: (.) dey abn– **–Did Mar:k– did**
Gordon get my ↓le↑tter?

In example 3 Leslie begins to name the 'wrong' language; and in example 4, as so often happens in families, Mum gets the name wrong (starting with the name of her son-in-law, when she meant to refer to her grandson). In each case the speaker corrects the error, or in example 3 the error in progress. The operation being conducted – correction – is evident in the comparison between the item initially selected by the speaker, the repairable, and the item she selects subsequently, the repair.

However, it's well known that we refer more generically to self-*repair* because so frequently speakers are in some way changing what they are in the course of saying, or have said, not in order to correct a mistake, but for some other interactional 'purpose'. *Purpose* has been placed in scare marks here to remind us that as analysts we cannot be sure what a speaker's purpose is, or was; we are reluctant to speculate about some cognitive state (purpose, intention) on the part of the speaker, so instead we explore analytically the interactional effect of a self-repair. In each of the three examples below, it doesn't appear that the effect was to change a factual error in what the speaker began to say; rather, they repair what they are in the course of saying, thereby adjusting their turn in some particular way.

(05) Goldberg:2:18 (Telephone call: talking about Dee's marriage)

Con: Ye:s but I mean its a relationship whe:reuh:
yihknow pa:ss the butter dear, hh
(0.5)
Con: Yihkno[w make a piece toa:st dear this type'v thing.
Dee: [N o not really
(.)
Dee: **We've actually hadda real health- I think we've**
hadda very healthy relationship y'know.

(06) BR:CM:18.2.76 (Care home for adolescent offenders; B is one of the adolescent inmates)

B: But there's sufficient ans- ashtrays in here to
u::se them, an' make sure a cigarette is ou:t. (.)
An' if it's n:ot, it's not gunna cause anywhere
near th'amount a damage, tha' could be done if it's
left inna bin.
(3.0)
B: An' if anybody thinks I'm bein' s:illy, I've been
on night duty before where **som'n: threw–**
carelessly threw a cigarette in a bin.
(1.1)
B: An' it caught fiyer

(07) Field:1:5 (Telephone call)

01	Nan:	=No:w I want t'morro:w (0.3) two sco:nes
02		(0.2)
03	Les:	Pa:r– (.) Sorry?
04		(0.5)
05	Nan:	Two s::co::nes

In example 5 Dee is disagreeing with Connie's assessment of his marriage, and adjusts his disagreement in lines 7/8 by redoing the turn in such a way as to omit *actually* (for the significance of which see Clift, 2001), to change *real healthy* into *very healthy*, and perhaps most significantly to insert *I think* – which works to moderate the disagreement by limiting his assessment. The speaker in example 6 is talking to his co-inmates about an incident the night before, likening it to a previous incident when 'some'n: thre- carelessly threw a cigarette in a bin'; the insertion of 'carelessly' (noting the emphatic stress or accentuation on the first syllable) works to detoxify the description, by making it clear that he is not accusing anyone of having deliberately thrown a lighted cigarette into a bin (on ascriptions of the 'mentality' of action see Austin, 1963). When in response to her elderly mother-in-law's request to get her 'two sco:nes', Leslie initiates repair through forms that attribute her problem to being a difficulty hearing – a difficulty that she begins to display with what looks as though was going to be *pardon*, but which she changes to *sorry*. The difference between *pardon* and *sorry* might be a matter of responsibility for the difficulty hearing, *pardon* indicating a lack of clarity on the speaker's part, whilst *sorry* might suggest that the shortcoming lies with the recipient (here, with Leslie) (for more on which see Robinson, 2006).

Whatever is the case in example 7 and the others, as regards what the self-repairs achieve interactionally, two things are clear. First, the original version, the repairable – that is the version that the speaker begins, though sometimes does not complete – can be compared with the eventual version, the repair, to identify in what ways the speaker has modified, altered or adjusted their turn to deal with something other than a factual error. The adjustments seem instead to be associated with better designing the turn for the work it is being constructed to do. Second, in comparing the initial (repairable) version with the subsequent (repair) version, we see exposed the *work that it takes to design a turn in the way the speaker treats as best suited to its interactional placement and needs*. In short, in instances of self-repair we see the work of designing a turn appropriately brought to the surface of the talk. We don't need to compare the design of a turn with putative alternative constructions for the 'same' turn/action, nor do we need to compare a turn's design in one conversation with that in another, nor employ any other kind of external comparative method. Self-repairs give us direct access to the alternative designs considered by speakers, the initially selected design being rejected by the speaker in favour of the subsequent version selected, the repair. Hence in self-repair we can discern speakers' orientations to how best to construct turns for their sequential environment, to do the interactional work they are designed to perform.

Much of the research effort has focused on the operations through which speakers manage self-initiated (same-turn) self-repair, operations that Schegloff sketches in his contribution to this volume. Research to date has revealed much about the techniques through which these operations – replacing, inserting, deleting and so on – are managed and accomplished. However, less attention has perhaps been given to the aspect of self-repair that Schegloff summarises as 'the systemic or interactional import that may be understood to inform the doing of a same turn repair in any given instance' (Schegloff, this volume). One reason for this relative neglect of the interactional significance or import of self-repair might be that this can seem to border on speculating about cognitive processing, including attributing to speakers some intentionality in changing the design of their turn (for example Levelt's important study of the cognitive processing involved in speakers' on-line monitoring of their talk; Levelt, 1983). Another reason is that there is, as far as we know, no association between the form of repair operations and the substance or 'content' of repair (or 'there do not seem to be systematic relationships between the types of trouble source and the form taken by the repairs addressed to them,' Schegloff, 1987: 216); since we set out to explore and identify the generic mechanisms or practices of talk-in-interaction, we have tended to look away from what's going on to focus instead on how it's going on.

However, there is no need for us to peer into the gloom of cognitive processing to discern something of the orderliness or systematics of the interactional significance of self-repair. Our starting point here is that the work that it takes to construct a turn appropriately – whatever 'appropriately' may mean, as will become clearer as we proceed – is laid bare, exposed or manifest in comparing the speaker's first, aborted attempt – the repairable – with the version that they subsequently select – the repair. One systematic basis for self-repair concerns the *selection of the appropriate form of action*, for the particular sequential environment in which it is being conducted. This will be the focus of this paper.

3.2 Self-repair as a means to alter the action

Comparing the version that Leslie first selects with her repair in the following example, it is clear that the interactional import of her repair is to have changed the action she has performed.

(08) Field SO88(II):1:3:1 (Telephone call; Leslie is caller)

Hal: Oh ’el[lo Lesl[ie?
Les: [.hhhh [I RANG you up- (.) ah: think it wz
la:s’ night. **But you were- (.) u-were you ↑ou:t?**
or: was it the night before per[↓haps.
Hal: [Uh:m night be↓fore
I expect we w’r dancing Tuesdee ni:ght.

In changing from the declarative form, ‘but you were’, to the interrogative ‘were you’, Leslie changes the action from one of telling to that of asking or enquiring. (In our account of each of these examples, we will not comment much on the repair operations and techniques involved, nor at all on the specific components through which we, and of course the participants, can tell that repair is being mobilised – here, the cut off of ‘were-’, the micro pause followed by the slight hesitation ‘u-’ before Leslie resumes with her repair, ‘were you …’.) So instead of asserting that Hal was out when she rang (i.e. tried to call), she enquires whether he was out. One can imagine all kinds of reasons for her backing away from asserting that he was out; all she knows is that she rang and no one answered, from which she might infer but cannot be sure that Hal was not home (see Pomerantz, 1980, on such matters), so she might realise that she’s not sure (she is after all not sure which evening it was that she called; her repair facilitates the addition of the clause in which she expresses this uncertainty, ‘or: was it the night before per↓haps’). But we don’t need to speculate on what she may or may not have realised as she was speaking to see that through her repair she has moved from *asserting* something about Hal’s life, something in his epistemic domain (Stivers, Mondada and Steensig, 2011; Heritage, 2012), to *enquiring* about whether he was out.

Moreover, if one wanted to push the matter of ‘appropriateness’ – and at this stage we are not keen to push this too strongly – there are grounds for suggesting that asserting something about Hal’s life, when she has only circumstantial, ‘my side’ evidence (again Pomerantz, 1980), is less appropriate than enquiring about whether he was out. Enquiring may be more appropriate insofar as Leslie thereby acknowledges Hal’s epistemic authority about where he was on which evening (displayed in his response in lines 5/6).

In this next example Edna has called Margy, in part to thank her for a luncheon party a short while ago; she’s apologetic about not having called sooner (starting line 1), which Margy brushes aside, finishing with the rather gracious suggestion in line 9 that they ‘do that’ (get together? do lunch?) more often.

(09) NB PowerTools

Edn: =I shoulda ca:lled you sooner b't I don't know
where the week we::n[t,
Mar: [u-We:ll::=
Mar: =Oh– yEdna you don'haftuh call me up=
Edn: =[I wa::nt [t o : .]
Mar: =[I wz jus [tickled] thetche–
(.)
Mar: nYihkno:w w'n you came u:p en uh–.hhh=
=W'l haftuh do tha[t more] o[:ften.]
Edn: [.hhhhh] [**Wul w]hy don't we:**
uh–m:=Why don't I take you'n Mo:m up there tuh:
Coco's.someday fer lu:nch.We'll go, bkuzz up there
tu[h,
Mar: [k Goo:d.
Edn: Ha:h?
Mar: That's a good deal. .hh-.hh=
Edn: =Eh I'll take you bo:th [up
Mar: [No:::: wil all go Dutch.=
Mar: =B't [let's do t h a t.]
Edn: [No : we wo:n']t.
(.)
Edn: Becuz uh:: u–may u-dz yer mom like t'shop ov'r 'n:
look arou:n' 'n th'stores

Edna responds in line 10 to Margy's suggestion that 'W'l haftuh do that more o:ften.' ('W'l' being a reduction of *we will*) initially by a matching form, 'Wul why don't we:', which is to firm up a more general suggestion ('have to do that more often') to one that is going to be more specific. So Edna begins by piggy-backing on Margy's suggestion (in line 9), with a follow-up suggestion that makes Margy's a little more concrete. But whatever that suggestion was going to be, Edna leaves it incomplete and instead in line 11 repairs that by replacing the first person plural *we* with the first-person singular pronoun *I* (in restarting her turn, though omitting the turn-initial *well*). The change in pronoun quite alters the action here, from what was going to be a suggestion about getting together, instead to an *invitation* or an *offer* to take them for lunch at Coco's (for a more detailed analysis of this example, see Drew, 2005: 89/90, 94/95).

(It might seem as though there is an alternative understanding of Edna's action here, and that she is offering to *take* Margy and her mother to Coco's, which is to say to drive them to Coco's: we happen to know from this and other calls that Edna does not drive, and therefore it is clear that Edna is offering to 'treat' Margy and her mother to lunch, when Margy's mother comes to visit, which Edna evidently knows about. This ensues, and specifically Margy's response in line 18/19 declining Edna's offer/invitation to 'take you bo:th up', line 17.)

Again, it might be that the action done through the repair is somehow more appropriate, in the circumstances. When Edna changes to offering to take (i.e., treat) Margy and her mother to lunch, she is reciprocating the hospitality for which she's called to thank Margy, and which is the immediate context of her turn; in this respect her offer/invitation is perhaps better fitted to its local environment than would have been just a suggestion to get together.

These examples illustrate how speakers may, during a turn's progress, change the action in which they are engaged, through self-repair. Comparing the initial and aborted version with the repair, speakers are evidently changing the action from telling/asserting something to asking the recipient, and from suggesting to offering/inviting. There is the hint of some normative dimensions involved in these examples; in excerpt 8 the speaker seems to be orienting to the epistemic authority the recipient has about where they were/ what they were doing, etc., and in example 9 Edna's offer/invitation is appropriately fitted as an offer of hospitality reciprocating the lunch party for which Edna is calling to thank Margy. But these normative considerations are not so clear and somewhat speculative. When we turn to examine repairs that do not so much change the action being conducted, but change instead the form selected for the same action, then the normative aspects of action design become more clearly apparent.

3.3 Repaired offers

So just to recapitulate: in the previous section we were considering examples in which speakers repair their turns-in-progress in such a way as substantially to change the action being performed. In this section, we will consider cases in which by contrast the repairs do not change the action itself, but rather alter the *form* in which some same action is conducted. In these cases the action remains the same, but the design of that action is altered – an alteration that is associated with normative aspects of action construction. In this section we'll focus on offering, and in the next on requesting.

To begin with, it will be worth considering an interstitial case in which both possibilities are present; that is, it is possible either that the speaker is changing the action she is performing, or that she is changing the format of the same action – offering to come over. Dana and Gordon have in the past been girlfriend/boyfriend, but each is at college, now home for the vacation; Gordon is shortly returning to his college and has called to see whether Dana would like to meet up one afternoon (data not shown). Dana has agreed, and the extract begins where they are talking about precisely when they'll get together, Gordon suggesting this coming Sunday (line 1).

(10) Field SO88:1:3 (Gordon and Dana are back for the vacation and arranging to get together to go out for a drink)

Gor: How 'bout Sun°day.°
(0.3)
Dan: ↑Yeh
(0.3)
Gor: .h[hhhhh]hhh h- (0.2)[Right]
Dan: [S u r e] [( ]),
(0.2)
Gor: Oka[y.
Dan: **[Ri:ght so I'll poh– eh w'l– (.) D'you wan'=**
=[me t' pop over.
Gor: [.p.hhhhhh
Gor: Please.

In line 9 it looks as though Dana is beginning to say 'Right so I'll pop over …', which she aborts in 'poh-' (pɒʔ), changing instead to *Do you want me to pop over*. She might, through the declarative form with which she starts her turn, be *suggesting* that she'll come over that afternoon (that's to say, that she'll come over to his house; they have not previously discussed or agreed where they will meet); in which case in her repair she changes the action from suggesting to offering to come over. However, there is another possibility, that her initial version was going/designed to be an offer, 'So I'll pop over' or even 'So I'll pop over shall I?'; and that rather than changing the action, she changes instead the *form* of the action of offering – changing from a declarative form to selecting instead a *Do you want* … form.

This example is poised between the possibilities outlined above; it is not clear whether in her repair Dana is designing her turn to do a different action, or whether she is changing the *form* of the same action – offering. It is unlikely that we could decide between these alternatives, in this case. However, the latter possibility – that Dana began with one form of offering and changes that to another form – serves to introduce a systematic basis for some self-repairs: that when speakers repair their turn in such a way as to alter the *form* of an action, they orient to normative aspects of action construction.

To explore this further, some background is necessary. Our research into offering in interaction has demonstrated that the three most common forms through which speakers make explicit, on-the-record offers in English – conditional *if* … *then* … forms, outright declaratives, and *do you want* … forms – are used in systematically quite different interactional environments (see Curl, 2006). First, when speakers call in order to make an offer, they use the conditional form, as is illustrated in this example.

(11) Field 2:3 (Telephone call)

Les: .hh And he now has: u-a:: um (1.1) I don't think
eez called it consultancy (0.2) They find positions
for people: in the printing'n paper (0.4)
indus[try:,
Mar: [Oh I see:[:.
Les: [hh An:d **if: i-your husband would**
li:ke their addre[ss.v
Mar: [Y e :[: s,
Les: [<As they're specialists,
Mar: Ye::s?
(.)
Les: Uhm: **my husband w'd gladly give it=**
=[t o h i m .]
Mar: [Oh ^thats ˇv]ery ^kind

This occurs shortly after the beginning of this call, in which, setting aside all the usual opening greetings and *How are you's?*, Leslie has straightaway moved to her business, which is to offer to put Mary's husband in touch with someone she (Leslie) and her husband know, who runs a kind of employment agency for personnel in the printing and paper industry (lines 1–4). The construction she uses to make the offer is the conditional form, 'if your husband would like their address (then) my husband would gladly give it to him' (lines 6–13).

By contrast, offers may be made in response to something that arises then and there during the conversation; that is, rather than having initiated an interaction in order to make an offer, we may find during a conversation that the other has a difficulty for which we can offer assistance. Thus offers may be interactionally generated during the conversation itself; offers of this second kind are done in the form of an outright declarative, as in this example (though a caveat about 'outright declarative' is in order here: there is more properly a cluster of such forms, including an interrogative construction *Can I* …, the key features being that they are *self*-focused or self-referential constructions, whereas *Do you want …?* is *other*-focused).

(12) NB:IV:4:4 (Telephone call)

Emm: W'l anyway tha:t's a'dea:l so I don'know what tih
do about Ba:rbra .hhhhh (0.2) c'z you see she w'z:
depe[nding on:=
(L): [(°Y*eh°)
Emm: =hhim takin'er in tuh the L.A. deeple s:- depot
Sundee so ['e siz]
Lot: **[I:'ll] take'er in: Sundee,**

Emma's difficulty (the details of which need not concern us here) is quite explicit in her reporting that 'I don't know what to do about Barbara', and then her formulation 'she was depending on him' (*was depending* being one of what Sacks called 'incomplete verbs', that is forms indicating non-success, that something didn't or won't now happen). Lottie responds immediately by offering assistance, using a declarative form, 'I'll take her in Sunday' (line 7).

The third form of offer found most frequently is *Do you want* …, used in circumstances when (i) making an offer was not the reason for calling, (ii) no problem or difficulty was mentioned explicitly in the immediate prior turn, but (iii) a problem might be educed from some prior existing circumstance or from something implicit earlier in the interaction.

(13) SBL:2:2:3:28 (Telephone call)

01	Chl:	We:ll it was[fu:n Clai[re, ((smile voice))
02	Cla:	[hhh [Yea::[:h,]
03	Chl:	[° M]m°
04	Chl:	[(an')
05	Cla:	[I enjoyed every minute o[f it,
06	Chl:	[Yah.
07		(0.4)
08	Cla:	Okay well then u-wi'll see: you:
09		Sa'urde[e.
10	Chl:	[Sa'rdee˘night.
11	Cla:	Sev'n thirty?
12		(.)
13	Chl:	Ya[h.
14	Cla:	[hhhh **D'you want me to bring the: chai:[rs?**
15	Chl:	[hahh
16	Chl:	Plea::: (.) NO: (0.2) °Yah,°
17		(0.3)
18	Chl:	I:'ve ˘got to get chairs.˘ Bring'em one more ˘time

Chloe and Claire belong to a group that plays bridge (the card game) on a regular basis, at one another's homes. They have been talking at length about the previous occasion hosted by one of their friends; Chloe is hosting the next event, this coming weekend (lines 8–10), and some considerable time earlier they have discussed something that Chloe doesn't have but will need (tallies, which are a form of scoring card used in bridge). In closing the call Claire asks Chloe 'Do you want me to bring the chairs?', thereby offering to bring something else Claire might need. Note that (i) there is no mention of a problem or difficulty in the immediate prior turn(s); this offer is made in a quite different sequential environment to that in which Lottie offered in example 12 to 'take her in

Sunday'; (ii) there has been no mention here or earlier in the talk that Chloe doesn't have sufficient chairs for all the gang; (iii) Claire seems to have figured – or educed – that Chloe might need extra chairs because she's needed them in the past; Claire refers to *the* chairs, rather than just 'chairs', the definite article alluding to what Chloe makes explicit in line 18, which is that she doesn't have enough chairs, she's needed them in the past, and probably that Claire has brought them in the past ('bring them one more time'). So this offer was neither the reason for the phone call nor interactionally generated by the mention of an explicit problem or difficulty. Claire has figured, from circumstances she knows about, that Chloe might need chairs, and offers to bring them. In our database, *Do you want ..?* offers are found only when the problem they propose to remedy or resolve is educed either from the prior talk or from known circumstances – when the problem has not been overtly displayed as such by the eventual offer recipient.

So we have identified a clear pattern of occurrence, in which systematically conditional forms of offers are used when the one making the offer has initiated the conversation in order to make the offer; declarative (and associated) forms are used when the offer is interactionally generated during the conversation, by the explicit mention, in the offer recipient's immediate prior turn, of some difficulty, problem or trouble; and *Do you want ..?* offers are used when the one making the offer did not call or initiate the interaction with that purpose, and when there has been no explicit mention of a problem in the prior turn (again, for the details of this pattern see Curl, 2006).

But what evidence do we have that this is anything more than a pattern that we, as analysts, can discern across a large data set? What evidence is there that this is anything more than a quasi-statistical artifact (we found only one or two cases, across approximately 150 cases of all three offer formats, that were anomalous)? What evidence do we have that this association between the particular form of the offer and the sequential environment in which they are used is 'real' for participants – and that they orient to the appropriateness of one form rather than another in a given sequential environment? In short, what evidence do we have that the selection of one from among these three formats is a normative matter?

The answer is that the evidence is to be found in the self-repairs when speakers change from one format for an offer-in-progress, and select instead one of the other formats.

We will review three examples, in the first of which Nancy begins to make an offer using the *Do you want ..?* format – which, as we've seen in the account given above, is in the 'wrong' sequential environment.

(14) NB:II:4:4 (Emma has just had a minor surgical operation to remove a toe nail, and is sitting outside relaxing; her friend Nancy has called, to ask Emma whether she'd like to go shopping)

Emm: I:'d LIKE TIH GET S'M LID'L[E slipper]s but uh:
Nan: [Y e :*ah.]
(0.7)
Emm: .t.hhh *I jis do:n't think I better walk it's jis
bleeding a tiny bid'n a:nd u-I think I'm gon'stay
o:ff of it it thro:bs: a liddle b*it. Yihknow
thet's no fun tuh have a nai:l tak[en *off.]
Nan: [°Y e a h]=
=r*ight.°hh[hh
Emm: [°Oh: G*o:d,°
(.)
Nan: -> We:ll dih you wanna me tuh be tih js pick you Can u
-> you (.) get induh Robins'n? so you c'buy a li'l
pair a'slippers?h
(.)
Nan: -> I mean er: **can I getchu somethin:g? er: sump'm:? er**
sum'n?

The multiple self-repairs in Nancy's turn in lines 12–16 result in, or are manifest in, her syntactically disfluent constructions, as highlighted. She transitions from her *Do you want ..?* construction with a component that retains some connection with the initial and aborted construction through repeating *to* (the second one, transcribed *tih*, is even more reduced than the first one), and in which 'pick you' connects back syntactically, and in terms of action, to the aborted construction. This second construction is in turn aborted, when Nancy selects a *Can you …?* construction, which turns into something that is not yet an offer ('Can you get into Robinson's so you can buy a little pair of slippers', lines 12/13). Finally, after an explicit repair marker 'I mean' (see Maynard, this volume), Nancy constructs an offer – though perhaps not quite the one she meant to make – using a format which is self-focused, and hence closer to the declarative form (*Can I …?* being one of the cluster of forms noted above that, like declaratives, are self-referential).

Nancy began to make her offer in her turn immediately following Emma's extended and explicit account of the problem with her toe, which she rounds off with the exclamatory 'Oh God' (lines 4–10). The *Do you want …?* construction is not found immediately after an explicit account of a trouble; the form used in that environment is the declarative (or associated) form. There is no need for us to speculate about what, for Nancy, might be difficult about constructing this offer, and how it is she comes to begin with the 'wrong' form – the form that is inappropriate in this environment. We can see that, through her repair, or rather series of repairs in lines 12–16, Nancy manages to discontinue her *Do you want …?* formatted offer and change the format instead to a more declarative-like format of the sort used in response to explicit troubles in prior turn. In her self-repairs, then, Nancy can be seen to orient to what is the appropriate form for offering, in this sequential position. The pattern that might appear to be only an analyst's construct is demonstrably real to participants; the speaker orients to the inappropriateness of one form of offer, and selects instead an alternative form that is appropriate for this position.

The self-repairs through which this orientation to the normative association between action construction and sequential environment is evident result in a mess; Nancy's turn in lines 12–17 is a syntactic mess, is repetitive, and she ends up not quite making the offer she might have wanted to make (if you'll excuse the psychologising, Nancy doesn't want to get Emma anything – she wants Emma to go shopping with her, so that she can tell her about the man she met the previous afternoon).

Just parenthetically, it is worth mentioning that this is the kind of mess that Chomsky threw in the trash bin of language performance, from which, in his distinction between competence and performance, nothing useful about linguistic structure was to be found. Well, be that as it may, his trash bin is full of the most exquisite evidence for the normative systems of the ways we use language (for a similar observation, though phrased in a more scholarly fashion, see Goodwin, 1981: 170/171).

This next example further illustrates a speaker initially selecting what he then treats as having been the inappropriate form in the sequential position for which it has been selected.

(15) TC1(a):14:2–5 (Albi has asked some guys over for the evening, to watch a football game on the TV, have some beers, etc. Ben has not been invited over but has heard about this, and has called Albi 'innocently', apparently fishing for an invitation, which is eventually forthcoming in line 1 here)

Alb: Uhhhhhh. So you guys coming over toni:ght?
Ben : Yeah.
(0.2)
Alb: You are.hh
Ben: Yah.
Alb: Okay. Good. We're havin a h–buncha people over
too[:.
Ben: [Oh are yih?
(.)
Alb: Yeh it sort'v uhhh stardih- started out ez sorta
impromptu en now it's, ended up tih be a party,
Ben: Oh yeaah?
Alb: Uhhhh hihh
(0.5)

Ben: -> So uh:m, (.) didju wan me to:: What time is this
-> thing sta:rt.
Alb: Oh I don'know, why don'chu g'mon over aboutah:: oh:
seven thirdy er: closer tuh ei:ght,
Ben: A–'ri:ght,=
Alb: =Right aroun the:re,
Ben: A'ri:ght,
(0.2)
Alb: Oka[y,]
Ben: [U:]:m,
(0.4)
Ben: 't! I got s'm Hawaiian Pu:nch,
(0.2)
Alb: hhh hhhheh–heh, .hh hh[heh–heh,]
Ben: [E n s'm] En s'm ah
lemona:de,
(0.2)
Alb: hhhhhhnh,
(0.2)
Ben: ->> **>Want me to bring anything?<**

The way in which Albi describes how this event – that he comes to depict as a 'party' – can be characterised as something that has got out of his control, as something that 'started out as sort of impromptu en now it's ended up to be a party' (lines 10/11). This is almost a complaint formulation, but anyway fairly overtly indicates a problem. In line 15 Ben embarks on offering to bring something to the 'party', using the *Do you want ...?* which, as in example 14 is the inappropriate form to use when the offer is adjacent to a problem. He pulls out of that and does not complete that construction, using a lengthened vowel in 'to::' (-ɾu::), with no break or pause between this and the start of 'what time', facilitating a seamless transition into a different action (inquiring about when the 'thing' starts; end line 15/16). After that's been settled, Ben manages some further displacement/delay before remaking the offer, by mentioning, ironically, some non-alcoholic drinks he has; only after that does he redo his offer, 'want me to bring anything' (line 34, now at some sequential distance from Albi's characterisation of the 'thing' as problematic, as complainable (on which see Sacks, 1992; e.g., Fall 1968 Lecture 4). So, although Ben's offer still follows an overt problem formulation, it is not in next position, but instead is substantially delayed. Notice, moreover, that he uses the elided form *Want me*, not the full form *Do you want me ...*, so that, whereas in this example the repair does not involve the selection of one of the other two offer forms, nonetheless the form of the offer is altered through the elision. Once again, therefore, the work in which Bill engages before reissuing his offer displays his orientation to the normative placement of such offers.

A final example further and rather dramatically illustrates how, through self-repairs, speakers may orient to the normative constraints on offering – though here those constraints are broader than the matter of which is the appropriate form of offer. In July 2006 Israeli soldiers were captured by Hezbollah, in Israeli territory, and then taken over the border into Lebanon. This developed into something of an international crisis, and there was much speculation about whether the US, and perhaps other countries such as the UK, might intervene or mediate. This incident occurred just a few days before the G8 meeting in St Petersburg, at which a private interchange between President Bush and Prime Minister Blair happened to be recorded. As delegates broke for lunch on the 17 July, Bush remained seated in his chair at the conference table, when Blair walked past behind him. Bush hailed Blair with the much-reported greeting 'Yo, Blair,' and Blair stopped to talk to Bush. Neither realised that Bush's microphone was still on (a few seconds after the extract shown below, Blair noticed the red 'on' light, but by then it was too late).

(16) 'Yo, Blair!': Overheard conversation and the 'special relationship'
(George Bush and Tony Blair, recorded at the G8 meeting,
St Petersburg, 17 July 2006.

Bsh: What about Kofi? (he seems alright. I don't like
his ceasefire plan.) His attitude is basically
ceasefire and everything else … (sorts
out/happens).
Blr: Yeah, no I think the (inaudible) is really
difficult. We can't stop this unless you get this
international business agreed.
Bsh: Yeah.
Blr: -> I don't know what you guys have talked about, but
-> as I say I am perfectly happy to try and see what
-> the lie of the land is, but you need that done
-> quickly because otherwise it will spiral.
Bsh: -> I think Condi is going to go pretty soon.
Blr: -> But that's, that's, that's all that matters. But
->> **if you ...** you see it will take some time to get that
-> together.
Bsh: -> Yeah, yeah.
Blr: -> But at least it gives people ...
Bsh: -> It's a process, I agree. I told her your offer to ...
Blr: ->> Well... it's only if I mean... you know. **If she's got**
->> **a ...,** or **if she** needs the ground prepared as it
-> were... Because obviously if she goes out, she's got
-> to succeed, if it were, whereas I can go out and
-> just talk.
Bsh: You see, the irony is what they need to do is to
get Syria to get Hezbollah to stop doing this
shit and it's over.

Whilst the world's press was transfixed by Bush's unusual greeting, mixing informality and last-name formality, by their joshing, by Bush seeming to continue eating a hamburger through the interchange, by Bush's expletive (last line above) and other such incidental matters, none commented on the diplomatic significance of this interchange. Blair comes close to offering to go to the Middle East on behalf of the allies and intercede to resolve the crisis. Clearly an offer of this kind has been made through diplomatic channels (see Bush's reference to 'your offer', line 19); here Blair comes close to making the offer directly. But (i) Blair is attempting to renew an offer that presumably has been declined, or more likely diplomatically held at the gate, (ii) offers of this kind are handled by the relevant ministers/secretaries of state and their departments, not by world leaders, and (iii) Blair begins his offer with the wrong form; the conditional form, as highlighted, is used when the purpose of initiating an interaction is to make the offer, which is plainly not the situation here – Bush initiated the conversation, and he initiated the topic of a ceasefire plan relating to the Israeli/Lebanon crisis.

For reasons of space, we will not go into further details about this example. Unlike the previous examples, the speaker (Blair) does not substitute a different form of offer for the one he first selected (presumably in view of points (i) and (ii) above). He continues with the same form, which is inappropriate for this sequential environment (point (iii) above); but crucially he does not ever complete the construction, and therefore does not complete an on-the-record explicit, fully formed offer – he hints at one, but doesn't quite make it. Once again, self-repair is associated systematically with normative aspects of the selection of an appropriate form of offer, in a given sequential environment.

3.4 Adjusting the format of requests

Just as there are alternative ways in which offers may be constructed – alternative morpho-syntactic constructions – so too there are a variety of ways in which requests are typically constructed (we refer here to explicit, on-the-record requests, not the myriad of contextually bound ways in which we may 'hint' at wanting something). Frequently used forms of explicit requests are, first, conditionals formed with modal auxiliaries *could* and *would*, and second the *I wonder if + complement clause* construction which moves the main verb into a dependent/subordinate clause. In the same research in which we investigated the use of the different constructions/formats for offering, we showed that speakers select from among the formats for requesting the one that reflects their assessment of their entitlement to ask, and the contingencies that might be involved in granting their request (Curl and Drew, 2008; Drew and Walker, 2010).

Just briefly, when these contingencies are known, and known to be unlikely to prevent the request being granted, speakers use the modal form of the verb, as in this example.

(17) Field SO88:2:8:1 (Leslie's son Gordon, who has just left home to live away at university, calls her first thing in the morning)

Les: Hello:?
(0.3)
Gor: It's Gordon.
Les: .hhhh oh Gordon. Shall I ring you back darling,
Gor: Uh:: no y⁻ I don't think you can,
(0.3)
Gor: But uh: just to (0.3) say (.) **could you bring** up a
letter.
(.)
Gor: -> When you come up,

When Gordon asks his mother to bring up a letter, he uses the modal form (line 7); notice that as well as the matter of his asking his mother (so highly entitled), he orients to the low contingency of his request, given that his mother and father are driving up to visit him, 'when you come up,' (line 10). So this is a high entitlement/low contingency request.

By contrast, in the next example Jenny orients to high contingency – of there being the possibility, at least, of there being some difficulty in granting her request. She is phoning her opticians, having previously called in (person) to make an appointment; she has been expecting the optician to call her, and the fact that she *hasn't heard anything* (line 6) is an indication that there might, for example, be a difficulty in finding her a slot in the near future.

(18) Rahman:1:2:JT 11 (Jenny phones her opticians)

Dsk : Hello Goodzwin,
Jen: Ehm good morning. eh it's Missiz Rah:man here, I
ca:lled in on Thursday: to see: if uh I could make an
appointment t'see Mister Fawcett,
(1.2)
Jen: -> An– I haven't heard anything'n I was wondering if:
uh:m >(it was possible)< to see him:(um) one day next
week

It commonly happens when calling/interacting with organisations that we are uncertain about what services they provide, what we are entitled to, what contingencies there might be in doing or getting what we want. We don't know their procedures, we don't know whether they offer a given service, we're unsure about someone's schedule or availability – uncertainties that Gordon did not have in example 17. Jenny has particular grounds for being uncertain about the contingencies that might be involved (again, beginning of line 6), and so uses a request form ('I was wondering if: uh:m >(it was possible)<') that conveys lower entitlement and higher contingency than the modal form of the verb (i.e., she does not ask *Could I see him* ...).

Taking into account other request forms besides the two illustrated above, especially imperative forms and *I need* ..., it appears that there is a cline or continuum of request forms, represented in Figure 3.1, ranging from those that index speakers' assessments of high entitlement and low contingency in making the request to those that by contrast index low entitlement and high contingency. There is, by the way, a certain respect in which moving the main verb into a dependent/subordinate clause through *I wonder if* ... somehow makes iconic sense as a marker of low entitlement/high contingency, because the other (left-hand) end of the scale is one where the verb is right at the start of the sentence and in an uninflected form.

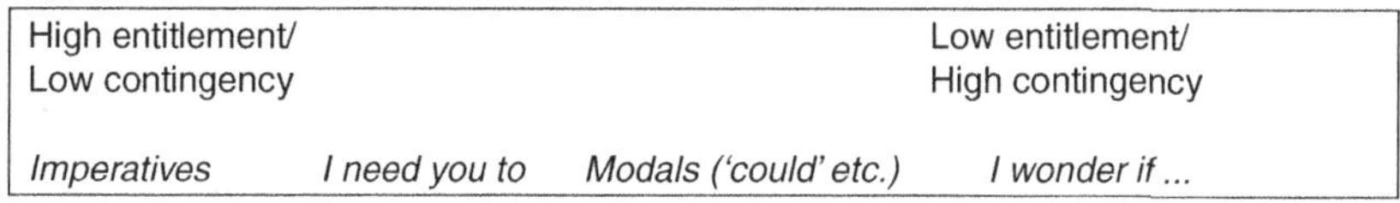

Figure 3.1: A cline of request forms.

There is evidence that speakers orient to what is the appropriate form of request in the particular interactional circumstances; hence there is a normative underpinning to the selection of a request form. This evidence is nowhere clearer than in the adjustments speakers make in request forms, as those circumstances – contingencies – alter, moment by moment.

In this first example, Kath responds rather indirectly to her mother's enquiry about when she'd like to come home (from college) for Christmas; reporting that her boyfriend, Brad, is going down on Monday (line 4) suggests that she'd like to come down with him (their family homes are in the same area, lines 16–18) – which is how Leslie understands that in lines 6/7, when she indicates that Kath's arriving on Monday would be difficult ('Monday we can't manage').

(19) Field X(C)85:2:1:4 (Leslie has called her daughter Kath, who lives away at college, but is returning home for Christmas)

Les: Anyway when d'you think you'd like
t'come home ↓love.
(.)
Kat: Uh:m (.) we:ll Brad's goin' down on Monday.
(0.7)
Les: Monday we:ll ah–:hh .hh w:Monday we can't manage

```
            becuz (.) Granny's ↓coming Monday.↓
            (0.4)
Kat :       Oh:,
            (0.5)
Kat :  ->   C'd– (0.3) Dad couldn't pick me up fr'm:: (.) ee–
            even fr'm Glastonbury could'e
Les :       .hh I CAN'T HEAR you very well cz a'this damn
            machine tht's attached to this telephone say it
            again,
Kat :  ->   Would it be possible: for Dad t'pick me up fr'm
            Glastonbury on [Monday.
Les :                      [Ye:s yes THAT would be ↓alright if
            the Kidwells don't mi↓:nd.
```

So between the moment of Leslie's rather 'open' enquiry in lines 1–2 and Kath's request in line 11, a difficulty has arisen (lines 6/7), a difficulty that changes and increases the contingencies involved in granting her request (for her father to collect her from Brad's home in Glastonbury). After a delayed token indicating that this difficulty is news to her (lines 8 and 9; on *oh* see Heritage, 1984b), Kath begins her request in line 11 with the modal (albeit a reduced or weak form, 'C'd-'), which she aborts and replaces with a negative construction ('Dad couldn't ...'). By changing from an interrogative to this negative declarative form Kath more firmly orients to the difficulty that has arisen (that her father may not be able to collect her), and hence to the changed contingencies (on the 'stronger' presuppositions of negative questions/constructions, see Heritage, 2002).

The form of Kath's subsequent request is also a self-repair, though in this case one that is initiated by her mother's difficulty hearing her previous request. Leslie evidently has difficulty hearing (lines 13/15) Kath's initial (though already repaired) request (lines 11/12). In response, Kath makes the same request, but changes the form once again to 'Would it be possible: for ...' – thereby sliding her request form even further from the left to the right of our cline (Figure 3.1).

So in the repair Kath makes to her request forms in lines 11 and 16, Kath is adjusting to the difficulty that has arisen. She adjusts to this change in the contingencies involved by altering her request forms from the relative low contingency 'C'd-' to one reflecting a higher contingency: 'Would it be possible: for ...' Through her self-repairs Kath manages to select a form that more appropriately reflects the change in her understanding of the circumstances, and the contingencies that may be involved in her arriving home on the day she first mentioned (line 4).

The following example similarly illustrates how a speaker may adjust (repair) the request form in response to changes in circumstances/

contingencies. The excerpt begins at the point at which Susi requests to be passed the salad dressing (line 1).

(20) Porch Dinner:4:45 (The family are sitting around a table outside on the porch, eating dinner. Mat is a neighbour who happens to walk by)

Sus: **Pass me** the Wishbo[ne,
Kat: [SHHHH WHA:T?
Dwn: Oh
(0.7)
Mat: I: don't think anybody gonna, pick me up I: think
I've been let down
Frn: NO:::::=
Kat: =UH HEH UH HEH
Frn: We'll bring you dessert over Matt
(0.6)
Sus: **Pa- may >I have a< c– c'n I have** the gravy Ross?
Frn: Boy everybody's really: hoggin [up things like
Sus: [Mother said to
sta[rt passing it=
Mrk: [ehYhheh uh huh
Rss: =[Hey look at the sa:lad.
Sus: -> =[Well you picked it up and you laid it back do:wn

In line 1 here, Susi asks Ross, sitting next to her, to her right, for the salad dressing (Wishbone is a brand name), placed at the end of the table nearest the camera and close to Ross's right hand, and which is not being used by anyone. Pointing to the Wishbone simultaneously with her request, Susi uses the imperative *Pass me*, thereby displaying her understanding that there are no contingencies apparent that might block her request being granted.

The next several lines (2–8) of transcript show the family interacting with a neighbour (Matt), who is off camera. Immediately before Susi begins her request in line 10, Ross – who had been serving himself gravy from the boat in front of his plate – puts down the spoon (held in his right hand) as Frank completes 'NO:::::' (line 7), and then pushes the gravy boat away with his left hand. That is to say, Ross pushes the gravy further from Susi, and with the hand that is closest to her. Her eyes track him making this gesture. Then as Ross lifts his hand to accept a dish that Martha is passing to him, Susi begins the first syllable shown in line 11, 'pa-'. This is most likely a beginning of the same imperative she employed before, *Pass*, as it has the same vowel quality. She cuts this word off, however, as Ross takes the bowl from Martha's hand, and restarts the request with 'may I have', only to abandon that for 'c'n I have'. So that whilst immediately before Susi's request in line 11 Ross's hand was free to pass the gravy, now by the time she begins her request the contingencies have changed – his hand is not free.

So although just before she began speaking the gravy was easily available and was not being used by anyone, just as she spoke the contingencies had changed; the gravy was moved away from her, and Ross now had something else in his hand. Her repair from the imperative to the modal form is precisely responsive to this change in contingency. She begins her request in imperative mood, the format with which she made her first request in this extract. However, she then repairs this first to 'may I have', then to 'c'n I have …' line 11. It is unclear what is involved in the change from *may* to *can*; but the outcome of her self-repair is to have changed the form of request from an imperative to a modal form, thereby again finally selecting a form that is to the right end of our continuum – moving from the least contingent a little way towards a more contingent form.

Furthermore, just as the speakers are explicit about their understandings of the contingencies involved in examples 17 and 18 ('when you come up' and 'I haven't heard anything', respectively), so too here in example 20 Susi makes explicit the situation as it was when she began to ask for the gravy, that is that having picked the gravy up (to use), Ross then put it back down in front of him, making it available for anyone else (low contingency). So here are participants' analyses of the contingencies that obtained, but which then changed, reflected in Susi's repairing the form of the same action – requesting – to select a form that is more appropriate to the changed contingencies.

3.5 Conclusion

We have had two principal aims in this account of self-repair in conversation. Our first aim has been to show that self-repair provides a particular, and generally overlooked, comparative 'methodology' for exploring and understanding the work that goes into constructing a turn at talk. There are other comparative methodologies for exploring turn design, and what speakers select in order to construct their turns at talk. However, self-repair affords us the most direct access to the alternative versions or selections considered by speakers, whatever was initially selected being rejected by the speaker in favour of the subsequent version, the repair. In self-repair we can see the work of designing a turn brought to the surface of the talk. Hence we can discern in self-repair speakers' orientations to how best to construct turns for their sequential environment, to do the interactional work they are designed to perform.

Our second aim has been to show that there is a *systematic* basis for (some) self-repairs – or rather we have explored one systematic basis for self-repair;

there are no doubt many others. That systematic basis arises from the action that the speaker is conducting in a turn, and how that action should 'appropriately' be constructed. The patterns of association we find between the form an action may take, and the interactional circumstances or sequential environment in which the action is being conducted, are evidently normative; the evidence for the normativity lies, in part at least, in self-repairs in which speakers begin producing one form of the action, and instead change the construction of the turn in such a way as to construct the turn – and the action – quite differently.

There are three take-home messages from this account of self-repair and action construction.

- Self-repairs give us access to the work of constructing a turn – they bring to the interactional surface the work in which speakers engage in order to construct the action.
- The action is constructed with respect to its interactional environment and sequential placement or position.
- Self-repairs provide the evidence that speakers orient to what are, and are not, the appropriate forms – that is, to the normative character of constructing social actions.

Thus in the mess of self-repair – in this aspect of linguistic performance, in Chomsky's trash – we find crucial evidence for the normative connections between turn design and sequence/interaction; because it is through self-repair that we see speakers orient to what is the appropriate form to do *this* action in *this* sequential place.

REFERENCES

Austin, J. L. (1963). Three ways of spilling ink. In *Philosophical Papers*. Oxford University Press.

Clift, R. (2001). Meaning in interaction: the case of 'actually'. *Language* 77(2), 245–291.

Curl, T. (2006). Offers of assistance: constraints on syntactic design. *Journal of Pragmatics* 38: 1257–1280.

Curl, T. and Drew, P. (2008). Contingency and action: a comparison of two forms of requesting. *Research on Language and Social Interaction* 41: 1–25.

Drew, P. (2005). Conversation analysis. In K. Fitch and R. Sanders, eds., *Handbook of Language and Social Interaction*, pp. 71–102. Mahwah, NJ: Lawrence Erlbaum,

(forthcoming). Turn design. In J. Sidnell and T. Stivers eds., *Handbook of Conversation Analysis*. Oxford: Blackwell-Wiley.

Drew, P. and Walker, T, (2010). Requesting assistance in calls to the police. In M. Coulthard and A. Johnson, eds., *The Routledge Handbook of Forensic Linguistics*, pp. 95–110. London and New York: Routledge.

Fillmore, C. (1997). *Lectures on Deixis*. Stanford, CA: CSLI Publications.

Goodwin, C. (1981). *Conversational Organization: Interaction Between Speakers and Hearers*. New York: Academic Press.
Heritage, J. (1984a). *Garfinkel and Ethnomethodology*. Cambridge: Polity Press.
(1984b). A change-of-state token and aspects of its sequential placement. In J. M. Atkinson and J. Heritage, eds., *Structures of Social Action*, pp. 299–345. Cambridge University Press.
(2002). The limits of questioning: negative interrogatives and hostile question content. *Journal of Pragmatics* 34: 1427–1446.
(2012). The epistemic engine: sequence organization and territories of knowledge. *Research on Language and Social Interaction*.
Levelt, W. J. M. (1983). Monitoring and self-repair in speech. *Cognition* 14: 41–104.
Pomerantz, A. M. (1980). Telling my side: 'limited access' as a 'fishing' device. *Sociological Inquiry* 50, 186–198.
Robinson, J. (2006). Managing trouble responsibility and relationships during conversational repair. *Communication Monographs* 73: 137–161.
Sacks, H. (1992). *Lectures on Conversation*, vol. II, ed. Gail Jefferson. Oxford: Blackwell.
Schegloff, E. A. (1987). Some sources of misunderstanding in talk-in-interaction. *Linguistics* 25: 201–218.
Ten operations in self-initiated, same-turn repair. This volume.
Stivers, T., Mondada, L. and Steensig, J., eds. (2011). *The Morality of Knowledge in Conversation*. Cambridge University Press.

4 On the place of hesitating in delicate formulations: a turn-constructional infrastructure for collaborative indiscretion

Gene H. Lerner

4.1 Introduction

Broadly speaking, this report investigates one way that technical practices associated with turn construction and turn construction repair enable emergent forms of participation in the social life of a society. One aim here is to show how the texture of interpersonal relations shaped by an orientation to matters of social propriety and impropriety can rest upon – and thereby be contoured by – a formal infrastructure of speech exchange in talk-in-interaction.

There is ample evidence that speakers and their recipients pay special attention to what can and cannot be properly said in conversation – and to when one is overstepping the limits of propriety (see Pomerantz, 1980, 1984b; Schegloff, 1980, 2003; Jefferson 1983, 1985a, 1985b; Jefferson, Sacks, and Schegloff 1987; Sacks, 1992 (e.g., vol. II, pp. 431–436); Clift, 2001; Whitehead, 2009). In discussing the range of such participant-administered breaches of conversational standards, Jefferson, Sacks, and Schegloff (1987: 160) note that: "In the course of ongoing talk someone may say something which breaches conversational standards of courtesy, propriety, tact, ethics, commonality, etc. etc., the breach in conversational standards at least potentially being offensive to other parties to the interaction."[1]

Participants can (but do not always) show a special concern for such interpersonally sensitive matters as the voicing of potentially offensive terms (e.g., vulgar expletives), aspects of apparently indelicate topics (e.g. sex or death), and derogatory references to persons. This concern can be explicitly attended to before the apparently offensive expression is voiced, as in extract 1 at line 2:

(01) HB10

01 Pet: I've already had one so:n. Uhm and basically the
02 hospital's complE::tly >**'scuse my language**< scre:wed
03 up on all my care one way or the other

Earlier versions of this report were presented to the National Communication Association, Chicago, 1999, to the "Conceptual Structures, Discourse and Language" Conference, Santa Barbara, 2000, and to the American Sociological Association, Anaheim, 2001. My thanks to Bob Arundale, Celia Kitzinger and Manny Schegloff for their very useful suggestions and to Celia Kitzinger, Geoff Raymond and Sue Wilkinson for bringing interesting cases to my attention.

or the indelicate item itself can be voiced in a manner that obscures its delivery in some fashion. Thus speakers sometimes deliver an item *sotto você*, as in extracts 2 and 3 or they can employ in-speech laughter that obscures the indelicate item as in extract 4.

4.1.1 Sotto você *delivery*

Whisper voicing can indicate that a term (or the TCU it is a part of) is being treated as in some way a delicate matter. This leaves it to recipients to inspect the whispered term for the way in which it might be offensive or otherwise indiscreet. This can be seen in the following excerpt from the telling of a story.

(02) Auto Discussion:7

01 Mik: … 'e takes his helmet off'n clunk it goes on top a'
02 the car he gets out'n goes up t'the trailer 'n gets
03 a °**god damn**° iron ba:r¿ ˙hhh r:aps that
04 trailer en away he starts t'go en evrybuddy seh
05 hey you don't need dat y'know, seh ye:h yer
06 righ'n 'e throws that son'vabitch down- ˙hhhhhhh

Here Mike voices "god damn" in a noticeably quieter manner than the surrounding talk, thus singling it out as a "quiet impropriety" (Schegloff, 2003), while nonetheless still producing it. For the purpose of this report, which will become apparent shortly, it is important to note that quiet delivery can be employed without delaying the progressive realization of the turn's talk. That is, the TCU continues without disturbing its "forward development" towards its next possible completion.

In extract 2 quiet voicing was employed to isolate a delicate term. By contrast, in extract 3 it is the character of the action *implicated* by a quietly produced sequence-initiating action that is at issue. In this case members of a family seated around the dinner table are discussing a crude letter a teenage boy has sent to a friend of one of the teenage participants (Beth).

(03) Virginia: 26

01 Mom: Well: I: tol' Beth >I didn' like that< bo:y, > °I didn'
02 wan' her havin' anything tuh do with him.<
03 (0.2)
04 Vir: °**Whattid it say.**° *((Leans toward Mom))*
05 (0.4)
06 Mom: (wull) I really can't tell yuh.

It is not so much the utterance itself which is marked as delicate, but rather it is the action implicated by Virginia's attempt to elicit a rendition of the boy's crude letter. Virginia not only produces her turn in a whisper but leans in toward Mom as she speaks, as another way to indicate that this (thereby delicate) matter is "just between us."[2] One reaches the limit of *sotto você* delivery when a speaker simply mouths a delicate without voicing it at all.

4.1.2 Speech-obscuring laughter

Jefferson (1985b) shows that speakers can deploy in-speech laughter that precisely covers delicate terms such as obscenities.

(04) GTS:I:2:33:r2 (From Jefferson, 1985b)

Ken: And he came home and decided he was gonna
play with his o:rchids from then on i:n.
Rgr: With his what?
Lou: mh hih hih[huh
Ken: [With hz orchids.=
Ken: =Ee[z got an orch[id-
Rgr: [Oh [hehh [hah .he:h] .heh
Lou: [heh huh .hh] PLAYN(h)**W(h) IZ**
O(h)R'N ya:h I [thought the [same
Rgr: [uh:: [.hunhh .hh.hh
Ken: [Cz ezz gotta great big
[gla:ss house] ( )
Rgr: [I c'n s(h)ee] im pl(h)ay with iz **o(h)r(h)g'(h)n** .uh

The in-speech laughter both obscures and distorts the impropriety, while the speaker can nonetheless still be understood to have voiced it. As Jefferson (1985b: 31) puts it, the laughter makes the obscenity "not-quite-said and difficult to hear." Obscuring the delicate expression in this way requires that a recipient dig out what was said, thus casting some of the responsibility for what was said on the recipient's ability to decipher it.

Each of these devices retains the indelicate element, but indicates that the speaker is treating it *as indelicate* – or in other words the speaker is exhibiting a stance toward what is being said as a delicate matter. Another common way to demonstrate that something is a delicate matter – that something is being delivered as a delicate matter – is to employ a less offending expression, but one that makes clear it is being offered up as an alternative to a more unvarnished formulation.

4.1.3 Euphemistic formulation

It is the use of a euphemistic formulation as a recognizably alternative formulation for a less guarded one that shows this formulation is being delivered as a delicate. This type of formulation can be seen in extract 5 at line 2 (and again at lines 3–4). Here what is being pointed to by what is said is left tacit, but nonetheless becomes available to the recipient.

(05) Heritage I–3

01 Iln: ((nasal)) ° –Oh well she doesn't do that he:re,°
02 Lsa: (Well) well she wants tih **git down t'th' bo:ys.**
03 Think about six uh'clock she **has th–**.hh she **has the**
04 **–u:rge.=**
05 Iln: =Oh I see::. Yes. Yeah.

A euphemistic expression ("get down to the boys") is employed to formulate an action associated with the mating of the caller's dog, but the mating itself is only insinuated. In this case, just what is being alluded to by the breeder at line 2 is apparently not recognized by the dog's owner until after a second somewhat less veiled formulation is produced at lines 3–4.

One could go on to catalog a considerable inventory of practices for delicate formulation and delivery employed in talk-in-interaction – a task that must be left for another occasion. In this report I focus on one family of methods for delivery of delicate formulations, all of whose members entail some form of delaying or hesitating in the course of turn-constructional unit composition and whose affordances allow for the co-production of delicate TCUs. These delaying practices, when employed as a way to deliver a matter delicately, allow for – and perhaps are even designed for – a co-participant to implicate themselves in the delivery of a not yet fully formulated delicate term, matter or action through other-completion of the in-progress TCU. I begin by examining one common site, searching for a next word in the course of composing a TCU, at which speaker hesitation can form an opportunity for other-completion to assist in the search (and thereby provide a way to realize a shared voicing of a delicate matter), and then I broaden the scope of the investigation by showing that other practices employed to suspend or abandon the progressive realization of a turn's talk prior to possible completion can also furnish an opportunity space for other-completion of a TCU that implements the formulation of a delicate matter. I then move on to describe what can be accomplished through a variety of sequence-organizational trajectories that such opportunities for other-completion of delicate-bearing TCUs can occasion, and I finish up by describing what additional actions can be accomplished through practices of what might be termed "delicate delay."

4.2 Doing 'searching for a word'

Recognizably searching for a word in the course of – and in the service of – composing a turn at talk constitutes one kind of repair procedure for conversation and other forms of talk-in-interaction (Schegloff, Jefferson and Sacks, 1977;

Schegloff, 1984; Goodwin and Goodwin, 1986; Sacks, 1992; Lerner, 1995, 1996b). Once *recognizably* underway, some word searches are worked at and completed solely by the speaker and include elements with solely turn-compositional relevance (as in extract 6), while others include elements with sequence-organizational relevance and expand into sequences of action that can include contributions by both the original speaker and other participants (as in extract 7). Here I am speaking exclusively about observable conduct involved in doing 'searching for a next word or other item' in its particular sequential environment and not about any underlying cognitive process.[3]

(06) SN–4:11

Kar: Oh my friend useteh make up the best insurance
stories. ˙hhh He **ha:d u:m (1.0) Whuh wuz iht. (0.3)**
Oh. He had some paint: (•) da:mage.on iz car.

(07) SF-2

Mrk: an' at what point did you find out
that **ah .hh her ah what shall we call**
him (0.2) uhm: (.) her [um
Bob: **[(her old) boyfriend?**

Of course, on some occasions it will be clear to participants that only the currently searching speaker will be able to supply the searched-for item (as is evidently the case in extract 6, where Karen is telling her recipient about something only she knows about), while on other occasions it may be apparent (to participants) that a co-participant may be best positioned to provide the solution (as in extract 7, where Mark is referring to someone only Bob knows about). Sometimes other participants' contributions are explicitly solicited by the original speaker as in extract 7 (at lines 2–3), but regularly enough these contributions can be volunteered without explicit solicitation as in extract 8.

(08) Holt 5/88-1-2

Joy: We were hoping to go toni:ght to see **thee uh:m:**
Les: **.h the film show.**=o:r the sli[:des.]
Joy: [Y:es.]

It is important to note that in this case Les evidently treats Joy's hesitation as indicative of *trouble ahead* and in particular trouble in delivering the strongly projected item that had been due next and that would bring the TCU to possible completion – even though such turn-constructional delaying tokens as “uh(m)” can lead to other forms of repair besides searching for the delayed next item.[4] For example, a speaker can abandon the TCU-in-progress and begin another TCU altogether, as in extracts 9 and 10.

(09) SBL:3:2R (simplified)

Cla: No: honey we go:t some it’s **no:t uh:: uh we I have**
another card table my (.) en my chai::rs arn’t very
good but (.) ah u we kin manage for th: three hours’n

(10) Clacia:10

Cla: … One other girl from the:re, ˙hh en I usetuh go
up almost every weeken’ t– well we did go up every
weekend to **uh (0.2) she dated another guy up** (0.5) in
another fratern‘n we’d go up there’n we’d hv good
time,

Thus when a speaker hesitates by deploying some form of “uh(m)” recipients cannot be certain what repair operation will follow on from this alert of possible turn-compositional trouble. Nevertheless, recipients can and do treat such hesitating as indicative of possible trouble – and in particular, as indicative of trouble in delivering the word (or other item) that had been due next by assisting in the production of the suspended TCU and they take this opportunity to furnish it even before a fully fledged (i.e., recognizable) search is underway. That is, such hesitating can be and recurrently is treated as a nascent search.

Furthermore, not all cases in which a speaker does search for a “word” are best characterized as doing *word* searching. For example, after having been asked a question, a hesitating speaker – employing the same tokens – may be better understood as searching for the answer-part of an answer turn as in extract 11 at line 4.

(11) Mid City 21:29

Dsk: Okay uh were you a customer at that store?
Clr: Yeah.
Dsk: What’s the address there. the um–
Clr: I’m right on **u::h (0.7) uh**

Here the repeated “uh(m)”s demonstrate a continued commitment to answering by showing a continuing commitment to producing the currently suspended answer turn. One upshot here (as virtually everywhere else in the organization of talk-in-interaction) is that just what hesitating in this way indicates – on its situated occurrence – depends upon participants’ real-time understanding of the sequential environment in which it is placed.

4.2.1 *On the relevance of "uh(m)" in conversation*

Speakers, in the course of producing a turn at talk, will occasionally stop the forward progress of their utterance prematurely – i.e., before a next possible completion of the unit-type that is currently underway and thus before voicing the word that is due next. Thus, in extract 12 a proposal (not shown) concerning a medical test performed on a friend currently in the hospital is rejected (at lines 1 and 2) and then shortly thereafter an alternative proposal is offered (at lines 4 and 5), but the progressive realization of that turn (after its recycled turn beginning) is delayed when the speaker hesitates.

(12) KC–4

01	K:	...I don think they grow a culture to do a biopsy
		:
02	K:	... I don't know if they– if they do that,
03	R:	[( )]
04	D:	[(w'll they di–)] they did have to grow a culture for
05		**thee: ahm (1.0)**

Speaker D produces an item ("*ahm*") that both indicates and constitutes a delay in the forward progress of the turn and makes *additionally relevant* a pause in speaking that in this case does follow and thereby extends the delay in the progressive realization of the turn's talk.

Stating that a pause in speaking is made "additionally relevant" after "uh(m)" is not to propose that such an interval is *exclusively* relevant. Rather, I am just saying that some "uh(m)s" not only promise a continuing commitment to the further realization of a turn's talk, but also make another sort of turn-construction-relevant action – a possible pause in talking before that continuation – additionally relevant. Hesitating in this way establishes a context for an interval without speech and thereby makes an immediately subsequent pause accountable (if one does occur). When a speaker shows him- or herself to be having some trouble in producing a turn's talk (by retarding and/or suspending its progressive realization), that having done so, having produced such an alert as "uh(m)", itself makes a pause in speaking relevant.[5] It is certainly not exclusively relevant, but for what can relevantly happen next in composing the TCU-in-progress, pausing is now an additionally relevant maneuver that a speaker might employ next.

Hesitating in this way maintains an active claim on the turn space here and elsewhere, but not everywhere.[6] This can be a "promissory note" that indicates resumption of a TCU-in-progress even if followed directly by an interval during which the current speaker refrains from speaking. In extract 12 there is even some indication of a slightly earlier onset of speaker hesitation in the sound stretch that prolongs the just prior word ("thee:") and thereby slightly *retards* the progressive realization of the turn's talk towards next possible completion before "ahm" *suspends* it – both of which relax the progressivity of the turn's talk, but do not in themselves constitute an abandonment of the TCU or the turn, while nevertheless making relevant and accountable an ensuing pause.

With some same-turn repair operations (e.g., replacing, inserting, or deleting) it may not be possible to establish what sort of operation is underway (or, indeed, whether repair is underway at all) from the trouble alert itself (e.g., a word cut-off); participants must wait until the repair solution is fashioned. However, in the case of word searching, speakers can make "doing searching" evident before a solution is produced as in extracts 6 and 7. Yet, as I have shown in extracts 9 and 10, not all "uh(m)"s – even when employed as trouble alerts – lead to a later production of the word due next, although, as extract 8 shows, recipients can treat some "uh(m)s" as indicative of trouble in producing a next term (more on this in the next section).

However, *recognizable* word searching can be implemented through the use of "uh(m)s" in some sequential environments. So, for example, in extracts 13 and 14 the *repeated* use of "uh(m)" in conjunction with a previously voiced word – which *on its second voicing* constitutes a "pre-frame" for a now-delayed next word – can indicate a commitment to continuing the TCU now in progress (and not just a continuing commitment to the turn), and thus a commitment to delivering up that next word.

(13) BCC369

Clt: .h h h h Well one of the people you might
try who:: (.) works **at uhm (0.5) at uh:m**

(14) BCC217

J: But .hhh uhm (.) although he tells me I'm an excellent
subject (.) and I'm sure I probably am for
hypnotherapy <I mean he was the person that my husband
and I had been to see: 'cause he does all sorts **of uhm**
(.) of uh

However, this cannot be said of the initial "uh(m)" on its occurrence. Rather, it can only alert recipients to possible trouble, with the speaker, at that point, remaining openly uncommitted as to what sort of trouble it might be, and therefore what sort of repair operation might be undertaken.

4.2.2 "Precises" and "delicates"

Even a casual inspection of a collection of such turn-compositional hesitating yields two observations. First, a recurrent place speakers engage in the practice of hesitating is in the lead-up to possible completion. And second, many that occur in this position fall into one of two distinct types – or one might say that many of them can be understood on their occasion and by their recipients to be connected to one of two distinct turn-compositional projects.

The first is the imminent production of a *precise* formulation such as the name of a particular person or place – that is, a formulation that does not have an easy substitute or for which the substitute could be hearable *as* a substitute for the more precise formulation itself. In other words, as a speaker begins hesitating, the term due next can be projected as an instance of a particular type of term and then, in those cases where the speaker subsequently does produce the projected item, they can be seen as having engaged in a search for that precise term as in each of the following cases:

(15) KC–4 (Formulating a different medical procedure.)

D: They did have to grow a culture **for thee: ahm (1.0) for the blood test.** didn't they?

(16) Mid City Calls, 10 (Formulating a place where the child will be taken.)

Call Taker: Well if the woman is not there the child will be taken
to: u:m: (.) Saint Joe's

(17) NB II.2, 4 (Formulating the name of a course.)

Nancy: I took my final Monday in A:nthro: en I took my: final in
.hhhhh I gave turned in my term paper **i:n h–uh:: (0.4)**
.tch **Psychology** on Thursday

(18) Mid City Calls, 35 (Formulating the place where the caller is located.)

Caller: I'm right on **u::h (0.7) uh (Dowling::)**=an' (0.2)
Freemont Avenue.

(19) Clacia:11 (Formulating the name of another girl.)

Clacia: B't, a–another one theh wentuh school with me wa:s a girl
na:med uh, (0.7) W't th'hell wz'er name.=**Karen.**

(20) HOLT 5/88–1–2, 6 (Formulating the name of the third item in a list offering a variety of frozen fruit.)

Leslie: Well what do you like gooseb'rys black curre:nts:
uhm::::::::: rhuba::rb?

In cases such as these the turn-so-far in its sequence-so-far makes it more or less clear that some particular item that was due next has been delayed, while nonetheless indicating the speaker's commitment to continue speaking and therefore – at least in the first place – a continued commitment to resuming and (regularly enough) completing the in-progress TCU with that item. So, this first type might be characterized as pre-precise hesitation – and as we saw in extract 8 this can furnish a recipient with both the opportunity and the turn-compositional resources to assist by offering up a precise other-completion for the TCU.

The second type involves hesitating just prior to a projectably *delicate* term or prior to a term that is part of a turn-constructional unit that formulates a delicate matter or implements a delicate action. When a speaker engages in, for example, negatively evaluating someone's actions or character, this can be composed in a straightforward and unhesitating manner, as Shane does at the end of extract 21.[7]

(21) Chicken Dinner

Mic: He might be: ˙hhhh (0.6) well known photographer some
day.
(0.2)
Sha: At's true.=
Mic: =Yihkno:w,
(1.7)
Sha: It's tru[e.
Viv: [You c'd s–]
Mic: [S : t r a_:]nger things have happ[ened.
Sha: [That's
ri:ght ennit: still won't keep'm fr'm bein'n **asshole.**

On the other hand, this sort of formulation can be composed with some hesitancy in applying the projected negative evaluation, thereby showing that it is a delicate matter. This can be accomplished by hesitating at the point the negative expression is due, as Al does at the end of extract 22.

(22) GTS

Al: We're trying to find out (.) why you came up with
this decision, why you came up with this idea of
(.) using this (0.4) u:mm, (0.4) **this fa:lsehood,**

Here Al produces his criticism of a co-participant in a fashion that shows he is somewhat loath to say it by voicing it hesitatingly as a search for just the right term, and by using what on its delivery can be understood as a somewhat milder substitute for another, more accusatory formulation (e.g., "this lie"). Composing a potentially delicate term or delicate matter one way or the other (i.e., straightaway or hesitatingly) can be consequential in that the one who voices it can be seen as either someone who speaks in this way freely or only reluctantly thereby showing one is loath to say something derogatory about another, while nonetheless still voicing it (cf. Whitehead, 2009). How one voices a possibly delicate term or a possibly delicate matter can also be consequential in another way: it can be "procedurally consequential" for what a recipient does next (Schegloff, 1991).

In such *pre-delicate* environments (as was shown for pre-precise hesitating) the addressed recipient can treat turn-compositional hesitating as a trouble alert that is indicative of a search for a less delicate term, and use the opportunity space it constitutes to assist the speaker by offering up a euphemism as a candidate search solution as in extract 23 at line 2. (Note that the "he" at line 1 refers to the family dog, whom Mom lets off the leash when taking him out for a walk. Here she is responding to Dad's objection to this practice.)

(23) Shaw AFB

Mom: He doesn't go very far, he's got a little ah:: (0.8)
Dad: **she dog up ther[e**
Mom: [Yeah she do:g up here,
(0.4)
Mom: mm huh huh
Dad: **tryin a think of a- nice word** huh huh=
Mom: **=I was gunna say hussy** °but°

In this case both the original speaker of the turn (Mom) and the recipient who produces an other-completion for the stalled TCU (Dad) go on to explicitly formulate the hesitation as indicative of a search for a euphemistic expression.[8]

Yet, more than searching for a less delicate term (e.g., a euphemistic substitute for a possibly offensive term), the delay in the progressive realization of a turn's talk can indicate that an about-to-be-voiced term (e.g., a derogatory appraisal) is being delivered *as a delicate*. This is a method for delivering a term, matter, or action delicately; it is as much a way of displaying a stance toward what one is saying, or is about to say, *as delicate* (i.e., as potentially transgressive) as it is a method for actually selecting a milder alternative. Launching a search may result in the production of an apparently less offensive alternative or the indelicate term itself may be issued – but with its delicate character having now been made evident. In either case a speaker demonstrates reticence about voicing a delicate. Here the turn-constructional delaying practices used in searching for a word can be employed to implement another action – displaying some unease or hesitancy about what one is saying or is about to say. The turn-compositional features of hesitating are reflexively constituted and accountable as reticence in environments that have been prepared as involving a possible delicate.

Jefferson (1974) has described an "error correction format" (featuring "word cut-off + replacement") that can be employed to show one is producing a formulation appropriate to the current setting and recipients. By way of contrast, she also describes an "error avoidance format" (featuring "delay + word") that can be employed for "avoiding inappropriateness." Jefferson notes that such hesitating can convey "'I am thinking about how to put it.' Subsequently, a term is produced [by the same speaker] which can be heard as a solution to the problem of how to put it" (Jefferson, 1974: 194). The present report can be understood as building on Jefferson's early observations on avoiding inappropriateness by focusing on the affordances such hesitating, as well as other forms of turn-compositional delay, furnish for the (technical) possibility of other-completion – and thereby for the social possibility of the collaborative realization of delicate formulations.

4.3 An opportunity for other-completion

The speaker of a turn-so-far in its sequence-so-far can project the delivery of a delicate term, matter or action, and then suspend or retard the TCU-in-progress before its next possible completion. Because hesitating to produce a prefigured delicate furnishes an opportunity for conditional entry into the turn space by another participant, it can furnish an opportunity for other-completion of the delicate-bearing TCU-in-progress (Lerner, 1996b).[9] This opportunity for syntactic co-construction enables the possibility for the shared voicing of a delicate matter. And this allows a recipient to show that an impropriety can be propitiously voiced "between us," and to demonstrate that they are "of the same mind" as the original speaker. In short, this opportunity space furnishes recipients with one way to take a stand concerning what is being said and what is being done *while it is being delivered.*

In each of the following extracts a speaker hesitates in the course of a delicate matter and the TCU is then completed by a recipient.

1. Other-Completion of a Complaint

(24) DA

Bet: I– I– I just couldn' take the constant
repetition of uh::[::
Fan: [**of the same <u>story</u>.**

2. Other-Completion of a Declination to Recommend a Person for a Job

(25) SBL

Bee: Well do you think she would fit i:n¿
(.)
Amy: Uh:m .hh (.) uh I don't kno:w=What I'm: hesitating
abou:t is uhm .hh uhm (.) maybe she wou:ld .hh (0.8)
uh but I: would hesitate to: uhm
Bee: **recommend her.**

3. Other-Completion of a Sexual Innuendo

(26) GTS:2

Rgr:	Think about it you gotta be strong, that's that's
	three bottles a' champagne, .h three exerting rides
	and uh (0.2)
Al:	**three exerting women**

In each case a speaker begins a turn that seems to implement a delicate matter in a fashion that apparently allows their recipient to recognize both its delicateness and project what could complete it, and then by hesitating they furnish an opportunity for a recipient to enter the turn. And in each case the recipient of the turn-so-far then finishes voicing the delicate formulation.

4.4 Suspending the progressive realization of a turn's talk

Pre-delicate (as well as pre-precise) hesitating suspends the progressive realization of a turn's talk toward its projected next possible completion. Yet this is not the only form of action that can arrest the progressive realization of a turn's talk. There is a range of ways to suspend the forward progress of recognizably delicate turns-in-progress. In this section I expand the domain of the investigation by examining other methods that speakers can use to suspend a turn's talk before possible completion, and I show that these practices can also furnish opportunities for other-completion of delicate terms, matters and actions.

4.4.1 Cut-off just as a delicate term is due

A speaker can design their speech in a fashion that shows they are not so much searching for the *next* (precise or delicate) word as restraining or suppressing its production by stopping just as the (TCU-completing) term is due, as in extract 27 at the end of line 5. Here a bilabial stop (transcribed as "(b)") – which indicates onset of the next word – is formed and held, but not released for the voiced vowel that ordinarily follows it.

(27) Auto Discussion

Cur:	God damn it,
( ):	hh hh
Car:	Wuhd she do.
	(0.4)
Cur:	Oh nothin she's just **a(b)– (0.4)**
Car:	**bitch.**
Cur:	tch! Ye:ah, .hhh

4.4.2 Cut-off after partial production of a term

A speaker can actually produce part of the delicate term and then withdraw it by cutting it off and attempting to replace it with a less delicate term as in extract 28. In this case the sole female member of a teenage therapy group, Louise, begins to voice an expression that can suggest a degree of intimacy among group members.

(28) GTS

Lou:	cause we're=just gedding **clo–** you know, [started
( ):	**[Close enough**

However, she cuts it off mid-word and replaces it with a more neutral formulation, while one of the group's male members voices the term she is apparently abandoning. (Here "you know" extends the opportunity space for other-completion; see Lerner, 1996b: 265ff.) One might say that whereas "u(h)m" can be understood (at least in the first place) as pointing out a possible trouble ahead in something that has not yet been voiced, cut-offs seem to point back to something already voiced (or partially voiced) as a possible source of trouble (see Schegloff, 1979: 273).

4.4.3 Trail-off of a turn's talk before voicing the delicate matter

A speaker can trail-off the final component of compound TCU as in extract 29.

(29) Valdez

C:	Well grampa it's bad enough when 'e when
	he uhm:: tells you how much t'make,
	but when 'e tells you what t' **coo:k,**
	(0.3)
M:	**then it's rilly bad**=yeah. yeah.

4.4.4 Unmarked suspension at pre-completion

The possible completion of a delicate TCU or delicate terminal item of a TCU (or both) can be delayed by a pre-completion pause that has not been preceded by any sort of pre-pausal alert as in extract 30.

(30) GTS

Dan:	Well I do know last week that
	uh Al was certainly very **(0.6)**
Rgr:	**pissed off**

It is important to underline the import of the sequential position of such pauses for projecting a possible delicate matter. By contrast, the pauses that occur in the following extract are accountable in a fashion that does not indicate that anything delicate is going to be forthcoming.

(31) HIC (in Lerner, 1996b:264)

Spr: Now Dad wants to ah wants to have ah four officers
For the coming year, president, **(0.5)** vice president
secretry=treasurer **(1.1)** an [dah agent
Dad: [agent

In extract 31 Sparky is enumerating a list of officers for a newly formed family investment club and as he is voicing the titles he is simultaneously writing them down. It is obvious to all those present that he suspends his utterance so as to finish writing what he has just said. Note that such (non-delicate) "coordination pausing" nevertheless furnishes an opportunity for other-completion. That is, the opportunity furnished by suspension of the progressive realization of the turn's talk is a more general feature of the suspended progressivity of a turn's talk and is not, for example, delicate-specific (Lerner, 1996b).

4.4.5 Emotive expressions

Progressivity of a turn's talk can also be suspended by emotive expressions such as the audible sigh in extract 32 at line 8. In this case the sigh extends the opportunity space already established by the preliminary component of a compound TCU at line 7 ("I figure").

(32) HYLA

H: I yihknow when 'e– nyeh' I wz deciding
if if I sh'd write im the thank you
no:te [fer the birthday gi:ft,
N: [Yea:h
H: hh.hh I decided no:t to [though
N: [How co:me,
H: 't hhhhh (.) Becuz **I figure**,
hhhh[hhh
N: [If 'e [hasn' written ye:t,
(H): [(He)
(0.4)
N: then 'e doesn' want to.
(0.2)
H: Oh:: don't say thahhh [a(h)t
N: [NO is tha'wtcher[think[ing?
H: [.hhhh [No::,
.hhhh

Here the questioner uses the opportunity space extended by the sigh (at line 8) to offer a rather delicate candidate answer (delivered as an other-completion beginning at line 9). Note that this other-completion is itself produced as a compound TCU which projects its own opportunity for other-completion (after line 9) and this is also extended by a delay at line 11 (i.e., after the preliminary component) and just before the TCU's final component which contains the delicate formulation itself ("he doesn't want to").

What these extracts have in common (alongside the word searches examined above) is the suspension of the progressive realization of the turn's talk toward a next possible completion, and in each case this delay furnishes an opportunity – but not an obligation – for a co-participant to assist in the production of the TCU, and thereby to endorse the admissibility of the delicate it implements (by voicing what the other has hesitated to say). In extract 27 Carney comes in and produces the delicate term after a cut-off extended by an interval during which talk is suspended. In extract 28 a next speaker comes in and reissues the abandoned word after a cut-off and "you know," which further delays a possible replacement for "clo-" and perhaps explicitly opens up her turn to recipient entry. In extract 29 M comes in after a trail-off and a short interval and in extract 30 Roger completes Dan's assessment of Al's emotional state after Dan suspends the progressive realization of his turn just before its key term. In extract 31 talk is suspended to coordinate with the concurrent activity of writing, and Dad completes the list of candidates (no delicate here), while in extract 32 a long sigh extends the opportunity space furnished by the preliminary component of a compound TCU Hyla has produced, and the recipient uses that extended opportunity to venture a rather delicate reason for not contacting the boy.

To recap, I have now described how turn-constructional practices employed when launching the search for a word are composed and how participants (both the originator of the delicate and their recipients) can explicitly orient to the delicate character of what is being done. In addition, I have shown that the turn-constructional features of word searches are designed for collaboration – i.e. they furnish an opportunity space for other-completion – and that recipients do, indeed, complete delicately composed TCUs. Finally, I have shown that other practices that suspend the progressivity of a turn's talk also furnish an opportunity space for other-completion of recognizably delicate formulations.[10]

4.5 Turn construction and the social life of a society

The common element found across the range of features associated with possibly delicate TCUs-in-progress described above – the retardation or suspension of the progressivity of a turn's talk toward next possible completion – leads to a quite general observation about the relationship of turn construction to the social life of a society. And registering this observation constitutes a central upshot of this investigation. I am proposing that one main way to indicate to recipients that a possibly delicate term, matter, or action is being delivered as a delicate (alerting them to inspect the turn-so-far in its sequence-so-far for how it might be delicate) is through hesitation of some sort – i.e., through delaying the further realization of a turn's talk. This has an important implication for understanding the relationship of the organization of the talk itself to the emergent interpersonal relations that are enabled through talk and other conduct in interaction. The very form this practice takes constitutes a sequential environment for other-completion – and thus for achieving the joint authorization of a delicate. In short, *the very enactment of delicateness is designed for collaboration* – that is, for collaborative indiscretion.

This is not the only environment in which delay operates systematically to enable and thereby privilege something like "interpersonal harmony" or "social solidarity" (Heritage, 1984). The delayed turn beginnings associated with many disagreeing or dispreferred sequence-responding actions (Pomerantz, 1984a: 70–71) also comes to mind. Here too, exhibiting reluctance by hesitating (which is only evident by reference to the normative character of turn taking and sequence organization in which it is embedded) takes a form that permits, by its very structure, the pursuit of a more agreeing or aligning relationship between sequence-initiating and sequence-responding actions (Davidson, 1984; Pomerantz, 1984b; Sacks, 1987). For example, Sacks (1987) offers the following case,

(33) Schenkein 2a–A (From Sacks, 1987: 64)

A: They have a good cook there?
(1.4)
Nothing special?
B: <No,
(1.7)
Everybody takes their turns.

and then states, "'A' first displays a preference for a 'yes'; when a silence intervenes, A shifts to a form which invites agreement with the negative" (p. 64). The practice of delaying dispreferred sequence-responding actions is one basis for claiming there is a *structurally enabled* preference for agreement.[11] Note that in the case of other-completion of a delicate search, delay is revealed by reference to the progressivity of the TCU in which it is embedded. This is a specification of progressivity in the domain of TCU composition. In the case of delayed sequence-responding actions, the delay is revealed by reference to the conditional relevance of a second pair-part for the adjacency pair in which it is embedded. Here pair-part contiguity is a specification of progressivity in the domain of action sequencing.

In addition, one might also register here the delay found in launching many next-turn repair initiations that contributes to a preference for self-initiation of repair. As Schegloff, Jefferson, and Sacks (1977: 374) put it, "In such cases, other-initiations occur after a slight gap, the gap evidencing a withhold beyond the completion of trouble-source turn – providing an 'extra' opportunity, in an expanded transition space, for speaker of trouble source to self-initiate repair."[12]

In a similar vein, the range of progressivity-delaying methods employed for delicate delivery affords a structurally enabled opportunity for collaborative indiscretion – an interactional fact that puts its stamp on the habitus of social life. One might say that here we see a preference organization operating within a turn at talk. Elsewhere I have shown that delaying the progressive realization of a turn's talk in a range of ways is treated by recipients as an (unprojected) opportunity space for other-completion (Lerner, 1996b). Thus, completing the delicate formulation of another speaker constitutes an application of a more generally available method to a particular domain of action. That is, a general-purpose tool (concerned with turn composition) is employed here, rather than a domain-specific device particular to delicate formulation.

In the next section, I describe a variety of sequence-organizational trajectories for delicate formulations including centrally but not exclusively the collaborative production of the delicate matter. In doing so I show how the admissibility of delicates and possible co-implication in their production is worked out in practice. When an opportunity space for other-completion becomes available, recipients are thereby given the chance to implicate themselves in the emerging impropriety by sharing in its voicing (cf. Jefferson, 1985b: 33); however, they do not always do so. There is an opportunity for other-completion here, but ordinarily not a mandate. When a recipient is given this opportunity to participate in the production of a delicate, what do they do next – and what does the turn's original speaker then do? Posed in sequence-organizational terms, the question is: what sequences of action follow on from this type of opportunity to participate?

4.6 The sequential arrangement of delicate formulations

The structural opportunity for collaboration provided by the composition of a TCU-in-progress that is designed to implement a delicate formulation (in the variety of ways described above) makes relevant the possibility but not the inevitability of its joint production, and thus in effect makes possible its co-authorization (if not its co-authorship). Establishing under whose auspices a derogatory or otherwise delicate remark appears can be understood as the outcome of sequentially organized "negotiations"; the contributions that can make up this small sequence of actions can be distributed among participants in a range of ways. There are opportunities to participate for both the original speaker of a delicate TCU-in-progress and their recipients – and these opportunities can be taken or passed up, by either one or the other or both. What one participant does or does not do at each opportunity is consequential for what another can do next. In other words, the collaborative construction of a delicate formulation should be seen as an interactional achievement – one outcome among several possible turn-constructional and sequence-organizational trajectories – arranged moment-by-moment over the course of the delicate's formulation (or abandonment).

The following array of data extracts exhibits some of these trajectories. In each case an opportunity space for co-participant entry (and recurrently for other-completion) is produced through the suspension and/or retardation of the ordinary progressive realization of the turn's talk toward possible completion. In each case I track what happens next.

1. Recipients pass up an opportunity for other-completion and then the original speaker completes the TCU.

(34) GTS I :70–71

Al: We're trying to find out (.) why you came up with
this decision, why you came up with this idea
of (.) using this (0.4) u:mm, (0.4) **this fa:lsehood,**
(0.4) not falsehood=I didn' mean tuh say (that).
This u:h
Dan: device.
Al: device, to hide your uh to present to us.

In this case, Al employs a comparatively mild term to complete the TCU (at line 3), and then explicitly withdraws the delicate formulation (at line 4), but nevertheless it is he alone who has voiced it, and thus he alone who has authorized its delivery. (He seems oriented to this in that he does try to dodge full personal responsibility for having said it with "I didn't mean to say that.") In Goffman's (1981) terms Al is the formulation's "animator" and "author" – although perhaps not its only "principal." Note that Al launches this accusatory interrogation on behalf of the members of this therapy group through the use of a collective self-reference ("we") at line 1.[13] Thus, it is also in point to note (for this multi-party interaction), that, given the structural opportunity for other-completion, these group members have passed up the opportunity Al has fashioned for others to join in. (Note that the search is then expanded at line 5 and a subsequent opportunity is, in fact, immediately taken up by the group therapist who produces a rather more neutral formulation at line 6, which Al then takes up at line 7.)

Something similar can be seen in extract 35. Here the recipient passes up an opportunity to offer the searched-for term (which in this case is not the terminal item of the TCU) and then the original speaker continues – but here using a method that requires the recipient to infer the delicate formulation.

(35) Holt: X(C)1:1:3

Les:	… are you going t'have the funeral i:n
	North Cadb'ry or i[:n
Phi:	[Yes in North Cadb'ry o:n
	Tuesday at twelve o'clock.
Les:	Oh[:.
Phi:	[°°(at uh)°°
Les:	[Yes.
Phi:	[°°Mmhm°°
Les:	Right.
Phi:	at uhm (0.2) Yeh the service's at uhm twelve o'clock
	'n then: **the .hwhhh the: uh:m: (0.5) it'**ll be
	in the ceh- the Cary cemet'ry afterwards
	(you kn[ow) .hwhh
Les:	[Oh yes.
Les:	[Yes
Phi:	[I mean **my father: is** we've got a double grave
	there °(so it's [ )°
Les:	[Oh °yes.°

Phil employs a pro-term ("it" at line 11) to index the delicate in place of an explicit formulation of the delicate term itself (presumably "burial"). Also, note that the same speaker again seems to veer away from "buried" when he subsequently leaves off after "my father is" (at line 16) and then recomposes the TCU from its beginning, employing another method of delicate delivery. At this point I just want to note that multiple methods can be employed in concert, with one method (e.g., euphemistic formulation) employed as a fall-back when delicate delay does not result in other-completion.

2. Recipient produces an other-completion of the TCU, then the original speaker produces an agreement token that confirms the proffered completion as the projected (but previously unvoiced) completion to their turn.

(36) Auto Discussion

Cur:	Oh nothin she's just a(b)– (0.4)
Car:	**bitch.**
Cur:	tch! **Ye:h**, .hhh

This type of entry into the turn of another speaker is "conditional" in two ways: first, such entries regularly further the action of the turn – here producing the derogatory term that brings the TCU-in-progress to a next possible completion; and second, the erstwhile speaker who began the turn retains practical authority over their turn's talk insofar as other-completion (in these cases) makes confirming specially relevant for next turn (Lerner, 2004).[14] Completing another's delicate formulation can demonstrate both a shared sentiment *and* a shared manner of voicing that sentiment, while confirming the proffered completion allows the original speaker to indicate that it is in fact a shared sentiment. This small sequence ("other-completion + receipt") can be elaborated in a number of ways – ways that also elaborate what is accomplished by each of the sequence's elements.

3. Recipient produces the next element of the TCU-in-progress, the original speaker repeats the proffered element and then produces an agreement token that accepts it as the projected next element to their turn.

(37) SF–2

01 Mrk: an' at what point did you find out
02 that ah .hh her ah what shall we call
03 him (0.2) uhm: (.) her [um
04 Bob: **[(her old) boyfriend?**
05 Mrk: **her old boyfriend (y)eah that's a good phrase**

In this case (at line 5), Mark first employs the [repeat + agreement token] format that can be employed to attribute authorship to prior speaker before accepting the proffered element (Jefferson, 1985b), and then he underlines this attribution of its authorship to Bob by assessing it in a manner that makes clear it is Bob's turn of phrase ("that's a good phrase").[15] Further details of the actions accomplished in this case will be developed below as part of a discussion of solicited other-completion. (See discussion of extract 46.)

4. Recipient first proffers an other-completion, and then goes on to agree with what they have voiced on the other's behalf. In extract 38 speaker M both completes the evidently trailed-off TCU (a doubly compound TCU) and then produces a response made relevant by the action that TCU has implemented.

(38) Valdez

01 C: Well Grampa it's bad enough when 'e when he
02 uhm:: tells you how much t'make, but when
03 'e tells you what t' coo:k, (0.3)
04 M: **then it's rilly bad=yeah. yeah.**

In terms of sequence organization, speaker M first shares in the voicing of the compound complaint and then concurs with the negative appraisal it carries, thus producing a sequence-responding action implicated as a next action after an assessment (Pomerantz, 1984a) – but doing so in a place at which a receipt of the other-completion by speaker C was a specially relevant next action (Lerner, 2004). Speaker M not only renders a completion that can be projected (in both form and action) from the compound TCU-so-far, but she asserts separate knowledge of and experience with Grampa by going on to agree with the now-completed negative appraisal, rather than deferring to the originating speaker to accept or reject the other-completion.

This is consistent with Heritage and Raymond's (2005: 23) observation that the use of a [repeat + agreement token] format in a different sequence-organizational environment (after a tag questioned first assessment) can convey that the second speaker's position on the matter is "held independently of the view that the first speaker's assessment conveys." In the case of other-completion, the recipient is not technically repeating what the prior speaker has actually said, but rather is offering a rendition of what the prior speaker was evidently about to say – i.e., what had been projected from the turn-so-far in its sequence-so-far – and thus is the one who first voices the negative assessment (cf. Jefferson, 1985b: 32).

This practice can be seen clearly in extract 39 when Fanny offers an other-completion for Betty's stalled TCU-in-progress and then produces an "oh"-prefaced confirmation (cf. Heritage, 1998) that explicitly formulates her access to the source of the complaint as separate from that of her co-participant.

(39) DA

Bet: I– I– I just couldn' take the constant
repetition of uh::[::
Fan: **[of the same story. Oh don't I know**

"Oh"-prefaced responses to assessments are a way speakers display "epistemic independence" (Heritage, 2002). And in this case, Fanny then goes on to make explicit that her opinion was arrived at independently of Betty's original formulation.

In both extracts 38 and 39, after the other-completion, there are two distinct types of relevant next actions: 1. receipt of the other-completion by the TCU's original speaker and 2. response to the action of the now-completed TCU by its original recipient. Accordingly, one might want to say that there are competing sequence-organizational claims on this slot. However, in-coming speakers regularly stop after having completed the TCU-in-progress (Lerner, 2004), thereby allowing the turn's original speaker to address the adequacy of the proffered completion as a completion to their TCU and turn, as in extract 36. This "second-order" practice reinstates the turn-taking-provided "first order" entitlement of a speaker "to one such unit"

(Sacks, Schegloff, and Jefferson, 1974: 703) in the face of a relaxation of this entitlement carried out through other-completion of the TCU. Moreover, other-completion counts not only as a shared voicing of the TCU-in-progress, but also as an "early" sequence-responding action to the action the turn-so-far can be seen to have been implementing. And so one can see cases (such as in extracts 38 and 39), where the recipient does continue, as invoking a now-superseded warrant for responding – a warrant superseded by the incoming speaker's own action of other-completion. Importantly, by continuing in this way, the incoming speaker moves to sequentially delete the relevance of a receipt to their just-produced other-completion and thereby treats their own other-completion as not in need of acceptance or rejection by the original speaker of the turn. By producing a rendition of the projected completion for a turn that makes agreement/disagreement relevant for next turn, a recipient can demonstrate agreement with the originator of the TCU. By continuing to speak at the point a receipt of the other-completion is specially relevant, a recipient claims some entitlement to produce the action implemented through the TCU, independent of the original speaker's authority over what is said in their turn.

5. Although an other-completion is not delivered by recipient, they do respond to the action being implemented by the TCU-so-far and in the slot an other-completion could have been volunteered – i.e., they respond to the recognizable *action-in-formation* of a turn-so-far given an opportunity to do so, rather than wait for possible completion to respond.[16] In extract 40 at line 1 Penny counsels Pat against continuing to talk about the recent traumatic experience of having had her house burn down and starts to give the reason for her advice, but then begins hesitating. At this point, Pat responds by rejecting Penny's concern in the slot other-completion could have occurred. When a speaker hesitates during the construction of a TCU that implements a sequence-initiating action, then producing an "early" sequence-responding action becomes a "slot alternative" to other-completion of the TCU.

(40) Houseburning: 2

Pen: .hhh I don't wanna, (0.3) .thhh I don'
wanna make yih ta:lk, cuz I don' wanche tu:h,
(.)
Pat: **mNo I f- I really do feel a lot [better.** I feel like–]
Pen: [u p s e t yerself]
all over agai:n,

In this case the original speaker of the TCU (Penny) then begins a delayed completion (Lerner, 1989) for her original delicate TCU – doing so in the course of Pat's response. In this way, she reclaims her turn and completes her own unfinished TCU, thereby sequentially deleting Pat's response, reasserting her own cautionary advice and doing so in the face of its nascent rejection.

The array of data extracts in this section exhibits a range of ways sequence-specific elements can be distributed between the speaker of record and recipients, and illustrates that and how the resulting sequence of actions is an interactional achievement in each case. That is, *who* undertakes *which* of the elements that make up this sequence of actions is not set, but is arranged case by case, action by action and on a moment-to-moment basis with a range of different outcomes depending upon which elements are produced by each participant (and which opportunities are passed up or pre-empted). And, of course, on some occasions both speaker and recipients can pass up the opportunity to complete the suspended TCU, and so the delicate remains allusive because the TCU has remained incomplete. In these cases, as Sacks (1992, II: 429–430) once observed about obscenities:

> a party will break off their talk before they say it, when they might well say it … Where, then, the sheer fact that others don't continue can in some way evidence that they see what you were saying. And furthermore, that you don't continue can inform them that that's what you were indeed going to say.

4.7 Accomplishing more than delicate delivery of a delicate matter

One of the ways in which the formal organizations of talk-in-interaction allow for great flexibility of use can be found in the myriad ways that practices employed systematically to accomplish one action can as well be exploited (in particular circumstances) to implement additional actions. Accordingly, it should not be surprising that the practice of delicate delivery can be used to accomplish more than the delicate delivery of a delicate matter. I show how this practice – how its formal features – can be exploited to transfigure an otherwise innocuous formulation into an ostensibly delicate one, and then I describe two ways this practice can be employed to do more than merely furnishing an opportunity for other-completion of a delicate. It can be configured to solicit other-completion.

4.7.1 Delivering a seemingly innocuous formulation as (if) a delicate

Even when searching for a word prefigures a yet-to-be voiced delicate, the formal features of this practice can be exploited by both speaker and recipients to accomplish other outcomes. So, for example, a speaker's (pre-delicate) hesitating can be exploited by a recipient to opportunistically voice a manifestly indelicate completion as Al does (at line 3) in extract 41 even as Ken continues on to produce his own formulation.

(41) GTS

01	Ken:	And you think I really got pleasure out of
02		getting **uh (0.6) well I getting** [in that debate.
03	Al:	**[Stomped on.**

As in this case, other-completions are sometimes delivered even after a speaker resumes the progressive realization of their turn's talk. (See Lerner (1996b) for a discussion of "early"- and "late"-placed other-completions.)

In addition, a search can be employed by a speaker even when no obvious delicate is forthcoming to nevertheless adumbrate delicateness. Formulating an upcoming person reference as delicate can be a not-so-subtle way to convey that a derogatory person reference is going to be produced – even when that reference itself, when it is actually formulated, turns out to be quite innocuous. In extract 42 Bob apparently slows the progressivity of the turn's talk (by producing an extended stretch on "the::") to insinuate that a disparaging person reference will be forthcoming, but then produces a pointedly neutral term – which in the context of the topic at hand can then be understood as a euphemistic solution to a search for a more delicate formulation.

(42) SF–2

01	Mrk:	No:::. uh:: Yih kno:w I mea:n uh::,
02		hh What happened t'er boyfriend.
03		(0.6)
04	Bob:	I don' kno:w,
05		(1.2)
06	Bob:	Never talk about **the::. person.**
07	Mrk:	hhhhh huhh

Note Mark's subsequent brief laughter, which can be understood to demonstrate his appreciation of Bob's faux-delicate formulation and the disparaging formulation it adumbrates. This use of a [delay + completion] format might be thought of as constituting a *formal allusion* because it is only the form of the turn's composition and not the particular term that adumbrates a delicate formulation. Here, the format in its sequential environment can lead recipients to project one sort of term (adumbrating an indelicate terminal item) and then the realization disappoints the projected term or type of term.[17] (One could even say that the stance Bob takes toward the referent trumps the reference term he ultimately employs.)

Hesitating in this way can also be exploited when referring to an action as in extract 43. Here a speaker suspends her turn for 0.6 sec (at line 9) before producing what can thereby be heard as a euphemistic formulation.

(43) Housemates:24

J: .hhh We need to hire that girl.=Annie.
T: What girl.=
J: =Do[n and Jane's friend.
B: [We need to hire a girl?
J: There's this [girl, A(h)nnie. ((laugh))
B: [((laugh))
J: Um, (I want to)
B&T: ((laugh))
J: hire a girl for some **(0.6) services?**
B&T: ((laugh))
T: Uh hu:h
J: ((laugh))
B: Are there any in Boulder?

In both extracts 42 and 43 a speaker exploits the delay to the progressive realization of a turn's talk by not delivering on the expectation this practice apparently educes. And in both cases this maneuver is itself then appreciated by recipients.

4.7.2 Soliciting other-completion to accomplish more than conjoint delivery of a delicate

I begin by showing how delicate delivery can be elaborated to actively solicit other-completion, and then I describe two cases in which soliciting other-completion of a TCU is exploited by a speaker. In the first of these cases soliciting other-completion is employed to prompt a more entitled participant to formulate a possibly delicate person reference, and in the second case it is employed to prompt an offending party to formulate the character of his own offense.

Soliciting other-completion of a delicate matter. It is possible for a speaker to overtly solicit aid in the course of a search (whether searching for a delicate or a precise), and thus other-completion can become more than a sequential possibility; it can become specially relevant.

(44) DA

Jen: =Ri:ght. Right. I mean basic'ly she had a lot'v
Good qualities en I adored being with huh when she
wz **eh::: yihknow**[uh:::::::
Gol: **[yeah when she was rational** end uh=
Jen: **=nYeh tha:[t's ri:ght]** becawss uh:uh=
Gol: [( )]
Jen: =She had one thing that few'v us don't have she had
the capacity t'laugh et herself.

The long stretch on "eh:::" (at line 3) constitutes not only an *opportunity* space for other-completion, but, as such, it also constitutes a "*monitor* space" (Davidson, 1984) in which absence of recipient action can be addressed. In this case Jenny adds "you know" – which here can amount to a solicitation of other-completion. At this point in the search, her recipient, Goldie, responds directly to the format of the solicit with "yeah" and then goes on to produce an other-completion of a rather backhanded compliment.[18]

In this section the focus will continue to be on the solicitation of delicate items in the service of searching for a word, but before continuing it should be noted that there are other methods speakers employ to prompt a recipient to deliver a delicate formulation *first*. Jefferson (1983) reports on one such method a speaker can use to prompt a recipient to contribute a delicate item – setting up a puzzle for a recipient, whose solution to the puzzle can be the voicing of the (as yet unspoken) delicate item. In describing an instance of this "puzzle-solution" method, Jefferson (1983: 11) states, "The situation here is that of a 'delicate' problem, delicately referred to as 'having a little trouble in the bathroom', and a delicate remedy, delicately arrived at via … a puzzle/guessing-game format." In this case, then, the troubles teller formulates the problem as a delicate matter by employing a euphemistic expression, but the advice-giver sets up and pursues a puzzle (to be solved by the troubles teller) rather than voice the rather delicate advice herself.

(45) SBL:2:1:8 (simplified)

Nor: … I was thinking this morning I was having little
trouble in the ba:throom 'n I thought oh boy I (.) I
This business of getting up at six o'clock'n: being
ready (t'eat) is no– is no:t fer me ihh[h huh huh
Bea: [Uh huh
(0.4)
Bea: **Well** (.) uh(th ekhh hkkhhem=
Nor: =Somehow yo[u endure it.
Bea: **[THERE'S 'N THERE'S 'N A:NSWER TIH**
THA:T t:oo. hh
(0.7)
Bea: .hhhhhh 'hhh ehhh **A physical a:nsw(h)er**
Nor: You mean takin: takin la:xative et ni::ght

In this case rather than directly presenting a remedy for a rather delicate problem, the recipient of this "troubles telling" (Jefferson and Lee, 1981) hints at a remedy and then waits for her recipient to guess. When the troubles teller (Nora) does not do so, the advice-giver (Bea) resumes speaking, but still does not offer the (delicate) remedy itself. Rather the original hint is elaborated (from "an answer" to "a physical answer"). It is at this point that the original troubles teller guesses at the solution to the puzzle.

This method of prompting a recipient to deliver a delicate first parallels the search-based solicitation practices to be examined in the remainder of this section: In both advice-giving and searching for a word a "solution" to a puzzle is made relevant. In the case of advice-giving, the whole of the turn can be given over to prompting the advice recipient (i.e., the troubles teller) to be the first to voice the advice in next turn (by delivering the solution to the puzzle). Whereas, in the cases to be described below both the soliciting of a recipient to join in and the delivery of a solution to the searched-for element are shaped by the activity of searching for a word – i.e., in the service of resuming the progressive realization of a turn's talk – and therefore the sequential environment prepared for voicing the delicate establishes a place for it to take the form of other-completion.

Interestingly, in extract 45 the solution is cast in terms of what the advice-giver (i.e., the troubles recipient) was on the way to offering as a remedy ("you mean X"), thereby casting her own voicing of the delicate as on behalf of the advice-giver. This shows us that methods to solicit another to be the first to voice a delicate can encounter resistance (i.e., countermeasures) and thus who turns out to be the eventual "author-owner" of an impropriety is a locally produced, interactional achievement in these puzzle-solution sequences – as is also the case when assistance is solicited in the course of searching for a word.[19]

Soliciting the assistance of a more entitled participant. In the next extract, which occurs shortly after the exchange shown in extract 42 and reproduces extract 37, Mark continues interrogating his friend Bob about a woman he (Bob) has recently begun seeing socially. Although Mark had previously referred to "her boyfriend" without any hesitation, he now treats the same referent as a delicate – perhaps in line with Bob having done so during the earlier exchange. Here Mark shows that he is treating this as a delicate reference by launching a search ("ah.hh her ah"). However, in this case, he does not simply leave it to his recipient to offer up a formulation – i.e., leave it as an optional opportunity to do so. Rather, he expands the search by explicitly soliciting a formulation from his recipient – thereby transforming it from a purely turn-compositionally organized search into one that now includes sequence organizationally-relevant features.[20]

(46) SF–2

01	Mrk:	an' at what point did you find out
02		that ah .hh her ah **what shall we call**
03		**him** (0.2) uhm: (.) her [um
04	Bob:	[(her old) boyfriend?
05	Mrk:	her old boyfriend (y)eah that's a good phrase

Note that Mark resumes the production of turn-compositionally organized features of searching after soliciting his recipient's assistance, but the relevance of assistance endures – and the turn-compositional features of continued searching furnish opportunities for delivering that assistance.

The move to make a contribution by Bob specially relevant seems particularly apt in this case because the reference in a sense belongs to Bob and not to Mark: the way this person is referred to is bound up with the way Bob constitutes his relationship with the woman he is beginning to see socially. Bob has a special entitlement to set the terms of this relationship – for all that that can connote. Mark's question (at lines 2–3) is used as a method for deferring to Bob in this matter. However, there are cross-cutting entitlements here, with the speaker – qua speaker – retaining some authority over what is voiced within his turn. Bob seems to grant Mark authority over what is voiced within his (Mark's) turn by voicing his own contribution to the TCU ("her old boyfriend?") as a confirmable candidate. On the other hand (as noted earlier for this case), Mark sustains Bob's entitlement to formulate his own social relationships first by employing the [repeat + agreement token] format (that attributes authorship to prior speaker) and then by adding an evaluation of Bob's formulation ("that's a good phrase") (See Lerner, 1996a: 305 and 313–318 for an examination of other cross-cutting entitlements to voicing a turn's talk.)

Soliciting the assistance of an offending party. The recurrent practice of interspersing sequence-organizational elements into what is initiated as a turn-compositionally designed search can be exploited when the delicate matter targets the speaker's addressed recipient, rather than a non-present person. Soliciting assistance seems particularly fitting in extract 47. In this case, the delicate matter concerns an oversight: Bob and his roommate neglected to inform Mark (a life-long friend of theirs) of a party they were planning. This was apparently the reason for Mark's call, having heard about the party from another person in an earlier (recorded) telephone call. Prior to this extract Mark has complained to Bob about not being "clued in." The extract begins with Bob's apology.

(47) SF-2

01 Bob: .t .hhhh Okay Mark en uh::: yihknow,
02 a (.) thous'n pard'ns. fer yer– the oversight.
03 (0.2)
04 Mrk: .t .hhhh=
05 Bob: =(Or[is it)
06 Mrk: [Oh: .uh no: .Well I wasn't I didn't fee:l
07 like I wu:z:: ah .hh **what's the wo:rd.** uhm=
08 Bob: **=rebu:ffed?,=**
09 Mrk: =.hh–.hh rebu:ffed,h
10 Bob: Well I hope not.

Here the offending party (Bob) is put in the position by the offended party's search-relevant question ("what's the word") to select and voice a hurtful possible outcome of his own misconduct – something he might otherwise be unlikely to volunteer. (See, for example, extract 34, where the addressed recipient, whose misconduct is also the target of the delicate formulation, passes up an opportunity to assist in the search.) Note too that (as in the previous cases) Bob does resist being put in this position a bit by composing his other-completion with questioning intonation – that is, it is delivered as a candidate completion that solicits confirmation from the original speaker.

4.8 Concluding remarks

The myriad practices that enable conversation and other forms of talk-in-interaction along with the organization of these practices into systems of practical action enable emergent social relations, and thus the affordances of these practices can add shape to the customs that are realized in and as talking in interaction. Because conversation, as a speech exchange system, is locally managed, participant administered and interactionally organized (Sacks, Schegloff, and Jefferson, 1974), the realization of the elements of a culture-in-action that are enabled by talking in interaction then must also necessarily be so organized – or at least must accommodate how talk-in-interaction is organized. A corollary of taking this empirically grounded stance is that aspects of a society's interpersonal relations ought to be described in terms compatible with the central features of their enabling organization. That is, they should be described as emergent, interactional products realized both in and as turn-by-turn talking and the moment-by-moment sequencing of actions that talk and other conduct put into practice.

In this report I have focused on one way that impropriety finds its way into the social life of a society. These practices can be understood to express some misgivings for speaking in a particular way, while at the same time furnishing an opportunity for co-participant ratification of this manner of speaking *before the speaking turn has come to its next possible completion*. Suspending the ordinary progressivity of a turn's talk in the course of a TCU can alert recipients to inspect the turn-so-far for not only what it might take to complete it, but also what action is being held up through delaying its completion. This can be done by temporarily suspending the progressive realization of a turn's talk at a point that allows recognition of a projected delicate term or matter or action (or alternatively a projected precise term). This can take various forms, but the launching of (what can be treated as) a possible word search seems to be one main method speakers employ. In some circumstances doing searching may be understood as displaying a reticence or hesitation to voice a delicate term or formulate a delicate matter or form up a delicate action, while concomitantly furnishing an opportunity space for a co-participant's conditional entry into the turn. This "structural semi-permeability" of turn-constructional units establishes a local venue for interpersonal affiliation on just such occasions when such affiliation might come into question. Of course unmitigated negative assessments and other fully indelicate improprieties are also possible, but that is another type of action with its own organization.

At the outset, I introduced *sotto você* delivery, speech-obscuring laughter and euphemistic formulation (among a larger inventory of available practices) in order to establish that hesitating and other turn-constructional delays encountered in the course of TCU production represents only one form of practice among others that speakers can call upon to compose a delicate term, matter or action – that is, to deliver them as delicate. The aim in introducing these other practices was to show that there are alternatives – that the hesitating involved in, for example, searching for a less offensive term is not simply a logical or natural feature of embodied hesitation, but a social-organizational form among alternatives available to a speaker, each with its own relevancies for recipients. Thus employing practices that retard or suspend the forward progress of a TCU-in-progress furnish a ready opportunity (but ordinarily not an obligation) for other-completion, while other practices do not.

Moreover, in the service of investigating delicate delivery, I have described some of the basic organizational dimensions of word searching and explicated how "uh(m)" operates as a trouble alert which may or may not lead to repair (and thus need not "initiate" a repair at all) and if it does may or may not lead to a repair solution that retrospectively reveals itself as having been a word search.[21]

Searching for a word – along with other turn-compositional practices that retard, suspend or abandon the progressive realization of a TCU – provide an opportunity for recipients to contribute to another participant's speaking turn and thereby furnish a means for an assisting speaker to endorse the admissibility of a possible impropriety or other delicate matter before it has been completed by the original speaker of the turn. Taken together these turn-constructional features – in these sequential environments, in these positions within their turns and TCUs and projecting a specific sort of (terminal) item as due next – afford an opportunity for recipient intervention. Doing hesitating and other turn-delaying and turn-abandoning practices are offset against the ordinary progressive realization of a turn's talk toward (next) possible completion that is a feature of the turn-taking system for conversation.

Let me underscore a key point here. Doing searching for a word, and, more inclusively turn-compositional hesitating, and, more inclusively still, any suspension of the progressivity of a turn's talk, establishes a systematic venue and a structural basis for recipients to implicate themselves as co-animators and thus as co-owners of delicate formulations of all sorts (culturally proscribed, occasion- or recipient-specific, and momentary). And as I have said, these methods for showing that a formulation is a delicate are designed for – and can elicit – shared voicing by recipients. Here, assisting in the production of a TCU is a way to co-authorize what is being done. In this way, the very structure of delicates (i.e., the very practices for composing formulations as delicately delivered) can be seen as instituting a sequential opportunity for what might be referred to as practical solidarity in the face of possible social impropriety. This observation then situates social solidarity as an *organizationally advantaged* (i.e., 'preferred') interactional outcome of situated practices of talking in interaction.

Finally, this investigation suggests, in its detailed treatment of individual specimens, a far-reaching connection between the organization of talk-in-interaction and a culture-in-action. Here we see how practices for talking-in-interaction establish structural affordances for accomplishing action in interaction – affordances for action that underwrite the possibility of collaborative production of culturally specified, occasion-specific or locally established forms of impropriety. One might want to say that the delicateness of a formulation – that is, the stance a speaker is taking toward what they are saying as in some way indelicate – is reflexively established in the production of just this term (or matter or action) in just this sequential environment for just this recipient by speaking in just this way. This is one way culture emerges as action at the point of its production in interaction.

REFERENCES

Brown, P. and Levinson, S. C. (1987). *Politeness: Some Universals in Language Usage*. Cambridge University Press.

Clift, R. (2001). Meaning in interaction: the case of "actually". *Language* 77: 245–291.

Davidson, J. (1984). Subsequent versions of invitations, offers, requests, and proposals dealing with potential or actual rejection. In J. M. Atkinson and J. Heritage, eds., *Structures of Social Action: Studies in Conversation Analysis*, pp. 102–128. Cambridge University Press.

Drew, P. (1984). Speakers' reporting in invitation sequences. In J. M. Atkinson and J. Heritage, eds., *Structures of Social Action: Studies in Conversation Analysis*, pp. 129–151. Cambridge University Press.

(1991). Asymmetries of knowledge in conversational interactions. In J. Markova and K. Foppa, eds., *Asymmetries in Dialogue*, pp. 29–48. Hemel Hempstead: Harvester Wheatsheaf.

Drew, P. and Walker, T. (2010). *Going too far*: Complaining, escalating and disaffiliation. *Journal of Pragmatics* 41: 2400–2414.

Goffman, E. (1967). *Interaction Ritual: Essays on Face-to-Face Behavior*. New York: Doubleday Anchor.

(1981). *Forms of Talk*. Philadelphia, PA: University of Pennsylvania Press.

Goodwin, M. H. and Goodwin, C. (1986). Gesture and coparticipation in the activity of searching for a word. *Semiotica* 62: 51–75.

Heritage, J. (1984). *Garfinkel and Ethnomethodology*. Cambridge: Polity Press.

(1998). Oh prefaced responses to inquiry. *Language in Society* 27: 291–334.

(2002). Oh-prefaced responses to assessments: a method of modifying agreement/disagreement: in Cecilia Ford, Barbara Fox and Sandra Thompson, eds, The *Language of Turn and Sequence*, pp. 196–224. New York: Oxford University Press.

Heritage, J. and Raymond, G. (2005). The terms of agreement: indexing epistemic authority and subordination in assessment sequences. *Social Psychology Quarterly* 68: 15–38.

Jefferson, G. (1974). Error correction as an interactional resource. *Language in Society* 2: 181–199.

(1983). On a failed hypothesis: 'conjunctionals' as overlap-vulnerable. *Tilburg Papers in Language and Literature* 28: 1–33.

(1985a). On the interactional unpackaging of a "gloss." *Language in Society* 14: 435–466.

(1985b). An exercise in the transcription and analysis of laughter. In T. A. van Dijk, ed., *Handbook of Discourse Analysis* vol. III, pp. 25–34. London: Academic Press.

(1987). On exposed and embedded correction in conversation. In G. Button, J. R. E. Lee, eds., *Talk and Social Organisation*, pp. 86–100. Clevedon: Multilingual Matters.

Jefferson, G. and Lee, J. R. E. (1981). The rejection of advice: managing the problematic convergence of a "Troubles Telling" and a "Service Encounter." *Journal of Pragmatics* 5: 399–422.

Jefferson, G., Sacks, H. and Schegloff, E. A. (1987). Notes on laughter in the pursuit of intimacy. In G. Button and J. R. E. Lee, eds., *Talk and Social Organization*, pp. 152–205. Clevedon: Multilingual Matters.

Kurri, K. and Wahlström, J. (2007). Reformulations of agentless talk in psychotherapy. *Text & Talk* 27(3): 315–338.

Labov, W. (1972). *Language in the Inner City: Studies in the Black English Vernacular*. Philadelphia: University of Pennsylvania Press.

Lerner, G. H. (1989). Notes on overlap management in conversation: the case of delayed completion. *Western Journal of Speech Communication* 53: 167–177.

(1992). Assisted Storytelling: Deploying shared knowledge as a practical matter. *Qualitative Sociology* 15: 247–271.

(1995). Turn design and the organization of participation in instructional activities. *Discourse Processes* 19: 111–131.

(1996a). Finding "face" in the preference structures of talk in interaction. *Social Psychology Quarterly* 59: 303–321.

(1996b). On the "semi permeable" character of grammatical units in conversation: conditional entry into the turn space of another speaker. In E. Ochs, E. A. Schegloff, and S. A. Thompson, eds., *Interaction and Grammar*, pp. 238–276. Cambridge University Press.

(2002). Turn-sharing: the choral co-production of talk-in-interaction. In C. Ford, B. Fox and S. Thompson, eds., *The Language of Turn and Sequence*, pp. 225–256. Oxford University Press.

(2004). Collaborative turn sequences. In G. H. Lerner, ed., *Conversation Analysis: Studies from the First Generation*. Amsterdam: John Benjamins.

Lerner, G. H. and Kitzinger, C. (2007). Extraction and aggregation in the repair of individual and collective self-reference. *Discourse Studies* 9(4): 526–557.

Lerner, G. H. and Raymond, G. (2007). Body trouble: some sources of interactional trouble and their embodied solution. Paper presented to the National Communication Association, Chicago.

Pomerantz, A. (1980). Telling my side: "limited access" as a "fishing" device. *Sociological Inquiry* 50:186–198.

(1984a). Agreeing and disagreeing with assessments: some features of preferred/ dispreferred turn shapes. In J. M. Atkinson, and J. Heritage, eds., *Structures of Social Action: Studies in Conversation Analysis*, pp. 57–101. Cambridge University Press.

(1984b). Giving a source or basis: the practice in conversation of telling "how I know." *Journal of Pragmatics* 8: 607–625.

Raymond, G. and Heritage, J. (2006). The epistemics of social relationships: owning grandchildren. *Language in Society* 35: 677–705.

Sacks, H. (1975). Everyone has to lie. In M. Sanches amd B. Blount, eds., *Sociocultural Dimensions of Language Use*, pp. 57–80. New York: Academic Press.

(1987). On the preferences for agreement and contiguity in sequences in conversation. In G. Button and J. R. E Lee, eds., *Talk and Social Organization*, pp. 54–69. Clevedon: Multilingual Matters.

(1992). *Lectures on Conversation*. Blackwell, Oxford.

Sacks, H., Schegloff, E. A. and Jefferson, G. (1974). A simplest systematics for the organization of turn-taking for conversation. *Language* 50: 696–735.

Schegloff, E. A. (1979). The relevance of repair to syntax-for-conversation. In T. Givón, *Syntax and Semantics*, vol. XII: *Discourse and Syntax*, pp. 261–288. New York: Academic Press.

(1980). Preliminaries to preliminaries: "Can I ask you a question?" *Sociological Inquiry* 50: 104–152.

(1984). On some gestures' relation to talk. In J. M. Atkinson and J. Heritage, eds., *Structures of Social Action: Studies in Conversation Analysis*, pp. 266–296. Cambridge University Press.

(1988). On an actual virtual servo-mechanism for guessing bad news: a single case analysis. *Social Problems* 35(4): 442–457.

(1991). Reflections on talk and social structure. In D. Boden and D. H. Zimmerman, eds., *Talk and Social Structure: Studies in Ethnomethodology and Conversation Analysis*, pp. 44–71. Cambridge: Polity Press.
(1996). Confirming allusions: toward an empirical account of action. *American Journal of Sociology* 102: 161–216.
(2000). Overlapping talk and the organization of turn-taking for conversation. *Language in Society* 29: 1–63.
(2003). The surfacing of the suppressed. In P. Glenn, C. LeBaron & J. Mandelbaum, eds., *Studies in Language and Social Interaction: A Festschrift in Honor of Robert Hopper*, pp. 241–262. Mahwah, NJ: Lawrence Erlbaum Associates.
(2004). On dispensability. *Research on Language and Social Interaction* 37: 95–149.
(2007). *Sequence Organization in Interaction: A Primer in Conversation Analysis.* Cambridge University Press.
(2010). Some other "uh(m)"s. *Discourse Processes* 47(2): 130–174
Schegloff, E. A. Jefferson, G. and Sacks, H. (1977). The preference for self-correction in the organization of repair in conversation. *Language* 53: 361–382.
Stivers, T. (2005). Modified repeats: one method for asserting primary rights from second position. *Research on Language and Social Interaction* 38: 131–158.
Treis, Y. (2005). Avoiding their names – avoiding their eyes: how Kambaata women respect their in-laws. *Anthropological Linguistics* 47: 292–320.
Whitehead, K. A. (2009). "Categorizing the Categorizer": the management of racial common sense in interaction. *Social Psychology Quarterly* 72: 325–342.
Wilkinson, S. and Weatherall A. (2011). Insertion repair. *Research on Language and Social Interaction* 44: 65–91.

NOTES

1 One can see the shadows of Goffman's (1967) abiding concern with "face" and "face-work" here and (building on Goffman's ideas), Brown and Levinson's (1987) specification of the operation of politeness, not to mention the ample linguistic anthropological literature (largely based on elicitation) describing euphemistic alternatives to taboo words and otherwise distasteful expressions. To give just one case in point, Treis (2005) describes an Ethiopian speech community in which daughters-in-law have traditionally avoided voicing the names of their in-laws, as well as "any word starting with the same syllable as their names" (p. 295), but who have a special vocabulary of respectful alternatives at their disposal for many words, as well as other ways to demonstrate respect through word avoidance including partially conventionalized methods of circumlocution (e.g. by turning verbs into nouns of agency).

2 Another routine practice here is to produce a quiet aside accompanied by, or rather obscured by, a hand placed near the speaker's mouth so as to show one is shielding what is being said as in the following case at the arrow. This exchange occurs during

a family dinner composed of a mother, her young, twentyish son and his same-aged buddy. Here the friend addresses a question to the mother (in defense against her criticism of their sloppy eating habits).

[GB07-9]

Frn: Did you ever kiss someone who doesn't kiss right?=It
feels like he just doesn't kiss right¿ Or it feels
like
(1.2) ((makes kissing face))
he's not a good kisser. Ever have that before¿
(1.4)
Mth: (I don't know.) Let me think, ((hand to chin))
(0.2)
-> ((**Son moves hand to shield mouth from Mother**))
Son: (°° [°°)
Mth: [Ah(p)– You know what,
you talk like that an you're gunna get slapped.

It is not possible to hear what the son says, but clearly the mother takes it to have been tactless.

3 In co-present interaction, accompanying visible aspects of a speaker's conduct may ratify that a search is underway. For example, Goodwin and Goodwin (1986) have noted that speakers sometimes assume a "thinking face" as part of searching for a word. However, a "thinking face" on its own does not indicate that a party is engaged in a *word* search. So, for example, after being asked a question that could require working out an answer, a recipient's assumption of this pose can indicate a party is engaged in "searching" for an answer in a sequence-so-far and not in searching for a next word in a turn-so-far.

4 In this report I adopt Schegloff's (2010) convention of referring to both "uh" and "uhm" together with the single form "uh(m)."

5 These features – retarding and/or suspending the forward progress of an action – are not limited to turn construction. Lerner and Raymond (2007) have shown that these are quite general resources that are also employed to remediate body-behaviorally implemented action as well as to alert recipients to such possible trouble (ahead). For instance, the recipient of an object in an object transfer can suspend the forward progress of the transfer (by not pulling the object away) as a method for indicating to the participant delivering the object that there is some trouble with the delivery.

6 For example, a "hesitation token" can also be employed in turn-initial position to claim a new turn at talk even when followed by a pause. In this regard, Sacks (1992: 547) notes that: "A characteristic form of an utterance turns out to be 'Uh,' pause, sentence. Why is the 'Uh' there? It's there in order to permit the pause to be after you started talking." That is, the "uh" shows that a turn at talk has begun and indicates a continued commitment to its production. However, not every use of "uh(h)" implicates further talk. For example, there is one sequence-organizational environment in which it implicates *no* further talk – or at least no further talk connected to the now-ending sequence. Schegloff (2010) shows that ["and uh(m)" + silence] can be

employed as a sequence (re-)exiting device after a first attempt at closing a sequence was ineffective. Rather than showing a continued commitment to talk, this use of "uh(m)" is treated as indicating a commitment to not continuing the sequence and therefore furnishes an opportunity for others to launch a next matter.

7 Of course, there are also practices available to speakers to indicate that they are going out of their way to produce an impropriety. For example, in the following case a person reference is interrupted in order to reformulate it in a more derogatory fashion. In this instance Bee cuts off the very beginning of what is apparently going to be a name ("*v-*") and then pauses before continuing speaking. When she resumes, Bee inserts "*fat ol'*" and then continues with the name she apparently had begun beforehand (thereby constituting "fat old" as an insertion).

[TG:10]

01	Bee:	Hey do you see v– (0.3) **fat ol'** Vivian anymore?
02	Ava:	No, hardly, en if we do:, y'know, I jus' say hello
03		quick'n, ˙hh y'know, jus' pass each othuh in the hall.

The cut-off of a word can indicate that voicing that word (as the next word of the TCU-in-progress) is being reconsidered. In this case, that reconsideration ends with a turn-compositional insertion repair (Wilkinson and Weatherall, 2011). Rather than indicating the deprecating descriptor is being produced as a delicate, Bee seems to accomplish something else. Here she shows her willingness to delay the forward progress of her turn in order to go back and add the unflattering descriptors to the reference she is formulating. One might say she is "going out of her way" to get it said; she is not hesitating to say it. (Perhaps, in this case, the speaker is increasing the specificity of a reference in the service of producing a recognitional reference and selects a deprecating descriptor to accomplish this.)

8 It seems to be the presence of Mom and Dad's young son at the dinner table that occasions the search for a delicate alternative to "bitch" for referring to a female dog. Indeed, Mom glances briefly toward her son after launching the search and then directly at Dad, who has been looking at her the whole time.

9 The opportunity for others to speak can be understood as "conditional" in that such entry by others is recurrently designed to contribute to or forward the speaker's within-TCU project of searching for a word. There is at least one systematic exception to this: when the action of searching for a word occurs within a TCU that is involved in implementing a sequence-initiating action. In this case furnishing a conditionally relevant sequence-responding action becomes an additionally relevant alternative – one that forwards the sequence.

10 The features described here as furnishing an opportunity for other-completion can also be found in abundance in circumstances of "competitive overlap," where they form a set of resources for resolving overlapping speech. As Schegloff (2000: 12) demonstrates, "when we examine the distribution of these hitches and perturbations in the developing course of overlapping talk, we may come to understand all the deflections as possible resources deployed by speakers in managing the course and resolution of the overlap, and of their position within it."

11 In addition to response turn delay, there are other turn-constructional and sequence-organizational practices speakers employ that put preference-dispreference

organization into action. See Schegloff (2007: 63–96) for a review. These too can furnish opportunities to build an agreeing – or a more agreeing – relationship between sequence-initiating actions and sequence-responding actions, and thereby promote, but not require, social solidarity among participants (see, e.g., Lerner, 1996a).

12 A similar observation can be made concerning one form of same-turn repair examined in this report. In the case of word search organization (when the projected term is not a "delicate," but a "precise" such as a name), I have observed (Lerner, 1996b: 262–263) that co-participants recurrently hold off offering a candidate at the beginning of the search, unless they are able to assert some special authority (e.g., the co-teller of a story).

13 Lerner and Kitzinger (2007) have shown that speakers can switch from individual self-reference to collective self-reference as a way to "diffuse responsibility" for what they are saying. Here the use of collective self-reference may be further evidence that Al is treating this as a delicate matter.

14 One might also draw a parallel to Schegloff's (1996) description of "confirming allusions" in which something only hinted at by one speaker is made explicit by another speaker and that then makes confirmation relevant. Both the "strong" (turn-taking-provided) authority of turn-construction and the somewhat "weaker" authority of allusion are instantiations from the broad range of practices that enable the organization of deference to and assertion of "authoritativeness" in talk-in-interaction (most centrally, but not limited to what might be dubbed "interactional epistemics"). Many investigators have explored how these practices organize talk-in-interaction from Labov (1972), Sacks (1975) and Pomerantz (1980, 1984b) to Drew (1991), Lerner (1996a, 2004), Heritage and Raymond (2005) and Raymond and Heritage (2006). For the most part these practices implement differential authoritativeness, but this domain also includes practices that can implement coequal authority (see, e.g., Lerner, 1992).

15 By contrast, in one case (previously displayed as extract 23) the original speaker begins with an agreement token confirming the completion and then follows up with a (modified) repeat of the other-completion. However, I do not believe this case instantiates another receipt slot format. Rather, this particular repeat might best be understood as implementing an embedded correction (Jefferson, 1987) of the other-completion. In this case Mom is describing what happens when she takes her dog for a walk and lets him off the leash.

[Shaw AFB]

```
01   Mom:    I take him in the school yard
02           (1.0)  ((Left hand thumb point over shoulder))
03           at night an let him run
             :
04   Mom:    He doesn't go very far, he's got a little ah:: (0.8)
05   Dad:    she dog up ther[e
06   Mom:                   [Yeah she dog up here
```

At first one might think of a change in the deictic place formulation as merely reflecting a change in speakership, while maintaining the same referent (as would ordinarily be the case in a telephone call when participants are in different locations). Dad's other-completion places the "she dog" "up there" (i.e., near the school), while Mom's modified repeat seems to place it closer to home. In this case, it seems to me that the post-receipt repeat (with deictic shift) reiterates Mom's acceptance of the other-completion as an adequate rendition for the focal matter at hand (formulating a euphemistic alternative), while correcting an error incidental to what Mom was aiming to produce. In this case the repeat-cum-embedded-correction allows Mom to fine-tune her confirmation. Some modified repeats can also be used as a systematic practice to demonstrate ownership over the repeated matter (Stivers, 2005). In the present case, the modified repeat simply continues Mom's already-established authority to dictate what her turn's talk will be even in the face of its other-completion by Dad.

16 See Lerner (2002: 234) for a characterization of "recognition" vs. "completion" as sequentially distinct loci for action.

17 This might be thought of as somewhat akin to taking an overly big in-breath after having been asked a question, but then producing only a terse reply.

18 In this case, Goldie does not simply produce the terminal item, but returns to an earlier constituent boundary, thus using Jenny's already spoken words to pre-frame the added element of the completion. It is worth considering the possibility that this is done here because of the intra-turn sequence [you know + yeah] that breaks up the syntactic contiguity of the other-completion with the turn-so-far.

19 Two additional methods for prompting a recipient to first voice a delicate have been described: 1. Drew and Walker (2010) examine complaint sequences in which, "'the complainant' does not initially go on record with a complaint, but instead secures the other's participation in co-constructing the complaint. Hence the 'complaint recipient' may be the first to make the complaint explicit" (p. 2400). 2. Schegloff (1988) describes a practice by which tellers of bad news get their recipients to guess the news (e.g., the death of a mutual friend), rather than deliver it themselves. Also, see Drew (1984: 137).

20 When a formulation is, in a sense, properly the property of another participant, a speaker can run the risk of producing a less than satisfactory formulation (cf. Raymond and Heritage, 2006). This can be seen in extract 32, where Hyla (who is obviously entitled to know what she is thinking and is about to say) passes on an opportunity for other-completion at line 11 – an opportunity furnished at line 9 by the preliminary component of a compound TCU and extended by a pause in speaking – and then Nancy, rather than soliciting other-completion as Mark does in extract 46, goes on to complete the TCU herself at line 12 (reproduced below). This rendition of what Hyla was about to say is then rejected by Hyla.

```
N:   then 'e doesn' want to.
     (0.2)
H:   Oh:: don't say thahhh [a(h)t
N:                          [NO is tha'wtcher[ think[ing?
H:                                                  [.hhhh [No::,
     .hhhh
```

Note that this is a rather complicated case in that the party who produces an opportunity space for other-completion (Nancy) is herself actually in the course of completing a TCU begun by her recipient (Hyla). In effect, this is an opportunity not taken within an opportunity that was taken. Here Hyla treats what Nancy says as if it were Nancy's property (i.e. as representing Nancy's opinion) – and when she does, Nancy denies this and makes explicit that she was speaking, not on behalf of herself, but on behalf of Hyla.

21 I am indebted to Manny Schegloff for long discussions of these matters of mutual interest.

5 One question after another: same-turn repair in the formation of yes/no type initiating actions

Geoffrey Raymond and John Heritage

This paper examines occasions in which speakers initiate repair in the midst of, or at/after the possible completion of, a question, and by virtue of this come to pose "one question after another." The data are drawn from ordinary and institutional contexts, though questions from the latter constitute the large majority of cases examined below.[1] Unlike the chapters in this volume that explicate practices associated with the organization of repair as such, this chapter makes a different use of these phenomena: we use occasions in which speakers encountering, and attempting to resolve, troubles in the posing of a question display their orientation to what they are entitled or expected to know, or what they cannot know or assume, and how these two alternatives are implicated in the organization of social action, and social relations more generally. That is, we use instances of repaired questions (and other bases for their in-course modification) as a method for opening a window on practices of questioning, expanding Raymond and Heritage's (2006: 701) analysis of the "distance-involvement" dilemma to show that "the twin risks of appearing disengaged from the affairs of the other, or appearing over-involved with and even appropriating of them" emerge in a broad range of sequence types, suggesting that this dilemma may be inherent in cooperative action more generally. In this way we also illustrate how the organization of repair can be exploited as a methodological tool to understand, and explicate, how speakers posing sequence-initiating actions reflexively position themselves in a multi-dimensional space of rights and obligations (see Drew et al., this volume).

As a backdrop to this discussion we begin by reviewing some recent findings regarding practices of questioning and their connection to participants' management of rights to knowledge in, and as, action.

5.1 Introduction: grammar and the epistemics of social relations

In organizing action in interaction, persons continually position themselves with respect to "the epistemic order" because persons cannot avoid taking a position regarding what they know relative to others, what they are entitled to know, and what they are entitled to describe or communicate (see Heritage,

2012: 16). Indeed, as various analysts have demonstrated, such matters are the subject of highly elaborate management through practices of turn design and sequence organization, suggesting their central import for action, and for the normative regulation of identities and social relations more generally (see, for example, Goodwin, 1979, 1984, 1987; Pomerantz, 1980; Heritage, 1984, 1998; Heritage and Raymond, 2005; Raymond and Heritage, 2006). These analyses established two key findings regarding the organization of this domain and the "practiced solutions" (Schegloff, 2006) that have emerged to manage the recurrent contingencies it poses for participants. First, epistemic rights are not solely (or even mainly) distributed on the basis of physical access to a state of affairs; they are socially distributed (Whalen and Zimmerman, 1990; Heritage and Raymond, 2005). Second, there appears to be a fundamental association between the positioning of an action and the epistemic claims implied by that positioning (cf. Heritage and Raymond, 2005; Raymond and Heritage, 2006). As a consequence, the practices used by participants and their deployment by speakers asserting distinct claims regarding their rights relative to co-participants will be sensitive to whether the utterance *initiates* an action sequence or is produced as *responsive* to prior action.

The relevance of sequential positioning for the assertion of rights can be illustrated if we consider the basic alternative grammatical constructions speakers use to initiate action sequences: declaratives and interrogatives. These alternatives are simultaneously the most ubiquitous resources available to speakers, and the most directly consequential for the actions they make relevant next. For example, in choosing between declarative and interrogative constructions (which are widely recognized as "language universals"; cf. Greenberg, 2005) speakers propose or project contrasting socio-epistemic *relations* with the recipient targeted by them (Raymond, 2010a, 2010b; Heritage, 2012).[2] The use of declaratives to compose a first position action indexes both the speaker's right to know and to assert what is being declared and the assumption that her recipient does not know it but *would have an interest in knowing*, as in example 1. In a conversation among long-time friends that is devoted to "catching up," among other activities, Bee tells Ava that, "Sibbie's sister had a baby boy" (line 1).

((*K+ = has knowledge/information; K– = lacks knowledge/information*))

(01) TG

01 Bee: -> Oh Sibbie's sistuh hadda ba:by bo:way. (K+)
02 Ava: Who¿ (K–)
03 Bee: Sibbie's sister.
04 Ava: -> Oh really? (K– -> K+)
05 Bee: Myeah,

The default outcome aimed for is a sequence in which the recipient will register having been informed by an utterance that conveys something that she does not yet know, but which is relevant for her. We can note that in line 4 Ava registers the telling as news: "oh really?" (see Heritage, 1984; see also Jefferson, 1981). Much as in the case of assessments, straight declaratives in a sequence initial position claim established knowledge of, or unmediated access to, the matters formulated in them, and thereby constitute an "unmarked" form, insofar as they contain no design features that either strengthen or weaken the declarative claim that is made by them.

By contrast, the deployment of an interrogative form proposes the opposite relationship: a speaker claims a relevant interest in obtaining information from a recipient who knows something – or is obligated or has rights to know something – that the questioner does not (see Heritage, 2008; Raymond, 2010a, 2010b). For example, in extract 2, line 2, Regan, who has just informed her sister about her own plans for the following evening, poses a reciprocal query, "Are you going to go downtown?", evidently anticipating the possibility of a shared outing.

(02) Sisters Call 1

01	Nik:		Wut are you doin tomorrow are< you goin downtown¯?	
02	Reg:	->	Yeah. Are you gunna go down–town?	(K–)
03	Nik:		˙hh I don't know I'm bro:ke*.	(K+)
04	Reg:	->	Oh °poo:per:°	(K– –> K+)
05	Nik:		I kno::w¯	

Nikki's response (in line 3), which dashes those hopes, is registered as news "oh," and assessed "pooper." In this way, interrogatives work to downgrade the rights otherwise asserted by a sequence-initiating action.[3] We use (K+ -> K–) and (K– -> K+) to refer to these alternative relationships; their embodiment in the grammar in languages around the world suggests that they are two basic occasions for action, and interaction, as such.

In the cases above we can note the connection between the rights asserted by these grammatical forms and the putative rights of the speakers who deploy them as a sequence-initiating action. In extracts 1 and 2, the social relation proposed by the grammatical form of the sequence-initiating action maps on to the putative "epistemic status" of the participants ("real world" distribution of knowledge and rights to knowledge between them); that is K– speakers use interrogatives; and K+ speakers use declaratives. We may thus speak of a general preference for congruency between a speaker's epistemic status and the epistemic stance indexed within a turn at talk. The connection between grammar, epistemic rights, sequential positioning and action can be further underscored, however, if we consider cases in which speakers exploit a mismatch between their actual circumstances and the social relation claimed by a grammatical form used in first position. For example, speakers can pose questions about themselves to recipients who evidently have subordinate rights in the matter, and they can use declaratives to formulate states of affairs associated with their recipients, even though their recipients can – and typically do – claim primary rights in the matter.[4] In such cases, however, the mismatch between the social relations claimed by the deployment of declarative and interrogative grammatical forms (K+ -> K– and K– -> K+ respectively) and the contrasting putative real-world circumstances of the speakers who use them, give rise to very different types of actions. Where speakers pose questions about themselves – e.g., "when other time have I ever done that?" – such utterances, which typically find a home in conflicts and other contentious environments, will be treated as especially strong *assertions* (or challenges) that make agreement (or acquiescence) relevant (for this reason they have been called "rhetorical questions" because they are formed up as "unanswerable" by the speaker who posed them; see Koshik, 2005; Heritage, 2002, 2012; Heritage and Clayman, 2010). By contrast, speakers can demonstrate various forms of affiliation using declaratives to formulate matters over which their recipients can claim primary rights, thereby making it relevant for recipients to confirm what has been asserted (in the case of "yes/no declaratives" or "b-event statements"; though, see Kendrick, 2010, Heritage, 2012, for a discussion of some borderline uses of declaratives and their implications).[5]

As these extracts suggest, declarative and interrogative forms (and the range of combinatorial forms made possible by associating two or more of them, e.g., as in declarative followed by tag questions) provide a central means by which participants can invoke, and thereby make relevant, the practical management of these basic social relations in interaction. As such, these forms, and the relations they index, figure in sequence organization across a range of action types, and thus constitute a central feature of action formation more generally. Despite their relatively formal character (i.e., asserting knowledge, or the relevant absence of it), the basic social relations indexed by these forms "take on specific practical import in the contexts in which they are used, thereby constituting a (local) basis for social action that speakers can exploit to make recognizable, with considerable precision, the import of their [sequence-initiating actions]" (Raymond, 2010a: 104).

As we shall see, there is considerable variation within this very broad domain of practices. For example, in contrast to the use of declaratives to assert a K+ position (relative to their K– recipients), speakers have a wide range of practices available for asserting a K– position.

5.2 The epistemic gradients of questions

In posing questions speakers can select from among a range of alternative grammatical forms to establish a K− position relative to a(n ostensibly) K+ recipient. These forms vary in terms of the "epistemic gradient" they claim between speaker and recipient (Heritage and Raymond, 2012). So-called "WH"-interrogatives (e.g., utterances beginning with, or including, what, when, where, why and how) establish the steepest epistemic gradient relative to a K+ speaker. Although they are often described as a distinct category of interrogative, speakers treat them as an alternative to other forms, such as YNIs, and yes/no declaratives. For example, in extracts 3 and 4 speakers alternate between WH- and yes/no type initiating actions:

(03) Sisters Call 1

Nik : -> Wut are you doin tomorrow are< you goin downtown¯?
Reg: Yeah. Are you gunna go downtown? (K–)
Nik : ˙hh I don't know I'm bro:ke*. (K+)
Reg: -> Oh °poo:per:° (K– –> K+)
Nik : I kno::w¯

(04) SF 1 (pg. 5)

Joa : Okay?
Mar: .khhhh
Joa : Nice talking to yuh.
Mar: -> Whuddiyuh doin tuhnight.Js sitting there?
(0.3)
Joa : Y'know I am so tired t'night. Came home en I wz
starving so I made en omelette ...

Evidently, in asking "what" someone is doing, speakers claim not to know anything about the recipients' plans (3) or present circumstances (4), other than to propose that the recipient is, or will be, doing something. In both of these cases, however, the FPP speaker goes on to produce a second query that establishes a different epistemic gradient. By posing a YNI (as in 3), or offering a "candidate answer" for confirmation (as in 4), the speaker formulates a proposition regarding the recipient's plans/circumstances, thereby claiming/asserting more knowledge about them than the initial question suggested (cf. Pomerantz, 1988, for an analysis of this question form). In such sequences, the preference for contiguity (Sacks, 1987) holds: preferred, type-conforming responses align with the proposition expressed in most proximate query (as in extract 3, line 2, "yeah"); by contrast, responses that take up the more distal question (and the action for which it is a vehicle) tend to indicate some trouble with the proximate assertion, or the action for which it is a vehicle, as in extract 4.[6] Leaving aside the specific action import of using these alternatives one after the other (though, see note 6 for some analysis of extract 4, and section 5.4 below for a consideration of how this combination can be used to manage specific institutional contingencies), for now we can simply note that in these two cases speakers treat WH- and yes/no interrogative/declaratives as alternative forms that, in (a) establishing different epistemic gradients, and (b) setting in motion different (interpretive) constraints on the responses they make relevant, provide very different bases for initiating action.

Speakers formulating a state of affairs for a recipient's agreement or confirmation can further choose from a range of alternative forms that establish different epistemic gradients relative to a recipient. Extract 5 contains instances of three basic forms: a declarative (assertion), declarative + tag, and interrogative. In this case, Richard intervenes in Vic's recitation of the fish tanks he owns to initially propose that they are actually owned by Alex, a mutual acquaintance.

(05) US (From Schegloff, 2007: 103)

Mik: You have a tank I like tuh tuh– I–I [like–
Vic : [Yeh I gotta
fa:wty:: I hadda fawtuy? a fifty,
enna twu[nny:: en two ten::s,
Mik: [Wut– Wuddiyuh doing wit [dem. Wuh–
Ric : -> [But those
were uh::: [Alex's tanks.
Vic : [–enna fi:ve.
Vic : Hah?
Ric : -> Those'r Alex's tanks weren't they?
Vic : Pondn' me?
Ric : -> Weren't– didn' they belong tuh Al[ex?
Vic : [No: Alex ha(s) no
tanks Alex is tryintuh buy my tank.

The alternative forms of initiating actions in extract 5 vary in terms of the epistemic gradient they encode, indicating "different degrees of information gap and different levels of commitment to a particular response" (Heritage, 2008): the declarative asserts matters for confirmation or acknowledgment, placing a speaker on nearly equal footing with a recipient, while interrogatives ostensibly treat a matter as genuinely "in question," posing more distance between them (see also Raymond, 2010a). Example 5 compactly reflects the precise ordering of these alternatives: in the face of a series of repair initiations that foreshadow Vic's ultimate rejection of his claim, Richard successively backs away form his initial assertion; in line 6 Rich asserts that third party (Alex) owns the fish tanks Vic refers to using a declarative that embodies a relatively flat epistemic gradient (deferring only to Vic's rights to confirm it); in the face of Vic's repeated indications of trouble, however, Richard comes to use a negatively valenced interrogative with a relatively steep epistemic gradient that treats those same facts as "in question."

This array of commonly used practices for asserting variations in a speakers' K− position stands in contrast to the single, basic resource – declaratively formed utterances – that speakers commonly rely on to establish a K+ position. This asymmetry in the range, and deployment, of such practices suggests a recurrent need for speakers to overcome the primary rights otherwise associated with first-position – or sequence-initiating – actions.

In addition, the grammatical form of each of these sequence-initiating actions makes a distinct range of responses relevant next. As the preceding cases suggest, there is a direct connection between the epistemic gradient asserted by a K− action and the range of responses that can be treated as conforming to the constraints set by its grammatical form (of course in response to any form, a responding speaker can produce a nonconforming response; see Raymond, 2000, 2003). Whereas WH-queries make relevant a type-conforming response, this form allows the recipient considerable leeway insofar as it leaves open who that person might be and how she will be formulated (e.g., using a recognitional reference form, a non-recognitional form, etc.; cf. Schegloff, 1996 on person reference; see Fox and Thompson, 2010, on responses WH-interrogatives make relevant). By contrast, forms that assert a relatively flat epistemic gradient make relevant a much more limited range of responses relevant next; for example yes/no initiating actions (YNIs, declaratives plus tag questions, and Y/N declaratives) pose the most limited range of options by making relevant a choice between either agreement/disagreement (for YNIs) or confirmation/disconfirmation (for Y/N declaratives), or some combination of these (as in the case of declaratives plus tag questions). In using such Y/N or polar questions, the respondent is invited to either assent to or reject a proposition concerning a particular state of affairs. These questions thus set the terms within which Y/N responses are to be constructed. Moreover because Y/N questions are unavoidably designed for, or tilted towards, either "yes" or "no", they exert a preference for the agreeing or confirming response discussed by Sacks (Heritage 2007; see also Pomerantz, 1988).

Thus, in posing such questions speakers maximally exploit the agenda-setting and subsequent conduct constraining potential of action in first position (Raymond, 2003) while simultaneously positioning the recipient as the participant with primary rights in the matter (Heritage and Raymond, 2012).

Having established some basic features of the repertoire or resources available to speakers initiating sequences using various interrogative, or

K−, forms, we now turn to cases in which speakers' use of self-initiated repair in the same turn and in or at the transition space suggest that just which form will be selected, and/or how a state of affairs is formulated by it, comes to be treated as problematic in some way.

5.3 Question design and domains of knowledge

As a backdrop to a more fine-grained consideration of the "distance-involvement dilemma," we begin by examining several cases in which speakers posing one question after another reveals basic considerations in their use as practices for managing the social organization of knowledge in action. In the following cases the alternative questions that speakers pose reflects their orientations to differences in the forms of knowledge or information that are available to their recipients. These include differences between forms of knowledge to which recipients can claim primary access or rights (e.g., as they are related to matters of personal experiences and preferences) and forms of knowledge to which the experiences of recipients may be expected to conform (because they reflect what "everybody knows"); or between forms of knowledge or information readily available to (or accessible by) recipients and matters that require some effort to recall or provide; and so on. These differences come most clearly into view where either questioners anticipate, or respondents encounter, some trouble in responding to a query, and questioners refashion them to deal with these problems (in many cases, drawing on practices of repair to do so; see Schegloff et al., 1977). As might be anticipated, the vast majority of such cases entail questions that are redesigned so as to promote recipients' preferred (or agreeing) responses to them (see Sacks, 1987; Schegloff, 2007). How and when such questions are refashioned, as well as the responses such refashioned questions are designed to promote (including the specific form or valence of them) reflect considerable variation in the ways that practices of questioning are, or can be, used to hold the recipients targeted by them accountable for knowing specific types of information or knowledge.

In designing questions, speakers orient to a distinction between what Schutz called a "common stock of knowledge" – what anyone knows – and knowledge domains associated with personal experiences and preferences. The difference between these alternatives, and their consequentiality for the organization of social action, are nicely illustrated in the following case. In this relatively short stretch of talk a doctor attempts to persuade an elderly patient visiting for a check-up to consider moving into a retirement center. In the first query, "what about going ..." (line 6) the doctor uses a WH-interrogative to formulate a proposal (to move to a retirement home). The use of "what about [solution]" as a format to suggest or propose a "remedy" for a recipient's consideration entails two relatively substantial presuppositions: (1) that the recipient is oriented to some aspect of his circumstances as problematic (or that the problem is known-in-common to both parties), and thus in need of remedy; and (2) that the proposal constitutes an acceptable remedy that is "new" to the recipient, and thus not already considered or tried by him.[7] The long silence that begins to grow foreshadows some problem with the query; anticipating one possible source of trouble (in this case the patient's likely rejection of the proposal it delivers) the doctor reformulates his prior query (retaining basic elements of it, "going to a/the retirement center"), now offering it as a YNI that solicits the patient's preferences ("would you like" …), as part of an effort to seek information about his wishes.[8]

(06) SG: 813:4

Doc: (°Lemme have you sit u–°) You still livin' by
yoursel:f?,
(0.5)
Pat: #A::lri:ght,#
(4.5)
Doc: –> What about goin' to uh retirement center.
(1.5)
Doc: –> Wouldju like to go to th'retirement center:,
(2.0)
Pat: L (.) u=No.=h
Doc: No,
(2.5)
Pat: Not yet.
(2.0)
Doc: –> It must be pretty hard tuh be by yourself though:,
(1.5)
Doc: –> Isn't it hard tuh be by yourself?
(2.3)
Pat: Well I have friends (I have:) I visit with.
(.)
Pat: An' they visit me so I keep company: hh uh- when I
need it

In this first pair of queries, the doctor anticipates that the patient will reject his proposal (based on the delay in his response to it), and retreats to safer ground by soliciting the patient's views as part of an effort to probe the basis for that resistance. The patient's initial unelaborated negative response (line 10) provides little room for the doctor to pursue the matter. His subsequent elaboration ("not yet," line 13, following the doctor's pursuit in 11) casts the doctor's query as premature, suggesting that the patient does not share the doctor's assumption that his current living situation is problematic.

The different ways that the doctor designs these two queries reflects an orientation to his patient's primary – if not exclusive – rights to express his preferences regarding where he wishes to live; as part of his effort to secure some form of agreement – or indeed response – the doctor refashions his initial question in a way that (a) downgrades its presumptiveness regarding a state of affairs that he treats as belonging to the patient, while (b) amplifying the query's preference for a "yes" (or agreeing response) by using a YNI.

The doctor's subsequent queries regarding the difficulties associated with living alone (in lines 15 and 17) reflect a very different dynamic. Despite the resistance he has encountered thus far, the doctor begins to probe what is problematic about the patient's living situation: using a yes/no declarative (that proposes a relatively shallow epistemic gradient) the doctor invites the patient to confirm that it's "hard to be by yourself." The design of this assertion is striking: first, the doctor *downgrades* the epistemic assertiveness of the query by formulating it as an inference (using "it must be") – albeit one grounded in worldly conditions that anyone can recognize; while this acknowledges that the doctor lacks first-hand knowledge of the patient's circumstances, it actually ratchets up the pressure to agree by marking disagreement as "strange" or "odd," or otherwise outside of common experience. Second, the use of a turn final "though" positions the point of view expressed in the query as contrasting with the one just expressed by the patient. In this way, the doctor invites the patient to consider at least one possible problem with the position he has adopted. In the face of yet another long stretch of silence (which again projects disagreement), the doctor again initiates repair, replacing one version of his query with another that retains its basic frame, but packages it in a different grammatical from. Although the doctor backs down again (in moving from declarative to interrogative syntax), he adopts a very different stance with this subsequent query (as compared with the version in lines 6 and 8). In using a negative interrogative, "Isn't it hard ..." the doctor treats the position formulated in his query as "settled" or established (see Heritage, 2002), thereby effectively skeptically probing the view expressed by the patient. In this way the doctor treats the assumption that informs his query – that "it's hard to be by yourself" – as a matter of common knowledge, as reflecting what anyone knows, and thus *not* a matter of personal preference. Apparently one can prefer not to live in a retirement center, but from this doctor's perspective, an elderly patient who refuses to acknowledge the difficulties of being alone has not recognized what anyone else would.

In this case, then, the doctor reformulates two questions in the face of a recipient's apparent trouble with them. In both cases, the doctor anticipates that the silence following his questions foreshadows disagreement. In the first case he backs down on the question's assertiveness, acquiescing to the patient's primary rights to decide on the best solution to the problem posed by living alone. In the second case, however, he upgrades the assertiveness of his query, treating the patient as, in effect, unwilling to acknowledge the problematic character of his circumstances. In very short order, then, we see the consequences of the doctor's distinct orientations to two very different domains of knowledge: while the doctor is willing to collaborate with the patient's expression of (what are treated as) idiosyncratic preferences, he appears unwilling to do so when it comes to what "anyone knows" about elderly patients living on their own. While this may seem overly assertive – and indeed "over-involved with and even appropriating of" matters to which the recipient can claim primary rights – the doctor's assertiveness here appears to be partly constitutive of his institutional role as a caregiver. For example, a doctor can readily work to help a patient understand that his drinking is a problem; however, a doctor who no longer holds such a patient accountable to the view that drinking to excess is a problem risks appearing to have given up on him. In the same way, for a doctor to let go of the position that elderly patients living alone risk being lonely would be to demonstrate a willingness to privilege matters associated with recipient design (or a concern with agreement) over established conceptions of health, thereby suggesting that the doctor had abandoned his position as an advocate of the patient's best interests.

5.3.1 What's optional? What's required?

Between these two poles – that is, between knowledge associated with personal experiences and preferences on the one hand and common sense knowledge that "everyone knows" on the other – speakers may find themselves navigating many other, differently composed knowledge domains. Perhaps most complex are those pertaining to third parties, especially where a recipient can be held accountable for knowing the circumstances of a third party because they are co-incumbents of mutually related categories (e.g., mother and child, spouse-spouse, etc.; see Sacks, 1972). Consider the following excerpt taken from the Health Visitor corpus, which consists of recordings of postnatal visits by a representative of Britain's National Health Service to monitor the health of new mothers and their babies. In these interactions, HVs pursue three main institutional imperatives with the mothers they visit: (1) they gather information through a survey; (2) use their expertise to provide advice, information, or counsel to new mothers; and (3) attempt to befriend the mothers through a mix of institutionally focused activities and conversational exchanges (Heritage, 2002: 315). In this stretch of talk, the HV invites the mother to collaborate in filling out the forms that constitute the central portion of the survey. Beginning in line 1, the HV solicits the names of the baby's father and mother. Although the HV initially asks the name of the mother's "boyfriend," she comes to revise this initial inference about their relationship (see line 8; in noting that the mother shares the last name of the father, she conveys that she has registered that they are married). In line 10 the HV projects her continuation of the survey, though the brief delay following the turn's inception (after the "and") suggests some trouble in posing a query (which turns out to solicit the father's birth date). And, indeed, as soon as she brings the first version of it to completion ("his date of birth") the HV initiates repair, reusing the frame from the last element of the query ("his {X}") to produce an alternative version that replaces it: "his age" (see Schegloff, this volume).

(07) 5A1:7

HV: What's your boyfriend's name?
M: Nigel.
HV: Nigel.(0.2) Wilkin.
M: Yeah.
(3.0)
HV: You're Carol.
M: Yeah.
HV: °Wilkin°.
(1.8)
HV: -> And uh (.) his date of birth=his a::ge?
(1.0)
M: -> He's twenty-one so what would his date of birth be.
(?): hhhhhh=
M: =six–
HV: -> Twenty one'll do:.=
M: =Yeah.
HV: -> =They can work it out from the[:re huh
M: [Yeah
(0.2)
HV: fr'm there. Were you working?

Although these two questions ask about the same basic subject matter (the age/birthdate of her partner) the HV treats the form of answer made relevant by each as differentially available to the recipient. Drawn as it is from the survey form she is filling out, the HV's first query reflects the bureaucratically preferred form for the response it makes relevant. The repaired version she subsequently provides, however, orients to the exigencies of recollection, anticipating that the mother can more easily retrieve, and thus provide, the age of her partner (thereby retrospectively casting "date of birth" as a potentially more problematic question to answer). While this evidently reflects a way in which the HV is actively reshaping institutional demands (posed by the survey) for the current recipient she is questioning (i.e., rather than requiring the person to adapt to the institution), her conduct also conveys an understanding that the mother may not readily know the year that her husband was born.

After a substantial delay the mother begins a response that asserts some independence from the terms of the question(s). While "he's twenty-one" provides precisely the item made relevant by "his age," by packaging this type-conforming response in a sentential turn-constructional unit (or TCU) that disengages it from the immediately prior query ("he's twenty-one" vs. "Twenty-one"), the mother conveys that her response will be doing something other than, or more than, what the most proximate form of the HV's query made relevant. This addition formulates the mother's effort to recall (or perhaps calculate) her husband's date of birth ("so what would his date of birth be ..."), expressing a commitment to providing a form of information that the standard survey question (initially posed by the HV) evidently anticipates she will have, and inviting the HV's assistance in the matter. Instead of participating in the search, however, the HV intervenes to accept the form of response the mother has already provided (see line 15), "twenty-one'll do," and elaborates her basis for accepting a response form that the mother initially treated as potentially inadequate by noting that "they" (presumably the users of the information collected in the survey) "can work it out."

Here it appears that the HV uses practices of repair to replace a query designed to solicit a bureaucratically preferred response form (the year of the father's birth) with one that solicits a form of information more readily available to (or retrievable by) the mother (i.e., the age of her partner). In this respect, although the mother and the HV conclude the sequence with fully aligned views regarding the response the mother provides, they adopt slightly different views regarding the questions used to make it relevant. The HV treats the information requested in the standard version of the question as something the mother might not be expected to know, and shouldn't be expected to work out. Once she has a related form that can suffice as an answer, she notes, "they can work it out." By contrast, the mother's effort to supply a response fitted to the standard survey question suggests an understanding that she should (or at least could) answer such a question, even if she readily abandons that effort at the HV's behest. And across both questions and response(s) we see reciprocal efforts to manage recurrent interactional exigencies: whose concerns, whose orientations, will prevail in the design and conduct of the interaction. The HV's repaired query reflects an effort to simplify the task for the mother and the mother's elaborated response reflects her effort to help the HV complete her institutionally mandated activities.

The following exchange entails a similarly reciprocal effort. In this case, however, the participants treat the matter inquired into as something that the recipient(s) *should* know, and be able to provide, more or less immediately. This turns out to be a problem, however, because their delay in responding to the HV's query suggests it is problematic for the parents in some way. Beginning in line 8, the HV poses a question to a mother as part of an effort to solicit information about her child's development (whether the child can visually track people and fix his gaze on caregivers). The first question posed by the HV, "Does he follow you around" is brought to completion suggesting that, for HV, the parents should be able to respond to it. When a silence begins to grow, the HV treats the design of her initial question as the trouble source, producing a second version that in replacing "follow" with "look" makes more explicit that the question concerns the infant's vision (as opposed to his mobility).

(08) 4A1:2

01	F:		Very much alert are[n't you feller (.) *eh?*
02	M:		['E's two weeks old on Friday.
03			(0.4)
04	HV:		Terrific.
05			(0.4)
06	M:		hhhuhuh
07			(.)
08	HV:	->	Does he follow you round–
09			(0.8)
10	HV:	->	Does he look around?
11	F:		Oh y[eh
12	M:		[He is starting to.=Yeh.
13	HV:		A[nd does he fix on you?=
14	M:		[Yeh
15	HV:		=Does he look at you?
16	F:		[Mm mm
17	M:		[Yeah.
18	HV:		Lovely.

In contrast to the prior extract (in which the HV *simplified* the question to solicit a form of information more readily accessible to the recipient) the HV in this case uses an alternative query to make the action it implements more intelligible, thus treating the information sought by the question as something that the parents are specifically accountable for knowing. This subsequent question attracts an immediate, oh-prefaced, positive type-conforming response from the father (in line 11), and a more carefully calibrated response from the mother, "he is starting to. Yeh." In this case, the HV's initial question ("follow you around") is retrospectively cast as involving a kind of quasi-specialist terminology to inquire about the child's ability to track motion with her eyes; the repaired version (which replaces "follow" with "look") makes the subject of the query, and thus the action it implements, more explicit by referencing the child's vision. Although this alteration resolves the problem, the very fact the parents encountered trouble in responding to the HV's query may raise the possibility that they had not been attending to a fairly basic (and readily apparent) developmental pattern. The parents' responses are telling for the ways they seek to counter such an inference. The father's oh-prefaced affirmative registers his late recognition of the question's import, suggesting that the initial question (or its design) was inapposite or unanticipated (see Heritage, 1998). By contrast, the mother (literally) goes out of her way to convey her close attention to the matter by delaying her type-conforming response (in 12) to respecify what she confirms with it at a more fine-grained level of detail (since "starting to" incorporates a reference to the recent onset of this development) than the HV's question made relevant. Thus, in this case, all of the participants treat the parents' ability to answer a question about their child's development as something they are expected to know. When recipients treated the initial query as problematic, the revised version offered in its place did not reduce the demands placed on the recipient (as in the prior case). Rather, HV retains the basic framework she established from outset by producing an alternative version of the "same" query that uses the practice of "replacing" (Schegloff, this volume) to make what a type-conforming response will confirm more explicit, and thus the action-implication of the response to which it will contribute.

5.4 Questions, and the responses they invite

In each of the cases so far, the occasion of posing one question after another has been associated with what recipients can be expected to know and what questioners can assert, or with issues relating to the agenda it establishes or its preferences and presuppositions. A quite different problem emerges when posing a question, per se, emerges as a possible source of trouble. If, in posing questions, speakers treat the matter they raise as relevant for both parties, then circumstances where they may not be are problematic in several different ways: for example, posing a question can, by virtue of making a response relevant, invite a recipient to convey – or even consider or adopt – a point of view that they had not previously held. In such cases, the problem for participants may be that, if questions propose that a domain of knowledge is relevant for a recipient, an especially compliant or concerned recipient may acquiesce in treating it as such. As a consequence, once a question has been raised, it can be difficult to disentangle whether the response provided to it was merely prompted by the question (or shaped by its design) or reflects the independently held view of the participant who expressed it.

This appears to be the conundrum facing the speaker posing a question in the following extract, taken from the HV data. In this extract an HV is probing the potentially delicate matter of whether a parent (in this case, the mother) might object to having her child vaccinated. At the time of the recording such vaccinations were controversial in some circles because a study published in the British medical journal *The Lancet* falsely linked them to increased rates of autism. In this case, the HV's concern with the mother's orientation to vaccinations seems to be prompted by her initial response to the HV's utterance in line 1: she responds to the HV's mention of injections with an oh-prefaced response that treats it as unexpected (Heritage, 1998), and then produces a few laugh tokens that further adumbrate a departure from the matter-of-fact view adopted by the HV up to this point. Although the HV appears to briefly entertain an alternative trajectory in line 4 (note the brief delay and the "uhm"), it is only after her next turn (in which she conveys the method by which appointments are scheduled) goes entirely unacknowledged (suggesting the mother's possible resistance to such appointments) that the HV poses a contingent, follow-up question that specifically solicits the mother's views. In so doing, the HV initially poses a question using a form that permits a wide range of responses by asking how the mother "feels" about injections; she then uses a transition space repair to replace that question with a YNI that asks about a more basic matter: whether she has "thought about them at all."

(09) 5A1:9

HV: The other thing that happens are the injections.
M: Oh yea:h. (.) huh huh
(.)
HV: .hh Uh:m (.) yeh (.) we have a computer (1.0) that
sends out appointments.
(2.5)
HV: -> How do you feel about the injections.=Have you thought
about them at all.
M: I just thought that she ought to have them a:ll.

While the mother's conduct thus far may hint at some potential resistance to injections, the source and strength of any such resistance are entirely opaque. For example, the mother may be opposed to the practice outright, or her conduct may simply reflect a parent's unease about the physical pain caused by "jabs" (and the prospect of holding her new baby as she suffers from it). Given this environment, and the HV's subsequent decision to probe the matter, various forms of the query present distinct problems.

On the one hand if the mother does not object to having her child vaccinated (or has not heard of the then current skepticism regarding the practice), the HV would be reluctant to introduce such matters since this would be tantamount to suggesting that the mother should be concerned (when most health professionals argued that the risks posed by vaccination – if there were any – far outweighed the possible consequences of the alternative). On the other hand, if the HV simply asks whether she has thought about vaccinations using a form that presumes that she has not (the addition of "at all" anticipates, or prefers, a "no") could effectively insult the mom if she has done so (and especially if she has negative views on the matter). The HV apparently struggles with just these alternatives: she initially invites the mother to express her "feelings" about vaccinations (thereby presuming that she has reportable ones) using a form that *permits* an expression of negative views without including a reference to them in the design of her turn (e.g., as "what are your concerns" would do). Before the mother can respond, however, the HV replaces that query with one that probes a more basic matter by asking whether she has considered the matter, using a form that makes relevant a more closed set of response options. Moreover, by including the negative polarity item ("at all") the HV allows a preferred, type-conforming response (confirming that the mother has not thought about vaccinations) to bring the sequence to a close. Notably the mother produces a nonconforming, "no problem" response (which she associates with the more proximate query via the repetition of "thought") – "I just thought she ought to have them all" – that she frames (with "I just") as delivering "less than" might have been anticipated, thereby tacitly addressing a possible implication in the HV's initial query.

In this way the mother conveys both that she has "thought about" vaccinations and that she supports the practice, providing for an exit from the sequence. In this case, then, the HV's replacement of one query that invites elaboration with another that projects closure enables her to probe whether the mother is skeptical about vaccinations without raising such skepticism directly, since doing so might very well prompt her to consider whether she should be.

A related concern with "contamination" (i.e., an orientation to the ways in which the terms of a query, and especially the preference it establishes, can prompt a recipient to confirm a point of view they may not actually hold, or prompt them to consider a point of view that is problematic from the questioner's perspective), can be observed in extract 12. In this case a doctor managing a patient's call on an "out of hours" line (see Drew, 2006) questions a mother about her daughter's symptoms as part of his attempt to determine whether a home visit will be necessary. After establishing the recent onset of her current symptoms – repeated vomiting (see lines 1–11) – the doctor asks the mother a follow-up query designed to rule out the presence of a significant symptom that would warrant immediate medical attention: namely the presence of blood in her vomit. As Boyd and Heritage (2006) suggest, in many cases doctors use yes/no queries with negative polarity to invite patients (or caregivers) to confirm the absence of a problematic symptom (e.g., "no blood in the vomit?"), thereby conveying an "optimal" view of the patient in the design of their questions. In the current context, however, such negatively formed questions may be problematic since it can be heard as promoting (or anticipating) a decision to *not* visit the patient (thus countering the project initiated by the caller in placing the call; see Drew, 2006). On the other hand, posing the query in positive terms ("is she bringing up blood?") may be problematic since it may invite a "false positive", indicate a pessimistic view of the patient (see Boyd and Heritage, 2006), and/or even imply that the mother may have left such a crucial matter out of her initial report. We can note, then, that the doctor here uses a WH-interrogative, "What's she bringing up?" Using a transition space repair, however, the doctor appends a "candidate answer" (see Pomerantz, 1988) – "anything exciting" – that transforms the response *form* it makes relevant (by making the query a YNI) and resets the *terms* for what will qualify as a positive response (since now any reported contents must be "exciting").

(10) DEC 1:1:01:1

```
Doc:        ˙hh Fine. ˙h So: ho:w ho:w: this was: all just
            started tonight, is it?
Clr:        Yes.<Well I didn't [come in from wo:rk unti:l uh:] =
Doc:                           [˙h  h  h  h       h  h  h  h]
Clr:        = ten past [seven and she'd already been sick three]=
Doc:                   [˙h   h   h   h             h   h   h   h]
Clr:        =times,
Doc:        ˙hhh Ri:gh[t,
Clr:                  [(And) since then, (.) [been sick
Doc:                                         [˙hhhh
Doc:        ((swallow))[mYeah,
Clr:                   [another three ti[mes,
Doc:                                    [Another three time ˙hh
       ->   What's she bringing up?<any[thing exciti°n–
Clr:                                   [(like just)
Clr:        [Just fluid rea[lly,
Doc:        [˙hhh          [hhh  Just fluid.
Clr:        [Nothing now. I don['– obviously I don't know what it=
Doc:        [Nuh–               [˙hhh
Clr:        =was earlier on, I wasn't her[e, you know,=
Doc:                                     [˙hh˙hh
Doc:   ->   =Right, but the: th I mean– n:othing nasty no blood er
       ->   anything ˙hhh and the diarrhea: you say is quite (0.9)
Clr:        Very strong, yea[h.
Doc:                        [Smelly.=What color is it.<is a
            hih! ˙hh
```

The initial question, "what's she bringing up?" is less than optimal for the doctor's project (evaluating the patient) because, in making relevant a reporting of the contents of the child's vomit as such, it invites the mother to report on matters that potentially have little or no medical significance. The transition space repair, "anything exciting," narrows the terms of the query, limiting what the mother should report by delineating a quality of it (i.e., unusual contents) as opposed to naming a specific item of interest (e.g., blood). As it happens, however, the mother began addressing the broader form of the query (initially in overlap, line 15, then in the clear) just as this qualification was added. Even in this response she orients to the query's specific institutional import by prefacing her report with "just" to convey the "nothing special" character of it (demonstrating her expertise as a caregiver). Perhaps because of this elaboration (which falls short of "no," as a response form that confirms the absence of special symptoms), however, the doctor pursues the matter for yet another round after acknowledging her response (with "right"). In doing so, he initially treats her just prior elaboration (in lines 18/20) as inapposite using the preface "but," though he subsequently mitigates this view by cutting off "I mean," which would have more clearly positioned the turn as a third-position repair (that the doctor does not provide the space for the revised response that third-position repair would have made relevant confirms this view). Nevertheless, the doctor's use of "nothing nasty no blood or anything" neatly confirms that the aim of the sequence was to rule out the presence of blood: this casts the presence of blood in the child's vomit as only one possible item among others that are of possible interest, but only names that one item. These features of the doctor's initial and follow-up question suggest that he has been pursuing whether there is blood in the child's vomit from the outset; its presence would constitute an emergency requiring immediate medical attention.

Here it appears that the doctor faces a specific institutional contingency (or indeed, dilemma) associated with the demands of medical questioning (particularly as conducted in an "out of hours call," which, as Drew (2006) notes, pose an additional set of concerns to be managed). On the one hand, seeking to simply rule out the presence of a symptom using a negatively formulated declarative (as routinely happens in office visits) may suggest that the doctor has already decided not to visit. On the other, a positively formed query naming the symptom would raise the mother's concerns (unnecessarily, if there is none), and otherwise risk eliciting a false positive – that is, a positive response prompted by the question's preference rather than the actual presence of the symptom. To avoid these outcomes the doctor finds a way to probe whether a symptom is present or not, without asking about it directly (at least initially) since doing so may contaminate the independence of such a report. In managing this dilemma the doctor settles on forms of questioning that provide an occasion for such a report (i.e., if one noted blood, surely it would be included in a response to the doctor's question at line 14), without soliciting it directly (by asking about it in so many words). Only after that form fails to invite an affirmative response does the doctor then attempt to positively rule out the matter with the negatively formulated query (in which he specifically mentions blood), thereby providing a second (or third) chance for the mother to note the symptom.

In these two cases, speakers using transition space repairs to pose one question after another appear oriented to a basic contingency associated with the use of questions to initiate actions: the very ways in which questions set topical and action-based agendas, assert presuppositions and establish preferences – and thereby provide a highly structured environment for lay participants' contributions – can complicate the responding speaker's efforts to exercise the primary rights they are treated as having in the matter (cf. Heritage and Raymond, 2012). Indeed, the very features of questions that promote their adoption for a wide range of action types in ordinary conversation and institutional activities have also led to specific regulations governing their use in specific institutional contexts (see Atkinson and Drew, 1979; Raymond, 2003). For example, in American courts attorneys can be sanctioned for "leading a witness" where they use YNIs in the direct examination of witnesses testifying on behalf of their case. In effect these rules reflect a concern with the possibility that responding speakers can (or will) simply acquiesce to the terms set by an interrogative (e.g., by producing preferred, type-conforming responses), thereby undermining the degree to which responses they produce reflect the personal experiences and independently held views of the speaker. Such explicit rules regarding question design in institutional contexts reflect systematic efforts to either enable or avoid specific outcomes associated with practices of questioning that are either central to (or problematic for) the workings of those institutions (see Romaniuk and Ehrlich, this volume).

Speakers in less formally organized institutions (i.e., lacking specific rules and/or a designated party to administer them) may nevertheless confront similar problems. The methods observed in these two excerpts (from different institutional contexts) reflect an ad hoc orientation to a related set of contingencies: where routine practices of questioning (i.e., such as the use of simple WH- or polar interrogatives) may generate problematic outcomes (or fail to enable desired ones), those methods can be manipulated to produce hybrid forms that are better suited to the interactional and institutional exigencies confronted by the participants. In these cases, speakers exploit the different division of labor between questioner and respondent enabled by polar and WH-interrogatives: in polar interrogatives, the terms are set by the questioner, whereas responses to WH-interrogatives specify a domain of phenomenon, and then allow respondents to formulate relevant matters with respect to it. In these two cases, however, speakers exploit these features of questions to produce a kind of hybrid question form (described in Pomerantz's 1988 paper on "offering a candidate answer"). The WH-question makes relevant a more open field of response, while the "candidate answer" delimits the materials that can go into it (see Pomerantz, 1988).

As we can see, however, these cases are somewhat special versions of that practice on several grounds: for example, in the last case, the terms of the response invited by the WH-interrogative are further delimited by the use of the *negative* polarity item ("anything") that, in anticipating a "no" response (i.e., "nothing exciting"), effectively cancels the *positive* presupposition of the WH-interrogative that there is *something* that has come up. Similarly, in the first case the HV's initial query, "How do you feel?", evidently presumes that the mother has "feelings" about vaccinations while the negative presumption embodied in the second query ("Have you thought about that *at all*?") actively undercuts that very presupposition. What may appear to be a "hodge-podge" combination of two interrogative forms turns out to produce a sequential environment for responding that is highly tuned to the precise exigencies confronted by the participants: i.e., enabling the introduction of delicate matters or problematic symptoms without necessarily presuming the presence of either.

Having run through a number of basic exigencies associated with the epistemics of questioning per se, we now turn to examine some ways in which cases involving self-repair reveal participants' efforts to struggle with what we have termed the "distance-involvement" dilemma: that is, the ways speakers manage the twin risk of appearing disengaged from the affairs of the other or over-involved with and even appropriating of them.

5.5 The distance-involvement dilemma in practices of questioning

In an earlier paper on the epistemics of social relations (Raymond and Heritage, 2006), we described the "distance-involvement dilemma" as critical to understanding the organization of assessment sequences. In such sequences, because the composition of a first position action cannot avoid establishing a set of claims regarding what the speaker knows (and has rights to know) about a state of affairs relative to a recipient, speakers (producing both first- and second-position actions) face a recurrent dilemma: on the one hand, a speaker posing an assessment that asserts (by reference to its sequential position) an overly deferential epistemic stance regarding a state of affairs that a recipient may claim as her own ("your grandchildren seem as if they might be nice"), or formulates a too cautious evaluation of the matter, risks appearing remote, detached or disengaged from that recipient. On the other hand, if the same speaker evaluating the same state of affairs uses a form that usurps or arrogates the rights her recipient would otherwise claim as her own, such "over-involvement" in the affairs of a recipient can complicate his or her basis for involvement in the sequence, and engender resistance, even in cases where the parties otherwise agree (e.g., see the extended stretch analyzed in Raymond and Heritage, 2006: 696–700). Thus, while the management of rights to knowledge may complicate the terms on which parties agree, how the parties manage the distance-involvement dilemma constitutes a central mechanism by which "who the parties" are for one another comes to be reflexively bound up with the rights to knowledge they assert in such action-sequences. It should not be a surprise, therefore, to find that speakers posing questions face the self-same dilemma: where a speaker poses a question about a recipient (or matters belonging to her) that the recipients treat as obvious, established, or even presupposed, the speaker risks appearing disengaged, distant, or even hostile. By contrast, where the posing of a question asserts (i.e., without some basis for doing so) an entitlement to know about a state of affairs its recipient (may) deem as private, or the epistemic rights asserted in the form of the question complicate the basis on which a recipient can respond, speakers risk appearing "over-involved" in the affairs of the other.

In this respect, participants' use of question design to navigate the distance-involvement dilemma constitutes a key interpretive resource by which parties to an interaction solve the sort of action being done by those questions (Schegloff and Sacks, 1973; Schegloff, 2007; Heritage, 2012). For example, a teacher asking a student participating in an activity, "do you want to be here?" treats a matter that might otherwise be presumed by his presence as actively "in question" – thereby adopting a relatively "distant" posture. It is by virtue of this that such a question may enact a challenge, and, by the same logic, project a possibly different future state of affairs (i.e., that he may not be here for long). By contrast, a question that explores a situation a recipient treats as private or personal may be treated as overly intrusive, particularly if the party posing the question lacks either a local (e.g., in the encounter) or extra-situational (e.g., by virtue of what one heard or knows, or via the rights associated with an institutional, familial, or personal category that links the speaker to the recipient) basis for grounding the action. In this section we consider cases in which the alternative versions of questions that parties pose – one after another – suggest an orientation to just these matters.

As our analysis of extract 6 (and to a lesser extent, examples 9 and 10) suggests, when speakers use questions to probe the presence of, or solutions to, problems or troubles associated with recipients, they may encounter some trouble in settling on just how to formulate them. The delicate nature of these inquiries may be especially pronounced in cases where a recipient's conduct thus far provides little or no evidence that they share the questioners' orientation to the matters as constitutive of a trouble or problem for which assistance may be relevant (e.g., as in extract 6). For the helping professions (including doctors, health visitors, counselors, and the like), such circumstances pose an all-too-common form of the distance-involvement dilemma: posing questions that do not raise possible troubles (explicitly, i.e., in so many words) in the surface design of the query may suggest that the questioner is disengaged from the recipient (and allow her to confirm a "no problem" state of affairs as a preferred response); by contrast, in raising such matters explicitly, and thereby treating the presence of troubles as a potentially confirmable state of affairs, may involve the professional in formulating, and thus appropriating, matters that the recipient may defend as ones to which they can claim exclusive rights. Certainly among the most challenging forms of this dilemma arise in circumstances where health professionals pose questions or claims about a recipient's mental health.

For example, in the following, an HV making her initial visit to a new mother probes the possibility that she may be depressed, setting in motion an extended sequence during which the parties struggle over the terms on which her current living situation, orientation to mothering, and mental health are to be discussed. The HV's initial question emerges in the context of the mother's friend's past-tense report (in the course of explaining how she knew the mother) that "they used to work together." This mention, in turn, leads the mother to mention that she "finished at [working at the café] on Christmas," implying that she no longer works outside the home. Despite the relatively innocuous circumstances under which this comes to be disclosed (e.g., there is no indication that the mother treats her circumstances as complainable; see Schegloff, 2005), the HV begins (after a considerable silence during which the mother appears to comfort her child, line 4) to cautiously probe whether the mother's changed employment situation might impact her mental health, asking "you don't feel too depressed." The HV's production of this query evidently reflects her orientation to it as "delicate" (see Lerner, this volume): she delays the initiation of her turn relative to the parties' last exchange (providing ample opportunity for the mother to initiate commentary about her situation), and, after delaying its actual onset (after "eh"), the HV further delays saying what her turn up to that point ("you don't feel") heavily projects – namely the condition she is aiming to rule out (i.e., "depressed"). While these intra-turn delays provide opportunities for the mother to relieve the HV from continuing her query (by contributing to its production, or responding to it preemptively; see Lerner, 1996, this volume), we can note that the HV designs her query to probe the mother's perception of her mental health without implying that she necessarily thinks it may be problematic: for example, the HV's use of a negatively formed declarative ("you don't feel too depressed") invites her to confirm the absence of depression, while the inclusion of "too" sets a fairly high bar for a dispreferred response (that would convey she *is* depressed). Nevertheless, in raising the matter at all, the HV reveals that she has at least entertained the possibility that the mother could be suffering in some way (which may not be unwarranted in light of the relative rates of post-partum depression for first-time mothers in similar circumstances).

(11) 1C1:15

01	M:		Ye:h I w's working the:re.=I finished at Christmas.
02	Fr:		Ye:h.
03			(2.7)
04	?M:		°feel better (1.0) feel better.°
05			(2.5)
06	HV:	->	Eh: (.) you don't fee:l uh (.) uhm too
07		->	depressed.=You're oka:y at ho:me.=
08	M:		=Fine. (.) Ye:s.
09	HV:		The thing is a bit uh- anti-climax you kno:w having
10			(0.5) Looked forward to the baby coming and then (.)
11			having a rough old ti:me (1.0) and then (.) everybody
12			leaving you: (kind) of being on your o:wn
13			(0.6)
14	M:		Oh I li:ke being on my o:wn.
15	HV:		([ )
16	M:		[I like the: uhm (0.6) the midwife coming again

((9 lines by mother omitted – regading her positive experiences))

26			(.)
27	M:		°You know,°
28			(0.5)
29	HV:		Lovely:.=
30	M:		=I enjoy spending the da:y with (h)er.
31			(0.4)
32	M:		Don't I.
33			(1.7) ((Sounds like M kisses baby))
34	HV:		Goo:d. That's uh– fantastic.

Before the mother can respond, the HV initiates repair (in the transition space), producing a second, positively formed query that replaces the first. This second question evidently retreats to safer ground, providing an embedded account for her prior question (using "at home" to link her prior query to the discussion of mother's job situation), and inviting the mother's confirmation that she is "okay." In these ways, the HV retrospectively treats the question she initially (and hesitantly) posed as overly intrusive: as intervening into territory to which she may not be entitled (particularly in light of the mother's conduct up to this point, which does not suggest she is depressed). The mother resists even the terms of this query, however, by initially responding with (a terminally intoned) "fine" that, in replacing "okay," treats it as an overly gloomy formulation of her current state. After a brief pause, the mother then adds a preferred type-conforming response that retrospectively accepts the (now adjusted) terms of the query, bringing the parties into alignment (cf. Raymond, 2000, 2010b).

Having solicited confirmation that the mother is "fine," the HV could move on. Instead, however, she continues the matter for a further round by recounting a standard sequence of events by which mothers may experience a let-down, and find themselves "on [their] own" (line 9–12). Although this continuation involves a further retreat – now to the HV's own professional experience – it also sustains the possibility that the mother may *not* be "okay" (her claims to the contrary notwithstanding) by (i) linking this account to the mother's earlier comments regarding her birth experience ("having a rough old time" indexes the mother's claim that giving birth was in "bloody agony"), (ii) producing it as a contrastive ("the thing is …") follow-up to the mother's just prior claim to be "fine," and (iii) inviting her confirmation of the position it reports (in part via the use of "you know," in line 9). The mother manages to (begin) assuaging the HV's concerns using an oh-prefaced declarative with contrastive stress (on "like") to convey that she has a positive view of "being on her own." Finally, following a further elaboration of her positive experiences with her newborn in the home, and explaining that she "couldn't wait to get home and (.) do it all on me own," the HV (with some additional prompting, see line 27) accepts the mother's report (line 29) and positively assesses her current situation (line 34), bringing the sequence to a close.

In this sequence, absent of a positive basis for asking whether the mother suffers from depression, the HV orients to raising the issue as entailing (a perhaps professionally motivated) over-involvement in the mother's affairs. Moreover, once she has posed even a mild form of the query, the HV successively retreats to the safer ground, first by adjusting the terms of the question so that it probes matters directly inferable from the parties' current experience and prior talk (that the mom will be "okay at home"), and then to her own professional experience (in lines 9–12). At the same time, the mother's careful delineation of her current state (in adjusting her response, line 8), and her ever more elaborate recitation of positive experiences (of, and) in the home, begin to flavor her assertion that she is not suffering from depression with a kind of defensiveness that may be difficult to avoid in circumstances where a health professional persists in questioning whether that is actually the case. The consistency and vigor with which the mother defends her views, and the delicacy with which the HV probes them, suggest that other-initiated questions about such intimate matters may be inherently problematic (except in the most propitious environments).

As the preceding case illustrates, speakers can vary the propositional content of a question (e.g., "feel too depressed" versus "doing okay") and its polarity (i.e., whether it prefers a "yes" or "no" response) as a method for managing the distance-involvement dilemma, using these alterations to move from ruling out a problematic state of affairs to inviting confirmation of a positive one. In the next case, by contrast, we see a similar set of practices being used to progressively entertain an ever more serious estimation of a mother's injuries. As this case illustrates, how speakers vary the grammatical form of a query, its polarity, its propositional content shapes the distinct action the query enacts, and even the social relation they propose for speaker and recipient. In this case, an HV administering a survey to a mother comes to pose a question concerning her birth experience (in line 5) that eventuates in a shift out of the survey as an institutionally focused activity (which "normalizes" her injuries), with the HV adopting a more "personal" interest in (and reaction to) the mother's experience (see Heritage and Sorjonen, 1994: 10–11, for a discussion of this case; see also Raymond, 2010a). In line 1 the HV poses a declaratively formed query that invites the mother to confirm that she is "feeling well." Although the mother responds with a preferred, type-conforming response, the substantial delay that precedes it may suggest an element of acquiescence on her part. After a further delay (in which the mother could have expanded her otherwise minimal response) it appears that the HV is prepared to move on to a further agenda-based question (see line 5; "and you're"). She cuts this question off, however, and belatedly begins to probe the basis for the mother's delayed response (in line 3), initially seeking to explicate an unstated feature of the mother's prior response using a declarative that (in its shallow epistemic gradient) asserts a local, proximate basis for the inference it seeks to have confirmed. Shortly after she begins this query, however, she cuts it off. The HV's successive efforts to design this question are of particular interest: the HV initially uses a negatively formed declarative question designed to rule out any injury ("you didn't have"; line 5), but abandons it in favor of a positively formed yes/no interrogative ("did you have stitches") that anticipates at least some problem (in preferring a "yes" response).

(12) 4A1:17

HV: And you're feeling well.
(0.7)
M: Yeah.
(1.5)
HV: -> And you'r– (.) You didn't ha- Did you have stitches?
(0.8)
M: Ye[:es

HV: [You did. [('N) are you so:[re=
M: [(nh hnhn) [I had a third degree
tea:r=
HV: =O::::::h. Did you::?
M: Yeah. (0.2) It's uh (.) they think what happened 'is
chin must 'ave caught me.
(0.3)
M: .hhh as 'e w'[z coming ou:t.
HV: [O::::h,

As with the prior case, a speaker formulating a query must choose between alternative forms that convey very different understandings of her recipient's circumstances: the first version the HV chooses reflects an optimistic evaluation of the mother's circumstances (i.e., it anticipates that she was not substantially injured); however, in using a declarative, negatively formed assertion to do so, the HV's question also reflects a less than substantial shift in her orientation. If the mother's prior delayed response (in 3) hints at such an injury – as suggested by the HV's decision to pose a contingent follow-up question – the form the HV initially selects barely acknowledges this. While the polarity of the question acknowledges the possibility of injury, it does so in the service of ruling the matter out. At the same time, by using a declarative to invite such confirmation, the query would provide for only a minimal response. In both of these ways, the form of query *retains the survey as a focal activity* by projecting an imminent return to it. In contrast, the positively formed, yes/no interrogative the HV uses to replace it – "did you have …" – alters both dynamics: in anticipating a "yes" response, the HV more strongly presumes the mother's injury; and by treating the matter as genuinely in question she invites the mother to elaborate the circumstances that gave rise to it (see Raymond, 2010a). In response, the mother remains troubles resistant, producing a delayed "yes"; after the HV's treatment of this as news (in line 8), however, the mother subsequently elaborates her substantial injuries in overlap with a further YNI ("are you sore") by the HV that specifically solicits aspects of her personal experience.

In this stretch of talk, we can see both participants struggling with whether, and how, and in what context, the mother's experiences (and her injuries in particular) will be introduced, elaborated, and appreciated. As the HV's subsequent versions of her question increasingly acknowledge the possibility that the mother suffered injuries, the mechanisms by which this is accomplished – the shift in polarity (from negative to positive) and grammatical form (from declarative to interrogative) – work to reshape the central activity to which the questions contribute, and thus the HV's alignment with the mother: she moves from institutional representative filling in a form to a conversational recipient, listening to the mother's birth experience. Over the same stretch of talk the mother similarly undergoes a progressive shift in her orientation: while her conduct initially reflects a striking degree of "troubles resistance" (Jefferson, 1984; Heritage and Sorjonene, 1994), as she begins to elaborate her injuries (and the HV sympathetically registers these), she ratifies the HV's proposed move into a conversational exchange by detailing the extent of her injury and its source. As this case illustrates, how participants navigate the distance-involvement dilemma can be directly implicated in more than the way a specific sequence unfolds; participants' management of these matters are directly constitutive of the very activities in which they are engaged, and even the social relations to which these contribute.

Questions pertaining to troubles or problems may also become complicated when the actions they accomplish involve possible solutions or remedies. As Curl and Drew (and their colleagues) have established in a recent series of papers (see Curl, 2006; Curl and Drew, 2008), the placement and design of offers (and requests) can entail precise considerations of (a) the problems or needs to which they are addressed, (b) what the parties (can accountably) know about a co-participant's ability to manage these, and (c) the speaker's entitlement to produce such actions based on their understanding of their recipients' ability to accept (or grant) them. In these ways, offers of help (and requests for the same) unavoidably involve speakers in efforts to balance the forms of entitlement asserted in producing these actions against the need to acknowledge the capabilities (and situations) of the recipients they target (including the contingencies that shape their acceptance, fulfillment, or completion; see Curl and Drew, 2008: 147). Evidently, speakers producing such actions can scarcely avoid managing the degree to which the type and design of the action they initiate may appear disengaged from the situation of the recipient, or over-involved with and even appropriating of them.

For example, in the following case, Edgerton has called his friend Michael to offer help on hearing that Michael's wife (Margaret) has suffered a back injury during the Christmas holidays. As with the prior case, a concern with the distance-involvement dilemma informs the design of the focal action and the alternative version he proposes on its completion, as well as shaping a range of other features of the call. Several features of the opening suggest that the parties know each other, but are not close or intimate friends. For example, although Edgerton recognizes Michael when he answers the phone, Michael misses several opportunities for a reciprocal identification of him (see the delay in line 3, and the greeting term in 4 that precede Edgerton's self-identification in 5). Moreover, as Edgerton formulates the reason for the call he indicates the second-hand nature of knowledge about Margaret's injury (i.e., he "heard" about it) and encounters some trouble in retrieving her name (see line 9, "poor um (0.4) Margaret"). The opening of this call evidently reflects Edgerton's efforts to convey his genuine (and even urgent) concern for Michael and his family, even as the derivative character of the knowledge on which it is based, and other infelicities (in recognition and person reference), position him in a less than intimate relationship with them. It is in the context of this opening – and the current state of the relationship between the parties instantiated by it – that we can appreciate Edgerton's offer of help, and the transition space repair he uses to modify it.

(13) Heritage 0II:4

Mic: Woking three five one six?
Edg: Michael?
(.)
Mic: Hullo:?
Edg: This is Edgerton:.
Mic: Yes Edger[t ['n.
Edg: [.h[Michael look ah:: I'm I'm phonin:g uh on
beha:lf of Ilene and myse:lf. =We just heard abou:t
poor um (0.4) Margaret.
Mic: Yes ma:ddening isn't it.=
Edg: =Oh:hh Lord.< And we were wondering if there's
anything we can do to help<
Mic: [Well that's]
Edg: [I mean] can we do any shopping for her or
something like tha:t?
(0.7)
Mic: Well that's most ki:nd Edgerton .hhh At the moment
no:. Because we've still got two bo:ys at home.
Edg: Of course

By including his own spouse as a party to the offer (see lines 7–8, and his use of "we" in 11) and placing it directly following Michael's confirmation of his own spouse's injury, Edgerton's offer may be heard to propose a rather intimate level of involvement in Michael's management of his family's affairs (especially relative to the fairly attenuated connection between the parties suggested by the call's opening). And yet Edgerton's use of "wondering if" to frame the offer as reflecting an ongoing concern ("we were wondering if …") suggests his orientation to the possibility of unknown contingencies that could make it problematic (see Curl and Drew, 2008, on the use of "wonder" prefaced requests; see also Raymond, 2010b). Edgerton's immediate addition to the offer (using an "I mean"- prefaced transition space repair) suggests a more or less literal concern with the distance-involvement dilemma: in specifying the terms of the offer – "can we do any shopping for her or something like that?" – Edgerton names candidate activities that take place *outside* of, and at a "distance" from, the home, thereby quite literally reducing the level of involvement otherwise implicated by his query. Finally, we can note that in rejecting the offer Michael's account specifies conditions *within* the house ("boys at home") that render Edgerton's offer of help outside of it superfluous. In the last three cases – 10–12 – we have examined some ways in which repaired questions open a window onto the ways in which speakers orient to, and contend with, the distance-involvement dilemma in sequence-initiating actions. In addition, by focusing on how alternative versions of the "same" initiating action can be reshaped – via the selection of different grammatical forms, the presuppositions they embody, their polarity, and the preferences these together establish for the form and valence of the response they make relevant – we have illustrated how the basic materials used to pose questions constitute a primary set of resources by which speakers manage to avoid "appearing disengaged from the affairs of the other, or appearing over-involved with and even appropriating of them" (Raymond and Heritage, 2006).

5.6 Conclusion

In analyses of responding actions, a range of contributors have shown that variations in response design can be a vehicle for (i) the weighting of a question's relevance, (ii) contesting its agenda, presuppositions or preference structure, (iii) whether it should have been asked at all, (iv) whether a response is an answerer's obligation or a voluntary dispensation, and (v) how committed the answerer is to the course of action projected in the answer (cf. Raymond, 2003; Heritage, 2010; Heritage and Raymond, 2012). In the current paper we have exploited the organization of repair as a methodological tool to demonstrate that variations in the design and implementation of initiating actions reflect a complementary set of concerns associated with first position actions. Across both positions, the intensity with which epistemic positions, rights and obligations are indexed and policed in practices of, and practices in, interaction, is vivid testimony to their fundamental status within social relations.

In these considerations one may hear echoes of Searle's and Austin's concern with felicity conditions, or Goffman's concern with the "traffic rules of interaction" (Goffman, 1967, 1971); it is likely that the observations of each were prompted, in part, by the systematic organization we have begun to describe. However, our approach differs in a number of respects: we do not approach these as logical conditions that participants can either meet or fall short of; instead we view them as practical problems to be managed by participants as they coordinate social action and social relations in concrete courses of action. Further, we do not treat these matters as conditions to be deduced by analysts or philosophers as *a priori foundations for action*; rather, we are interested in how the participants orient to, and exploit, them in organizing social action, personhood, and social relations. As the cases analyzed in this chapter suggest, speakers initiating action sequences using interrogatives must contend with a distinct range of contingencies in managing the "distance-involvement" dilemma as practical matters associated with the production, recognition, and coordination of action, and the social relations accomplished through them.

Finally, we note that these considerations suggest the degree to which the "epistemics of social relations" – and the ways that alternative grammatical forms used to initiate question-answer sequences constitute a basic mechanism for their expression and management – are central to the organization of social action, and thus interaction. It appears that, in addition to the capacity of grammar to project the course and duration of an utterance, and, in that way, facilitate the organization of turn taking (cf. Sacks et al., 1974; Schegloff, 1996; Raymond and Lerner, 2009), the capacity of grammatical forms to embody or assert distinct epistemic relations between speaker and recipient may be another – if not *the* other – primary way in which grammar is adapted to the exigencies of interaction. That is, if the projectable structure of grammatical forms provide a central resource for organization of turn-taking (see Sacks et al., 1974; Lerner, 1991, 1996), then the alternative epistemic relations embodied in distinct grammatical forms constitute a basic resource for the organization of *sequences* of action (see Heritage, 2012). Moreover, while the capacity of grammatical forms to project utterance completion appears to be a *generic* feature of grammar (i.e., all forms project completion, and the production of each inexorably leads toward a next possible completion), the distinct epistemic relations indexed by the deployment of alternative grammatical forms (declaratives, interrogatives, and commands) constitutes a basic source of variation between them, and thus the key mechanism by which sequentially sensitive deployments of them come to have a distinct action import. Thus, while the projectable structure of grammatical forms enables participants to organize their participation as *speakers*, variations in the distinct epistemic relations asserted by alternative grammatical forms provides a basic mechanism by which such participants organize their participation as social actors.

REFERENCES

Atkinson, J. Maxwell and Drew, Paul (1979). *Order in Court: The Organization of Verbal Interaction in Judicial Settings*. London: Macmillan.

Bolden, Galina B. (2006). Little words that matter: discourse markers "so" and "oh" and the doing of other-attentiveness in social interaction. *Journal of Communication* 56:4: 661–688.

Boyd, Elizabeth and Heritage, John (2006). Taking the patient's personal history: questioning during verbal examination. In John Heritage and Douglas Maynard, eds., *Practicing Medicine: Structure and Process in Primary Care Encounters*, pp. 151–184. Cambridge University Press.

Curl, Traci (2006). Offers of assistance: constraints on syntactic design. *Journal of Pragmatics* 38: 1257–1280.

Curl, Traci and Drew, Paul (2008). Contingency and action: a comparison of two forms of requesting. *Research on Language and Social Interaction* 41: 1–25.

Drew, Paul (2006). Misalignments in "after hours" calls to a British GP practice: a study in telephone medicine. In John Heritage and Douglas Maynard, eds., *Practicing Medicine: Structure and Process in Primary Care Encounters*, pp. 416–444. Cambridge University Press.

Drew, Paul and Atkinson, Maxwell (1999). *Order in the Court: The Organisation of Verbal Interaction in Judicial Settings*. London: Macmillan.

Du Bois, John W. (2007). The stance triangle. In R. Englebretson, ed., *Stancetaking in Discourse: Subjectivity, Evaluation, Interaction*, pp. 139–182. Amsterdam/Philadelphia: John Benjamins.

Fox, Barbara, and Thompson, Sandra (2010). Responses to "wh" interrogatives in English conversation. *Research on Language and Social Interaction* 43(2): 133–156.

Goffman, Erving (1967). *Interaction Ritual: Essays in Face-to-face Behavior*. Chicago, IL: Aldine Publishing.

(1971). *Relations in Public: Microstudies of the Public Order*. New York: Harper and Row.

Goodwin, Charles (1979). The interactive construction of a sentence in natural conversation. In George Psathas, ed., *Everyday Language: Studies in Ethnomethodology*, pp. 97–121. New York: Irvington.

(1984). Notes on story structure and the organization of participation. In Max Atkinson and John Heritage, eds., *Structures of Social Action*, pp. 225–46. Cambridge University Press.

Goodwin, Charles and Goodwin, Marjorie Harness (1987). Concurrent operations on talk: notes on the interactive organization of assessments. *IPrA Papers in Pragmatics* 1(1): 1–55.

Greenberg, Joseph Harold (2005). *Language Universals: With Special Reference to Feature Hierarchies*. Berlin: Mouton de Gruyter.

Heritage, John (1984). A change-of-state token and aspects of its sequential placement. In J. Maxwell Atkinson and John Heritage, eds., *Structures of Social Action*, 299–345. Cambridge University Press.

(1998). Oh-prefaced responses to inquiry. *Language in Society* 27: 291–334.

(2002). Ad hoc inquiries: two preferences in the design of "routine" questions in an open context. In Douglas Maynard, Hanaka Houtkoop-Steenstra, Nora K. Schaeffer and H. van der Zouwen, eds., *Standardization and Tacit Knowledge: Interaction and Practice in the Survey Interview*, pp. 313–333. New York: Wiley Interscience.

(2007). Intersubjectivity and progressivity in references to persons (and places). In T. Stivers and N. J. Enfield (eds.), *Person Reference in Interaction: Linguistic, Cultural and Social Perspectives*, pp. 255–280. Cambridge University Press.

(2008). Conversation analysis as social theory In Bryan Turner, ed., *The New Blackwell Companion to Social Theory*, pp. 300–320. Oxford: Blackwell.

(2010). Questioning in medicine. In A. Freed and S. Ehrlich, eds., *"Why Do You Ask?": The Function of Questions in Institutional Discourse*, pp. 42–68. New York: Oxford University Press.

(2012). Epistemics in action: action formation and territories of knowledge. *Research on Language and Social Interaction* 45: 1–29.

Heritage, John and Clayman, S. E. (2010). *Talk in Action: Interactions, Identities and Institutions*. Boston: Wiley-Blackwell.

Heritage, John and Raymond, Geoffrey (2005). The terms of agreement: indexing epistemic authority and subordination in assessment sequences. *Social Psychology Quarterly* 68: 15–38.

(forthcoming). Navigating epistemic landscapes: acquiescence, agency and resistance in responses to polar questions. In J. P. de Ruiter (ed.), *Questions: Formal, Functional and Interactional Perspectives*. Cambridge University Press.

Heritage, John and Sorjonen, Marja Leena (1994). Constituting and maintaining activities across sequences: and-prefacing as a feature of question design. *Language in Society* 23: 1–29.

Jefferson, Gail (1981). The abominable "ne?": An exploration of post-response pursuit of response. In P. Shroder, ed., *Sprache der Gegenwaart*, pp. 53–88. Düsseldorf: Pedagogischer Verlag Schwann.

(1984). On the organization of laughter in talk about troubles. In J. M. Atkinson and J. C. Heritage, eds., *Structures of Social Action: Studies in Conversation Analysis*, pp. 346–369. Cambridge University Press.

(1988). On the sequential organization of troubles talk in ordinary conversation. *Social Problems* 35(4): 418–442.

(1991). List construction as a task and resource. In G. Psathas, ed., *Interactional Competence*, pp. 63–92. New York: Irvington Publishers.

Jefferson, Gail and Lee, John R. E. (1992). The rejection of advice: managing the problematic convergence of a "troubles telling" and a "service encounter." In P. Drew and J. C. Heritage, eds., *Talk at Work*, pp. 521–548. New York: Cambridge University Press.

Kendrick, Kobin (2010). Epistemic relations: two polar interrogative formats in Mandarin Chinese conversation. Unpublished Dissertation. University of California, Santa Barbara.

Koshik, Irene (2005). *Beyond Rhetorical Questions: Assertive Questions in Everyday Interaction*. Amsterdam and Philadelphia: John Benjamins.

Lerner, Gene H. (1991). On the syntax of sentences in progress. *Language In Society* 20: 441–458.

(1996). On the "semi-permeable" character of grammatical units in conversation: conditional entry into the turn space of another speaker. In E. Ochs, E. A. Schegloff, and S. Thompson, eds., *Interaction and Grammar*, pp. 238–276. Cambridge University Press.

Lerner, Gene H. and Raymond, Geoffrey (forthcoming). *Adjusting Action: Some Elementary Forms of Social Co-ordination in Interaction*.

Pollner, Melvin (1987). *Mundane Reason: Reality in Everyday Life and Sociological Discourse*. Cambridge University Press.

Pomerantz, Anita (1980). Telling my side: "limited access" as a "fishing" device. *Sociological Inquiry* 50(3–4): 186–198.

(1988). Offering a candidate answer: an information seeking strategy. *Communication Monographs* 55(4): 360–373.

Raymond, Geoffrey (2000). The structure of responding: type-conforming and nonconforming responses to yes/no-type interrogatives. PhD dissertation, University of California–Los Angeles.

(2003). Grammar and social organization: yes/no type interrogatives and the structure of responding. *American Sociological Review* 68: 939–967.

(2010a). Grammar and social relations: alternative forms of yes/no type initiating actions in health visitor interactions. In Alice F. Freed and Susan Ehrlich, eds., *"Why Do You Ask?" : The Function of Questions in Institutional Discourse*, pp. 87–107. Oxford University Press.

(2010b). Opening up sequence organization: Formulating action as a practice for managing "out of place" sequence initiating actions. Paper presented at the Max Planck Institute for Psycholinguistics, Nijmegen, the Netherlands.

Raymond, Geoffrey and Heritage, John (2006). The epistemics of social relations: owning grandchildren. *Language in Society* 35: 677–670.

(forthcoming). Constructing epistemic landscapes: variations in the design and deployment of yes/no type initiating actions.

Raymond, Geoffrey and Lerner, Gene (2009). Towards a sociology of the body-in-action: the body and its multiple involvements. Unpublished MS. Department of Sociology, UCSB.

Sacks, Harvey (1972). An initial investigation of the usability of conversational data for doing sociology. In D. Sudnow, ed., *Studies in Social Interaction*, pp. 31–74. New York: The Free Press.

(1987). On the preferences for agreement and contiguity in sequences in conversation. In G. Button and J. R. E. Lee (eds.), *Talk and Social Organization*, pp. 54–69. Clevedon: Multilingual Matters.

Sacks, Harvey, Schegloff, Emanuel A., and Jefferson, G. (1974). A simplest systematics for the organization of turn-taking for conversation. *Language* 50: 696–735.

Schegloff, Emanuel A. (1986). The routine as achievement. *Human Studies* 9: 111–151.

(1987). Analyzing single episodes of interaction: an exercise in conversation analysis. *Social Psychology Quarterly* 50(2): 101–114.

(1996). Turn organization: one intersection of grammar and interaction. In E. Ochs, E. A. Schegloff and S. Thompson, eds., *Interaction and Grammar*, pp. 52–133, Cambridge University Press.

(2005). On complainability. *Social Problems* 52(3): 449–476.

(2006). Interaction: the infrastructure for social institutions, the natural ecological niche for language, and the arena in which culture is enacted. In N. J. Enfield and S. C. Levinson, eds., pp. 70–96, *Roots of Human Sociality: Culture, Cognition and Interaction*. Oxford: Berg.

(2007). *Sequence Organization in Interaction: A Primer in Conversation Analysis.* Cambridge University Press.

Schegloff, Emanuel A., Jefferson, Gail and Sacks, Harvey (1977). The preference for self-correction in the organization of repair in conversation. *Language*, 53(2): 361–382.

Schegloff, Emanuel A. and Harvey Sacks (1973). Opening up closings. *Semiotica* 8(4): 289–327.

Watson, D. R. (1978). Categorization, authorization and blame: negotiations in conversation. *Sociology* 12: 105–113.

Whalen, Marilyn R. and Zimmerman, Don H. (1990). Describing trouble: practical epistemology in citizen calls to the police. *Language in Society* 19: 465–492.

NOTES

1 We suspect two sources contribute to this disparity: Many, if not most, institutional occasions are largely built from question-answer sequences, and thus questions occur much more frequently in these interactions than in mundane ones. In addition, in very many cases such institutional occasions consist of institutional representatives posing routine questions to lay participants in order to better understand them and their circumstances. Thus, in contrast to occasions of interactions among family members, friends and acquaintances, the circumstances of such lay participants are largely (or relatively) unknown to the institutional representatives who must nevertheless fashion their questions in a manner that satisfies recipient design constraints (cf. Sacks et al., 1974; Boyd and Heritage, 2006), as well as other constraints related to institutionally specific imperatives.

2 Most approaches to interrogatives and declaratives in linguistics (see, e.g., Du Bois, 2007) formulate these matters in terms of a speaker's state of mind (or in relation to the object or state of affairs being formulated); in our view, such an individualistic approach to these basic resources misses their fundamentally *social*, and therefore *relational*, import. For example, it is only by approaching these forms as proposing a *relevant* relationship that we can begin to compare declaratively formed actions with their interrogatively formed alternatives, or the ways in which recipients manage the epistemic landscapes they set in motion (cf. Heritage and Raymond, 2012). Similarly, this perspective sheds light on what makes "commands" such a distinctive form relative to declaratives and interrogatives (which are much more common). Commands differ from both declaratives and interrogatives insofar as they assume that speaker and recipient share relatively equal epistemic rights regarding the circumstances formulated in them (instead of asserting a difference in epistemic access to one key feature of them, as in "can you X," which establishes a speaker's K– position regarding a participant's ability to fulfill a request), while asserting rights to *compel action* by recipients that speakers otherwise avoid (e.g., in using an interrogative that asserts a K– position regarding a recipient's willingness or ability to comply).

3 Speakers can manage the lack of fit between their epistemic rights in a matter and those otherwise asserted by the sequentially initial positioning of their action in other ways. In addition to using grammatical resources to downgrade the rights asserted by a first-position action (e.g., by asking a question), speakers with subordinate rights can downgrade the "firstness" of the action by marking it as derivative in some way (e.g., using discourse markers such as "so"; see Bolden, 2006), or by otherwise constituting the action as part of "retro sequences," which, as Schegloff (2007: 217) observes, are sequences "launched from their second position."

4 Occasions in which one party registers or informs a recipient regarding a personal matter that s/he cannot be expected to know about (e.g., "you have food in your teeth") are a notable exception.

5 Although we cannot take up the matter here, it is notable that these two uses (i.e., so-called "rhetorical questions" and yes/no declaratives) are not merely formally contrasting alternatives. In fact, they are substantially different in both moral and distributional terms. A consideration of these alternatives, and the use of interrogatives and declaratives to form sequence-initial actions more generally, is the subject of a forthcoming paper by Raymond and Heritage, (forthcoming).

6 In extract 4, Mark has called Joan; his query in line 3 is launched directly after Joan has made an initial move to close the call (i.e., with "nice talking to you"). The question, "what are you doing" is hearable in this context as a possible pre-invitation, an analysis strengthened by the subsequent query he adds to it ("Just sitting there"), which anticipates a preferred response. If Joan confirms that she is "just sitting there" she opens herself to – and indeed positively encourages – the invitation projected by Mark's initial query. It is notable, then, that, although it appears that Joan is, "just sitting there," she formulates her current circumstances ("hungry," "just so tired," etc.) in a manner designed to block an invitation or proposal involving her.

7 These two features of "what about" formulated suggestions are nicely illustrated in the data below in which a doctor uses this form as part of an effort to convince a patient to quit smoking. Into a fairly unpropitious environment (note the patient's refusal to respond to the doctor's question in lines 1 and 7), the doctor launches a "what about"-formatted proposal suggesting the patient use (nicotine) "patches" to facilitate an effort to quit smoking. The tacit claim that such proposal is novel turns out to be problematic, however, since the patient has already used nicotine patches in a previously unsuccessful effort to quit.

[SG 813:3]

Doc: You still smokin'?
(4.0)
Doc: Didju hear me?
Pat: Yes I [did.
Doc: [Heh heh heh hah
Pat: £You know the answer.£
Doc: h– (When) am I gonna getcha tuh quit.
Pat: Ah.
(5.0)
Doc: Huh:?
(2.0)
Doc: –> What about– D'you wanna try thuh patches again?
(3.0)
Pat: I don't think they'll do any good.I put 'em on
an' (I s=eh eh°) As soon as I get 'em on I want
uh cigarette.

The doctor replaces the "what about"-framed query with a different one (do you wanna …") that formulates the suggestion as an "nth" effort ("try … again"), thereby acknowledging the patients' prior (failed) attempt. Nevertheless, across each of these alternatives the doctor *retains* the presupposition that the patient's continued smoking constitutes a known-in-common problem for which some solution is relevant. In his responses, the patient does so as well. In rejecting the suggestion (lines 14–16, "I don't think they will do any good") the patient uses a format that specifically implicates such understanding of his circumstances as problematic: to claim that a remedy won't "do any good" acknowledges a state of affairs where some "good" needs to be done.

8 One reviewer asked whether the revised queries posed by the doctor were not simply ways of pursuing a response (or agreement), using this formulation to suggest that they may not count as instances of "same-turn, self-initiated repair." While it should be acknowledged that such classifications are not an issue for the participants, it is worth noting that in this extract (1) the progress of the sequence stalled after the initial version of each query, and (2) the revised version offered in its place did not merely pursue a response (as in the cases analyzed by Drew and Atkinson, 1979), but, in recognizably repeating aspects of the query, also specifically altered elements of its design, thereby treating the prior version as having been problematic in some way – as having been a source of trouble. While these cases may involve repairs designed to promote agreement, that would not differentiate them from many instances of both self-initiated, same-turn repair (Schegloff, 1987) and other-initiated repair produced in next turn (see Schegloff, 2007: 100–106).

9 We can note, however, that HVs anticipated that some references would be problematic for parents, and provided "translations" to make them recognizable. In such cases, these matters were handled in a different manner: the HV anticipated trouble instead of waiting for evidence of it to emerge. For example,

[1A1: 13]

M:		°Oh I thought you we[re (big) did[n't we.°=
HV:		[Ri:ght [
F:		[Mmghm
HV:		=So you had a– uh:
		(1.0)
HV:		You didn't– Did you– You didn't have forceps you had
		a:
M:		=Oh [no:: nothing.
F:		[( )
HV:		An– and did she cry straight awa:y.
M:		Yes she did didn't sh[e.
F:		[Mm hm,
		(1.0) ((Wood cracking))
HV:	->	Uhm (.) you didn't go to scboo: you know the
		spe[cial care unit.
M:		[Oh: no: no:

By contrast, in extract 11 the HV treats her use of "follow" as unproblematic, only offering a translation when neither parent responds. The issue of specialist vocabularies and expertise are taken up by C. Kitzinger and J. Mandelbaum in a forthcoming paper.

6 On the interactional import of self-repair in the courtroom

Tanya Romaniuk and Susan Ehrlich

6.1 Introduction

Research on self-initiated, same-turn repair (Schegloff, Jefferson and Sacks, 1977) in English has tended to focus on its formal aspects, for example, its "technology" (i.e., practices for marking its initiation and completion, for locating the repairable, and for performing operations on them; see Wilkinson and Weatherall, 2011; Schegloff, this volume), or its relation to syntax (e.g., Fox, Hayashi and Jasperson, 1996; Fox, Maschler and Uhmann, 2009). In general, this work has taken such facets of self-initiated, same-turn (henceforth self-repair) as the starting point of analysis, and has, in some cases, also addressed the interactional import of repair. One exception in this respect is an article by Gail Jefferson (1974) entitled "Error correction as an interactional resource", in which she suggests that speakers can use error corrections to signal to their recipients that what they are saying is not what they would typically say, but rather has been chosen in response to the contingencies of the current situation. That is, rather than beginning with a description of the formal properties of self-repair, Jefferson begins by focusing on the possible *actions* repair can accomplish. For example, Jefferson (1974: 192) argues that, when defendants in traffic court are on the verge of using a term such as "cop" but replace it with "officer", they are signaling to recipients that they 'are the sort of person who habitually uses the term cop and replaced it with officer out of deference to the courtroom surround'. In this paper, we take Jefferson's (1974) article as our point of departure and examine the interactional work accomplished by self-repairs in the institutional

Earlier versions of this paper were presented at the International Conference for Conversation Analysis in Mannheim, Germany (July 2010) and the Sociolinguistics Symposium in Southampton, England (September 2010). In addition to thanking those audience members for their comments, we would also like to extend our gratitude to our Toronto-area CAsts for their observations during a very helpful data session: Jeffrey Aguinaldo, Lynda Chubak, Shannon Cunningham, Ross Krekosi, and Linda Wood. We are particularly indebted to both Celia Kitzinger and Jack Sidnell for their thorough and insightful comments on an earlier draft of this chapter, which have helped us significantly in refining our argument. Any remaining shortcomings, however, are our own.

context of the courtroom. Like Jefferson, our data show that participants use repairs "out of deference to the courtroom surround"; however, our examples are less about style-shifting (as the shift from "cop" to "officer" seems to be) and more about participants using self-repairs in the service of setting-specific tasks and constraints of the courtroom.

Within the adversarial context of the Anglo-American legal system, two parties come together formally, typically with representation (e.g., lawyers), to present their versions of the dispute to a third party (e.g., judge, jury, tribunal) who hears the evidence, applies the appropriate laws or regulations and determines the guilt or innocence of the parties. Lawyers have as their task, then, that of convincing the adjudicating body that their (i.e., their client's) version of events is the most credible. However, Atkinson and Drew (1979: 70) note that trial discourse is conducted predominantly through a series of question-answer sequences. Indeed, apart from making opening and closing arguments, lawyers use questions to elicit testimony from witnesses. Such questions are designed to build a credible version of events in support of their own clients' interests, and to challenge, weaken and/or cast doubt on the opposing parties' version of events. And, not only are there restrictions on the types of turns that courtroom participants can take (i.e., lawyers are mandated to ask questions and witnesses to answer them), there are also rules of evidence that can constrain the *nature* and the *form* of these turn types.

What we see from this description of courtroom interaction, then, are some of the setting-specific tasks and constraints the particular institutional context of the courtroom imposes on participants. This is consistent with what Heritage (2005: 109) observes about institutional interaction generally, in that it "involves a *reduction* in the range of interactional practices deployed by the participants" (emphasis added), and *restrictions* in the contexts in which they can be deployed, relative to ordinary conversation. Indeed, our analysis of self-repair shows it to be one such interactional practice to the extent that it is not "deployed in pursuit of every imaginable kind of social goal," as in ordinary conversation (Heritage, 2005: 109), but rather is reduced in accordance with the setting-specific tasks and constraints of the courtroom. A comparable use of self-repair in a different institutional setting, one with its own set of interactional tasks and constraints, is provided by Clayman's (forthcoming) discussion of broadcast news interviews. One of the professional norms that operates within this context is that of neutralism – the idea that journalists should restrict themselves to designing turns at talk that exhibit a "neutralistic" posture. Clayman shows, for example, how, in beginning to formulate an assertion as though it were his own perspective, a journalist implements the practice of self-repair so that the repair solution maintains a neutralistic posture, thereby orienting to this institutional norm. In a similar way, we present examples of self-repair from courtroom interaction in which the repair solution allows participants to address some of the interactional contingencies related to the norms of the courtroom. In other words, the self-repairs that we focus on in this paper "do not seem to be necessary in terms of correcting something that was problematic or mistaken" (Sidnell, 2010: 117), but rather serve other kinds of interactional purposes.

Following Jefferson (1974), we are interested not only in the interactional work accomplished by a given repair solution, but also that accomplished by a repair's trouble source. Under Jefferson's account, the speaker initiating a repair segment is not attempting to cancel out the repairable item; rather, she is displaying to her recipient that the repair solution has been selected "in light of this interaction" and, *in addition*, that the errors or the error avoided (i.e., the trouble source or repairable item) is the term "customarily" used by the speaker (Jefferson, 1974: 195). Like Jefferson (1974), we are also interested in the potential of self-repairs to accomplish multiple interactional goals, given that speakers can use self-repairs to keep alternative ways of saying things "on the record". Thus, in what follows, not only do we demonstrate how self-repairs show courtroom participants responding to single interactional goals, we also illustrate how self-repairs may be used to orient to the multiple – and often conflicting – demands that courtroom settings impose on both witnesses and lawyers.

6.2 Trial data

The data for this chapter come from an American rape trial, Maouloud Baby v. the State of Maryland, which took place in the state of Maryland in 2004. At the trial, the accused, Maouloud Baby, was convicted of first-degree rape and some lesser offenses and was sentenced to fifteen years in jail. Maouloud appealed this decision and, upon appeal, the Maryland Court of Special Appeals (the second highest court in Maryland) reversed Maouloud's convictions in September of 2006 and ordered a new trial. In April of 2008, after Maouloud and the state cross-appealed to the Maryland Court of Appeals (the highest court in Maryland), the Court of Appeals also reversed Maouloud's convictions and ordered a new trial. This new trial has not taken place and, according to the prosecuting attorney in the case (personal communication), will probably not occur because the complainant is reluctant to testify again.

In order to provide some contextualization for the excerpts that follow, we briefly describe the events that were under investigation in this trial. The complainant, Jewel Lankford, and the accused, Maouloud Baby, met at a McDonald's restaurant the night of the events in question – December 13,

2003. Jewel was with her best friend, Lacey Simmons, and was introduced to Maouloud because he was a friend both of Lacey's younger brother and of Lacey's boyfriend. When Jewel and Lacey were about to leave the McDonald's, Maouloud asked whether he and his friend, Michael (Mike) Wilson, could get a ride in Jewel's car. Jewel drove the four of them to a community centre, where they believed there was a party. Upon discovering there was no party, Jewel drove to a clearing between two townhouses and the four passengers exited the car. Maouloud and Mike smoked marijuana and joked with the young women about getting a hotel room. The four then drove back to the McDonald's in Jewel's car and Lacey left the group to be with her boyfriend. Jewel then agreed to drive Mike and Maouloud to a residential neighbourhood, where she parked her car and agreed to sit in the back seat of the car with the two young men. It was at this point that the accounts of Jewel and Maouloud began to diverge.[1] According to the prosecution, Mike and Maouloud then sexually assaulted Jewel in a variety of ways, including Maouloud fondling her breasts, removing her jeans, and inserting his fingers in her vagina, and Mike attempting to put his penis in her mouth, and to put his penis in her rectum. Following this sequence of events, Mike asked Maouloud to leave the car and Mike continued to sexually assault Jewel.[2] After some time, Mike got out of the car and Maouloud re-entered, and again, against her will, pushed his penis into Jewel's vagina. Eventually he stopped, after which Mike got back into the car and drove Jewel's car to a neighbourhood across the street from the McDonald's, where the three parted ways. As will become evident in the examples below, the prosecution argued that all of the sexual acts of aggression described above were non-consensual, while the defense argued that they were consensual.[3]

6.3 On the interactional import of self-repairs

Our collection of self-repairs in over eight hours of audio-recorded data during the trial yielded a total of 252 examples.[4] In the majority of instances, we found repair implemented by all participant roles (i.e., witnesses and lawyers) in the service of error-correction (Schegloff and Sacks, 1977), most commonly to correct apparent troubles in speaking (e.g., examples 1–4) or to correct factual inaccuracies (e.g., examples 5–9).[5]

(01) #17–Defendant–Direct examination

'She said she doesn't do oral sex. When he asked for **air– oral** sex,'

(02) #101–Complainant–Direct examination

'Like they could've **tooken– taken** thuh sidewalk to go there.'

(03) #205–State Lawyer–Opening statement

'Unfortunately she got in thuh back seat and that's a decision that Jewel Lankford will **regwet– regret** for thuh rest of her life.'

(04) #225–State Lawyer–Closing statement

'Two active lacerations plus **feeding– bleeding** from inside thuh vaginal wall.'

(05) #4–Defendant–Direct examination

'And at that point we was walking to thuh vehicle. (.) **Lacey's–I mean: Jewel's** car,'

(06) #97–Complainant–Direct examination

'I know I kind of yelled a little bit **when they put– when he put** his fingers in.

(07) #139–Defense Lawyer–Cross–examination

'Michae– Maouloud left.'

(08) #200–State Lawyer–Opening statement

'At one point Michael Wilson. was trying to put his penis in her vagina, and he put it **in his re–in her rectum.**'

While the above examples are all considered instances of self-repair, they are not the focus of this paper. Instead, our analysis is based on interactionally significant instances in which an emerging utterance is halted in some way and is then aborted, recast or redone in ways that serve other kinds of interactional contingencies, namely: (1) presenting a preferred version of events; (2) restricting the epistemic status of claims; and (3) conforming to constraints on asking questions.

6.3.1 *Presenting a preferred version of events*

In previous work on repair in courtroom testimony, Drew (1990) demonstrates how witnesses use other-initiated repairs to contest and amend the version of events put forward by cross-examining lawyers' questions in an attempt to avoid the damaging implications that may be conveyed by such questions. In other words, Drew addresses the issue of the interactional import of repair, even though his paper is not framed in these terms. However, while Drew discusses the function of other-initiated repair in the courtroom, his treatment of self-initiated repair is limited because, according to Drew, witnesses generally avoid self-initiated repairs in cross-examination, as such corrections and amendments can have the effect of undermining their credibility.[6] More specifically, Drew (1990: 43) says that, if witnesses in court were to engage in the kind of self-repair common in ordinary conversation, "they could easily be challenged about the accuracy of their evidence (e.g., whether it was a chip or a crack), about their ability to recall (e.g., whether it was the same day or the day after) – thus raising questions about the verisimilitude, credibility, or consistency of their evidence and hence about their competence as witnesses." Ultimately, Drew's argument is that witnesses engage in other-initiated repairs while avoiding self-initiated repairs in the courtroom in order "to make descriptions count toward their preferred version of events about which they are being cross-examined" (p. 63). (See also Sidnell and Barnes, this volume.) Interestingly, many of the self-repairs in our data function in a way similar to the other-initiated repairs that Drew talks about; that is, the speaker repairs an utterance so that it is more in keeping with their side's "preferred version of events" (Drew 1990: 63). This is the case for the defendant and both the defense and state lawyers at various points during the trial. We begin our discussion of these kinds of self-repairs with examples from the defendant's testimony.

Example 9 comes from early on in direct examination, when the defendant, Maouloud Baby (MB), is asked about his relationship with the complainant, Jewel Lankford, before and after the incident.

(09) 8:22:10–8:22:3 (#1)

DE: You heard Jewel Lankford testify.
MB: Yes.
DE: Did you know her before that night,
MB: No I didn't.
(0.4)
DE: How do you feel about her now as you testify.
MB: Uhhh:m=hh
(1.8)
I'm sorry for having to put her– goin– uh havin–
(.) put her– goin' through this (0.2) really.
DE: How do you feel about your family.
MB: Sorry for putting my family through it too.

At line 6, Maouloud is asked by his lawyer how he feels about the complainant "now." After first exhibiting some degree of thought in formulating a response in lines 7–8, Maouloud begins to express regret "for having to put her" but cuts this off before completion. The candidate replacement initially offered ("goin") is temporarily suspended and Maouloud exhibits further difficulty, vacillating between two ways of formulating his response. He ultimately opts for the one that removes himself as the agent responsible for the difficulties that Jewel has endured.[7] Since the defendant has been charged with rape, it is not in his interest to admit that he is the agent responsible for the complainant's suffering. Indeed, the altered version of his response – "I'm sorry for … her goin through this really" – removes him as the cause of her difficulties and, thus, represents a version of events that is more consistent with consensual sex than with rape. It is also revealing to note how Maouloud's answer to the following question regarding how he feels about his family ("sorry for putting my family through it too"; line 12) suggests that he was likely on his way to saying "I'm sorry for having to put her through this" (indeed, the "too" actually locates this formulation as the same as the previous one). In this first example, then, we see self-repair, specifically, grammatical reformulation, being mobilized to replace one version of events with a version that is more in keeping with the defendant's claim of consensual sex; that is, the defendant removes himself as the subject and agent of the complainant's suffering.

Example 10 illustrates a different kind of repaired version of the situation; this time, rather than removing or obfuscating responsibility, the self-repair has the effect of representing the complainant in terms that are better understood as fitting the defendant's version of what happened. In this example, again from direct examination, Maouloud is describing what happened after the alleged incident had occurred and Mike began to drive Jewel's car back to the McDonald's (line 1).

(10) 8:30:54–8:31:03 (#14)

MB: At that ti:me when we w's on our way back
she w's putting back on her clothes, (.) .h
She w's putting on her pants **she didn't hav–**
her shirt was still on she w's putting on her
pants. and her undergarment.

When beginning to describe what the complainant was doing in the back seat at the time (line 2), Maouloud does so with a description that focuses on the absence of something the complainant had on at line 3 (presumably clothes). However, this gets cut off before completion and the repaired version focuses on the clothes she had on ("her shirt was still on"; line 4). If the defendant had completed the aborted turn-in-progress, characterizing Jewel as *not* having clothes on, an inference could be drawn that he had removed those clothes. By contrast, a description in terms of the clothes she *does* have on does not generate any such inference. Notably, "still" at line 4 projects backward into the incident in question, implying that her shirt was always on, which, together with the repaired version of events, blocks an inference that could be compatible with rape.

Like the first two examples, the repaired version in example 11 also puts forth a more favorable representation of the event in question but, unlike those examples, it does so at the level of lexical choice.

(11) 8:51:35–8:51:54 (#31)

DE: And then what happened.
MB: An' then basically I placed myself i:n between her
legs, (0.6) a:n' (0.2) I tried tuh–I tried tuh uh::
(.) put my penis in her vagina but .h it wouldn't
go in after a few tri:es, .hh **she backed up– she sat**
up and said...

At line 1, the defense lawyer asks Maouloud to report "what happened" after he got back in the car. In his euphemistic depiction of his attempt to have sex with the complainant (lines 2–4), Maouloud says, at line 5, that after "a few tries" she "backed up." This particular lexical choice suggests a type of retreat and thus suggests resistance on her part. Before completing that description, however, (i.e., the production of "p" in "up" is hearably cut off) Maouloud initiates repair and redoes the formulation by replacing "backed up" with "sat up." This lexical reformulation replaces the term suggesting resistance with a descriptive term more consistent with consensual sex. In general, then, examples 9–11 show Maouloud beginning to produce an utterance that does not support his version of the "facts" but subsequently repairing it so that it is more consistent with the defense's, and his, claim of consensual sex.

As noted above, we also have examples in our collection where lawyers use self-repair to perform a similar kind of function, that is, amending an utterance so that it is more in keeping with the argument they are trying to make about the events under investigation. Examples 12 and 13 both come from the opening statement of the state lawyer (SE). In 12, the lawyer is introducing the complainant and depicting her as relatively inexperienced, "unsophisticated" and "naïve" (lines 1–4).

(12) 1:10:01–1:10:22–Opening statement (#195)

SE: Now you're gonna meet Jewel Lankford and you'll
↑see: (.) that Jewel is young for her age. (0.3)
Jewel i:s (.) unsophisticated, (0.2) she's
unworldly, (.) she's naïve, and she's trusting.
(0.2) Jewel Lankford. (0.3) **pla:ced her trust.**
her trust–↑misplaced her trust. (0.2) in Maouloud
Baby and his friend Michael Wilson.

After stating in line 4 that Jewel Lankford is "trusting", the lawyer seems to be on her way to saying that Jewel placed her trust in Maouloud Baby and his friend Michael Wilson. However, possible trouble is already indicated in the recycling of the words "her trust," only a partially realized turn constructional unit (TCU)-in-progress which is then cut off. This marks the initiation of repair, and, following a pitch reset, the lawyer stresses the inserted material (i.e., the prefix "mis" before "placed"). This prefix is hearable as an insertion by virtue of the fact that the lawyer repeats the elements that followed it (i.e., "her trust"), which Schegloff (n.d. a) refers to as "post-framing." While the repairable item, "placed," as in "Jewel Lankford placed her trust …" does not depict the young men in a negative light, the lawyer's repair solution and its corresponding emphatic production, which draws attention to it as the solution, "misplaced," conveys the idea that the two young men were *not* to be trusted and that Jewel's trust in them was misguided. Thus, the transformation achieved by the lawyer's self-repair (i.e., from "placed" to "misplaced") coupled with her prior description of Jewel in lines 1–4 characterizes the young men as having taken advantage of Jewel's naïveté and innocence – a characterization that is more consistent with the state's contention that Jewel was the victim of sexual assault and rape and not a participant in consensual sex.

The self-repair in example 13 also appears in the opening statement of the state lawyer and also involves the operation of inserting (see Schegloff, this volume; Wilkinson and Weatherall, 2011). It occurs as the lawyer is describing how Jewel and the two young men ended up parked in a residential neighbourhood in Jewel's car.

(13) 1:14:57–1:15:25–Opening statement (#209)

01	SE:	Jewel drove them to thuh place that Maouloud Baby,
02		(0.2) and Michael Wilson directed her. (0.3)
03		It's uhm (.) a place called Dandridge (.) Way:,
04		I–I'm sorry Dumbridge Way. It's a street in
05		Montgomery Village not far from that McDonald's.
06		.hh And you're gonna hear: that it's a dead end
07		street. (.) with a few isolated houses. (0.3)
08		A:nd **she:–=at their direction she parallel parked.**

In lines 1–2 of this example, the lawyer states that Maouloud Baby and Michael Wilson "directed" Jewel to drive to the residential street in Montgomery Village. After further describing this street by name, location, and characteristics (lines 3–7), the lawyer begins to describe how Jewel parked her car, "A:nd she:-" (line 8). However, repair is initiated at this point following a sound stretch and cut-off intonation on "she." The lawyer then restarts the TCU, inserting the prepositional phrase "at their direction" before "she parallel parked." Like (12), "at their direction" is hearable as an insertion upon the production of the post-framed material ("she"), which marks this as a return to what was previously in progress. If the lawyer had brought her initial utterance to completion (i.e., had not initiated repair), it presumably would not have contained the prepositional phrase that specifies the conditions under which Jewel parallel parked. The repair solution, by contrast, suggests that Jewel has not parked her car of her own free will, but rather was directed to do so by Maouloud and Mike. Given that the state is arguing that Maouloud and Mike forced Jewel to engage in non-consensual sex, it is also in their interest to portray the events leading up to the sexual assaults as coercive. Thus, again, we see that the state lawyer's repair solution is more in keeping with the state's argument that Jewel was sexually assaulted than the original formulation would have been otherwise.

The final example in this section comes from the closing argument of the defense lawyer (DE). Immediately prior to where example 14 begins, the defense lawyer has been describing the events that resulted in Maouloud's charge of rape from Maouloud's point of view. These events occurred once Maouloud reentered the car after Mike exited. Maouloud testified that, upon reentering the car, he said, "Can I hit that?" and Jewel responded by saying that he could as long as he stopped when she said so. Maouloud then put on a condom and, according to his testimony, tried to penetrate Jewel but was unsuccessful. Jewel testified, by contrast, that Maouloud was able to penetrate her.

(14) 9:40:00–9:40:09–Closing statement (#158)

DE: >This is not< the: actions of a gang rapist
this's a sixteen year old bo:y. (0.4) in a car
with a CO:llege girl, (.) **having–or ↑trying tuh**
have sex.

Beginning at line 1, the defense lawyer is suggesting, it seems, that Maouloud's actions were not malicious, but rather the natural inclinations of "a sixteen year old boy in a car with a college girl." In characterizing the sexual activity that Maouloud engaged in, the defense lawyer's description-in-progress is brought to a halt after producing the word "having-." Repair is then initiated with cut-off intonation at the end of this word, and the lawyer next produces the repair preface "or" which indicates that an alternative formulation is forthcoming (Lerner and Kitzinger, 2010). Following a pitch reset, the repair solution is offered, which reformulates the sexual activity as "trying tuh have sex." The lawyer's initial version, "having-," clearly projects that he was on his way to saying that Maouloud was "having sex" despite the fact that he does not bring this to completion. Through the initiation of repair, he abandons that TCU-in-progress to introduce an alternative version. Notice that both formulations (i.e., the repairable item and the repair solution) represent the sexual activity as consensual, which is consistent with the defense's argument; however, the repair solution represents events in a way that is more fully consistent with Maouloud's testimony, specifically, that Maouloud only *tried* to have sex with Jewel.

We began this section by commenting on the similarity between the work accomplished by other-initiated repairs in the courtroom, as described by

Drew (1990), and by many of the examples of self-initiated repairs in our collection. That is, in both cases speakers are repairing utterances (the utterances of others or their own utterances) so that they are more consistent with their, or their side's, version of the "facts." Given that lawyers and witnesses have as their primary task convincing judges and/or juries that their version of events is the most credible, it is not surprising that their talk, in general, is oriented to this institutional goal. And, what is interactionally significant about our examples is the way in which self-repair makes this orientation visible.[8]

6.3.2 *Restricting the epistemic status of claims*

The previous section described one interactional contingency that self-repairs can be mobilized to address (i.e., putting forth a more favourable version of events); in this section, we present examples of self-repairs that show witnesses oriented to another interactional contingency, namely one concerned with the epistemic status of the information they convey. The examples below illustrate witnesses using self-repairs to alter utterances in ways that restrict their testimony to that which is within their territories of knowledge (Heritage, 2011a) or epistemic domain (Stivers and Rossano, 2010). More specifically, they do so by limiting their testimony to what they know from first-hand experience, what Pomerantz (1980) calls a "Type 1 knowable," and not from report, hearsay or inference, what Pomerantz calls a "Type 2 knowable." And, interestingly, in the Anglo-American legal system, there is a rule of evidence that prohibits witnesses from testifying about "hearsay." According to Schane (2006: 95), for example, "a witness taking the stand during a court trial, can testify about events directly perceived through any of the five senses." Put another way, an ordinary witness (as opposed to an expert witness) "must have firsthand knowledge of what she is testifying about, or have had sensory experience of it" (Philips, 1992: 253). Although we have no way of proving that the defendant and the complainant in our data are orienting to this particular rule of evidence in any individual case, their use of self-repair often has the effect of reformulating their utterances in such a way as to adhere to this rule.[9] Moreover, there is other evidence in the conversation analytic literature that witnesses orient to this rule of evidence: Galatolo (2007), in her investigation of reported speech in an Italian criminal trial, has argued that witnesses use direct quotes in their answers as a way of demonstrating that they have had direct access to the conversation in question and, thus, that they have first-hand knowledge of what they are testifying about (i.e., that they are testifying about a Type 1 knowable).

Consider example 15 below. Prior to the beginning of this example, the defense has just established that Jewel agreed to go along with Maouloud and Mike, without being accompanied by her friend, Lacey. At this point, the defense asks Maouloud whether he told Jewel where they planned to go at line 1 and for what purpose at line 5.

(15) 8:43:17–8:43:31 (#22)

DE: Well didju tell Je:wel where you were gonna go?
(0.4)
MB: Nah:: we didn–we didn't tell em where we gonna go
we w's (0.2) jus' (.) gonna go (.) s:omewhere.
DE: To do what.
(0.4)
MB: **In our-in my: mind (.) to have sex with thuh girl(s).**

Maouloud begins his response at line 7 by saying that having sex with the girls was something both Maouloud and Mike had in mind ("in our"). However, before bringing this formulation to completion, Maouloud initiates repair with cut-off intonation on "our," and then restarts his response. The repaired version replaces the collective pronominal "our" with the individual self-reference "my" ("in my mind") (Lerner and Kitzinger, 2007), transforming his response into one where he is reporting only on his *own* thoughts/ideas and not on those of Mike.

Now consider example (16).

(16) 9:30:46–9:31:05 (#46)

PR: Mike wanted everyone to see that he was driving
someone else's car:,=so he drove right up under
those flood lights there,
MB: **I don't think he wanted anyb– I don– I don't know**
if he wanted anybody to see him dri[vin' but–
PR: [It would–It
wouldn't make sense if you didn't want someone to
see you driving to drive right up to thuh parking
lot with all those flood lights over you, (.)
That–that would be a foolish thing to do, (0.3)
Right,

At line 1, the state lawyer (PR) questions a suggestion put forward by the defendant that he and Mike simply dropped the complainant off at a location used earlier on in the evening. Maouloud begins to speculate about why Mike "drove right up under those flood lights" at lines 2–3, saying "I don't think he wanted anyb-" at line 4. After the cut-off on "anybody," Maouloud replaces "I don't think" with "I don't know if" and, in this way, replaces his speculation about what motivated Mike's behavior with an utterance that downgrades his ability to know Mike's motivations. That is, rather than inferring Mike's motivations, a Type 2 knowable, Maouloud's repaired version of events is limited to that which he knows from direct experience, a Type 1 knowable.

Example 17 also shows Maouloud restricting his response to what he knows from direct experience.

(17) 8:51:34–8:51:54 (#28)

01	DE:	How did she appe:ar when you got back in thuh car.
02	MB:	She was quiet (.) **She was:– (.) She appea:red**
03		**uh:m (1.2) I don't really know where to say how**
04		**she appea(l)ed-appeared but (.) she appeared (.)**
05		**normal** like–like how she appe:aled thuh whole day=
06		=she was quiet,

At line 1, Maouloud is asked how the complainant appeared when he got back into the car. After saying "she was quiet" at line 2, Maouloud begins his next utterance with "She was:" and then, instead of producing what the particular "next" would be (i.e., an adjective), he cuts off this description and replaces it with "She appea:red.," also on line 2. If the defendant had brought this utterance to completion, saying something like "she was normal," this would suggest that he had access to the complainant's internal state – something *outside* of his epistemic domain. However, in replacing "was" with "appeared," the defendant's reformulation (i.e., the semantics of the word "appear") restricts his observations to what he can directly experience, which is *within* his epistemic domain. In other words, he cannot definitively know what state the complainant "was" in at that time, only how she "appeared." It is interesting to note that, before completing this replaced version, i.e., describing how "she appeared," begun at line 2, Maouloud also introduces a qualification (lines 3–5), which exhibits his caution in formulating this description of her. In general, then, Maouloud's self-repairs in examples 15–17 show him modifying his testimony so that information that he represents as acquired on the basis of inference is re-presented as information that he knows from first-hand experience.

The next two examples, from Jewel's direct testimony, also contain self-repairs that involve epistemic issues. However, in these two examples, the trouble sources concern matters that Jewel has directly witnessed and her self-repairs function to downgrade the definitiveness of her claims to knowledge. Specifically, rather than overstating the certainty with which she knows the matters at hand, Jewel shows herself to be a reliable witness by carefully modulating the status of this first-hand knowledge. Example 18 occurs early on in Jewel's direct testimony as the state lawyer is questioning her about what happened before Jewel and Lacey arrived at the McDonald's on the day of the sexual assault.

(18) 8:44:40–8:44:53 (#61)

SE: What were you and Lacey going to do.
(0.2)
JL: .h Uhm: we really didn't have like a focused idea
on what we were gonna do:, **We:– (0.3) I believe we**
stopped by: a C:D store 'cause I wanted to pick up
some CDs 'cause I had just gotten paid.

Jewel begins to describe their activities using the subject pronoun "we" in line 4, but progressivity is suspended via the sound stretch, cut-off, and brief pause that follows. At this point, Jewel restarts the TCU inserting the evidential, "I believe," before producing the subject pronoun "we" again. The repaired utterance, "I believe we stopped by a CD store" (lines 4–5), provides a more qualified description of what Jewel and Lacey did on that day, compared to the utterance Jewel was presumably on her way to producing: "We stopped by a CD store."

In example 19, the state lawyer (SE) is questioning Jewel about aspects of her cross-examination, specifically, what she meant when she used the word "blunts" when the defense lawyer, Mr. Shalleck, was questioning her (lines 1–6).

(19) 11:45:58–11:46:18 (#103)

SE: .h Now: ((flipping pages)) you mentioned thuh
wo:rd when Mister Shalleck was asking you about
Maouloud and Mike smoking. I think he used thuh
word rolling (.) uh– a cigarette and you– you
mentioned something about blu:nts. What– what
does that mean Jewel,
JL: Ya– **it was like a– I think it was a** (Black n' Mild)
(0.2) .h cigar that they were putting it into.

Jewel begins to answer the question, saying "it was like a-," but her pronunciation of the indefinite article is hearably cut off (line 7). Similar to example 18, she inserts an evidential phrase as part of the repair solution – "I think it was a …." The insertion of these evidentials in both examples 18 and 19 has the effect of attenuating the certainty with which Jewel reports her knowledge about the matters being questioned (see also Wilkinson and Weatherall, 2011: 83). These self-repairs, then, function to modulate Jewel's utterances so that her formulations are consistent with the status of her knowledge; that is, she is not completely certain about "stopping by a CD store" in example 18 and what the word "blunts" means in 19. In sum, for both of our witnesses, self-repair is one means by which they accomplish the work of limiting their testimony (in terms of its content and/or its formulation) to what they know from direct experience and how definitive that first-hand knowledge is.

Heritage (2011a: 182) has argued that "the distribution of rights and responsibilities regarding what participants can accountably know, how they know it, whether they have rights to describe it, and in what terms, is directly implicated in organized practices of speaking." The examples in this section show that self-repair is one such practice of speaking, specifically, a vehicle through which participants can carefully show what they know and how they know it.

6.3.3 Conforming to constraints on asking questions

Given that courtroom interaction is organized primarily around question-answer sequences, it is perhaps not surprising that self-repairs are deployed by lawyers in a way that adheres to constraints on asking questions. While it is well known that the turn-taking system governing courtroom interaction restricts lawyers' turns-at-talk to the asking of questions (what Atkinson and Drew, (1979) termed "turn-type pre-allocation"), what is perhaps less well known is the fact there are also constraints on the *form* that lawyers' questions can take. Indeed, our next two examples show a lawyer using self-repair to modify the grammatical format of his questions in ways that seem to satisfy one such constraint, namely, a rule in the Anglo-American legal system that prohibits lawyers from asking leading questions in direct examination. While leading questions are defined in legal terms and not grammatical terms, that is, as questions that suggest a particular answer to a witness, Eades (2010: 43) points out that "they most commonly have the syntactic form of yes/no questions." Despite the fact that we have no way of definitively proving that the lawyer in examples 20 and 21 is orienting to this rule of evidence, his self-repairs do have the effect of reformulating "leading" questions so that they become less "leading."[10]

Consider example 20 below. It comes from direct examination of the accused and shows the defense lawyer (DE) questioning Maouloud about the area in the residential neighbourhood where Jewel parked her car and where the events under investigation took place.

(20) 8:45:28–8:46:01 (#117)

DE: What kind of: uh– (0.4) you parked around here.
(0.6) What–what kind of structure was–was over
here.
MB: It's a town(home) right there.
(0.5)
DE: **Were there a lotta town hou-h-how would you**
describe the: area.
MB: Uh:: (0.2) there was a lotta–it's like lil courts
you can go into (0.4) and then there's a street

tuh (lead to thuh courts) n' there's a lotta
townhouses like– (0.5) cannot say exactly how many
townhouses but there's a lotta townhouses and–
it's like uh (1.2)
DE: You been there before,
(0.3)
MB: Not really. Not–(probl'y). Prolly been there::,
(0.8) drove by there but I don't think I w'd ever
(been inside there before).

In line 6, the lawyer begins to ask a yes/no interrogative, but halts its production with a cut-off that initiates repair just before the final syllable of the word "house." The projected yes/no interrogative that was almost brought to completion is then aborted, and after a slight stumbling on the first sound ("h-"), the lawyer restarts the question with a new syntactic organization (i.e., with a WH-format: "how would you describe the: area."; lines 6–7). The repair solution, then, highlighted by the emphatic stress on its beginning, accomplishes grammatical reformatting of the question. The question that is produced via the repair, a WH-question, is more open-ended and less "leading" than the one the defense lawyer was initially formulating in that it does not "suggest" an answer to the witness, i.e., that there were "a lotta townhouses" in the area.

A similar instance of grammatical reformatting can be discerned in example 21, also from Maouloud's direct examination. Here we see Maouloud's lawyer asking whether he knew anything about what Mike and Jewel were doing in Jewel's car once Maouloud had exited it.

(21) 8:50:59–8:51:17 (#122)

DE: At any time did you–while you were:, (1.1) outside
thuh car.
MB: Mhmm.
DE: Did you he:ar any: (0.4) any– didju hear Jewel's
voice or Michael's voice at all,[11]
MB: No I didn–I didn't hear nothin'.
(0.4)
DE: Didju roll all thuh windows up before you got
outta thuh car?
MB: No I didn't.
(2.3)
DE: So Michael gets out (.) **you didn–=didju have any**
idea what they were doin' in there,
(1.4)
MB: Uh::: I had a–I–I had an idea what they w's doin'
in there.
DE: Didju see,
MB: No I didn't see but I–I kinda knew what they w's
doin' in there.

At line 12, the lawyer begins to produce what is projected as a negative declarative but abandons this formulation and restarts the TCU as an affirmative yes/no interrogative: "didju have any idea what they were doin' in there." While the preference structure of the two formulations is the same in the sense that they both prefer a "no" response (Heritage, 2010), the declarative is more leading than the interrogative because it *asserts* the proposition, as opposed to merely *interrogating* the proposition. Put in Heritage's (2010) terms, the declarative question has a shallower epistemic gradient than the interrogative, meaning that the producer of such a question projects a more "knowing" stance towards its propositional content than the producer of an interrogative. In substituting an interrogative question for a declarative question, then, the lawyer is presenting himself as less knowledgeable about Maouloud's thoughts than his projected formulation would have done. Thus, we are arguing that in examples 20–21, the defense lawyer produces questions that are less strongly suggestive of an answer (i.e., are less leading) by projecting a less "knowing" stance towards its content. And it is via the practice of self-repair that the defense lawyer alters his questions so that they satisfy the rule that prohibits leading questions in direct examination.

In considering why leading questions would serve a lawyer's strategic goals and, by extension, why the defense lawyer in examples 20 and 21 would initially formulate his questions in this way, it is helpful to consider the participation structure of trial discourse. As Drew (1985: 134) explains, while talk ostensibly occurs between witnesses and lawyers, "much of what is said in courts is designed for the benefit of recipients who are for the most part nonspeaking participants, that is, the jury." As a result, "speakers may design their utterances not only for their placement within the exchange with the other speaker but also with an eye to their effect upon and treatment by jurors." Leading questions, then, by "suggesting" answers to witnesses, allow lawyers to indicate to juries what kind of answers they expect from witnesses and, thus, what they believe the facts of a case to be. Put in a slightly different way, Woodbury (1984: 208) argues that leading questions give lawyers "a greater measure of control over how the evidence will be understood by the jury." The idea that leading questions allow lawyers to control juries' understanding of evidence is clearly related to the defense lawyer's initial formulations of questions in examples 20 and 21 (lines 6–7 and 12–13, respectively). Given that the defense lawyer must design questions that support his client's (Maouloud's) version of events, it is in his (and Maouloud's) interest that the jury understand, first, that: "there were a lotta townhouses" in the area where the events in question took place (presumably a young man would not take a woman he wanted to rape to a populated area); and, second, that: Maouloud "didn't have any idea" what was happening between Jewel and Mike when they were in the car (presumably

Maouloud's claim of consensual sex would be undermined if he had known what was happening; indeed, he could be found to be an accomplice).

6.3.4 The dual import of repair

We have argued throughout this paper that self-repair is a mechanism by which courtroom participants accomplish some of the specific tasks and constraints presented by the courtroom setting. Witnesses, for example, may use self-initiated repairs to retreat from knowledge claims based on inference or hearsay and lawyers may use them to amend utterances so that they conform to institutional norms regarding appropriate turns at talk. What we have not discussed up to this point is the possibility of self-repairs being mobilized to meet multiple interactional goals. As discussed earlier in the chapter, Jefferson (1974) talks about the potential for self-repairs to keep alternative formulations of things "on the record," given that a repair solution does not necessarily cancel out or erase the item that has been repaired. Similar claims about the dual import of self-repair can be discerned in the work of Fox et al. (1996) and Stokoe (2011). Fox et al. (1996: 216), for example, argue that self-repair does not always have the effect of correcting or replacing the trouble source; rather, they illustrate speakers in both English and Japanese making use of self-repair "to accomplish several competing interactional goals" within a single TCU. Stokoe's (2011) argument is similar: she shows how speakers can demonstrate a commitment to both formulations of a repair (i.e., the repairable item and the repair solution) such that both formulations remain "on the record" (p. 111). Below, we consider two of our previous examples in light of these claims about self-repair.

In example 22 below, originally example 15, we argued that Maouloud, through his self-repair in line 7, transforms his response into one where he is reporting on his own thoughts and desires, and not on those of Mike.

(22) 8:43:17–8:43:31 (#22)

01	DE:	Well didju tell Je:wel where you were gonna go?
02		(0.4)
03	MB:	Nah:: we didn–we didn't tell em where we gonna go
04		we w's (0.2) jus' (.) gonna go (.) s:omewhere.
05	DE:	To do what.
06		(0.4)
07	MB:	**In our-in my: mind (.) to have sex with thuh girl(s).**

While we are not retreating from this analysis, we also think it is important to consider the interactional work that the trouble source may be doing in this context. Previous research on courtroom discourse (Ehrlich, 2001) has demonstrated the way that defendants in trials can employ a variety of grammatical resources in their testimony to mitigate, diffuse, obscure, and/or eliminate their agency in relation to the criminal acts they have been accused of/charged with. Indeed, Maouloud's initial formulation in line 7 ("in our") indicates that he was on his way to doing precisely this; that is, by starting to say that having sex with the girls was something on the mind of *both* Mike and Maouloud, Maouloud "diffuses his responsibility" for the sexual acts of aggression he has been accused of (Ehrlich, 2001: 46). Thus, the self-repair in line 7 not only allows Maouloud to present himself as a careful witness – a witness that only reports on his first-hand knowledge – it also allows him to downplay his role in the sexual acts of aggression that are at issue in the trial.

Example 23, originally example 20, also illustrates the potential for a speaker's self-repair to address multiple – and competing – contingencies in the courtroom.

(23) 8:45:28–8:46:01 (#117)

DE: What kind of: uh– (0.4) you parked around here.
(0.6) What–what kind of structure was–was over
here.
MB: It's a town (home) right there.
(0.5)
DE: **Were there a lotta town hou–h–how would you**
describe the: area.
MB: Uh:: (0.2) there was a lotta–it's like lil courts
you can go into (0.4) and then there's a street
tuh (lead to thuh courts) n' there's a lotta
townhouses like– (0.5) cannot say exactly how many
townhouses but there's a lotta townhouses and–
it's like uh (1.2)
DE: You been there before,
(0.3)
MB: Not really. Not–(probl'y). Prolly been there::,
(0.8) drove by there but I don't think I w'd ever
(been inside there before).

We suggested above that the lawyer's repair in line 6 transforms a leading question into a non-leading one and thus can be understood as orienting to a rule of evidence that prohibits leading questions in direct examination. However, notice that the trouble source – "Were there a lotta town hou-" – is almost completely verbalized before it is repaired and, as such, succeeds in keeping the answer "suggested" by the leading question "on the record" for the benefit of jurors. As we argued above, this is no doubt in the defense lawyer's interest, given the inference it conveys, namely, that a highly populated residential area would not be the kind of place where two young men would take a young woman they wanted to rape. Notice also that even though the lawyer's leading question is repaired, it seems to have a second effect: in Maouloud's response to the reformatted WH-question, he states twice (with one aborted attempt) that there are "a lotta townhouses" (lines 10–12) in the area. We believe that example 23 is a particularly good example of the expansive power of self-repair. As noted above, Fox et al. (1996: 214) argue that self-repair can serve as a way of expanding a speaker's linguistic resources; more specifically, they say that self-repair can enable a speaker "to create two different syntactic projections within a single TCU that otherwise could not be 'grammatically united.'" We have not discussed our examples in terms of the expansion of *syntactic* possibilities; however, we are suggesting, like Fox et al., that because the technology of self-repair allows alternative formulations to remain "on the record," self-repair can serve as a resource for expanding the expressive possibilities available to a speaker at a given point in an interaction. Moreover, with respect to examples 22 and 23, we are arguing that both the witness and lawyer exploit the multiple linguistic resources that self-repair makes available (i.e., the trouble source and the repair solution) in order to meet the kinds of competing demands that the courtroom imposes on its participants.

6.4 Conclusion

We began this paper by noting that most research on self-repair has taken as its starting point the analysis of components and operations, and has then, at least in some cases, moved to addressing the actions accomplished in relation to these facets of repair. Following Jefferson's (1974) pioneering work on the interactional import of self-repair, we have reversed this usual trajectory by classifying self-repairs according to the actions they are used to do, regardless of their formal properties. The context of the courtroom has proved to be a useful one in which to adopt such an approach, given that it restricts the range of possible actions participants are engaged in. In this respect, our paper makes an important methodological contribution: the investigation of the interactional import of self-repair is greatly facilitated in settings where participants are demonstrably oriented to a restricted set of actions.[12] This particular approach has also been useful in revealing the range of repair operations that can be deployed in the name of single actions. That is, in altering an utterance-in-progress so that it is consistent with a preferred version of events, for example, our examples show participants reformatting, aborting, replacing, or inserting information in the service of a single interactional goal.

Like other work on institutional talk, our paper has demonstrated the way that interactional practices in institutional settings "may be shaped by reference to constraints that are goal-oriented or functional in character" (Drew and Heritage, 1992a: 23). In particular, we have shown how the practice of self-repair has been "shaped by" some of the goal-oriented constraints that the courtroom imposes on witnesses and lawyers in the context of an adversarial legal system. Within such a system, as previously discussed, two sides of an issue are presented, in part, through the testimony of witnesses and, in part, through the opening and closing statements of lawyers. Indeed, examples 9–14 have shown both witnesses and lawyers using self-repair to alter their utterances such that their side's version of events is supported; for instance, both Maouloud's and the defense lawyer's self-repairs replace a version of events that could be construed as supporting a charge of rape with one that is more compatible with the defense's claim of consensual sex. The adversarial nature of the legal system also means that much time and attention is devoted to undermining the credibility of opposing witnesses, while simultaneously bolstering the credibility of one's own witnesses. Witnesses are no doubt aware of this credibility contest, and examples 15–19 show our defendant and complainant modifying their utterances, via the practice of self-repair, in ways that enhance their credibility as careful and reliable observers. That is, in keeping with a rule of evidence that restricts the nature of witness testimony, the repair solutions in 15–19 report on what the witnesses have directly perceived or experienced as opposed to what they know based on hearsay or inference. Finally, our last two examples, 20 and 21, demonstrate one way that the practice of self-repair may be shaped by constraints on the asking of questions in the courtroom: specifically, the lawyer uses self-repair to reformat the form of his questions in ways that conform to a constraint on leading questions in direct examination. In addition to illustrating how participants conform to these various constraints – something the practice of self-repair exposes – we have also argued that the design of self-repair, in particular, its ability to keep alternative formulations "on the record," enables speakers to accomplish multiple, and potentially conflicting, tasks in the courtroom.

Overall, then, we are suggesting that in the same way that, for example, turn-taking systems can be adapted to the exigencies of institutional contexts, our examination of the interactional import of another organizational practice, self-repair, shows that it may also be adapted in accordance with institutionally specific tasks and constraints. And, while turn-taking systems may be constrained in terms of the allocation of turn-types, with respect to the practice of self-repair we want to suggest that the constraints seem to manifest themselves in terms of the *directionality* of the repair. In other words, in ordinary conversation, where Heritage (2005: 109) notes that interactional practices may be deployed "in pursuit of every imaginable social goal," speakers may repair utterances in a range of ways, for example, so that they conform to a version of events that serves their own self-interests, *or* so that they conform to a version of events that serves the interests of others. In the courtroom, however, where lawyers and witnesses must persuade a judge and/or jury that *their* version of events is the most credible, we do not find participants repairing their utterances in ways that support the opposing side's version of events. Similarly, in ordinary conversation speakers conceivably repair utterances to restrict their descriptions to what they know from first-hand experience, *or* to claim greater knowledge than they actually have (see, for example, Heritage, 2011b). And yet in the courtroom, we do not find witnesses repairing utterances so that their claims to knowledge go beyond their direct experience. Likewise, while in ordinary conversation the format of questions could presumably be repaired in a variety of ways, for example, so that they are more open-ended *or* so they are less open-ended, in direct examination, where there is a prohibition on the asking of leading questions, we do not find lawyers repairing their questions so that they are more leading. Thus, we are claiming that the directionality of self-repair in the courtroom is shaped by the kinds of actions lawyers and witnesses perform in orienting to setting-specific tasks and constraints. Of course, none of the actions we have described above are accomplished solely through the use of self-repair. Drew and Heritage's (1992b) groundbreaking collection of studies on conversation analysis and institutional talk, for example, outlines some of the dimensions of the organization of talk through which participants evoke and orient to the institutional context of their talk (e.g., lexical choice, turn design, sequence organization, overall structural organization, etc.). In this chapter, then, we have identified another feature of organization, namely, self-repair, through which participants situate themselves in relation to the tasks and constraints of institutions and, in this particular case, the courtroom.

REFERENCES

Atkinson, J. M., & Drew, P. (1979). *Order in Court: The Organisation of Verbal Interaction in Judicial Settings*. London: Macmillan.

Clayman, S. E. (forthcoming). Conversation analysis in the news interview context. In J. Sidnell and T. Stivers, eds., *The Handbook of Conversation Analysis*. Oxford: Blackwell-Wiley.

Drew, P. (1985). Analyzing the use of language in courtroom interaction. In T. van Dijk, ed., *Handbook of Discourse Analysis*, vol. III: *Discourse and Dialogue*, pp. 133–147. London: Academic Press.

(1990). Strategies in the contest between lawyer and witness in cross-examination. In J. N. Levi and A. G. Walker, eds., *Language in the Judicial Process*, pp. 39–64. New York: Plenum Press.

Drew, P. and Heritage, J. (1992a). Analyzing talk at work: an introduction. In P. Drew and J. Heritage, eds., *Talk at Work: Interaction in Institutional Settings*, pp. 1–65. Cambridge University Press.

(1992b). *Talk at Work: Interaction in Institutional Settings*. Cambridge University Press.

Eades, D. (2010). *Sociolinguistics and the Legal Process*. Buffalo, NY: Multilingual Matters.

Ehrlich, S. (2001). *Representing Rape: Language and Sexual Consent*. London: Routledge.

Fox, B. A., Hayashi, M. and Jasperson, R. (1996). Resources and repair: A cross-linguistic study of syntax and repair. In E. Ochs, E. A. Schegloff and S. A. Thompson, eds., *Interaction and Grammar*, pp. 185–237. Cambridge University Press.

Fox, B. A., Maschler, Y., and Uhmann, S. (2009). Morpho-syntactic resources for the organization of same-turn self-repair: Cross-linguistic variation in English, German and Hebrew. *Gesprächsforschung* 10: 245–291.

Galatolo, R. (2007). Active voicing in court. In E. Holt and R. Clift, eds., *Reporting Talk: Reported Speech in Interaction*, pp. 195–220. Cambridge University Press.

Garfinkel, H. (1974). The origins of the term "ethnomethodology." In R. Turner, ed., *Ethnomethodology: Selected Readings*, pp. 15–18. Harmondsworth: Penguin Books.

Heritage, J. (2005). Conversation analysis and institutional talk. In K. L. Fitch and R. E. Sanders, eds., *Handbook of Language and Social Interaction*, pp. 103–147. Mahwah, NJ: Lawrence Erlbaum.

(2010). Questioning in medicine. In A. F. Freed and S. Ehrlich, eds., *'Why Do You Ask?': The Function of Questions in Institutional Discourse*, pp. 42–68. New York: Oxford University Press.

(2011a). Territories of knowledge, territories of experience: empathic moments in interaction. In T. Stivers, L. Mondada and J. Steensig, eds., *The Morality of Knowledge in Conversation*, pp. 159–183. Cambridge University Press.

(2011b). The epistemic engine: sequence organization and territories of knowledge. *Research on Language and Social Interaction* 45: 25–50.

Jefferson, G. (1974). Error correction as an interactional resource. *Language in Society* 2: 181–199.

Labov, W. and Fanshel, D. (1977). *Therapeutic Discourse: Psychotherapy as Conversation*. New York: Academic Press.

Lerner, G. (1996). On the "semi-permeable" character of grammatical units in conversation: conditional entry into the turn space of another speaker. In E. Ochs, E. A. Schegloff and S. A. Thompson, eds., *Interaction and Grammar*, pp. 238–276. Cambridge University Press.

Lerner, G. and Kitzinger, C. (2007). Extraction and aggregation in the repair of individual and collective self-reference. *Discourse Studies* 9(4): 526–557.

(2010). Repair prefacing: preparing the way for same-turn self-repair. Paper presented at the International Conference on Conversation Analysis. Mannheim, Germany.

Philips, S. U. (1992). Evidentiary standards for American trials: just the facts. In J. H. Hill and J. T. Irvine, eds., *Responsibility and Evidence in Oral Discourse*, pp. 248–259. Cambridge University Press.

Pomerantz, A. M. (1980). Telling my side: "Limited access" as a "fishing device." *Sociological Inquiry* 50: 186–198.

Raymond, G. (2003). Grammar and social organization: yes/no interrogatives and the structure of responding. *American Sociological Review* 68(6): 939–967.

(1984). On doing "being ordinary." In J. M. Atkinson and J. Heritage, eds., *Structures of Social Action: Studies in Conversation Analysis*, pp. 413–429. Cambridge University Press.

Sacks, H. (1995 [1965–1968]). *Lectures on Conversation*, vols. I and II. Oxford: Blackwell.

Schane, S. (2006). *Language and the Law*. London: Continuum.

Schegloff, E. A. (n.d. a). *Doing Inserting*. UCLA.

(n.d. b). *The Technology of Self-Initiated, Same-Turn Repair*. UCLA.

Schegloff, E. A., Jefferson, G. and Sacks, H. (1977). The preference for self-correction in organization of repair in conversation. *Language* 53(2): 361–382.

Schulhofer, S. (1998). *Unwanted Sex: The Culture of Intimidation and the Failure of Law*. Cambridge, MA: Harvard University Press.

Sidnell, J. (2010). *Conversation Analysis: An Introduction*. Oxford: Blackwell-Wiley.

Stivers, T. and Rossano, F. (2010). Mobilizing response. *Research on Language and Social Interaction* 43(1): 3–31.

Stokoe, E. (2011). "Girl – woman – sorry!": On the repair and non-repair of consecutive gender categories. In S. A. Speer and E. Stokoe, eds., *Conversation and Gender*, pp. 85–111. Cambridge University Press.

Wilkinson, S., and Weatherall, A. (2011). Insertion repair. *Research on Language and Social Interaction* 44(1): 65–91.

Woodbury, H. (1984). The strategic use of questions in court. *Semiotica* 48(3–4): 197–228.

NOTES

1 We note that the Court of Special Appeals remarked in its opinion that the accused's testimony "was surprisingly consistent" with the complainant's (Maouloud Baby v. State of Maryland, Court of Special Appeals of Maryland, 2005).

2 Michael Wilson did not have a trial as he pleaded guilty to his charges.

3 An important aspect of rape law reform in the United States has been the requirement in many states that consent be "affirmatively" and "freely-given" (Schulhofer, 1998). Indeed, the rape statute in Maryland defines consent in precisely this way: consent is "actually agreeing to the act of intercourse" as opposed to "merely submitting as a result of force or threat of force." That is, agreement that is coerced as a result of force or the fear of force is not deemed to be consent in Maryland, nor in many other American states.

4 Both the complainant's and defendant's testimony lasted approximately two hours each (roughly 1 hour of direct examination and one hour of cross-examination each), and the lawyers' opening statements lasted approximately forty-five minutes while closing statements lasted over three hours. All instances of self-repair involving the operation of recycling (whereby speakers say again some stretch of talk that was just said) were excluded from our collection either because their occurrence could be explained by turn-taking considerations (i.e., the recycling emerges as a surviving turn from overlap) or because their occurrence could not be explained in terms of interactional import (see Schegloff, this volume).

5 The facts that are corrected via self-repair in examples 5–9 are those that were uncontested in the trial.

6 It is possible that self-repair has not generally been the focus of previous work on courtroom discourse (e.g., Atkinson and Drew 1979), because it has relied

on official court transcripts for data. Presumably, most instances of self-repair would be heard as mere perturbations in the talk, and as a result "cleaned up" in the process of producing such transcripts.

7 In terms of grammatical and thematic relations, Maouloud is the grammatical subject and agent of the transitive verb "put" (with Jewel as the object and the affected participant of the verb) in the trouble source, whereas Maouloud is absent (with Jewel as the subject and experiencer of the intransitive predicate, "go through") in the repair solution.

8 We are grateful to Celia Kitzinger for helping us to clarify this important point.

9 Of course, these kinds of examples are not restricted to courtroom talk, as is illustrated by the excerpt from "ordinary" talk below, where Madge repairs her utterance so that she is only reporting on her own (but not also on Bea's) experiences of car wrecks.

['Being ordinary' Sacks (1984: 424)]

01	Mad:	Ruth Henderson and I drove down, to, Ventura
02		yesterday.
03	Bea:	Mm hm,
04	Mad:	And on the way home we saw the– most gosh awful
05		wreck.
06	Bea:	Oh:::
07	Mad:	**we have ev– I've ever** seen. I've never seen a car
08		smashed into sm– such a small space.

Such examples suggest that the rule of evidence restricting lay witnesses' testimony to that which they have experienced first-hand may be a variant of a more general norm of social interaction. (See Pomerantz (1980) and Sacks (1995) for elaboration.) Indeed, consistent with Garfinkel's (1974) observations about juries, the fact that witnesses can conduct themselves in institutionally relevant ways with respect to this rule of evidence (and without any special training) is one indication that the "hearsay rule" may be an instantiation of a more general rule of ordinary conversation. We are grateful to Jack Sidnell for bringing this example to our attention and for alerting us to the connection between the "hearsay rule" and social interaction more generally.

10 That lawyers can be sanctioned for asking leading questions in direct examination is illustrated in the example below. Here the state lawyer is questioning the complainant during redirect examination about her motivations for allowing Maouloud "to take his turn." The initial question posed by the lawyer, "Did you think that if you: (.) allowed that to happen then you would be able to leave and go home" (lines 2–3), is a yes/no interrogative composed of a compound TCU (i.e., an "if-then" construction; see Lerner 1996) with the suggested answer formulated in the "then" clause: Jewel allowed Maouloud "to take his turn" because *then … [she] … would be able to leave and go home*. This question is objected to by the defense on the grounds that it is "leading". The judge ratifies this objection (line 5), thereby forcing the state lawyer to reformulate the question. She recasts it as a WH-question (i.e., a more open-ended kind of question) and, in so doing, does not "suggest" an answer to the complainant.

[11:53:15-11:53:43 (#193)]

SE: And so by thuh time Maouloud got back in thuh car:,
and you said– and– and he said to you. (.) "Are you
gonna let me have my turn." (1.0) Did you think that
if you: (.) allowed that to happen then you would be
able to leave and go home.
DE: Objection your Honour. Leading.
JL: Sustained as leading.
SE: What did you think Jewel would ha:ppen if you let him
(.) do it at that poi:nt,

11 Although self-repair also occurs in the course of this yes/no interrogative (lines 4–5), it does not alter the form of the question (i.e., the question remains a yes/no interrogative), nor does it alter the question's preference structure (i.e., the question prefers a "no" response in both formulations). Thus, the interactional import of this repair is different from the examples we focus on in examples 20 and 21.

12 We owe this observation to Celia Kitzinger.

7 Defensive mechanisms: I-mean-prefaced utterances in complaint and other conversational sequences

Douglas W. Maynard

Defense mechanisms, in Sigmund Freud's (1915 [1961]: 126–127; 1926 [1961]: 163–164) famous approach, are the means by which an ego handles its motive forces or instincts, especially of a sexual kind. In a more contemporaneous view (Fenichel 1945; Baumeister, Dale, and Sommer, 1998), defense mechanisms are the means by which self-esteem is protected. In either case, these mechanisms are powerful intrapsychic phenomena that ward off unwanted thoughts and feelings from conscious processing in the individual. This chapter, reflecting a scholarly orientation in conversation analysis to *overt* mechanisms and orientations in action and interaction, is an investigation of the practices by which participants defend stances of social rather than psychological consequence, where the incursions that are anticipated and blocked are not those potentially emanating from the individual but rather from the other. It turns out that particular I-mean-prefaced utterances (IMPUs, for short) in conversation[1] overwhelmingly appear in the context of complaint-type sequences to explicate those complaints in a defensive manner. The overall purpose of this paper is to distinguish and examine the interactional circumstances of this defensiveness, including the mechanisms by which it is achieved, and to answer the question of what kind of work IMPUs do in relation to complaints as a type of social action. I will also address three related issues.

The first issue about IMPUs is their formatting (the use of I-mean) and their sequential placement. The utterances with which I am working, by virtue of this formatting and placement, have at least the appearance of being self-

I wish to thank Elizabeth Weathersbee and Matt Hollander for able research assistance in the early stages of this project. Financial support was provided by two grants from the Wisconsin Alumni Research Foundation. I was able to devote substantial effort to the project during the fall of 2006 while visiting in the Department of Sociology at Helsinki University in Finland as a Fulbright Scholar. I am particularly grateful to Ansii Peräkylä (as faculty host) and the community of conversation analysts in Finland for invaluable feedback at data sessions and presentations. The paper benefited from discussions at a "Workshop on Repair," organized by Jack Sidnell and Tanya Stivers, at the University of Toronto in March 2008. Ceci Ford and Geoff Raymond offered invaluable comments on a previous draft of the chapter.

repair, and, more specifically "transition-space" self-repair. So the paper begins with a consideration of self-repair. Later I will address whether these utterances are "real" or "virtual" or only "boundary" cases of repair. The upshot is that, insofar as repair – or in this case a repair-formatted utterance – "supercedes other actions" (Schegloff, 1997a: 208), it exerts a kind of "immensely powerful privilege" on behalf of the complaining action that a speaker is producing and can prevail to elicit alignment from a recipient to that action.

The second issue is the linkage between these IMPUs and the complaints they explicate. In environments where recipients appear to resist a complaining turn of talk, IMPUs work to defend the complaints with accounts that encourage acknowledgment, confirmation, agreement, affiliation and other aligning types of responses to complaints. However, IMPUs also appear in environments where alignment is unproblematic. In these cases, IMPUs defend not so much the content or understandability of the complaint as they preserve the speaker's right to finish off a complaining action. Using this practice, speakers recontextualize the complaining action so far to provide for its just-now completion and therefore implicative thrust for recipient appreciation. More specifically, IMPUs can skip-tie to a previous utterance of the speaker and sequentially delete or at least disattend either a silence or a recipient's claim to a turn that had followed the previous utterance.

A third issue is that, although IMPUs appear overwhelming in the context of complaint sequences, they can manage other types of sequences or actions as well. That is, IMPUs can work to defuse inapposite actions, ones that, although not doing complaining, share a property with complaints, which is that they may be *complainable* in their own right. In working this way, IMPUs are fundamental to sustaining the social organization of courses of interaction that co-participants engage in assembling. It is in this sense that defensive mechanisms are social rather than psychological phenomena.

7.1 Repair organization

Before getting to the collection of IMPUs with which I'm concerned, a review of some features of self-initiated repair will help to both characterize and distinguish this collection. Self-initiated repairs appear in three main places relative to their trouble source or item they propose to fix. The first place is within the same turn as that trouble source, but I am not concerned with same-turn repair because these often are a means of completing an utterance with a particular operation such as replacing, inserting, searching and others that revise the turn (Schegloff, 2008; this volume). A subsequent place for self-initiated repair is the transition space, as that occurs upon the possible completion of a turn of talk. Here is an example of transition-space use of I-mean:

01) From Schegloff, Jefferson, and Sacks (1977: 364)

N: She was givin me a:ll the people that were go:ne this yea:r I mean this quarter y'know

While the IMPUs with which I am concerned reside in the place where transition-space repair occurs, when they are clearly doing correction – as in example 1, where the IMPU replaces "year" in the original utterance with "quarter" – and are often not grammatically complete on their own, such items utterances are excluded from my collection.

A variation on transition-space self-initiated repair is what Schegloff (1997b) calls "third turn repair." The reason for considering third turn repair as nevertheless in transition space is that, after the turn with the trouble source, the recipient produces a token such as a continuer like "mm hmm." And this is more like a "quasi-turn" (Schegloff 1997b: 33) that passes up any opportunity to display trouble with hearing or understanding the turn to which it responds:

(02) SBL 1:1:12:10 (from Schegloff 1997b: 32)

01 B: hhh And he's g:oing to make his own paintings,
02 A: Mm hmmm
03 B: And– or I mean his own frames.
04 A: Yeah

In this extract, "frames" is a correction for "paintings." Once again, these kinds of particularized corrections – what Schegloff et al. (1977: 370) call "word replacement" – are not included in my IMPU collection. However, third turn repair also can follow turns that are more than "quasi," where the intervening talk is still rather brief and regularly the second turn is incidental to the development of the talk. The third turn repair is just like transition-space repair in initiating self-repair as soon as possible after the turn with the trouble-source (Schegloff, 1997b: 35). So also third turn IMPUs are relevant to my analysis.

This brings us to third *position* repair, which occurs when the recipient of speaker's first turn does display a problematic understanding of it. (They are called third position repairs because they follow a turn (second position) subsequent to the trouble-source turn (first position) and because they sometimes can be displaced (delayed by intervening talk) relative to the turn that is proposed to have misunderstood the first turn.) The speaker suggests repair on this misunderstanding through a regular form, "No, I don't mean X, I mean Y" (Schegloff, 1992, 1997b). An I-mean utterance is usually the last component of this form.

We now have some leverage to describe IMPUs that occur relative to complaint and related social actions. Previous treatments of "I-mean" utterances often do not distinguish the very different sequential positions in which these utterances can occur, implicitly suggesting that "mean" or "I mean" has some inherent sense and/or semantic function apart from the particularities of its placement relative to other utterances and who (in terms of discourse identity as speaker or recipient of an initial action), for example, is producing those utterances.[2] The collection of IMPUs with which I'm working overwhelmingly includes transition-space self-repair (including third turn repairs). In addition, considering examples 1 and 2, these IMPUs are not correcting some misspoken word by replacing it. Nor do the IMPUs in my collection appear to be doing any of the other eight or so "operations" that Schegloff (2008) has explored, for example, with respect to self-initiated, same-turn repair. Rather, in explicating the complaint or other action they follow, and doing so relatively immediately, they are doing something more global with respect to the first turn. However, we can note a curiosity about the use of "I mean" for these complaint-subsequent utterances. Where, for example, Schegloff (1992: 1310) has noted that "I mean" is the most common formatting and "repair marker" for third position repair, and thus can be a canonical indicator,[3] the IMPUs in my collection, as already indicated, are questionable as to whether and how they are doing repair. This issue will be lurking in the background as we explore fragments containing the IMPUs.

7.2 Complaint sequences

Complaining in conversation has been subject to several disparate analyses including those in a recent special issue of *Journal of Pragmatics*, edited by Heinemann and Traverso (2009). Schegloff (1988: 120–122) has suggested that complaining often consists of noticing a "negative" event. An example of this is "formulating a failure," as in one occupant of a dormitory room saying to a returnee, "You didn't get an ice cream sandwich." Such an utterance is the first part of a complaining adjacency pair (Drew, 1998; Schegloff, 1988), and it occasions the relevance of a responsive second to the complaint – a remedy, account, excuse, or the like. When complaints are directed outward – toward circumstances or third parties – and not toward the recipient, acknowledgment and agreement are the occasioned responses.[4] The interactionally preferred second pair part to a complaint is some kind of aligning as opposed to misaligning response.

In that complaining can involve formulations of transgression, expressions of moral indignation, and descriptions of deliberateness (Drew, 1998), it is related to criticizing, accusing, and other conversational actions. Stated differently, there are different kinds of complaining actions in that one or both participants may complain about their jointly experienced circumstances, co-participants may complain about some third party in a gossipy kind of way, one participant may engage in troubles talk to another, or one may be accusatory about that other's conduct (Heinemann and Traverso, 2009). In examining these different kinds of complaint sequences, a caveat is that they are not rigid classifications (Ruusuvuori and Lindfors, 2009: 2415). There can be overlap among them. Recognizing that it is difficult technically to define or differentiate these actions, I may use such terminology as criticizing and accusing from time to time when it seems appropriate to the data.

The matter of complaints being the first part of a complaining adjacency pair is also complex. In this paper, I mostly am considering complaints as initiating actions, but of course complaints also can be responsive – for example, they can be used to agree or disagree with a speaker's prior turn. Moreover, there can be an identifiable four-part stage-like structure to complaining (Traverso, 2009) and, as Drew and Walker (2009) recently have shown, complaints generally can be part of a series in which co-participants collaborate in an overall, step-by-step, course of action in which a complaint recipient may escalate in a way that the speaker resists. For my purposes, it is important to be aware that some conversations turn out to be constituted by prolonged episodes of complaining and complaining back so that, when examining a particular instance or sequence of complaint, it becomes difficult to track who is the initiator and who is the respondent in the overall course of action. Nevertheless, across sequences at different points in a complaint series, practices associated with the use of IMPUs have generic defense-oriented features.

7.3 IMPUs in relation to other pursuits of alignment

A main interactional effect that IMPUs can have is to pursue aligning uptake relative to the complaints they accompany. They work to avoid displays of misalignment by recipients, including resistive silences and the like, by practices that retrospectively propose to constitute responses so far from recipients as incidental to the development of a complaint-in-progress. In this regard, as we will see, they are a little like, and in fact often accompany, the idiomatic expressions that Drew and Holt (1988) have studied, finding that participants use idioms, as formulaic and non-literal expressions, in environments of talk where recipients withhold or can be anticipated to withhold sympathizing or affiliating with a complaint or complainant. Idioms summarize the complaining in a way that solicits alignment and proposes to close the activity of complaining.

IMPUs may enhance this feature of the idiomatic expression. In the conversation from which example 3 is taken, and which Drew and Holt (1988: 401) analyze for its idiom at line 6, Emma has been complaining about and criticizing a hotel at which she and her husband Bud had stayed when the latter was attending a golfing event. In particular, when they went to breakfast, there were "only about two people to help." Emma continues her complaining and criticizing at lines 1–3, which depicts how Bud had to leave before being served, such that she gave away his breakfast.

(03) NB:IV:10:18 (24)

Emm:	Bud couldn't e:ven eat his breakfast. He o:rdered he
	waited forty five minutes'n he'a:dtuh be out there tuh
	tee off so I gave it to uh: (.) Karen's: liddle bo:y.
	(0.7)
Emm:	((swallow)) I mean that's how bad the service was .hhh
	(.) It's gone tuh pot.
Lot:	°u–Oh*:::° (.) e–[Y_e_:_:_ a h .]Ye<]
Emm:	[°But it's a° be] auti]ful ↓go:lf
	↓°c*ourse.°
	(0.9)
Lot:	Oh: ye:ah gee:

Then, at line 4, there is a silence, indicating Lottie's refraining from any kind of sympathetic or other uptake. While Drew and Holt focus on the idiomatic expression at line 6, of further note is the interjection of an IMPU at line 5, which, with its "how bad" assessment, itself summarizes and explicates the complaint and criticism before the line 6 idiom. Notice that the in-breath at the end of line 5 and micropause at the start of line 6 exhibit lack of uptake at that point, which suggests that the IMPU is an initial but unsuccessful pursuit of alignment subsequent to the line 4 silence. It is then (after line 5) that Emma deploys the idiom (line 6), whereupon Lottie registers the complaint in line 7 with a kind of laconic news-mark (spoken with scratchy voice and quieted volume) and agreement tokens.[5] Thus, Lottie (line 7) firstly treats lines 5–6 as news and then shows alignment with her stretched "yeah." The idiomatic expression, as part of Emma's IMPU (despite the in-breath and micropause, it continues the turn), and the repair formatting and overall reconstruction together elicit Lottie's displayed change of state and subsequent agreement. In a sense, the I-mean preface backdates the turn at lines 5–6 to suggest that these characterizations of "service" at the restaurant are what the complaining has been about all along.[6]

A possibility this extract raises is that the IMPU is a milder way of soliciting alignment to complaint-relevant talk than the idiomatic expression. As Drew and Holt (1988) observe, idioms are related to "extreme case formulations" (Pomerantz, 1986), putting things in egregious terms and being figurative expressions that are somewhat invulnerable to critique. Emma's IMPU at line 5 references "how bad the service was" on a particular occasion; as an assessment, it retains the concreteness of the original complaint, whereas "it's gone to pot" is a more generalized evaluation.

There is more to be said about this example and the IMPU it contains, and we will return to it. In the meantime, to further explore the facet of IMPUs as pursuing alignment, it is useful to distinguish these utterances from other ways in which speakers work to obtain such uptake to particular social actions.

7.3.1 *Subsequent versions*

In two papers that examine what she calls "subsequent versions" to invitations, offers, requests, and the like, Davidson (1984: 107; 1990) shows that when such actions meet with potential or actual rejection, a speaker may review the utterance for its inadequacies or sources of its unacceptability. Then the speaker may "produce some revision, modification, addition, 'correction,' etc. of the original invitation or offer" (Davidson 1990: 153).

Two things distinguish IMPUs in complaint sequences from Davidson's phenomena. First, in dealing with invitations, offers, and requests, Davidson (1984: 107; 1990) analyzes what can be called "prosocial" or positive activities that are, in conversation analytic terms, "preferred" actions, done with relatively little hesitation, circumlocution, or other accompaniments. The actions are not dispreferred or possibly "antisocial" or negative actions such as complaints and criticisms. Second, a search through Davidson's (1984: 107, 1990) examples suggests that such preferred social actions can be modified and embellished in various ways but do not need defending as such. That is, offers, invitations, and the like are revised with subsequent versions that are unmarked additions to the original rather than marked, defensive accountings or explications as such.[7] Moreover, while subsequent versions provide a "next place" for recipient response (Davidson 1984: 105), an IMPU's connection to a component of complaining that it follows suggests that upon completion of the IMPU a complaint is only then complete enough for recipient response. That is, in the face of apparent withholding on the part of a complaint recipient (as at line 4 in extract 3), a subsequent IMPU can propose that a response is not absent but merely dependent on sufficient explication of an in-progress complaining action by its speaker. Rather than a next place for response, the IMPU provides a first place because the complaining action is just now complete.

7.3.2 *Pursuing a response*

Davidson draws upon Pomerantz's (1984b) investigation of how speakers pursue responses when they have produced assertions that meet with silence or other forms of resistance. Speakers do so by reviewing an assertion for the source of trouble and displaying facets of this review as they propose to solve the trouble in various ways. One way is through clarification, as when the referent of a term is unclear, which involves canonical repair. Another way is by "checking presumed common knowledge," as by going through a narrative recounting of the "facts" of some event or proposed event to evoke the recipient's understanding, which is also a matter of repair.

A third way of pursuing a response, particularly relevant to the topic of complaining, is by changing one's position. An example (Pomerantz, 1984b: 159–161) involves a speaker who, with another member of a social club, is selling fruitcakes as a fundraising activity, and engages in a criticism of their customers for being rather cheap. When the other member is silent after hearing this criticism, the speaker takes a turn of talk and utterly reverses her position. By way of contrast with this kind of pursuit of response, I-mean-prefaced accompaniments to complaints either sustain the speaker's original position or exacerbate the complaining. Overall, in my data there are two patterns to the complaining actions that culminate with IMPUs:

Pattern 1: Complaint specificity and detail + IMPU that summarizes the complaint
Pattern 2: Complaint summary + IMPU providing specificity and detail

In example 3, Emma's "I mean that's how bad the service was" and idiomatic extreme case formulation ("it's gone to pot"), given that they follow a listing of problems, fit Pattern 1, where the speaker has provided a kind of complaining narrative (see also examples 4 and 10 below). Pattern 2 may predominate where a speaker is responding to another's telling, as in examples 6, 7 or 8 below. With either Pattern 1 or Pattern 2, the IMPU preserves rather than alters the overall complaining course of action a speaker is prosecuting.

7.3.3 Linguistic forms and pursuing alignment

An approach to pursuing response that focuses on the grammar of turns is to be found in Ford's (1993) study of turn extensions and the ways that speakers use them to handle lack of recipient uptake. Turn extensions, including prepositional phrases, adverbial noun phrases, and adverbial clauses are "increments" (nonmain-clause continuations after possible points of turn completion) that secure recipient response – gaze as well as verbal tokens – for a variety of utterances pursuing social actions. Extensions have in common with IMPUs that they are not starting something new, and instead are continuing what was just said. However, whereas extensions grammatically could have occurred as constituents of the turns to which they are subsequent (Ford et al., 2002: 25), IMPUs overwhelmingly are grammatically independent of the complaints they follow, as when Emma in example 6, after criticizing the breakfast situation she and her husband experienced, says, "I mean that's how bad the service was."

Different from increments are what Ford et al. (2002) call unattached noun phrases (NPs), which are grammatically independent assessments, evaluations, or other summary devices that display a stance toward some referent in prior talk (such as a storytelling or news announcement).[8] Although NPs, like increments or turn extensions, provide second opportunities for an aligning uptake when a turn has already reached possible completion, they are syntactically independent of the prior turn *and* "display an assessment or stance with respect to the referent" (Ford et al., 2002: 30), virtually modeling a position for the recipient to take up. Once again we can compare IMPUs. Like unattached NPs, they are grammatically independent of the preceding, and they can be in pursuit of alignment. However, when IMPUs follow complaints, they are adding to actions that already embody the speaker's stance – their critical assessment of some person, experience, or situation. IMPUs defend a stance previously exhibited, as when Emma (in the way that fits Pattern 1 tells about the breakfast at the hotel as having "only about two people to help ... with all these guys gonna play golf," characterizes the golfers (in an unnoticed pun) as "all teed off," states that her husband couldn't eat his breakfast after waiting for forty-five minutes, and reports giving away the breakfast. "I mean that's how bad the service was" may articulate a stance in different words from the complaining, but that stance as a critical evaluation was clearly articulated in the previous complaining.

To summarize the foregoing: I-mean-prefaced utterances often cluster in complaint-type sequences and thereby are different from the subsequent versions added to the prosocial preferred social actions that Davidson (1984, 1990) studies. And, unlike the pursuits that Pomerantz (1984b) discusses, they do not involve reviews of the assertions they follow in such a way as to clarify or fill in background knowledge in a technically reparative way. Nor do they involve a change in position. Instead, IMPUs sustain and even exacerbate the complaints they follow. Finally, in linguistic terms, IMPUs largely are not syntactic constituents of speakers' prior turns. Rather they consist in unattached sentences and noun phrases that are grammatically independent although, crucially and something *like* constituents or increments, speakers build them and recipients treat them as continuations of previous complaining turns. Thus, IMPUs also suggest a possible incompleteness to initial components of complaints. Rather than providing a next place for response, they propose a freshly unique opportunity for recipient alignment with a designed, just-now completeness to the complaint.

7.4 I-Mean-prefaced utterances in pursuit of alignment

When complaints occur in contexts where recipients are silent or give other indications of resistance to the complaint, IMPUs suggest closure to the sequence in a conjunctive way – that is, not just providing a next component but rather an explicative completion to what has so far been said. In example 3, it is after Emma's summarizing IMPU that there is alignment by Lottie and a change of topic. Another example of pursuing alignment to complaining is in the example below, which also shows that speakers may employ more than one IMPU in the effort. Leslie is talking with her mother, who asks her about whether she had hosted her mother-in-law, Mrs. Field, that evening. Leslie answers this question in a narrative way, starting with a report that she "went to see her," and "there's hardly anything the matter with her," continuing with story components about the doctor calling on Mrs. Field and not giving her an antibiotic but only a cough mixture, and the mother-in-law being in bed for a week, and that she "won't get up." Additionally, Leslie had gone shopping for her "and so on," and prepared her dinner. Mum's responses to Leslie's rather animated pronouncements are weak and distanced from the outset of Leslie's complaining.

Accordingly, after the component about getting the "dinner ready" (line 1), there is a 1.1 second silence (line 2). Then Leslie continues (lines 3–5) with a narrative and animation of what her mother-in-law "said."

(04) Holt 1.1: 7 [2] (modified)

01	Les:		A:nd uh so on an:d (0.3) an' I: got her dinner ready:?
02			(1.1)
03	Les:		But uhm (0.2) .hh she said oh I did think'v getting up
04			t'da:y .hh b't– (0.3) i–the o:ld lady nex'door said
05			(.) do:n't get up you're t:↑oo:: wea:-:-:k.h (.) hh
06			huh ↑huh .u
07			(.)
08	Les:		↑SO[SHE STAYED in BED again all day. ((smile voice))
09	Mum:		[(Ah–)
10	Mum:		W'l was that toda::y?
11	Les:		No that wz yesterday.
12			(1.8)
13	Les:	–>	But ↓really: (.) I mean: talk abou:t making the best'v
14			it,h
15			(1.3)
16	Les:	–>	I m'n th'z ha:rdly anything th'matter with'er.
17			(.)
18	Mum:		No:. ( ),
19			(0.7)
20	Mum:		Ah well– (0.2) y'won't cure'er ↓now love it's too late

Les: No an'she wz ever so na:sty tuh Mark when'ee ca:lled
l[as'week]
Mum: [Was she]:?
Les: Oh: ↓yes

Embedded in this reported speech is a quotation of the "old lady nex'door's" talk, and here Leslie's utterance exhibits a mimicking and parodying or mocking stance. At line 5, she raises her tone on the "too," emphasizes and stretches that word and the subsequent "weak." As Couper-Kuhlen (1996: 390) has suggested, speakers can engage in prosodic parody by modifying the register of reported speech to depart from the speaker's own and to match that of the reported speaker.[9] Of course, Couper-Kuhlen's data (1996) have quoted utterances that are adjacent to, and therefore can be compared directly with, those on which they are based, while here the reported speech is twice removed from its original source (Leslie is animating a quotation from her mother-in-law, who had reported on her neighbor's speech), and there is no recording of the source with which to strike a measured comparison. However, the device of raising register of the reported speech (in a way that contrasts with the reporter's own) appears to work in a similarly mocking way, and Leslie also appends tokens that would suggest "laughing-at" (Glenn, 1995; Jefferson, 1979) this quoted advice of the neighbor lady.

Mum, however, neither takes up this possible laughter invitation nor shows any other appreciation of the story. Following a micropause (line 7), Leslie with elevated volume and smile voice produces a further, recompleting punchline to the story (line 8). At another point (line 10) where story appreciation is due, Mum receives this punchline by asking a factual question about the timing of the event – a prototypical way of resisting or disattending a complaint (Mandelbaum, 1991/1992; Traverso, 2009: 2393). And, after Leslie's answer (line 11), there is another silence and still no uptake on this complaining line of talk. Leslie goes on with what may be a form for storytellers to re-mark their own – in this case, somewhat astonished – stance toward a story, "But really" (line 13). Following that, and a micropause, she produces a Pattern 1 IMPU offering an idiomatic form of ironic commentary ("talk abou:t making the best'v it," also lines 13–14), achieved in part by placement of the idiom immediately after details that would support a contrasting assessment (Clift, 1999). This also meets with silence (line 15), and then (line 16) Leslie offers a second IMPU ("I m'n th'z ha:rdly anything th'matter with'er"), an advertence to the gloss with which she started her complaint and criticism, and a more literal version summarizing it. With this "return to the beginning," Leslie can be offering to close the sequence and implicating ever more strongly a preferred type of response – sympathetic alignment – from Mum. However, Mum at line 18 replies with minimal confirmation ("No:") that precedes something indecipherable on the recording, and she follows with a token at 20 ("Ah well") that can project a "doesn't matter" kind of stance,[10] after which she provides an exhibit of understanding in an aphoristic form that also represents a much blander stance than Leslie's. Thus, for whatever reason, from the outset Mum appears disinclined to fully subscribe to Leslie's complaining talk, but the IMPUs do succeed in extracting a measured form of alignment. At the same time, they help bring this set of complaints to a close. Leslie at 21 confirms the aphorism, and then starts up a different complaint about her mother-in-law, thereby offering a step-wise shift in topic.[11]

An issue this extract raises is what the exact work of the I-mean preface is in the two utterances where Leslie deploys it. After all, as Jefferson (1978: 233) has shown, "the relationship of a story to subsequent talk is negotiated between teller and recipients," and a "teller will search for ways to elicit recipient talk" when it is withheld upon story completion. And her examples have speakers using story components without an I-mean preface. An initial observation is that Jefferson (1978) was not studying complaint-type stories per se. In instances where stories do embody complaining, as in example 4, the suggestion is that, when the storytelling lacks for recipient uptake, a main task of I-mean prefaces is to conjoin or interlock details of the complaint – the components of the storytelling – with their gloss in a specific way. The I-mean defends the complaining against the lack of recipient alignment by suggesting that what so far may have been tacitly available simply requires some summary or idiom for its full understandability. The utterances "I mean that's how bad the service was, it's gone to pot" in example 3, "I mean talk about making the best of it," and "I mean there's hardly anything the matter with her" in example 4, in other words, represent summarizing statements that retrospectively connect to the preceding, detailed complaining and bring it to a point where recipient appreciation is by now due where it wasn't necessary before.

IMPUs thus conjoin in a particular way to a speaker's statements of complaint that they follow. To put further flesh on this conjunctive quality of IMPUs, we can now turn our attention to their use after a recipient, instead of withholding response, produces an utterance aligning to a speaker's complaint.

7.5 I-mean-prefaced utterances in the context of alignment

In his lectures on "tying" and how pro-terms (including pronouns and pro-verbs) accomplish the task of relating one utterance to another, usually on a turn-by-turn contiguous basis, Sacks (1992: 718–720) discusses I-mean utterances as tying not to an immediately previous utterance but rather to one that is prior to the previous. That is, I-mean utterances can "skip-tie":

(05) From Sacks (1992: 720)

01 A: It's not hard enough
02 B: Age before beauty?
03 A: I mean strong enough

According to Sacks (1992: 720), the use of I-mean is to "signal" explication or clarification of something in the utterance to which the current turn is being tied. In the extract above, in that the trouble source is in A's initial turn, and B takes a next turn that may be predicated on erroneous talk in A's prior, A's clarification ("I mean strong enough") is an instance of third position repair (Schegloff 1992).[12] Important for our purposes is how the I-mean, in Sacks's (1992: 734) words "locates 'last utterance by same speaker.'" Crucially, skip-tying permits a speaker to avoid the usual constraint, described by Sacks, Schegloff, and Jefferson (1974: 728), requiring a display of understanding in current turn of the previous turn of talk: "a turn's talk will be heard as directed to a prior turn's talk, unless special techniques are used to locate some other talk to which it is directed." This skip-tying property can shed more light on I-mean-prefaced utterances occurring in the context of complaints, and specifically the way that they may sequentially delete and thereby disattend just what has transpired immediately before the IMPU. Here we turn to instances in which alignment to a speaker's complaint is unproblematic. These are environments in which co-participants display similar, aligning views regarding a complainable object, person, or situation. Still, the IMPUs can be said to be defensive in that they vie for explicating the speaker's complaint rather than ceding turns and topic to a recipient.

7.5.1 Using I-mean to complete a complaint

Prior to the next example, Sally and Judy have been discussing an acquaintance, Vickie, with whom Sally has been "really having problems," and who, as Sally tells Judy, announced to Sally in a conversation from the previous day that her mother "is terminal." Judy, however, rejects the newsworthiness of this report by saying, "Yeah but we knew that before," thereby claiming prior knowledge about the situation. Sally, in a sense, rescues the announcement with "now I guess it's official," and observes about Vickie (line 1 below), "she's very, very upset."[13] Then, in answering Judy's question about "how long" the mother was given, Sally does not just report the figure to Judy. She prefaces the report with a phrase whose initial component has increased volume ("GET this," line 3) and that proposes a particular stance toward the report, which Judy (line 5) interprets as "not bad at all." This assessment, prolonging the complaining about and criticism of Vickie, is produced in an interactional environment that is hospitable for it, and it is received with a strong claim of knowledge on Sally's part (line 6) – the claim is animated with increased pitch on "know." And while it aligns to Judy's criticism, it also may bid for a turn of talk that would instantiate the claim with a display of Sally's side or version of the criticism.

(06) Frankel:I:1:4 (retranscribed)

Sal: .t.hhh So she's very very upset. hh
Jud: W'l how long did they give'er.
Sal: GET thi:s. Fifty percent chance of three years.
(0.7)
Jud: W'l that's not bad at a::11.=
Sal: =I ↑kno:w.
Jud: I mean my(g) go::d. Some people find out'n they've
only got like six mo[:nths.
Sal: [.hhhhhhh hOh: I wz talking tih
this friend of Wendy's the other day. .hh whose
father, (.) collapsed.They found out he hadda brain
tumor. En he died the nex' da:y.
(1.0)
Jud: .tch.hhhhh Well (.) I mean there's reason tuh be upset
on her par[t,]
Sal: [S:]u[:re,]
Jud: [But–]
(.)
Jud: there's also reason tuh (.) feel very lucky.
Sal: .hhhhhhh ↑Well I look at it this way. yihknow, her
mother, is over sixty ...

After Sally's "I know," Judy in line 7 produces an IMPU with a "my god" imprecation and reference to "some people" who only have "like six months." Thereby, fitting Pattern 2, it reaches back (skip-ties) and explicates her slightly cautious "not bad at a::ll" assessment, suggesting a contrast with the mother's situation. If the utterance at lines 7–8 recognizes Sally's alignment by upgrading the criticism with the detail about "some people," it otherwise disattends it as it formulates a categorical reference conjoining in a contrastive way to the previous "not bad" assessment and the mother's situation. Sally responds at line 9 with a marker of realization (Heritage, 1984) and a story that instantiates the formulation. Although the story has a dramatic upshot (line 12), it meets with silence (line 13), and then Judy takes an extended in-breath and produces a "well"-preface to her next turn (line 14). Whereas there is an overall compatibility in the participants' stances, these features of the interaction project a local misalignment between the previous and current utterance (Pomerantz, 1984a), and Judy then produces another I-mean utterance skip-tying to the series of turns concerning Vickie, including, most immediately, her own (lines 7–8). In skip-tying, Judy's turns may have the effect of sequentially deleting Sally's line 6 and lines 9–12 contribution. As Jefferson (1973: 75) suggests about sequential deletion, it is a way that a speaker (with cooperation from a recipient) can render some object as "sequentially nonimplicative" or consequential for immediately subsequent talk.

Judy (lines 14–15) acknowledges Vickie's right "to be upset" (which also connects the turn with Sally's line 1 utterance), and this acknowledgment is the first part of a compound turn constructional unit (Lerner 1991) ending with a proposal (line 19) that can be heard to conjoin specifically with Judy's line 5 critique of Vickie's state regarding her mother and her subsequent explication (lines 7–8), explaining even further why the situation is "not bad at all." Thus, there is a just-now completeness to the complaint, accomplished in part by the way that the contrast developed in her turn at lines 14–15, 19 can offer a third and finalizing component to Judy's contingently developed complaint and criticism:

(1) The mother's chances (fifty per cent chance of three years) are "not bad at all" (line 5).
(2) "Some people" only get "like six months" (lines 7–8).
(3) There's "reason to be upset" but there is also "reason to feel very lucky" (lines 14–15, 19).

And Sally may hear things that way, *as* complete and finalized. Following Judy's compound TCU, Sally (line 20) immediately draws an in-breath, produces a "well," and launches a series of characterizations regarding the mother and her situation, starting with she's "over sixty" (line 21) and continuing with ones not on the example – "done everything," "been around the world like four times," done "significant work in bacteriology," etc. And the upshot is that Wendy's "getting so upset" is from her "feelings about her mother" and not from "losing" her.

In this episode, Judy's and Sally's versions of Vickie and her situation, although not completely concordant, are both critical and complaining. Their knowledge about Vickie and her mother's situation appears to enter into the saying of their respective versions. Sally, having recently talked to Vickie, has the more proximate knowledge, and projects and eventually builds an accusation of overreaction and unresolved feelings on Vickie's part to the recent news. Judy has claimed prior and independent knowledge regarding the terminality of the mother's condition, and treats the "fifty percent chance of three years" announcement as "not bad" news[14] and "reason to feel very lucky." Accordingly, the disparity in versions is slight – more a matter of emphasis than real difference. However, on the basis of having her own "mentionables" (1973), Judy vies for her critical perspective to be articulated.

The I-mean utterances are competitive with a line of talk that Sally projects with her claim of knowledge and story about another illness and death, and may sequentially delete those attempts of Sally to pursue her own trajectory. That is, Judy's I-mean-prefaced utterances connect her own articulations of stance while initially eschewing the direction that Sally proposes with her claim of independent knowledge and narrative about a "friend of Wendy's." When Judy arrives at a completion point, Sally returns to territory with which she has proximate epistemic familiarity, and revivifies the argument (whose incipiency Judy had quashed) suggestive of Vickie's unresolved feelings regarding her mother as Judy finally yields speakership over an extended series of turns.

On Judy's part, the I-mean-prefaced utterances are mechanisms defending her own speaking rights. It can also be said that, if the IMPUs are a speaker's device for sequentially deleting a co-participant's immediately preceding turns of talk, they may do something similar when the co-participant has not spoken, and a silence ensues after speaker's initial action or actions of complaining. As a skip-tying mechanism, they may propose to disattend or delete such silences, as in examples 3 and 4, thereby reinforcing a tacit proposal that the complaining action had been incomplete and now, with the addition of an IMPU or IMPUs, recipient appreciation is fully due.

7.5.2 *I-mean-prefaced utterances and epistemics*

We are seeing that complaining and the use of I-mean-prefaced utterances can involve what Raymond and Heritage (2006) have called the "epistemics of social relations" or the rights to speak on the basis of one's identity-bound knowledge. In the previous example, Sally and Judy each claim, with different kinds of knowledgeable access, to speak authoritatively about Vickie. An example in which a speaker repairs an utterance to include an I-mean preface shows further how dealing with topical speakership in complaint sequences may involve the epistemics of social relations. The extract is drawn from a conversation that Raymond and Heritage (2006) examine extensively, involving the friends Vera and Jenny.

Prior to the example below, Vera had been extolling her experiences with her own family but then, in a shift of topic, tells about another family member (Jean), the less favorable parenting the grandchildren of Jean receive, Vera's own negative experiences with the children, and Jean telling her she "just can't stand it" when "they come up," and she (Jean) is "praying for them to leave." Vera reports saying to Jean that she was glad she wasn't the "only one" who had such an attitude. Then, as Raymond and Heritage (2006: 691) say about line 1 below, "Jenny offers an assessment built to display her understanding of Vera's telling." Jenny's position, accordingly, is comparable to Judy's secondary position vis-à-vis Sally's telling about Vickie in example 6 above. That is, Jenny's knowledge about the family is less immediate than Vera's. In a Pattern 2 IMPU, after Vera's "yes" tokens (produced in overlap), Jenny produces an utterance (line 6) that, with its assessment plus tag question, "explicates the basis for her prior evaluation and cedes epistemic authority to Vera" (Raymond and Heritage 2006: 691). Observation of further details regarding the I-mean at the beginning of the line 6 turn can add to this analysis.

(07) Rah 14:6; 149

01	Jen:	Yah .h bec'z you'd a'thou:ght they'd'v grown out'v it
02		by now r[eally.
03	Ver:	[Yes
04		(.)
05	Ver:	[Yes
06	Jen:	[Th– ah mean theh not ba:bies ahr they.
07	Ver:	Theh not no:,
08		(.)
09	Ver:	.h 'R yih[goin yih won't be goin t'th'town tomorrow
10		will you.

Notice that the turn starts in overlap with Vera's "yes" token at line 5 and appears to project the "theh" (they're) of the forthcoming utterance. However, Jen cuts off and repairs the utterance. Ordinarily such repair – that is, a restart of the utterance – involves *recycling* the part of the utterance that occurs in overlap. Although Jen's repair does involve recycling of "th" apparently to "theh" ("they're") it also involves insertion of the I-mean preface, raising the question of what work that preface is doing such that the repaired utterance now includes it.

What seems to be afoot is that this IMPU skip-ties to Jenny's turn at lines 1–2 rather than overtly dealing with Vera's "yes" tokens at lines 3 and 5. The first of these is in overlap with Jen's turn at line 2, such that both speakers, possibly bidding to resolve the overlap, stop talking. Then, after the beat of silence (line 4), they simultaneously start up again (lines 5–6). Nevertheless, if Jenny tacitly has heard Vera's "yes" as aligning, she may project that she has put Vera in a mildly untenable position. At line 1, her "you'd a'thou:ght" preface, although categorical and something like "one would have thought," is inclusive of her recipient Vera, who is positioned as the more knowledgeable about her grandsons. Accordingly, Jenny is close to proposing a statement about what Labov (1977: 62) calls a "B-event" to which Vera has primary epistemic access,[15] and nevertheless obtaining Vera's agreements. Line 6 is a roughly similar assessment to that at line 1 but removes the possible implication that Jenny knows what Vera should think, and then (with the tag question) clearly defers to her on the matter. Following Raymond and Heritage's (2006: 691) analysis, we can observe that Vera's line 7 response is designed in such a way (first confirming Jenny's assertion and then agreeing with it) as to reverse the preference for contiguity, which would prioritize agreeing over confirming (Sacks, 1987). By confirming instead of agreeing (initially), Vera thereby displays her having held the position about the children not being "babies" prior to Jenny's assessment. This display and breaking of preference order in part may be encouraged by Jenny's skip-tying IMPU, by which, instead of recognizing the yeses (even though they may be working toward topic closure),[16] she disattends them, proposes to complete her complaint rather than accept Vera's inapt alignment to a borderline B-statement, and asks for Vera's confirmation.

7.5.3 *Equal epistemic status, complaining, and IMPUs*

Even when co-participants occupy relatively equal epistemic positions, the speaker of a complaint who obtains a display of alignment such as "I know" may follow it with an I-mean utterance to connect with the complaint, possibly hearing that alignment as an epistemically formatted self-oriented topic proffer on the recipient's part. For example, the extract below follows extensive talk in which Leslie and Joan have each been complaining about their economic circumstances, which started with Joan reporting that her husband had gotten "no bonus from his firm this year," and Leslie responding with "I think we're all in the same boat this year," and then telling Joan that she and her husband also were getting "no bonus or nothing extra." As the talk progresses, Joan's circumstances seem more dire than Leslie's and they explore possible remedies, including making things and selling them or finding an item for export. After each reports that "nothing" comes to mind for making such money on their own, the following ensues:

(08) Holt X(C)-2-1-2 [34]

Joa: You know ... if you do things by ha:nd it's so much
more expensive than people c'd buy them for aren't
the[y.
Les: [iYes[I kno:w.]
Joa: [I mean I c]'n knit 'n (.) an' do that sorta
thing. 'n I know someb'dy 'oo made a lot with a
knittin' machine.
(.)
Les: iYes.
(0.4)
Joa: Made it a proper business: you know (that future),
.hhhh (0.2) But ba:sic'ly (0.7) u–h you know, u–it js

wouldn't –suit me that sorta thing I doh– I think I–
if I wz at ho:me I'd be doin' (.) house-work. 'n I
wouldn' be able a'get (.) stuck into[it.
Les: [No:. I know ah–
it's the seh– .hhh I– I[make silhouettes you know.=
Joa: [( )
Les: =[an'
Joa: =[Do you,
(.)
Joa: Yes,
Les: And they look (.) really an-ti[que
Joa: [ukh–hih ukhh
(0.9)
Les: But um (0.7) 't's –not worth my while selling
them[becuz
Joa: [Ohh no:[:.
Les: [people c'n –buy them for about four
pounds fifty in[the shops.]
Joa: [That's it.]
Joa: That's i[t, (yeah.)
Les: [you know made by machine.
(.)
Joa: That's it

Leslie, in an utterance (line 4) that overlaps with the tail end of Joan's complaint at lines 1–3 regarding the expense of making "things by hand," consists of a "yes" and a claim of knowledge, which itself gets overlapped with the start of Joan's I-mean utterance at line 5. Leslie's "yes" can act as a confirmation of the tag question, but Joan may be treating it as projecting a shift of speakership, such that rather than aligning as a "passive" recipient of Joan's talk, Leslie is bidding to assume the discourse role of topical speaker.[17] The IMPU, by tying back to Joan's complaint (lines 1–3) and proposing a more detailed (Pattern 2) explanatory explication of it, can intersect fulfillment of Leslie's possible trajectory towards speakership by treating her "Yes I know" as a display of recipiency only, or it may simply be disattending it. To the extent that Joan's turn at lines 5–6, which builds a contrast between her ability to "knit" and someone using a "knitting machine," can be launching a small story, then with her slightly delayed standalone "iyes" (line 9) plus silence (line 10), Leslie may be aligning as a story recipient while still projecting an eventual my-side telling. Then Joan offers further components to her own story, which returns to a claim that reinforces her stance about not being able to earn money by making things; she would be "doin' (.) housework" were she "at home" (lines 14–15). Now Leslie confirms Joan's upshot with a "no I know" utterance, which has the structure of her "yes I know" but with an acknowledgment token fitted to the negative polarity of the utterance it follows, just as the "yes" at line 3 can be treating an utterance with positive polarity. Leslie then produces a series of hesitations[18] that lead into her own story.

While the eventual production of this story is evidence that Leslie had a mentionable relevant to Joan's initial complaint, the suggestion is not that Joan somehow knew that other than by what she could project from Leslie's just subsequent "yes I know" claim at line 4 as a possible bid for shifting from recipiency to speakership. Instead of aligning to that bid as a recipient of topical talk, or producing her "I can knit ..." comment without an I-mean in a way that would be a misfit with Les's "Yes I know" prior utterance, Joan uses the preface in a skip-tying utterance that deletes or disattends that utterance and connects with her complaint at lines 1–2 and further propels her own topical speakership.

As I-mean-prefaced utterances, in the context of aligning acknowledgments by recipients to a complaint, locate "last utterance by same speaker," their conjunctive work in these complaint sequences appears as competing for topical speakership. That is, unlike IMPUs that seem to deal with lack of alignment, they do not need to defend the content of the complaint but they may need to defend the speaker's right to articulate the complaint beyond its initial formulation and suggest a just-now completion. Such defensiveness may arise from being in a subordinate epistemic position relative to the complaint recipient, but may also be due to a situation in which a speaker's complainable experience is of roughly equal epistemic stature and the problem is one simply of getting a turn or turns to tell that experience in advance of recipients' possible bids to tell theirs.

7.6 Defensiveness: repair formatting of complaint explication

In the introduction to this paper, I suggested that there might be an issue as to whether transition-space IMPUs are real or virtual or boundary cases of repair. "Boundary" instances of what could appear to be other-initiated repair are utterances that have terms ("huh," "what") ordinarily associated with such repair but are doing other kinds of actions (Schegloff, 1997a), such as pursuing a response, engaging in "ritual remedy" (as when saying "excuse me" after a sneeze), progressing through a sequence, and challenging. Is it that I-mean-prefaced utterances in the context of complaining are only using a phrase associated with self-repair but are doing other actions and not repair?

The proposal here is that I-mean utterances accompanying complaints are indeed doing, or at least proposing to do, self-initiated repair, but in a way that is complicated and possibly virtual. One criterion for an utterance to be repair is that it replaces or defers what is "due next" (Schegloff, 1997a: 498) including a next turn in a sequence. By this criterion, IMPUs officially defer a response to the complaints as such that they follow, and solicit a response to the "repair" action they can be embodying. However, they do this deferral in a complicated way. Sometimes it is in a post-hoc way, after there has been no response to an initial complaint formulation, and an IMPU's skip-tying disattends or sequentially deletes the implicativeness of the silence. Other times, IMPUs work in a competitive way by skip-tying to the speaker's previous utterance when a recipient has just provided a construable aligning response. In either case, as repair, they occasion the relevance of talk that accepts or acknowledges the repair, and here is the crux: speakers can take that response to the repair as also aligning to the complaint in its full flower. Instead of deferring response, however, they tacitly extend the action underway and suggest that a response is only now (with completion of the IMPU) particularly due.

Accordingly, there is a sense in which the repair is more virtual than real, more pragmatic than technical. This is because, with an IMPU, speakers suggest a problem in need of repair without showing there to be one in any strong sense (as when they replace an errant word or phrase) or having encountered a misunderstanding in their recipient's responsive talk. That is, there is no errant or indecipherable talk per se on speaker's part and no exhibit of difficulty on the recipient's part. It is as if IMPUs *propose* a problem in understanding, and the original turn is a *putative* trouble source in its incompleteness, which is one sense in which these IMPUs as explications are defensive. As noted earlier, utterances formatted as repair embody actions that "supersede other actions" (Schegloff, 2000: 208) and thereby exert a "powerful" sequential privilege. If virtual, pragmatic self-repair accurately characterizes these IMPUs, it is a feature that again raises a question of what work repair formatting of complaint explication does, beyond eliciting alignment to the original complaint by gaining acknowledgment and acceptance. There are three points to revisit from earlier discussion, one about the conjoining of turns that I-mean can do, another about complainability and preference structure, and still another about the epistemics of self-repair.

7.6.1 I-mean as a complaint conjunct marker

Speakers have ways of signaling (as with "by the way," or "incidentally") that a turn of talk is not fitted relative to the immediate sequential environment. Schegloff and Sacks (1973: 315–316) have called these signals "misplacement markers," while Jefferson (1978: 221) and others have referred to "disjunct markers." I-mean prefaces in the context of complaining do something of the opposite. They propose that a speaker's next utterance after an initial complaint, rather than being a next turn as such, is a conjoined part of the speaker's own turn to which they are subsequent. In this sense, I-mean prefaces are "conjunct markers." In situations where the initial utterance lacks subsequent uptake, an I-mean utterance purports that the complaint is in need of a clarifying upshot or detail for its full understandability – they are reparative. From our earlier discussion of pursuing alignment, however, we know that, other than explicating the original complaint, they neither modify the original substantially by lessening or withdrawing a critical formulation nor show an analysis of a recipient's silence to revise or reverse their stance. And while they are grammatically independent of the complaining utterances they follow, IMPUs only continue or exacerbate a critical stance rather than (as in unattached noun phrases) formulating that stance in the first place. They are more like turn extensions or increments with the exception of their grammatical independence.

At times, IMPUs can be said to pursue alignment, as do these other devices, but their construction with the I-mean preface essentially ignores a lack of responsiveness as it builds a conjoint relationship to the original complaining utterance. The I-mean suggests a seamlessly complaining turn of talk, rather than one that is resisted in the course of its production. They do similar work in the context of alignment: demonstrating that an aligning "yes" or "I know" or other recipient utterance is not consequential for the pursuit the IMPU is fashioning, and that this pursuit skip-ties to speaker's own prior turn. In this respect, IMPUs in complaint sequences fit what Schegloff (1997b: 33, 35) has suggested about third turn repair, treating a recipient's intervening utterance as a "quasi-turn" or "organizationally incidental occurrence." Unlike the examples of third turn repair that Schegloff examines, however, IMPUs are not working to replace errant references. Recall extract 2, in which B says "paintings" when she meant to say "frames":

(02) SBL 1:1:12:10 (from Schegloff 1997b: 32)

01 B: hhh And he's g:oing to make his own paintings,
02 A: Mm hmmm
03 B: And– or I mean his own frames.
04 A: Yeah

Rather, I-mean-prefaced utterances in complaint sequences claim that an initial formulation of the complaint is incomplete. The initial component needs explication or accounting, and this is what the I-mean component is doing. The I-mean preface suggests an explanatory move that is doing the work of accounting or preserving speakership; in either way it is a defensive mechanism.

7.6.2 *Complaining as "complainable" and dispreferred*

Complaining, as Schegloff has written (2005: 466), is a dispreferred conversational action. Preference in conversational interaction is not about speaker's intentions but rather concerns how there may be alternative ways of initiating or progressing a sequence. In terms of initiation, for example, we know that offers are preferred over requests, when such things as invitations or help are at issue: Participants work to obtain offers rather than having to ask for these social objects. Given a problem that is complainable, nevertheless complaints are dispreferred relative to other actions such as apologies or other actions that preempt an actual complaint. Therefore, complaining is a very delicate action to perform, and were speakers to explicate an initial complaint without an I-mean preface, without proposing the explication as a repair, that is, it could not only prolong the dispreferred activity of complaining but also render those speakers vulnerable to a charge of "being a complainer" more than they already are by doing a complaint at all, a matter about which Sacks (1992) has written.[19]

To illustrate the complainability of complaining, we can consider a conversation in which Leslie calls Robbie to discuss school and classroom decorum with respect to a particular class of children at a local school. Robbie is their regular teacher and Leslie has been a substitute, so both are familiar with the class and the children. Robbie, although being the call recipient, initiates first topic by suggesting she was "thinking" about Leslie "today," and by launching a complaining utterance about the "lotta' children" in her class. As the conversation continues, she produces a series of complaints about the staff, a particular teacher, the children as a group, and several individual children. Leslie shares and sympathizes with these complaints, although not completely. At a point well into the conversation, and just after talking about one child who "really worries" Robbie, the following takes place:

(09) Holt 5/88-1-5:1

Rob: –Well ↓and the other thing I wz disgusted b– I'm
↓sorry you're getting'n earful'v this you couldn't'v:
phoned't a better ti:me,hheh he[h
Les: [.hh –Oh that's
alri:ght,
Rob: Well the –other thing ↓I've (.) found very strange is
–there weren't any dictionaries in the classroom
Les: .t.k.hhh[h
Rob: [Not actua[l
Les: [–No children's dih– e–w'l not many
children's dictionarys,hh
Rob: W'l, they–have those little (.) bookley ↓things

Robbie, at line 1, starts to produce yet another complaint, stops, and apologizes, also suggesting (lines 2–3) that the timing of Leslie's call was propitious for herself. Leslie (lines 4–5) accepts the apology and grants absolution (Robinson, 2004), whereupon Robbie then continues with the complaint, although it is now slightly mitigated ("disgusted," line 1 becomes "very strange," line 6). As Schegloff (2005: 465) has observed, apologies like Robbie's in lines 1–2 indicate an understanding that some piece of prior conduct can be complainable even though there has been no complaint. In this case, by taking the initiative to apologize, Robbie preempts possible protesting from Leslie, and it permits the production of another in her series of criticizing actions. The regularity with which participants do such preempting of complaints is one indication of their dispreferred status in conversation. If complaining is itself a complainable and dispreferred activity, then an advantage of producing one or more IMPUs after a complaint is that, rather than constituting a *series* of complaint-type turns (as they would without the I-mean preface), they embroider complaints with the looks of repair, which is another sense in which these IMPUs are something like *virtual* repair utterances.

7.6.3 I-mean prefacing, epistemics, and "A-statements"

In formatting these utterances as repair, thereby avoiding the potential for perseverating in the production of a dispreferred action, speakers accomplish an epistemic feat as well, in that it is within a speaker's domain to say what is meant by an utterance. By defending a complaint through a repair-formatted utterance, it accords the complaint an element that would be difficult to dispute because the speaker is defining what he or she meant or intended, whereas a recipient is not equally privy to the speaker's intentions.

The epistemic strength of IMPUs is in their character as "A-events," which a speaker has "privileged access" to and "can deal with … as an expert without fear of contradiction" (Labov and Fanshel, 1977: 62). If, epistemically, IMPUs forestall disagreement with what they assert about the speaker's meaning, this is another way in which they are defensive gambits. Although certainly they do not prevent disagreements and counter-complaints on grounds different from what the complaints and their IMPU attachments assert, IMPUs, because of the repair formatting, protect themselves and the complaints they follow from dispute, at least then and there. Consider an example in which the speaker produces a complaint, and then starts to explicate it cleanly or without any I-mean prefacing, and then repairs the utterance to include the preface. In the next extract, Leslie is talking to Mum, and Mum has just asked how Katherine, the daughter of Leslie and granddaughter of Mum, is doing. Katherine has had a cold (previous talk to line 1) and this is a report on her current status (lines 1–3), which occasions an announcement of and complaint about a visit from Coleen Bates. At line 6, Leslie reports that Coleen is "hou:nding" Katherine and her brother Gordon:

(10) Holt 2.09:4:36 (Corrected transcript.) [11]

01	Les:	t.hh Ye:s sh–u–she: um (0.2) She wz alright this
02		evening but she's .hhh but– (.) after Coleen's visit
03		i–you know Coleen Ba:[tes,
04	Mum:	[Yes,
05		(0.7)
06	Les:	Well she keeps hou:nding Kathrine 'n:::d Gordon no:w,
07		(0.7)
08	Les:	Sh[e keeps– (.) nagging Mark'n I becuz they don:'go=
09	Mum:	[(Really.)
10	Les:	=t'see her.
11		(.)
12	Mum:	eh–Oh:::.
13		(.)
14	Les:	Well she c'n jus' stuh–uh–stop that cz I'm not having
15		that, she– I mean she's nagged– (0.2) every generation
16		so fa::r,
17	Mum:	Yes.
18	Les:	I m'n she's not gonna sta:rt on the younger generation
19		no:w.h=
20	Mum:	=Now: that that Coleen usetuh come t'see (Esther) at
21		Maidstone.
22	Les:	Yes that's ↓ri:[ght

We have already seen how IMPUs may get used in pursuit of alignment when a person is complaining and criticizing and not getting some kind of satisfactory uptake. Leslie's turn at 6 is followed by a silence (line 7) and then a further complaint about Coleen Bates' "nagging" Leslie's husband Mark and herself (line 8) and a reason for the nagging. In overlap (line 9), Mum produces the kind of news receipt that, with its downward intonation discourages elaboration (Jefferson, 1981; Heritage, 1984: 339–341; Maynard, 2003: 101–103), and after Leslie's completion, she emits a slightly elongated "oh" change of state token (line 12), also discouraging of elaboration. Subsequent to a micropause, Leslie (line 14) produces an utterance that could finalize her complaint: it completes a three part list (whose prior two components are at lines 6 and 8), depicting opposition to the behavior formulated in the components so far produced with a summary version that "she c'n jus' stop" because she (Leslie) is "not having that." She reaches a transition relevance place (at the start of 15), yet Leslie continues and appears to start the utterance that culminates with a Pattern 1 generalizing utterance, "she's nagged every generation so far" (lines 15–16), a justification for her opposition. Also with a kind of "extreme case formulation" (Pomerantz, 1986) – "she's nagged every generation so far" – that exaggerates the prior components, it upgrades the complaint. However, she stops, and restarts the utterance to include an I-mean preface.

Here, in a similar fashion to the insertion of I-mean at line 6 in example 7, it is not that I-mean is, in the first place, being used to do repair. Rather, repair is being used to do I-mean. Or, more precisely, Leslie repairs an utterance that started without an I-mean preface to include such a preface, as the utterance that then emerges from the same-turn insertion repair comes to be built as repair form relative to the complaining utterances it follows and explicates. Now, with this conjunct marker in place, the utterance at 15 is positioned to explicate the stance Leslie exhibits at 14, drawing together in a general way ("nagged every generation so fa::r") what has been said particularly (about "hounding" Katherine and Gordon, the younger generation, and "nagging" Mark and Leslie, the older generation) and finally (she can "stop that"). With an exaggerated quality, and without an I-mean preface, this turn could be vulnerable to a display of skepticism, as regularly occurs after construable overstatements (Drew, 2003). Mum, however, in just the way that repair is to be treated with acknowledgment, treats this utterance with a "yes" (line 17), thereby also aligning momentarily to the trajectory of complaining action that Leslie is pursuing. Leslie produces another IMPU at lines 18–19, again conjoining an explication to the prior components of her complaining. At this point (line 20), Mum proposes to shift topic in a way that may tie back to Leslie's request about recognition at lines 2–3. Her utterance at lines 20–21 is a preface to a brief narrative about Coleen Bates that occurs after the extract, and which serves as an interlude before Leslie proposes returning with an "Well anyway …" utterance to complaining about Coleen.

From the example above, two points can be drawn. First, insofar as there is clear effort to include I-mean as a preface to an explication in the transition space after a complaint, it is a nontrivial matter. I-mean prefaces are not haphazardly used discourse markers. Second, although Mum provides an aligning "yes" after the first IMPU, and produces further discussion about Coleen after the second IMPU, consistent with her previous treatment of the complaint, Mum withholds full endorsement of the criticism. However, she does not dispute the IMPUs, which, as Leslie's A-statements, would be difficult to do because Mum lacks primary access to Leslie's thoughts, feelings, or opinions. Instead Mum focuses on a tangential matter, introducing recognitional and reminiscent talk about Coleen's earlier years. This is emblematic of a more general pattern in my collection of complaint-subsequent IMPUs: Although recipient talk may at times show misalignment with complaints, such talk does not disagree with what a speaker says they mean or have meant by the complaint.

6.7 IMPUs in relation to inapposite actions

I-mean-prefaced utterances accompanying complaining actions are numerous, and in conversation far outweigh any other use of I-mean. However, my collection of IMPUs includes some utterances in which the actions the initial utterances perform are not complaints as such. As I examined these exceptions, they ultimately showed a pattern that is related to the complaint-oriented IMPUs. Transition-space repairs-as-IMPUs, when not explicating complaints, often deal with *inapposite* initiating actions of various kinds. That an action can be inapposite has to do with the sequential environment in which the action takes place (Heritage, 1998). If that action, by way of its presuppositions or relevance, is ill fitted to that environment, or that environment is not propitious for the action, it is an inapposite one.

The topic of IMPU accompaniments to inapposite actions is one that deserves article- or chapter-length consideration in its own right. Here, I can provide only a sketch, using one example that we have already examined in which an I-mean utterance does tie to a complaint but across a more prosocial kind of claim, and another example that has some similar properties when the IMPU occurs skip-tied to a praising rather than complaining action. The two examples have in common that this skip-tying mechanism focuses off of a more immediately previous and possibly inapposite action of the speaker.

If we return to example 3, a detail to notice there is that Emma not only is complaining. At a particular point, she inserts a bit of what can be construed as self-praise (lines 2–3), a little brag, when she says that she gave Bud's breakfast to "Karen's little boy" (line 3). It *claims credit* for her handling of the situation, and such credit can ask for appreciation or "prospect" for compliments (Maynard, 2003: 203). Insofar as there is a conversational preference to avoid self-praise (Pomerantz, 1978), however, the brag as a small detail in an environment of complaining about circumstances affecting others, may be inapposite, and makes relevant an IMPU that, in explicating her complaint, also focuses away from the self-reported generosity.

(03) NB:IV:10:18 (24)

Emm: Bud couldn't e:ven eat his breakfast. He o:rdered he
waited forty five minutes'n he'a:dtuh be out there tuh
tee off so I gave it to uh: (.) Karen's: liddle bo:y.
(0.7)
Emm: ((swallow)) I mean that's how bad the service was .hhh
(.) It's gone tuh pot.
Lot: °u–Oh*:::° (.) e–[Y_e_:_:_ a h .]Ye<]

Lottie's withholding of response at line 4 may be dealing with the inappositeness of the brag as well as its insertion in an otherwise complaining course of action, such that the I-mean utterance, then, may perform dual functions in explicating the brag in such a way as to refocus on those who were the injured parties and bring the complaint to its completion. Notice also that, whereas the complaining was on behalf of others, the claim to have given Bud's breakfast to the little boy is on Lottie's own behalf. The I-mean utterance returns the focus to the plight of the others.

IMPUs in general suggest a shift from self- to other-oriented talk. A second example has a possibly inapposite self-reference in the context of praising rather than complaining. It involves women friends who are playing a game of Pictionary but who have taken a break as the host, Pam, is talking on the telephone and another participant has left to get ice cream (Ford et al., 2002: 24, 28–29). The three remaining participants discuss a picture on the wall near the game table of the "Café Yin Yang" (line 1 below), drawn by a ten-year-old nephew of Pam.

(11) Game Night

01	Rch:	The cafe thuh Yin Yang? When he was tw– te:n?
02	Ter:	Yeah:.
03		(1.2)
04	Rch:	[(°That looks really complicated.°)]
05	Ter:	[An– An– no:te, (.)] the uh:
06		(.)
07	Rch:	Is that a re[al feather on there?]
08	Ter:	[Y'see on the dress?]
09		The yin yang? symbol? [(there?)
10	Rch:	[Oh my go:sh.
11	Ter:	I was so impressed. I mean this kid.
12		(1.4)
13	Rch:	°Ten years o:ld.°
14	Ter:	Yeah.

As Terry gets up from her chair and points to the picture (lines 5, 8–9), she asks for others to attend to "the dress" (line 8) and to its "yin yang? symbol" (line 9). Rachel immediately produces an appreciative assessment at line 10, whereupon Terry announces, "I was so impressed." As Ford et al. (2002: 29) observe, the I-mean is not suggesting a repairing replacement of anything prior. Rather, given a possible lack of fit between the dramatic build-up toward assessment and Rachel's laconic "oh my gosh," which also was partially overlapped, and the lack of turn transition as well as gaze from a recipient after "impressed" at line 11, the I-mean utterance provides a "further stance display toward the referent (how amazing and impressive this child is)" (Ford et al., 2002: 29). In so doing, the utterance can be eliciting Rachel's gaze as well as providing a "standard" for the recipient response. In addition, if we consider that "I was so impressed" represents a momentary focus slightly away from the nephew's artfulness and claims a capacity on the speaker's part for artistic discrimination, it is like the small brag in extract 3. It is a momentary boast about her own agency in the act of other-appreciation, a partly self-oriented turn that is inapposite when the topic so far has been about the nephew and his achievement. "I mean this kid" minimizes the boast while returning focus on the nephew and what has been said about him. Rachel subsequently offers a remark that (with quieted volume) in fact reverts to admiring of the boy's achievement by re-mentioning his youth: "°ten years o:ld°."

Example 11 is emblematic. When IMPUs as transition-space self-repairs are not doing technical repair by replacing references or terms in a previous turn, when they are not explicating complaints per se, and when they are not dealing with something inapposite in an otherwise complaining environment,[20] they may regularly deal with interactional circumstances surrounding the delivery or report of an action that ordinarily would be apposite and even welcome or "supportive" (Pomerantz, 1978) prosocial ones. In my data, such actions include telling an entertaining story, offers or reports of helping, invitations, praise, and the like. Due to interactional circumstances – i.e., the sequencing within which they occur – the action or report is accountably inapposite, and the speaker uses the devices of self-initiated repair to propose an understanding that is more appropriate to the circumstances. The examples we have seen show a speaker using I-mean utterances to deflect attention from claims about self to experiences involving or belonging to others. More technically, transition-space self-initiated repairs that follow inapposite reports or circumstances may be dealing with a feature they share with complaining actions, which is the complainability of what they have done in the talk. These self-initiated repair forms, something like instances of other-initiated repairs done with apologies (Schegloff, 2005: 471–474), can preempt complaints that would target the inappositeness of what the speaker has just said.

7.8 Conclusion

If repair concerns problems in speaking, hearing, or understanding, the I-mean-prefaced utterances in my collection are something of an anomaly. They are not dealing with problems in speaking or hearing – not correcting a word or phrase or utterance trajectory that was in error – and they are not handling a recipient's turn that displays a wayward understanding of the speaker's original turn. Occupying the transition-space immediately after the turn of talk that they propose to repair, and explicating otherwise intact, understandable utterances, IMPUs seem to propose solving troubles where so far none has been overtly exhibited except that a speaker may have launched a risky type of action. In that respect, they may anticipate trouble with recipiency, and engage a repair form ("I mean") suggesting that some clarification or explication is in order such that the action underway is to be understood as complaining and not some other action.[21]

Then, as defensive mechanisms conjoining to previous utterances, they perform three kinds of tasks. First, they can defend the content of the complaint – in Pattern 1 by glossing or summarizing the details that are so far offered, or in Pattern 2 by providing specific components to a so-far generalized complaint – and thereby provide for its complete articulation. As conjunct-markers, they do this by skip-tying to the speaker's previous complaining turn and virtually deleting or at least disattending silences or a recipient's talk subsequent to that turn. Second, particularly when recipients may show alignment to a complaint component, IMPUs also defend the right to speakership in order to complete the complaint. Third, although IMPUs mostly are *not* attached to interactionally preferred first turns, such as offers, invitations, or praise, which are in a contrast class with complaints, they can accompany these actions when they are, because of their sequential placement, accountably inapposite. By defending dispreferred and inapposite talk, IMPUs encourage alignment to the action that a connected-to utterance projects, providing a completion rather than next point for response, and they do so with a certain kind of epistemic authority simply because it is speakers who have relatively sole access to what they mean by what they say.

In some ways it should be no surprise that speakers can work to explicate dispreferred or inapposite social actions so that they can take on the appearance of being appropriate and inoffensive – i.e., deserving of recipient alignment. However, at present research has concentrated on ways that recipients of actions produce second turns of sequences that resist first turn actions, whether it is to disagree with a first assessment (Pomerantz, 1984a), counter the presuppositions of a yes-no interrogative (Raymond, 2003), suggest the inapposite quality of a question (Heritage, 1998), or exhibit an independence of perspective relative to a speaker's own evaluation (Heritage, 2002). The practice or mechanism identified here is a speaker's rather than a recipient's practice, and speakers' use of it has a paradoxical quality. When using an I-mean utterance subsequent to initial complaint component(s), speakers work to establish that the objects of complaint, whether these are shared circumstances, other persons, their own troubles, or their co-participants, are what speakers propose them to be – complainable objects – and that the component or components produced so far are part of an entire turn whose completion is underway for recipient appreciation. On the other hand, for speakers who have engaged in inapposite actions that are (like complaints) dispreferred and therefore are complainable objects – that is, when the actions of the speakers themselves are potential complainables – IMPUs propose that they are not. In all these cases, I-mean-prefaced utterances serve the course of action a speaker is engaged in while dealing with a recipient's actual or potential responsiveness. With this interactional sensibility, rather than approaching defensive mechanisms as features of psychology and intrapsychic, individual conscious or unconscious motivation, scholarly inquiry can investigate them as fully social and sociological phenomena.

REFERENCES

Bakhtin, Mikhail M. (1978[1929]). Discourse typology in prose. In L. Matejka and K. Pomorska, eds., *Readings in Russian Poetics: Formalist and Structuralist Views*, pp. 176–196. Ann Arbor: University of Michigan Press.

Baumeister, Roy F., Dale, Karen and Sommer, Kristin L. (1998). Freudian defense mechanisms and empirical findings in modern social psychology: reaction formation, projection, displacement, undoing, isolation, sublimation, and denial. *Journal of Personality* 66: 1081–1124.

Bergmann, Jorg R. (1993). *Discreet Indiscretions: The Social Organization of Gossip*. Trans. J. John Bednarz. New York: Aldine De Gruyter.

Clift, Rebecca (1999). Irony in conversation. *Language in Society* 28: 523–553.

Couper-Kuhlen, Elizabeth (1996). The prosody of repetition: on quoting and mimicry. In E. Couper-Kuhlen and M. Selting, eds., *Prosody in Conversation: Interactional Studies*, pp. 366–405. Cambridge University Press.

Davidson, Judy (1984). Subsequent versions of invitations, offers, requests, and proposals dealing with potential or actual rejection. In J. M. Atkinson and J. Heritage, eds., *Structures of Social Action*, pp. 102–128. Cambridge University Press.

(1990). Modifications of invitations, offers and rejections. In G. Psathas, ed., *Interaction Competence*, pp. 149–180. Washington: International Institute for Ethnomethodology and Conversation Analysis and University Press of America.

Drew, Paul (1998). Complaints about transgressions and misconduct. *Research on Language and Social Interaction* 31: 295–325.

(2003). Precision and exaggeration in interaction. *American Sociological Review* 68: 917–938.

Drew, Paul and Holt, Elizabeth (1988) Complainable matters: the use of idiomatic expressions in making complaints. *Social Problems* 35: 398–417.

Drew, Paul and Walker, Traci (2009). Going too far: complaining, escalating, and disaffiliation. *Journal of Pragmatics* 41: 2400–2414.

Fenichel, Otto. (1945). *The Psychoanalytic Theory of Neurosis*. New York: Norton.

Ford, Ceci, Fox, Barbara A. and Thompson, Sandra A. (2002). Constituency and the grammar of turn increments. In C. Ford, B. A. Fox, and S. A. Thompson, eds., *The Language of Turn and Sequence*, pp. 14–38. New York: Oxford University Press.

Ford, Cecilia E. (1993). *Grammar in Interaction: Adverbial Clauses in American English Conversations*. Cambridge University Press.

Freud, Sigmund (1961 [1915]). Instincts and their vicissitudes. In *The Standard Edition of the Complete Works of Sigmund Freud*, vol. XIV, ed. J. Strachey, pp. 111–142. London: The Hogarth Press.

(1961 [1926]). Inhibitions, symptoms, and anxiety. In *The Standard Edition of the Complete Works of Sigmund Freud*, vol. XX, ed. J. Strachey, pp. 77–178. London: The Hogarth Press.

Glenn, Phillip (1995). Laughing at and laughing with: negotiations of participant alignments through conversational laughter. In P. t. Have and G. Psathas, eds., *Situated Order: Studies in the Social Organization of Talk and Embodied Activities*, pp. 43–56. Washington DC: University Press of America.

Goffman, E. (1974). *Frame Analysis: An Essay on the Organization of Experience*. New York: Harper and Row.

Heinemann, Trine and Traverso, Véronique (2009). Editorial: Complaining in interaction. *Journal of Pragmatics* 41: 2381–2384.

Heritage, John (1984). A change-of-state token and aspects of its sequential placement. In J. M. Atkinson and J. Heritage, eds., *Structures of Social Action*. Cambridge University Press.

(1998). Oh-prefaced responses to inquiry. *Language in Society* 27: 291–334.

(2002). Oh-prefaced responses to assessments. In C. Ford, B. Fox, and S. Thompson, eds., *The Language of Turn and Sequence*, pp. 196–224. New York: Oxford University Press.

Jefferson, Gail (1973). A case of precision timing in ordinary conversation: overlapped tag-positioned address terms in closing sequences. *Semiotica* 9: 47–96.

(1978). Sequential aspects of storytelling in conversation. In J. Schenkein, ed., *Studies in the Organization of Conversational Interaction*, pp. 219–248. New York: Academic Press.

(1979). A technique for inviting laughter and its subsequent acceptance/declination. In G. Psathas, ed., *Everyday Language: Studies in Ethnomethodology*, pp. 79–96. New York: Irvington Publishers.

(1981). The abominable "ne?": a working paper exploring the phenomenon of post-response pursuit of response. Occasional Paper No.6, Department of Sociology, University of Manchester.

(1983). Notes on a systematic deployment of the acknowledgement tokens "yeah" and "mmhm." In *Tilburg Papers in Language and Literature. Department of Language and Literature, Tilburg University*. The Netherlands: Tilburg.

Labov, William and Fanshel, David (1977). *Therapeutic Discourse: Psychotherapy as Conversation*. New York: Academic Press.

Lerner, Gene H. (1991). On the syntax of sentences in progress. *Language in Society* 20: 441–458.

Mandelbaum, Jenny (1991/1992). Conversation non-co-operation: an exploration of disattended complaints. *Research on Language and Social Interaction* 25: 97–138.

Maynard, Douglas W. (2003). *Bad News, Good News: Conversational Order in Everyday Talk and Clinical Settings*. Chicago: University of Chicago Press.

Ono, Tsuyoshi and Thompson, Sandra (1994). Unattached NPs in English conversation. *Berkeley Linguistics Society* 20: 402–419.

Pomerantz, Anita (1978). Compliment responses: notes on the co-operation of multiple constraints. In J. Schenkein, ed., *Studies in the Organization of Conversational Interaction*, pp. 79–112. New York: Academic Press.

(1984a). Agreeing and disagreeing with assessments: some features of preferred/ dispreferred turn shapes. In J. M. Atkinson and J. Heritage, eds., *Structures of Social Action: Studies in Conversation Analysis*, pp. 57–101. Cambridge University Press.

(1984b). Pursuing a response. In J. M. Atkinson and J. Heritage, eds., *Structures of Social Action*, pp. 152–164. Cambridge University Press.

(1986). Extreme case formulations: a way of legitimizing claims. *Human Studies* 9: 219–229.

Raymond, Geoffrey (2003). Grammar and social organization: yes/no interrogatives and the structure of responding. *American Sociological Review* 68: 939–967.

(2004). Prompting action: the stand-alone "So" in ordinary conversation. *Research on Language and Social Interaction* 37: 185–218.

Raymond, Geoffrey and Heritage John, (2006). The epistemics of social relations: owning grandchildren. *Language in Society* 35: 677–704.

Robinson, Jeffrey D. (2004). The sequential organization of "explicit" apologies in naturally occurring English. *Research on Language and Social Interaction* 37: 291–330.

Ruusuvuori, Johanna and Lindfors, Pirjo (2009). Complaining about previous treatment in health care settings. *Journal of Pragmatics* 41: 2415–2434.

Sacks, Harvey (1987). On the preferences for agreement and contiguity in sequences in conversation. In G. Button and J. R. E. Lee, *Talk and Social Organisation*, pp. 54–69. Clevedon: Multilingual Matters.

(1992). *Lectures on Conversation*, vol. I: *Fall 1964–Spring 1968*. Oxford: Blackwell.

Sacks, Harvey, Schegloff, Emanuel A. and Jefferson, Gail (1974). A simplest systematics for the organization of turn-taking for conversation. *Language* 50: 696–735.

Schegloff, Emanuel A. (1987). Some sources of misunderstanding in talk-in-interaction. *Linguistics* 25: 201–218.

(1988). Goffman and the analysis of conversation. In P. Drew and A. Wootton, eds., *Erving Goffman: Exploring the Interaction Order*, pp. 89–135. Cambridge: Polity Press.

(1992). Repair after next turn: the last structurally provided place for the defense of intersubjectivity in conversation. *American Journal of Sociology* 95: 1295–1345.

(1997a). Practices and actions: boundary cases of other-initiated repair. *Discourse Processes* 23: 499–545.

(1997b). Third turn repair. In G. R. Guy, C. Feagin, D. Schiffrin and J. Baugh, eds., *Towards a Social Science of Language*, vol. II: *Social Interaction and Discourse Structures*, pp. 31–40. Amsterdam: John Benjamins.

(2000). When "others" initiate repair. *Applied Linguistics* 21: 205–243.

(2005). On complainability. *Social Problems* 52: 449–476.

(2008). Self-initiated, same turn repair: three core topics. Paper presented at the Workshop on Repair. University of Toronto: March.

Schegloff, Emanuel A., Jefferson, Gail and Sacks, Harvey. (1977). The preference for self-correction in the organization of repair in conversation. *Language* 53: 361–382.

Schegloff, Emanuel A. and Sacks, Harvey (1973). Opening up closings. *Semiotica* 8: 289–327.

Schiffrin, D. (1987). *Discourse Markers*. Cambridge University Press.

Sidnell, Jack. (2007). "Look"-prefaced turns in first and second position: launching, interceding and redirecting action. *Discourse Studies* 9: 387–408.

Stivers, Tanya (2008). Stance, alignment, and affiliation during storytelling: when nodding is a token of affiliation. *Research on Language and Social Interaction* 41: 31–57.

Traverso, Véronique (2009). The dilemmas of third-party complaints in conversation between friends. *Journal of Pragmatics* 41: 2385–2399.

NOTES

1 This chapter adds to the study of turn beginnings, which conversation analysts recognize as significant structural places in conversation, particularly for the sequential work that they do in locating a turn relative to what has preceded it. For a review of this literature, see Sidnell (2007: 388).

2 Along these lines, see Schiffrin (1987: 295–311), although she also specifies four conditions that qualify an expression as a discourse marker (Schiffrin, 1987: 328): its syntax, turn-initial position, prosody, and operation at "local" and "global" levels in discourse. "Local" level could include sequential position.

3 Ford, Fox, and Thompson (2002: 29) observe that "I mean" can be an "epistemic 'discourse marker.'"

4 The conversation analytic literature on complaining tends to employ the term "affiliation" for the preferred response to complaining utterances. Schegloff (1988: 122), in discussing "responsive seconds" to complaints, uses the term "alignment" (among other terms). This is the term I shall use, along with its obverse, "misalignment." The topic of responsiveness to complaints is complex and cannot be fully addressed here, but I also draw on the research in a different domain by Stivers (2008) that suggestively distinguishes between alignment and affiliation.

5 Subsequent to Lottie's alignment, Emma changes the topic to a more upbeat one, which suggests that she notices the laconicism. Given that Emma's series of complaints and criticisms occur after Lottie had initiated the critical talk by a negative comment about the hotel where the restaurant was housed, this may be an instance where a recipient (Emma) of the first complaint "goes too far" (Drew and Walker, 2009) in her own complaining response.

6 In a sense, IMPUs work to re-complete the complaining action that they accompany. For a contrasting device, see Raymond's (2004: 190–193) discussion of "so" prefacing and how it can be used to close off a sequence and initiate another; such utterances are action-projective rather than or in addition to action-retrospective.

7 Examples 6 and 8 in Davidson's (1984: 106–107) paper contain offers that are followed by I-mean-formatted subsequent versions. However, there are inapposite features to the offers these IMPUs follow. I investigate the use of I-mean utterances in the context of inapposite turns of talk later in this chapter but for reasons of space do not further discuss the Davidson examples.

8 See also Ono and Thompson (1994).
9 On the use of prosody for parody and mimicry, see Couper-Kuhlen (1996: 389–390) and her discussion of Bakhtin (1978[1929]: 176–196) on parody and Goffman (1974: 537) on mimicry.
10 That is, "oh well" can propose to minimize the untoward aspects of some experience. For another example, in the extract below Leslie has reported being up with family "until half past three this morning":

[Holt:1:1]

01 Mum: Oh:; gosh y'been up all ni:ght the:n
(0.3)
02 Les: .t Oh well I went back t'bed,

Leslie treats Mum's offer of a sympathetic, extreme-case formulation ("up all ni:ght") with an "oh well" and a report ("I went back t'bed"), suggesting a situation within the realm of easy remediation.
11 As Mandelbaum (1991/1992: 116) notes, "In response to a recipient's disattending, the complainer can reassert the complaint." Here Leslie does not reassert the complaint but she does add fuel to the fire (so to speak) by raising another aspect of the mother-in-law's complainable conduct.
12 Sacks (1992: 734) discusses "No, I mean" as an instance for skip-tying, and Schegloff (1992: 1304–1317) refers to "No I mean" as the canonical way in which third position repair is formatted. So both Sacks 1992 and Schegloff, when dealing with I-mean, adduce clear instances of repair, whereas when I-mean utterances tie to complaints they may be doing something else besides repair as such, but under the auspices of repair formatting.
13 For discussion of this instance and how it constitutes a episode of gossip (Bergmann, 1993) in which Sally and Judy collaborate in their critical stance toward how bad the mother's condition is and how upset Vickie deserves to be, see Maynard (2003: 99–100).
14 See Maynard (2003: 88) on how the quality or valence of news "is not inherent in events and instead is something that is, relative to the exhibited concerns, perspectives, and identities of co-participants, their own interactional production."
15 Jen's proposal may thus embody an inapposite remark that the subsequent IMPU can remedy. See the discussion of IMPUs in relation to inapposite actions below.
16 As such they may also prepare for Vera's own speakership (see discussion below and note 16).
17 Jefferson (1983: 4) remarks, "Roughly, 'Yeah' can exhibit a preparedness to shift from recipiency to speakership, while 'Mm hm' exhibits what I will call 'Passive Recipiency'. And roughly what I mean by 'Passive Recipiency' is that its user is proposing that his co-participant is still in the midst of some course of talk, and shall go on talking." In these terms, Leslie's line 3 appears (and is apparently heard) not to be doing passive recipiency and is doing something more like working toward speakership.
18 The "it's the seh" phrase sounds to my ear like it is projecting "it's the same," as if Leslie were going to say "it's the same with me." If so, then Leslie may be revising

the preface to her story and avoiding portraying what it reports (making antique silhouettes) as the "same" as Joan's "doing housework" story.

19 Recall Sacks's (1992: 634–638) discussion concerning complaints in the context of turn-taking. Participants regulate most violations of turn-taking through competing for the turn and/or engaging in such activities as dropping out of simultaneous talk, and complaining that someone has interrupted is another (and more overt) means of enforcement for the system. However, utterances such as "you just interrupted me" have the built-in danger that they "are capable of being scrutinized for what action they're doing" (Sacks, 1992: 637–638) – namely complaining – and such expression can itself be subject to complaint.

20 Besides example 3, see also example 7.

21 As Schegloff (1987: 208–210) has shown, a potential source of misunderstanding in talk in interaction occurs when recipients hear an utterance as a complaint rather than as some other action (such as initiating closure or topic). Such displays of misunderstanding may result in repair by the speaker on behalf of the other action. IMPUs, by contrast, work to ensure that the action a speaker is pursuing is understandable *as* a complaint. By explicating or clarifying that complaint, the speaker may preempt possible alternative hearings and enhance the prospects for a preferred, aligning response to the complaint.

8 Availability as a trouble source in directive-response sequences

Mardi Kidwell

A fundamental requirement of interaction involves participants' coordination of, and ongoing monitoring for, one another's readiness, commitment, and ability to interact. In this chapter, I examine troubles in this basic sort of interactional coordination, what might very generally be subsumed under the term *troubles with availability*, whether that be at an interaction's outset or once interaction is underway. Drawing on 500 hours of videotaped very young children's naturally occurring interactions in two different American daycare centers (i.e., children between one and two and a half years of age), I present situations involving children who, in the course of some activity, are called upon by an adult caregiver to alter what they are doing, as in the following instance:

(01) "Dan" (*D is about to dump box of toys in vicinity of other child's head.*)

```
01    CG:    Da::n! Da[:n!
      D:               .   .
02    CG:    [We're not throwing that.
      D:     [X   ((shifts gaze to CG, lowers box of toys))
```

I consider how caregivers' initiation of what turns out to be a directive-response sequence involves practices targeted at getting children to attend to them, particularly as displayed by children's gaze shifts. These practices include summoning the child at the outset of the sequence, and, when this fails, other attention-recruiting practices that serve as mending devices for the basic alignment of two parties for interaction. These attention-recruiting practices locate troubles with children's compliance with children's inability and/or unwillingness to attend to the caregiver, and, as such, they target for remedy a very particular aspect of children's embodied conduct: their gaze direction.

The attention-recruiting practices to be considered here locate a quite different trouble than that demonstrated in the following example:

(02) "Hair" *(Amber has grabbed a boy's hair.)*

01 CG: A:mber let go plea:se.
02 (1.0)
03 *let go (0.1) LEt go. (.) LET Go:.
*((*said as CG tries to pull A's hand off boy's hair))*

In example 2, the caregiver's action in line 3 is a multiple directive produced in conjunction with her efforts to physically remove Amber's hand from the boy's hair. As such, it targets as a trouble the child's hand in the act of grasping the boy's hair, not the child's gaze direction. Indeed, getting the child's gaze, or other show of attention, is not part of the course of action the caregiver engages in here. The caregiver utters the child's name in line 1, but immediately follows this with the directive, "let go." In other words, the child's name is used to address the directive to her, but not to get her to make a display of attention in the same way that a summons is, which builds into its production a "place" for that display (e.g., in example 1, the elongation of the first summons component; or, canonically, a silence following the summons component that "waits" for the display). A question to consider, then, is what sort of interactional work is accomplished by targeting for action the child's attentional focus? And, what role does this play toward the end of effecting compliance from the child that is different from action directed toward the offending conduct itself?

The practices for procuring another's gaze as a display of availability for interaction that I examine here fall within the domain of practices of *pursuit* for how they are directed to the "noticeable" absence of a response (here, an answer to a summons; Davidson, 1984; Heritage, 1984; Pomerantz, 1984; Stivers and Rossano, 2010) due upon issuance of an initiating action, and they locate *recipient inaction* as an interactional trouble. In prior research, Pomerantz (1984) notes that the practices of pursuit, and the sorts of troubles to which they are directed, can be carried out as an ordered set of options by reference to the maxim, "try an easy solution first" (p. 156). An "easy solution" might be, as Pomerantz demonstrates, treating a recipient's non-response to an assertion as a problem of understanding, rather than as a problem of agreement: the former can be remedied (more simply) by clarification; the latter, (more complexly) by speaker's modification of her position. Bolden, Mandelbaum, and Wilkinson (2012) note, too, that, in so far as pursuit locates a failure with recipient action, speakers may employ practices to circumvent this implication and pursue a response by more covert means, specifically by self-initiated self-repair of their own talk, a move that shifts ownership of the problem from *other* to *self*.

In the case of directive-response sequences that are presented in this chapter, I also consider the interactional complexities, and sensitivities, involved in pursuing a response from another. As I demonstrate, the pursuit of an attentional display such as we see in example 1, in contrast to the pursuit of compliance such as we see in example 2, deals with a potential trouble, or attempts to preempt a potential trouble, at the earliest possible sequential point in an encounter, that is, before a trouble can emerge in the "interaction proper" space. In these cases, this is the space in which the directive utterance will be issued and the child's compliance called for. Further, pursuing another's attentional display versus pursuing their compliance entails rather different character implications: in particular, that the other is not so much non-compliant as he or she is inattentive.

While the practices for procuring another's gaze or other displays of availability that I examine here fall within the domain of practices of pursuit, they also have consequences for our understanding of the domain of repair. In line with work by Schegloff (1968) on the summons-answer sequence, and C. Goodwin (1980, 1981) on participant techniques for eliciting recipient gaze as a display of recipiency, I consider how caregivers work to set up an "optimal environment" for interaction with young children, one in which they have an attentive and available recipient. This is an environment that is resistant (but not immune) to the sorts of phenomena that repair is directed to: "troubles in speaking, hearing, and understanding" (Schegloff, Jefferson, and Sacks, 1977: 361; Schegloff, 2004).

Before continuing, I discuss the terms "pursuit" and "repair" in more detail, and the different domains of interactional trouble to which they are addressed.

8.1 Pursuit versus repair

The term "repair" refers to the practices laid out in a significant body of work by conversation analysts that focuses on talk-in-interaction. As mentioned above, this body of work has quite explicitly dealt with "troubles in speaking, hearing, and understanding," and the sequentially afforded opportunities and practices for initiating and carrying out repair on these troubles as they differentially emerge for self and other across the unfolding of turns at talk.

As Schegloff and others have demonstrated, the mechanisms of repair are critical to the maintenance of intersubjectivity in talk-in-interaction (Schegloff, 1992; cf. Wootton, 1994), and designed to handle the contingencies and imperfections that are quite naturally a part of two or more people using talk as their primary resource for interaction. In its historical use in the field, repair refers to the domain of practices aimed at dealing with troubles in talk that are, of essence, deployed with respect to the turn-based, sequential organization of talk, and the actions that talk implements, including, as many chapters in this volume demonstrate, actions that deal with a variety of interpersonal and institutional matters. The term, in this sense, does not easily transfer to other domains that have to do with dealing with other sorts of troubles in interaction (e.g., embodied action troubles, troubles with interactional alignment and affiliation, troubles with securing a response to an initiating action, and so on) that, while important in their own right, and for the advancement of an interaction, are not subject to the same set of turn-based, sequentially organized constraints and opportunities for handling troubles as is the repair of talk.

The sorts of practices that I examine here, as a sequential matter, locate troubles with *other's* action following other's non-response (or otherwise inadequate response) to an initiating action, and, as such, constitute practices of pursuit. In some ways, these practices resemble the practices of third position repair: following the position in which a response is due, that is, in the *next turn,* or second position, the producer of the initiating action reformulates that action in the third position, having located a trouble with his or her own initiating action by way of how the other does or does not respond (Schegloff, 1992). Arguably, however, in the cases of non-response, such as I examine here, this is done in a way that does not *repair* the talk used to implement the action – although modifications to the talk are made – but rather *pursues* a response with resources that call upon, even demand, that "other" produce that which is due. Such resources, as we will see, consist quite powerfully of repetition (as opposed to reformulation; cf. Schegloff, 2004), as well as sound stretches, sound stresses, and volume shifts (typically volume increases, but sometimes decreases), and, when these fail, other resources that more strongly call on "other" to remedy their actions having to do with what and whom they are attending to, including the use of physical intervention.

An aim of this chapter, then, is to consider, within the context of other chapters on repair, how participants go about dealing with a different set of troubles than troubles with talk. The sorts of troubles, actual and potential, that are examined in this chapter have to do, on the one hand, with getting another to respond to an initiating action, and, on the other, with setting up and maintaining the conditions that make interaction possible in the first place. The practices for doing this, for securing interactional alignment, particularly at the start of interaction, are the topic of some of the earliest work in conversation analysis.

8.2 The summons + directive sequence

Schegloff (1968), in his classic paper on the summons-answer sequence, demonstrates how this two-part structure is a powerful tool for the coordinated entry of participants into an encounter, and, moreover, for committing them to a possibly more extended engagement. The summons, as an initiating action, seeks to elicit a response from a would-be recipient. This response, which might take a verbal form such as "yeah?" or "what?", or an embodied form such as a shift of gaze to the summoner, works as a show of availability for interaction and a willingness and ability to be a recipient of an action that is to follow. A summons sets in motion a sequence of four actions (p. 1091):

> Action 1: *A summons B.*
> Action 2: *B answers A's summons.*
> Action 3: *A produces action that B has been summoned for.*
> Action 4: *B produces responding action to A's action.*

Example 3 provides a demonstration of this four-part sequence. Brittany has taken a toy from another child, and the caregiver intervenes:

(03) "Sandbox 4" *(Brittany has taken a toy from another child.)*

```
01   CG:   Britta ny:[:
     B:          . .[X
02   CG:   I'd like you to give her something. Okay? You
           just keep grabbing everything.
           Le[t-  give her something to play with.
03   B:      [((shifts gaze down, hands over object to child))
04   CG:   Thank you.
```

We see that the caregiver summons the child by calling her name, and, before she has even finished the utterance, the child has begun turning toward her. In this way, the child demonstrates a ready willingness to be a recipient of the caregiver's next action, a directive. The directive seeks to get the child to do something, and we see that it is effective: Brittany hands over an object to the other child. Of note is that the caregiver here, as in example 1 above, produces the directive once Brittany has shifted her gaze to her; the elongation of the summons allows Brittany time to accomplish the gaze shift such that they will be in a state of mutual gaze when the caregiver produces the directive (C. Goodwin, 1980).

Directives, as initiating actions that seek to compel another to act in a particular way (M. H. Goodwin, 1980, 1990; West, 1990; Kidwell, 2006; Craven and Potter, 2010), are usually terminated when the directive recipient demonstrates that s/he is going to, or about to, comply with the directive.[1] Together, directive and response form a sequence. As one can imagine, however, compliance with a directive action is not always immediately forthcoming: as mentioned above, the directive recipient may not want to, or be able to, comply. Getting another to comply with a directive (in contrast to getting them to make a display of attention) may involve a variety of directive and other persuasive actions that pursue compliance as the proper response to the directive: for example, accounts, suggestions, hints, coaxings, urgings, pleadings, threats, and even the use of physical force. As we see in example 3, the caregiver employs a variety of actions in the directive space but, unlike example 2, does not use "repeat" as a resource for pursuit. The caregiver follows the initial directive, formulated as a want/need statement ("I'd like you to ...") with a tag question that explicitly pursues a show of compliance from the child ("Okay?"); an account that warrants the directive by providing a negative characterization of the child's actions ("You just keep grabbing everything"); and another directive that starts out, it appears, as a proposal ("Let('s)–"), but is cut off and reformulated as an imperative ("give her something to play with") when the child shifts her gaze downward. These actions coincide with the unfolding actions of the child: the caregiver produces a stream of verbal actions, TCU by TCU, as she awaits, and seeks to motivate, the child's compliance, which occurs in line 3 in overlap with the caregiver's last directive. Upon achieving compliance from the child, the caregiver ceases her line of directive action and, further, produces a *thank you* that explicitly acknowledges receipt (and shows appreciation) of the child's compliance and closes the sequence.

8.3 A collaborative intervention technique

In the cases that are of interest in this paper, the directive-response sequence is initiated via a summons: as just discussed, an effort by the caregiver to secure the child's availability for the next action, which will be the directive. When the child "answers" the summons, the caregiver produces the directive. Of note is that this is an intervention technique that calls on the child to alter her or his own behavior and, as such, is to be distinguished from cases in which the caregiver simply effects the altering herself through direct physical intervention. For example, in example 4 the caregiver sees Marcus push Checco as he sits atop the sofa. She quickly, urgently reaches out her arm to stop him, but is too late, and Checco goes tumbling to the floor (figure 8.1).

Interventions in which the caregiver works directly, and unilaterally, to bring about change in a child's behavior, such as we see in example 4, are typically associated with situations in which the child's actions present a clear danger to her- or himself or to another child; there is also the quite practical matter that the caregiver needs to be close enough to the site of action to get there in time to intervene if, in fact, a physical intervention is going to be successful. In contrast, the use of a summons, followed by a directive, represents a more collaborative intervention approach, one that explicitly targets the child as an agent of change over her or his own behavior. This is done as part of an orientation by the caregiver to the child, pedagogically and culturally, as an actor who can author her or his own actions, and, thus, as someone who understands the speech that is directed to her or him – or is in the developmental process of coming to be able to understand it. It is also done as part of the practicalities of the daycare setting: the caregiver, in

Figure 8.1: Caregiver tries to stop push/fall (example 4).

charge of several young children at once, sometimes in a large space, cannot physically get to every trouble and must attempt to solve problem incidents by *telling* children what to do and getting them to alter their own behavior. Additionally, the caregiver typically has the task of selecting a particular child for action out of a cast of many children. The summons is *the* device for handling these cultural and environmental contingencies: it calls on a particular child out of many children, sometimes from a distance and/or in the context of the caregiver's other preoccupations, to not only be a recipient of the caregiver's summons, but, of particular consequence, to ultimately be an agent of change over her or his own conduct in accord with the action that has been set up by the summons, the directive.

8.3.1 Summoned for "cause": preemptive compliance

Indeed, so suited for this task is the summons that sometimes it is all that is needed to get a child to alter her or his actions. The summons, in calling on a child to attend, sets up the expectation that the child has been called *for cause*, "a reason" (i.e., *Action 3* in Schegloff's four-part sequential model) and before one can even be articulated, children may make the connection that it is their own conduct that is the "reason." As we see in the next two examples, the caregiver calls the child's name, and as the child is in the process of shifting his gaze to the caregiver – in other words before he has fully made the gaze shift and before the caregiver has issued a directive – he ceases the problem conduct:

(05) "Firetruck Short" *(Derrick pushes Eathan; his arm is still outstretched when CG intervenes.)*

01 CG: Derrick?
02 (.)
03 D: (0.5) *((shifts gaze to CG, retracts his hand in the process))*
04 CG: Gentle please.

(06) "Grabbing" *(Eathan is trying to pull a toy out of Brian's hand.)*

01 CG: Eathan? *((Brian is crying))*
02 E: (1.0) *((shifts gaze to CG, retracts hand in the process))*
03 CG: He's telling you that he doesn't want you to touch that broom right now.

In examples 5 and 6, the children not only respond to the caregiver's summons by shifting their gaze to her and thus comporting themselves as recipients, but show that they are oriented to the fact that they are summoned for cause, and that, in anticipation of the action they have been summoned for – that is, one directed at getting them to alter their current conduct – they preemptively do this. We see, too, that the caregiver follows through on the action she had committed herself to delivering with the summons: she goes ahead and produces the directive. That she does so, even though the child has in effect already complied, speaks to the power of the summons to sequentially commit the summoner to a subsequent action (the "reason" or "cause" as discussed above) once she has elicited a display of attention from the child, independent, it seems, from whether or not she has accomplished what motivated her use of a summons in the first place, namely, getting the child to alter his conduct.

Children, too, may *refrain* from shifting their gaze upon being summoned, but nonetheless preemptively alter their conduct. In example 7, Alex is pushing a child when the caregiver calls his name. He quickly withdraws his hand, but shifts his gaze downward rather than to the caregiver.

(07) "Alex" *(Alex has been pushing Derrick.)*

01 CG: *A: le: :x: ? *((*said as Alex pushes Derrick))*
02 A: (0.3) *((retracts hand, shifts gaze downward in the process))*
03 CG: No push: ing: .

We see that Alex refuses to comport himself as a recipient to the caregiver's projected action, but he nonetheless orients to the reason for the summons with his quick termination of pushing. In other words, he complies without acknowledging that he is being asked to comply, in this way designing his actions so as to suggest that they are not motivated by the caregiver's directive.

We see in examples 5, 6, and 7 that children, whether or not they shift their gaze to the caregiver, are responsive to being summoned for how this action is the start of a course of action designed to get them to alter their conduct. As such they may alter their own actions *before* the caregiver has in fact produced an utterance explicitly aimed at setting them to do this. Another kind of evidence of children's orientation to what they are being summoned for comes from their acts of "defiance" toward adults: upon being summoned and registering such with their gaze shift, they nonetheless carry on with their current conduct in an escalated or intensified fashion. Alternately, children may "ignore" the caregiver altogether.

8.3.2 Defying and ignoring: two different trouble types

In example 8, a child who is trying to get a ball away from another child turns to the caregiver when she summons him and then hurriedly turns back to resume the activity he was engaged in before. In other words, he tries to "get away with" taking the ball before the caregiver takes stronger action, such as a physical intervention, to stop him:

(08) "His Ball" *(Brian tries to take ball from M, it drops to floor, M cries out.)*

01	CG:	Brian.
02	B:	(1.0) *((turns, shifting gaze to CG))*
03		(1.7) *((turns quickly back to resume trying to get ball on floor; M is also trying to get ball))*
04	CG:	Brian. (0.1) Michael was *playing with the blue ball. *((*CG begins to move to physically intervene to help return ball to M))*

In example 8, Brian, like the children in the prior three cases, exhibits a responsiveness to the reason that he has been summoned for but, to not be impeded in his project, intensifies his efforts to get the ball. When he turns back to resume this project, the caregiver summons him again. When he does not respond (she leaves a bit of space for him to do so in line 4), she begins an utterance that formulates a particular scenario: Michael's prior possession of the ball ("Michael was playing with the blue ball"). Such formulations invoke "ownership," or rights of use; as stand-alone accounts, they are produced to motivate a child's cessation of efforts at possession of an object and/or justify the caregiver's moves to effect such a cessation. The child's failure to heed the second summons and beginning of an account, following his visible registering of the first summons, results in the caregiver's move to physically intervene.

In addition, children may simply refrain from shifting their gaze to the caregiver to avoid being a recipient of a directive action and carry on with the problem conduct – as if they have not heard the summons. In example 9, Willy pushes a child and the caregiver summons him a number of times; in other words, she pursues a display of attention from him:

(09) "Throwing" *(Willy pushes J)*

W: *((pushes J))*
CG: uh: Willy Willy,
(0.3) *((W pushes J again))*
CG: Wi:lly,
(0.6) *((W turns back to play with blocks))*
CG: Wi:lly,
(5.2)
W: *((runs away from the scene))*

In example 9, the caregiver is not able to secure a response to her multiple summoning attempts. In this context, and considering also that the child terminates his problem conduct in line 5, the caregiver does not deliver the subsequent action, the directive, that is projected by the summons.

In examples 8 and 9, the caregiver is confronted with a problem recipient – and a non-compliant child – in two different ways: one who acknowledges the summons, yet carries on with the problem conduct (example 8); and the other who neither acknowledges the summons nor terminates (in a timely way) the problem conduct (example 9). In example 8, the trouble is *not* the child's inattention toward the caregiver, but rather his carrying on with the problem activity in the context of having made a display of attention, making of his conduct something on the order of an act of defiance. As such, the caregiver, registering that the child has made a display of attention, focuses her efforts at getting compliance on the offending act itself by ultimately moving to physically intervene, an issue to be considered below in light of cases of multiple directives. In example 9, the trouble, as constituted through the caregiver's actions, is with the child's unwillingness to make a display of attention toward her. By his actions he shows himself to be actively ignoring the caregiver, and it is this trouble that the caregiver works on via multiple summoning actions. However, the sequence, as one that projects a second, third and fourth action, is prematurely terminated: in the context of the child failing to produce the second action by shifting his gaze to the caregiver and thus displaying himself as a recipient, the caregiver withholds the third action, the directive. We see that in so far as the point of the summons is to set up the necessary conditions for interaction, the summoner may simply abandon her project when this work is unsuccessful – or, as we see below, pursue via other techniques.

To be considered in more detail next is how caregivers orient to children's inattention itself as a problem, the resources they mobilize to pursue their attentional displays as a go-ahead for subsequent interaction, and the consequences of this for a line of directive action.

8.4 Managing the inattentive recipient

Caregivers have at their disposal a number of resources for securing the attention of a child for a directive action when a single summons is not, or does not seem to be, enough. Such resources include verbal summoning methods and physical methods. Verbal summoning methods include the use of repetition (as opposed to reformulation), sound stretches, sound stresses, and volume shifts. Physical methods may be used in conjunction with verbal ones to more strongly call on *other* to provide the response that is due, or, as I demonstrate, to preempt troubles from occurring in the first place.

8.4.1 The multiple repeat summons vs. the repeat single summons

As we see in example 9 above, a caregiver may try more than once to summon the child when the child fails to make a display of attention. For example, the initial summons in example 9 at line 2 is composed as a *multiple repeat summons*, a successive calling of the child's name (here, twice) without pause:

(09) "Throwing"

```
01   W:    ((pushes J))
02   CG:   uh: Willy Willy,
```

The repeating components of this summons type may undergo variation as they are produced one after another that include sound stretches, stresses, and increases or decreases in volume (e.g., example 1) – or they may not, as is the case in example 9 in which both components are produced in virtually the same way, without pause, and within the same intonational contour (Stivers, 2004). This is a summons type that stands out more conspicuously in the acoustic environment than a single summons, and constitutes a more insistent, urgent way of calling another to attend. Produced as it is as a single unit of talk, its first job is to *distract* the child from a current course of action by getting him to shift his gaze to the summoner, rather than to get him to shift his gaze in order to be a recipient to something the summoner has to say. Indeed, at the moment the caregiver issues the action in line 2 in example 9, the child, having just pushed another child, is poised to do so again, and the action seeks to intervene in and prevent this second push. In contrast, the single summons actions, which allow a silence following their production for recipient to respond, are issued in an environment of less threat: Willy, having pushed the other child a second time, is summoned by the caregiver in line 4 with a single summons, then again in line 6 after he has turned back to play with a pile of blocks.

03 (0.3) *((W pushes J again))*
04 CG: Wi:lly,
05 (0.6) *((W turns back to play with blocks))*
06 CG: Wi:lly,

The first single summons at line 4 is stressed and elongated, while the second summons is not stressed, only elongated; it is a weaker version of the first. Such production differences of the first and second single summons are responsive to an environment in which the child is visibly disengaging from the activity of pushing and resuming the activity of playing. These subsequent summonses are designed less to prevent an imminent act of peer aggression than to get Willy's attention to sanction his just prior conduct. Such an action by the caregiver might be done either in the form of a directive or directive related utterance (as in, "don't push," "we don't push here," or "be gentle"), or as a negative characterization of his actions – a reprimand (as in, "That's not okay"). But, as already discussed, Willy refuses to answer the caregiver's summonses, and the caregiver gives up trying to engage him.

Going back to example 1, presented at the outset of the chapter, we see another example of the multiple repeat summons, which, in contrast to example 9, does secure a show of availability from the child. As with example 9, the action that the caregiver addresses is one that she urgently seeks to have the child abandon: he is about to dump a box of toys in the vicinity of another child's head; further, the caregiver is some distance from the child when she calls him. The caregiver's summons is produced with a sound stretch on the first component that allows for a response from the child before a second, shorter, sharper summons is produced. When the child shifts his gaze to the caregiver, a move by the child that starts as she nears completion of the second summons component, she produces the action that has been projected by her summons, the directive.

(01) "Dan" (*D is about to dump box of toys in vicinity of other child's head.*)

01 CG: Da::n! Da[:n!
D: . .
02 CG: [We're not throwing that.
D: [X *((shifts gaze to CG, lowers box of toys))*

In the cases presented so far, getting a child to answer a summons is done solely with verbal techniques. On what might be thought of as a collaborative continuum scale, verbal techniques allow a child the most agency in conforming to the constraints posed by the conditional relevancy of an initiating action, with, of course, multiple repeat summonses being stronger versions of the single summons. As we saw, too, the summoning components of either a single summons or multiple repeat summons may entail production characteristics that enhance or weaken its strength as an initiating action, especially in response to the perceived urgency of a child's behavior at a particular moment.

To be considered next is how a caregiver may employ physical means to "force" an answer to the summons.

8.4.2 Gaze tracking, "face holds," and other "forced recipiency" techniques

In the data set, caregivers can be seen practicing techniques of "forced recipiency" of varying degrees of strength: tracking children's gaze shifts away from them with their own gaze; pulling children to them and bringing their faces close to children's faces; and taking children's faces and turning and holding them toward their own – this latter technique, a "face hold," being the most forceful in terms of how it maximally constrains the other's freedom of movement. These techniques are typically produced in conjunction with verbal summonses, as in the following case:

(10) "Sand Throw" *(Alex has thrown sand on another child's head.)*

01	CG:	*Uh:: Alex. *((*CG takes A's hand, begins pulling A to her; A is resisting, looking at other child))*	
02		(0.3)	
03		*Alex. *((*CG takes A's other hand, still pulling; he is still resisting, looking at other child))*	
04		(0.1) *((CG leans her face in toward A's))*	
05		*ALex. *((*CG gives a tug to bring bring A closer; A simultaneously shifts his gaze to her))*	⎤ CG and A are in mutual gaze (lines 05–10)
06		(0.2)	
07		That's not okay.	
08		(1.2)	
09		We're not throwing sand	
10		on people ( ).	⎦

In example 10, the caregiver goes about the work of getting a display of recipiency from the child in a number of ways. First, in line 1, the caregiver takes Alex's hand and begins to pull him toward her; as she does so, she produces a hesitation, "uh::," that shows her to be preparing to produce an utterance, the summons; after doing so, she pauses for him to answer. Then, in line 3, as she takes hold of his other hand, still pulling him toward her, she summons him again, again pausing for him to answer. Finally, in lines 4 and 5, she leans her face in close to his and gives him a tug as she summons him a third time. Upon the third summons and embodied action, the child shifts his gaze to her, and she delivers the action that these prior actions have been preparing the way for: first, a reprimand, then a rules invocation that, on the one hand, warrants the reprimand and on the other, is its own sort of directive action (i.e., a version of "don't throw sand on people"). In other words, the caregiver *only* produces the reprimanding/directive action when she has an available and attentive recipient, a circumstance that she has gone to some lengths to secure.

While example 10 demonstrates how a caregiver deals moment by moment with the unfolding contingencies of an inattentive recipient and undertakes measures of increasing strength to get him to attend to her, caregivers may also work preemptively to circumvent this kind of trouble.

8.4.3 Preempting recipiency troubles

In examples 11 and 12 we see a technique for assuring that a child is available and attentive from the start of the interaction: the caregiver does not use a verbal summons at all, but instead immediately uses a physical means to get the child's attention: taking hold of the child's face in what might be termed, the "preemptive face hold". In example 11, a child is about to bite another child, and the caregiver moves in swiftly to stop this.

(11) "My Seat" *(A is about to bite D when caregiver runs to scene and intervenes.)*

01 CG: *I don't want you to put your **<u>mou</u>th on 'im.
*((*CG pulls A's hands off B; **cups A's chin and pulls her face toward hers; **Figure 2))*

Example 12 provides a similar example:

(12) "Bite" *(E is about to bite D. CG rushes to intervene.)*

01 CG: *((puts hand on E's face to block bite, pulls his face away from D and toward her face))*
Stop.
02 E: *((shifts gaze down and tries to squirm away))*
03 CG: *Stop. *((*pulls child's face toward her again; *Figure 3)*

Figure 8.2: Caregiver pulls child's face to her (example 11).

We see in examples 11 and 12 that the caregiver first intervenes, that is, stops the impending bite, and then, as part of the physical trajectory of this action, pulls the child's face to her own and produces a directive. In example 12, when the child tries to squirm away and shifts his gaze down in the process, the caregiver pulls his face to hers again and repeats the directive. In these cases, the children are not being called upon – summoned – to be recipients of caregiver action that directs them to alter their conduct, but in effect are being *forced* to be recipients to this action by the caregiver. This is a method that circumvents problems with recipiency (such as we saw in example 10), and might be considered especially stern on the collaborative continuum scale of getting children to alter their conduct. Yet, in contrast to a way of handling children's problem conduct in which the caregiver intervenes and simply attempts to effect the change herself (example 4 above), it still calls on children – here, once caregivers have intervened and stopped the impending offense – to regulate their subsequent conduct in accord with the directive, and, further, ensures that children have been attentive recipients of the directive.

As has been argued, caregivers via their summonses and other attention-recruiting actions are working to ensure an optimal interaction space, one in

Figure 8.3: Caregiver pulls child's face to her (example 12).

which the interactants (here caregiver and child) are displaying their mutual attentiveness and availability for interaction, specifically for caregivers to address children's problem conduct via a directive, and for children to attend to and heed the directive. Such actions treat children as (more or less) capable recipients of adult talk, as well as capable social actors (more or less) who have agency over their own conduct. In the cases presented thus far, the caregivers, having secured children's displays of attention, go on to produce talk that is trouble-free – that is, free from dysfluencies, hitches, restarts and the like – directed at getting children to alter their behavior (consider especially examples 1, 3, 5–7, and 10–12 again). Indeed troubles in procuring and maintaining children's attention that cannot be solved can result in troubles in the directive space: troubles with caregivers' talk, as well as with getting compliance from the child.

8.5 Troubles with talk in the "directive space"

In the following two cases, we see that, in the context of being unable to secure or maintain a child's display of attention, in line with work by C. Goodwin (1980, 1981), the caregiver's directive talk is produced with cut-offs and restarts as she negotiates trying to get the child's attention and trying to produce directive talk. As Goodwin has demonstrated, such methods work to elicit recipient gaze to speaker's actions. However, cases such as these seem to be rare in the data set, suggesting, perhaps, that a method that works with adults in situations of "ordinary conversation" may not be effective – or interactionally appropriate – in the case of young children, especially ones engaged *not* in conversation, but other, primarily embodied activities (pushing, throwing sand on peers, etc.) that an adult is trying to get them to stop.

Consider the following:

(13) "Shark" *(Brian has taken hold of a toy shark in Alex's hand and is trying to pull it away. Alex is upset. The caregiver intervenes.)*

01	CG:		Br [ian,
	B:		[..X
02	CG:		He:'s playing right now,
03			(0.3) *((B shifts gaze away from CG, holds onto toy))*
04	CG:	–>	An:d– >yeah<, he is playing.
05		–>	*>>And<< he feels comfo:rtable playing with
06		–>	this. *((*begins to disconnect A and B's hands))*
07			*Brian! (.) Brian! *((*B is backing away from CG))*

In example 13, the caregiver initially secures the child's gaze shift with the summons at line 1, and then she goes on to produce the directive (here, a rights-of-use formulation: "He:'s playing right now,") at line 2. Similar to Case 8 above, the child acts in defiance of the caregiver's directive action: having shifted his gaze to the caregiver, he then shifts his gaze away (back to the target object) at line 3, and maintains his hold on the object. In line 4, the caregiver continues with her talk ("An:d–") but cuts off and repeats talk from line 2 (">yeah<, he is playing."). She then goes on at line 5 to produce the utterance that was first projected by "An:d–" (">>And<< he feels comfo: rtable playing with this."). The caregiver has not resecured the child's gaze when she does this, but has managed to disconnect the hands of the two disputing children, and thus achieve some measure of a solution to the problem. However, the child's problem conduct continues. In line 7, Brian backs away from the caregiver, with object still in hand, and she begins the summoning process again.

In example 14, the caregiver, after multiple summoning attempts over the course of lines 1–8, begins to produce the directive at line 9 (what will turn out to be a rights-of-use formulation, as in "Robert's playing with that"). However, she cuts off when she is overlapped by the child's cry and, similar to example 13, handles the child's ongoing problem conduct by reverting back to summoning the child at line 11:

(14) "Bucket" *(Kelly is pulling on a big bucket that another child has a hold of. The caregiver tries to get her to let go.)*

01 CG: Kelly. *((pulling gently on K's shoulder))*
02 (0.8)
03 °Kelly°. *((pulling a little harder))*
04 <u>KE</u>lly. *((moves two hands to pull K))*
05 (1.0)
06 K: ah [hhhuh!
07 CG: [Kelly *((pulling on K with both hands, K's hand lets go of bucket))*
08 –> R [obert's–
09 K: [AH [HH!
10 CG: [Kel [ly

As the interaction continues below, we see that at line 11 the caregiver pulls Kelly to her lap and, at line 12, addresses her. But at line 13, Kelly shows herself to be completely unable to be a recipient: she collapses in an anguished heap in the caregiver's lap as she cries. While Kelly is in this position, the caregiver nonetheless continues to address her, and then pulls the child up to eye level starting at line 16, a technique of "forced recipiency" as discussed above:

11 [*uhhruhh [uhh *((*CG pulls K to her lap))*
12 CG: [You know wha::t?
13 K: –> [*K collapses in CG's lap*
14 (0.5)
15 CG: Robert's playing with that right now.
16 K: –> (1.0) *((begins lifting K up to look her in the eye))*
17 CG: Yeah. A:nd *you're just gonna get frustrated? *((*CG is holding K at eye level))*
18 (1.0)
19 Yeah. And I saw that happening already?

We see in both examples 13 and 14 that caregivers are sensitive to the interactional environment in which they might produce their directive talk to children, that is, sensitive to the quality of alignment between children and themselves as available and attentive co-interactants. Caregivers may cut off, then restart, a line of directive talk when this alignment is disrupted, and then revert back to summoning (example 13); or they may cut off and seek realignment by reverting back to summoning immediately, and, when this is ineffective, by "forcing recipiency" (example 14). In other words, caregivers are unwilling to go forward with their directive project until they have secured an attentional display from the child (Sidnell, 2011: 142–143.). Moreover, there is an ordering to their attention pursuit techniques. In these two cases, troubles that emerge in the directive space are remedied by increasingly strong techniques of getting the child to attend that range from operations on the talk itself (i.e., speech cut-offs and restarts) to explicitly calling on the child to attend (i.e., via summoning) in accompaniment with physical techniques that attempt to force recipiency. Techniques such as these warrant further consideration in light of how caregivers treat problems with children's compliance as a problem of basic interactional alignment.

8.6 Mending alignment troubles: the mid-encounter summons and other exposed techniques

As discussed above, in C. Goodwin's (1980, 1981) work on gaze-recruiting techniques and speaker-recipient alignment, he describes techniques such as speech cut-offs and restarts for recruiting recipient gaze. We see in the two cases above, however, that these techniques – ineffective in eliciting children's gaze or getting them to alter their conduct – are quickly supplanted by the caregiver's return to summoning. The distinction between what may be considered "embedded" techniques versus "exposed" techniques of gaze pursuit, and their connection to a line of directive action by the caregiver, warrants consideration here (Kidwell, 2006).

The techniques described by Goodwin are ones that work *within* talk to elicit recipient gaze and, embedded as they are within the talk, they work to preserve the business of the turn (i.e., whatever actions the turn is seeking to accomplish) as the main line of action. Indeed, returning to example 13, we see that these are techniques that the caregiver tries in lines 4–6 before turning to more exposed techniques, that is, ones that interrupt (or otherwise put on hold) the business that the talk is directed to in order to explicitly return to the business of calling for the child's attention, starting at line 7:

(13) "Shark" *(Brian has taken hold of a toy shark in Alex's hand and is trying to pull it away. Alex is upset. The caregiver intervenes.)*

01 CG: Br[ian,
B: [..X
02 CG: He:'s playing right now,
03 (0.3) *((B shifts gaze away from CG, holds onto toy))*
04 CG: An:d– >yeah<, he is playing.
05 >>And<< he feels comfo:rtable playing with
06 this.
07 -> Brian! (.) Brian!
08 (.)
09 -> *Excuse me, excuse me. *((*takes B's hand and pulls him to her; B begins to shift gaze to her))*
10 (.)
11 He is *playing. I am [– *((*B is gazing at CG))*
12 B: [AEHhhhh! Ahah hh
13 CG: -> Brian.
14 B: mumumumu
15 CG: -> BRIan.

At line 7, the caregiver summons the child by calling his name twice. She has thus abandoned her line of directive talk to now explicitly call for his attention again. When this fails, she produces a more general summons in line 9 ("Excuse me, excuse me.") as she takes hold of the child's hand and pulls him to her, in other words, attempting to also physically compel recipiency as part of her course of pursuit. As we see in line 11, the caregiver, having been successful in getting the child to shift his gaze to her, produces again the directive action that she issued in line 2. But as she continues her talk, the child cries out, in this way refusing to be a recipient, and we see the caregiver at lines 13 and 15 return to the project of summoning him.

To summon someone this way, mid-encounter as it were, once interaction has gotten underway (even a relatively short spate of interaction such as that examined here), locates, and attempts to remedy, a very basic failure of interaction. This is one in which one of the participants is showing himself to be unavailable and/or unwilling to be a participant – even though in example 13 the child initially committed himself to interaction via his gaze shift to the caregiver. Summonses, as Schegloff (1968) showed, are typically used at the outset of interaction to initially coordinate participants' availability and readiness to enter into an encounter – and, as we have seen, caregivers will go to some lengths via multiple summoning methods and embodied techniques to effectively secure the child's attention at the *outset* of interaction to set her or him up as a proper recipient for the directive. But when caregivers move to the directive space to embark on their directive project, and must then deal with subsequent or ongoing troubles with an inattentive – and noncompliant – child, one option the caregiver has is to put the directive project (and getting the child's compliance with the directive) on hold, and return to the business of securing the child's attention. A technique such as this is something that is, perhaps, akin to trying to push the interaction reset button.

Consider the following as another case in point:

(15) "Boxhit" *(Eduardo is hitting two children over the head with a box.)*

01 CG: *That's not okay Eduardo! *((*trying to pull E away from children))*
02 (2.2)
03 CG: *We're not hitting him on the hea::d
04 (0.1) with the box. *((*trying to pull E to her))* *A– are you looking
05 at me? I want you to look at me.
06 *((*CG brings face closer to E's))*
07 (0.2)
08 I want you to look at me Eduardo.
09 We're *not hitting him on the head.
10 *((*E squirms out of CG's hold and runs away))*

E does not look at CG, keeps gaze on children (figure 8.4)

Figure 8.4: Eduardo keeps gaze on children he was just hitting as caregiver addresses him.

In example 15, the caregiver begins addressing the child in the absence of *any* display of attention from him. His head is turned to the far right over his shoulder as he steadfastly maintains his gaze toward the children he was just hitting (see figure 8.4). In lines 1–4, the caregiver produces a reprimand (as a negative characterization of his actions), followed by a rules invocation, and she tries to pull the child to her. We might note that, as a physical technique of trying to elicit the child's gaze, this, too, works as an embedded method (as does gaze tracking and the "face hold") insofar as it does not intrude on the business of the talk. But when this fails, the caregiver moves to an exposed technique, not a summons, but multiple directives that request, and then command (via a "want" directive) the child to look; at the same time, she brings her face close to his and tries to track his gaze with hers. It should be noted that the child, in keeping his gaze toward the other children – and the site of his offense – maintains a body orientation of resistance to the caregiver's directives, both the directives to "not hit" (lines 3–4 and 10) and the directives "to look" (5–6 and 9). The caregiver is unable to get the child to shift his gaze to her, in spite of her repeated efforts to do so, and she is unable to get him to comply with her directive: as soon as he squirms away from her, he runs away and picks up another box and begins hitting another child. The child's unwillingness to conduct himself as a recipient of the caregiver's directives seems to foreshow his subsequent noncompliance with her directive to "not hit."

In examples 13, 14, and 15, caregivers, as a matter of pursuing children's compliance with a directive, pursue their attentional displays *after* having issued the directive (or started to issue it in example 14). In other words, rather than directly pursuing their compliance with the directive (e.g., through multiple directives), they treat children's noncompliance as tied to the problem of recipiency, and toward aligning children to the task of complying, they seek to align, or re-align, children to the task of being a recipient. This is a technique that speaks to the questions considered at the outset of the chapter: what sort of interactional work is accomplished by targeting for action children's attentional focus as part of a course of action designed to get them to alter their activities? And how might this be different from action that is targeted at the offending conduct itself?

8.7 Managing the non-compliant child

The following cases are of interest for how caregivers target children's problem conduct as a site for remedying work, and pursue their compliance with the directive via multiple directives.

Consider example 2 again, presented at the outset of the chapter:

(02) "Hair" *(Amber has grabbed a boy's hair.)*

01 CG: A:mber let go plea:se.
02 (1.0)
03 *let go (0.1) LEt go. (.) LET Go:.
*((*said as CG tries to pull A's hand off boy's hair))*

In example 2, the caregiver, arguably, makes a choice about where to target her intervention: toward the child's attentional focus, or toward the child's offending conduct? We see at line 3 that she targets the child's offending conduct by producing multiple directives ("let go (.1) LEt go. (.) LET Go:.") in conjunction with physical moves to pull her hand off the boy's hair. In this way, the caregiver foregoes the opportunity to attempt to get the child to be a recipient, to adequately listen and heed what she might have to say about the child's conduct, and rather seeks to *compel* her to alter her conduct. Directive-response sequences such as we see in example 2 do not promote children's agentful self-monitoring and regulation of their conduct, but rather quick compliance.

Consider another case in point:

(16) "Let Go" *(Eathan is holding a plastic toy in his mouth that another, very upset child wants. CG envelops him as she tries to get him to release it.)*

01 CG: *Let go ↑Eathan. *((*CG gently tries to pull object from E's mouth; Figure 5))*
02 (0.4)
03 Eathan.
04 (0.3)
05 ↑Let go.
06 (0.2)
07 *↑°Let go°. *((*CG squeezes E's cheek to get object to pop out))*

In example 16, a child has taken a plastic toy from another child and put it in his mouth. As in example 2, the caregiver produces multiple directives (although she does summon him at line 3) as she also attempts to physically effect compliance with her directive, "let go": first by restraining the child and gently trying to pull the object from his mouth (line 1; figure 8.5); then by squeezing his cheeks to get the object to pop out (line 7). While such methods

Figure 8.5: Caregiver tries to pull object from Eathan's mouth (example 16).

are especially forceful and promote the child's compliance over the child's self-regulation, they seem to be rare in the data, used only for situations that – for everyone's benefit (in these cases, for the child whose hair is being pulled, and for the child who might swallow the plastic object) – should come to an end as quickly as possible.

In the kinds of cases examined in this chapter (those involving very young children and their adult caregivers), we see that, apart from situations that entail some sense of urgency, as in the last two cases (also example 4), caregivers are rather inclined to *call on* children to alter their untoward conduct, rather than *making* them do so, and they will expend a great deal of interactional effort toward this undertaking, even treating outright troubles with compliance as troubles with children's attentional displays. On the one hand, this treats children not so much as non-compliant as "caught up in their own affairs." In this way, we see that *what* sort of response is pursued from another in interaction can entail choices that, in the cases examined here, work to subvert a negative character casting in favor of a more benign one – a matter that may prove even more critical in directive-response sequences involving adults. On the other hand, caregivers' targeting of children's attentional focus also works to set up an "optimal interaction space," as discussed at the outset, and thus helps to promote important interactional – and critically – caregiving business: this is business that involves substantively addressing children's problem conduct with the child acting as a properly attentive recipient to what the caregiver has to say. Hence, through the attention pursuit practices examined in this chapter, the caregiver orients to the directive space as an interactional space not only for dealing with problems of the moment, but for the ongoing and long-term work of socializing children as self-monitoring and self-regulating social agents who can adjust their actions in accord with the standards of proper conduct that are being imparted to them with the caregivers' directive actions.

8.8 Conclusion

As we have seen in this chapter, how participants go about the work of coordinating their availability for interaction, and dealing with troubles with this coordination, is closely tied to the work, the business, of the interaction. In the cases examined here, this business – which often must be handled with some immediacy – has to do with adult caregivers getting children to alter their problem conduct. This is conduct that entails such activities by children as their pushing, hitting, hair pulling, taking toys from others, and the like. It has been somewhat of a curious matter to see in the preponderance of interactions in which caregivers attempt to get children to alter such conduct, interactions that take the form of directive-response sequences, that caregivers undertake quite extensive work to secure and maintain children's attentional displays.

As has been argued, calling for children's attention at the outset of interaction, including pursuing their attentional displays when they are resistant or unwilling to make a display, is a sort of containment measure: it attempts to remedy actual or potential troubles at the first sequential opportunity in an encounter, before troubles emerge in the interaction proper space, the directive space. Troubles in the directive space, as we saw, are handled via a range of practices that can include focusing directly on getting compliance (e.g., as with the multiple directives in the last two examples, 15 and 16), to focusing, in a rather different way, on getting children's attention. Practices directed to this latter effort include embedded methods that work within speech (i.e., speech cut-offs and restarts of the caregiver's directive utterances; examples 13 and 14), although, as discussed, these practices are rare in the data set, and are perhaps more typically found with adult speakers using talk in conversational contexts other than directive-response sequences. Rather, we see that caregivers are more inclined to use practices that work to "reset" the interaction by returning to summoning and/or using other exposed techniques of attentional pursuit (e.g., "I want you to look at me"; example 15; also examples 13 and 14), often in conjunction with physical techniques such as pulling the child to the caregiver or turning the child's face to her. Such practices prioritize securing an available and attentive recipient as one who can be *told* to do something over one who has to be *made* to do it – although getting the child to comport her- or himself as a proper recipient, as we have seen, may entail its own element of coercion. What the range of practices examined in this chapter reveal, then, is a clear organizational tendency that is connected not only to the sequential biases and requirements of interaction, but also to how the adults in these particular children's worlds value and seek to nurture children's adherence to the standards of proper conduct in the daycare center, not as one motivated by force, but by reason and shared understanding.

REFERENCES

Bolden, G., Mandelbaum J., and Wilkinson, S. (2012). Pursuing a response by repairing an indexical reference. *Research on Language and Social Interaction* 45: 137–155.

Craven, A., and Potter, J. (2010) Directives: entitlement and contingency in action. *Discourse Studies*, 12(4), 419.

Curl, T. and Drew, P. (2008). Contingency and action: a comparison of two forms of requesting. *Research on Language and Social Interaction* 41: 1–25.

Davidson, J. (1984). Subsequent versions of invitations, offers, requests, and proposals dealing with potential or actual rejection. In J. M. Atkinson and J. Heritage, eds.,

Structures of Social Action: Studies in Conversation Analysis, pp. 102–128. Cambridge University Press.

Goodwin, C. (1980). Restarts, pauses and the achievement of a state of mutual gaze at turn beginning. *Sociological Inquiry* 50: 272–302.

(1981) *Conversational Organization: Interaction between Speakers and Hearers*. New York: Academic Press.

Goodwin, M. H. (1980). Directive-response speech sequences in girls' and boys' task activities: In S. McConnell-Ginet, R. Borker, and N. Furman, eds., *Women and Language in Literature and Society*, pp. 157–173. New York: Praeger.

(1990). *He-Said-She-Said: Talk as Social Organization among Black Children*. Bloomington, IN: Indiana University Press.

Heritage, J. (1984). *Garfinkel and Ethnomethodology*. Cambridge: Polity Press.

Kidwell, M. (2006). "Calm down!" The role of gaze in the interactional management of hysteria by the police. *Discourse Studies* 8(6): 745–770.

Pomerantz, A. (1984). Pursuing a response. In J. M. Atkinson and J. Heritage, eds., *Structures of Social Action*, pp. 152–164. Cambridge University Press.

Schegloff, E. (1968). Sequencing in conversational openings. *American Anthropologist* 70: 1075–1095.

(1992). Repair after next turn: the last structurally provided defense of intersubjectivity in conversation. *American Journal of Sociology* 97(5): 1295–1345.

(2004). On dispensability. *Research on Language and Social Interaction* 37(2): 95–149.

Schegloff, E., Jefferson, G., and Sacks, H. (1977). The preference for self-correction in the organization of repair in conversation. *Language* 53(2): 361–382.

Sidnell, J. (2011). The epistemics of make-believe. In T. Stivers, L. Mondada, and J. Steensig, eds., *The Morality of Knowledge in Conversation*, pp. 131–156. Cambridge University Press.

Stivers, T. (2004). "No no no" and other types of multiple sayings in social interaction. *Human Communication Research* 30: 260–293.

Stivers, T. and Rossano, F. (2010). Mobilizing response. *Research on Language in Social Interaction* 43: 1–31.

West, C. (1990). Not just "doctors' orders": directive-response sequences in patients' visits to women and men physicians. *Discourse and Society* 1: 85–113.

Wootton, A. J. (1994). Object transfer, intersubjectivity and 3rd position repair – early developmental observations of one child. *Journal of Child Language* 21(3): 543–564.

NOTES

1 The definition of directive that is used in this paper necessarily includes the provision that caregivers terminate their directive action(s) upon an indication of compliance from the child – this provides the proof procedure that the variety of utterance and action types produced by the caregiver is indeed targeted at getting children to alter their conduct. It is beyond the scope of this chapter to discuss in detail the variety of forms that directive actions may take, and the sorts of contingencies that affect directive selection (cf. Craven and Potter, 2010; Curl and Drew, 2008). Briefly, however, these include the use of imperatives (e.g., "stop!"),

want/need directives (e.g., "I don't want you to put your mouth on him"), negative action characterizations (e.g., "that's not okay"), rules invocations (e.g., "We're not throwing sand on people"), rights-of-use formulations (e.g., "That's his"), "speaking-on-behalf-of-another" formulations (e.g., "She doesn't like that"), and, sometimes, requests (e.g., "Could you give that back to him, please?"). Further, the positioning of the directive action relative to the child's conduct can vary. For example, the directive action may be made *as* the child engages in problem conduct, or just following its cessation. In the former situation, the caregiver seeks to interrupt or prevent some untoward act; in the latter situation, the caregiver seeks to remedy, or prevent a future recurrence of, the untoward act (e.g., note the difference in positioning of a similarly formatted "rules invocation" directive in examples 1 and 10). These sorts of complexities, too, await further consideration.

9 Epistemics, action formation, and other-initiation of repair: the case of partial questioning repeats

Jeffrey D. Robinson

It has been forty years now since Gail Jefferson (1972) published her groundbreaking chapter titled "*Side Sequences*," wherein she identified the *questioning repeat* as a class of practices for implementing other-initiation of repair. The current chapter examines one sub-class of questioning repeats that involve repeating part of a trouble-source unit (vs. a full repeat; cf. Robinson and Kevoe-Feldman, 2010), virtually identically (vs. being modified; cf. Jefferson, 1972; Heritage, 1984a; Schegloff, 1996, 1997; Stivers, 2005), with *non*-astonished prosody (vs. astonished; cf. Selting, 1996), and with unit-final-*rising* intonation (vs. falling or "level"; cf. Bolden, 2009; Jefferson, 1972). For economy, this sub-class practice will be referred to as a *partial questioning repeat*. For two examples, see examples 1–2. In example 1, Moe's partial questioning repeat of the noun phrase "My heater?" (line 12) initiates repair and identifies Bob's "your heater" (line 11) as the trouble source.

(01) BUS

```
01  Moe:  How's your bus running otherwise.
02        (0.5)
03  Bob:  Pretty good I need a tune up real ba:d, but (.)
04        [duh :    ]
05  Moe:  [Mm hm,]
06        (0.4)
07  Bob:  It's runnin' real goo:d.
08        (.)
09  Moe:  (>Mm=hm,</>Mm:,<)
10        (1.2)
```

The author thanks Galina Bolden, Heidi Kevoe-Feldman, Jenny Mandelbaum, John Heritage, and the editors of this book for their comments on previous drafts. Different parts of this chapter were presented at the 2007 conference of the National Communication Association in Chicago, Illinois (with Heidi Kevoe-Feldman), and the 2010 International Conference on Conversation Analysis (ICCA) in Mannheim, Germany.

Bob: How's your heater been working these last few w:eeks.
Moe: -> My heater?
Bob: Yeah=in your car.
Moe: Thuh bu:s?
Bob: Yeah=or do you use it that (m[uch.)]
Moe: [Oh]: yeah I been
using it, well it's s:low to heat u– you know you
>got a lot a< (.) cubic feet a a:ir in the:re,
Bob: Yeah.

In example 2, Mom's partial questioning repeat of the noun/proper name "Playbo:y?" (line 11) initiates repair and identifies Ula's "Pla:yboy" (line 7) as the trouble source (*Playboy* is an American men's magazine featuring photographs of nude women, as well as journalism and fiction).

(02) PLAYBOY

Mom: .hh Well this is something ve:ry impo:rtant.
Ula: .h [Yeah]
Mom: [We go]t thuh Washing>tonian,< ((a magazine))
Ula: Uh hu:h?=hh
(0.4)
Mom: #A#n'
Ula: But did you get [Pla:ybo[y.] ((a magazine))
Mom: [The:y [s:]aid–
(0.4)
Ula: Hh=hh
Mom: -> Playbo:y?
Ula: H .hh Yeah. a girl in my class was in it.
(1.3)
Mom: Wh(h)a(h)(h)t,=huh huh [huh huh]
Ula: [I ↑to]:ld you↓ about
th#a:t.#

This chapter attempts to answer the question of how recipients of partial questioning repeats – such as Bob in example 1 at line 13, who is the recipient of Moe's "My heater?" (line 12), and Ula in example 2 at line 12, who is the recipient of Mom's "Playbo:y?" (line 11) – understand the particular, contextualized social action that such repeats are designed to accomplish. As such, this chapter contributes to a core concern of ethnomethodology (Garfinkel, 1967) and conversation analysis (Heritage, 1984b; Schegloff, 2007) with explaining members' socially organized methods for designing recognizable social action, which Schegloff (*ibid.*) articulated as the analytic *problem of action formation*. This chapter argues that a necessary part of the answer to the aforementioned question involves *epistemics*, or what interactants know about each other's knowledge (Heritage and Raymond,

2005; Raymond and Heritage, 2006; Heritage, 2012a, 2012b; Stivers, Mondada, and Steensig, 2011). Prior to analysis, this chapter begins by reviewing partial questioning repeats and how they bring into relief the problem of action formation, and then presents the chapter's central arguments regarding epistemics.

Practices of other-initiation of repair have the formal-organizational goal – that is, relative to the organization of talk-in-interaction (Sacks, Schegloff, and Jefferson, 1974; Schegloff, Jefferson, and Sacks, 1977) – of resolving some type of "problem" or "trouble" with prior talk. Conversation analysis identifies "trouble" *post hoc* based on participants' orientations (Schegloff, Jefferson, and Sacks, 1977), and the range of repair-related troubles is vast; some empirically robust categories of "trouble" include that with *speaking* (e.g., mispronunciation, or saying something untrue, irrelevant, inappropriate, or hurtful; Sveenevig, 2008), *hearing*, and *understanding*. Although the initiation of repair by others can itself be characterized as an action, this type/level of action is a general (i.e., non-particularized, non-contextualized) formal-organizational one (Schegloff, Jefferson, and Sacks, 1977). A concurrent yet different type/level of action involves what a practice of other-initiation of repair is being used to do *in situ*, that is, embedded within all relevant particularities of "context," liberally defined (re. context, see Sacks, Schegloff, and Jefferson, 1974; Schegloff, 1987).

The final-rising intonation on partial questioning repeats contributes to their being understood as types of interrogatives (Quirk, Greenbaum, Leech, and Svartvik, 1985). Grammatically, a partial questioning repeat is a request for (dis)confirmation that initiates a sequence of action that makes (dis)confirmation conditionally relevant (re. conditional relevance, see Schegloff and Sacks, 1973). However, the interactional constraints of grammar can be different from those of action, and participants privilege the latter over the former (Schegloff, 2007). The *particular action* implemented by a partial questioning repeat is the resolution of a *particular* trouble (e.g., speaking, hearing, understanding) toward some *particular interactional* and *relational/interpersonal end* (re. relational/interpersonal dimensions, see Jefferson, 1987; Pomerantz and Mandelbaum, 2005; Robinson, 2006). Recipients must understand the particularities of repair-initiation actions in order to relevantly respond to them.

For a variety of formal-organizational reasons, there is *not* a one-to-one correspondence between the composition and position of practices of other-initiation of repair and trouble type (Schegloff, Jefferson and Sacks, 1977). This raises the question of how participants work within formal-organizational constraints – such as the organization of other-initiation of repair, which is an "organization of action" (Schegloff, 1997: 504) – to design recognizable *particular* actions. As noted earlier, this is what Schegloff referred to as the analytic *problem of action formation*: "[H]ow are the resources of the language, the body, the environment of the interaction, and position in the interaction fashioned into conformations designed to be, and to be recognizable by recipients as, *particular* actions" (ibid., p. xiv, emphasis added).

The problem of action formation is brought into stark relief by partial questioning repeats in the following way. A survey of prior research (ranging across English, Finnish, Korean, and Mandarin conversation) reveals that, even when partial questioning repeats – which already have a similar unit design/composition (i.e., a virtually identical repeat of the trouble-source unit) and a similar unit prosody (i.e., a *non*-astonished format with unit-final-rising intonation) – are positioned after similar trouble-source-unit actions (e.g., after requests for information, as in examples 1–2, above), share similar sequential positions (e.g., a post-first insertion sequence, as in examples 1–2; Schegloff, 2007), target similar grammatical objects (e.g., nouns/noun phrases, as in examples 1–2), and are produced in similar environments of non-embodiment (e.g., over the telephone, as are examples 1–2), *partial questioning repeats can be produced and understood as implementing radically different particular social actions* (Jefferson, 1972; Sorjonen, 1996; Kim, 2002, 2003; Koshik, 2005; Wu, 2006; Svennevig, 2008).[1] For instance, in example 1 (above), Bob's clarifying response (which is prefaced by a confirmation, *Yeah*, which addresses the grammatical constraints of the partial questioning repeat), "Yeah=in your car." (line 13), displays his orientation to Moe's partial questioning repeat as indexing his trouble *understanding* Bob's reference to "your heater" (line 11) whereas in example 2 (above), Ula's justificatory response (which is again prefaced by a confirmation), "Yeah. a girl in my class was in it." (line 12), displays her orientation to Mom's partial questioning repeat as indexing her trouble *accounting for the relevance* of the softcore-pornographic magazine *Playboy*.

While acknowledging that (at least) unit composition, unit position, embodiment, and environment are essential resources for action formation, the case of partial questioning repeats suggests that they are not (always) sufficient resources for the production of recognizable social action. This insufficiency is evident regarding other actions as well, such as asserting/requesting information (Heritage, 2012a), soliciting accounts for human conduct (Bolden and Robinson, 2011), and counter-informing (Robinson, 2009). There are, of course, other resources for action formation, many of which can be subsumed within "perhaps the most general principle which particularizes conversational interactions, that of *recipient design*," which refers to "a multitude of respects in which the talk by a party in a conversation is constructed or designed in ways which display an orientation and sensitivity to the particular other(s) who are the co-participants" (Sacks, Schegloff, and Jefferson, 1974: 727, emphasis original). That and how practices of action systematically involve the principle of recipient design is a nascent area of investigation within conversation analysis and a trove for future research. However, one resource for action formation, which is a robust facet of recipient design, is the *epistemics of social relationships* (or *epistemics* for short).

This chapter argues that, at least in the case of partial questioning repeats, epistemics is a necessary resource for action formation. Specifically, this chapter argues that, in order for a recipient to understand the *particular* social action being accomplished by a partial questioning repeat, the recipient must determine how much the producer knows about the repeated item in context, that is, how thoroughly, accurately, and/or authoritatively the producer understands the meaning of the repeated item in the context of the unit of talk that contains the putative trouble (e.g., in example 2, above, Ula, as the recipient of Mom's partial questioning repeat, must determine how much Mom knows about or understands the meaning of the repeated item, *Playboy*, as it was used by Ula in her trouble-source question: *But did you get Playboy?*). Along these lines, this chapter attempts to support two arguments. The first argument is as follows: If the recipient figures that the producer *has* knowledge of the repeated item in context – in which case we will say that the recipient figures that the producer is in a [K+] position relative to the repeated item – then the recipient will be more likely to recognize the partial questioning repeat as implementing a particular class of repair-related actions, which will be referred to as [K+] actions. [K+] actions index their producers' "disagreement" (for lack of a better term)[2] with the repeated item (Schegloff, Jefferson, and Sacks, 1977; Pomerantz, 1984), where "disagreement" can range from *pro forma* disagreement, which can result in actions that constitute claims of ritualized disbelief or surprise concerning the repeated item (Heritage, 1984a), to "serious" disagreement, which can result in actions that constitute challenges to the relevance, appropriateness, accuracy, and so on of the repeated item (Sacks, Schegloff, and Jefferson, 1974). [K+] actions involve repair-related troubles that are predicated on producers hearing and understanding repeated items (i.e., trouble sources) in context. The second argument is as follows: If the recipient figures that the producer of the partial questioning repeat does *not* have knowledge of the repeated item in context – in which case we will say that the recipient figures that the producer is in a [K−] position relative to the repeated item – then the recipient will be more likely to recognize it as implementing a different class of repair-related actions, which will be referred to as [K−] actions. [K−] actions index either their producers' lack of understanding of the repeated item, or a lack of adequate hearing of the repeated item (adequate hearing is a prerequisite for understanding).[3]

9.1 Data and method

This chapter is part of a larger project dealing with actions that get implemented through turns involving repetitions of others' talk. The larger data set is drawn from approximately 130 hours of naturally occurring, "ordinary" conversation between friends and family members (including 275 telephone calls and 8 videotapes). This paper draws on a sub-collection of 154 cases of partial questioning repeats (as defined above). By design, all of the cases analyzed in this chapter (with the single exception of example 14, in the discussion) occur over the telephone, which allows for analytic "control" over non-vocal behavior (Schegloff, 1968), which is consequential for the operation of other-initiation of repair (Seo and Koshik, 2010). All cases were transcribed by the author using Jefferson's notation system. The method used is conversation analysis (Heritage, 1984b).

9.2 Analysis

The analysis section is organized into three sub-sections. The first two sub-sections examine cases in which partial questioning repeats are understood as implementing [K+] and [K−] repair-initiation actions, respectively. The third sub-section examines a deviant case. Throughout, it is argued that, at least regarding partial questioning repeats, epistemics is a necessary feature of action formation.

9.2.1 When partial questioning repeats are understood as [K+] repair-initiation actions

In this sub-section, seven cases are examined in which partial questioning repeats are understood as implementing [K+] repair-initiation actions, or ones that index their producers' "disagreement" with the repeated item. As discussed earlier (and in note 2), "disagreement" can range from *pro forma* disagreement, which can result in actions that constitute claims of ritualized disbelief or surprise regarding the repeated item in context (Heritage, 1984a), or "serious" disagreement, which can result in actions that constitute challenges to the relevance, appropriateness, accuracy, and so on of the repeated item (Schegloff, Jefferson, and Sacks, 1977).

The first two cases involve partial questioning repeats that are positioned after requests for information. These cases can be compared to examples 1 and 9 in the next sub-section, where partial questioning repeats are similarly sequentially positioned (see again note 1). For the first case, return to example 2 (above), which is drawn from a long-distance call between a college-aged woman and her mom. At line 1, Mom uses a story preface, "Well this is something ve:ry impo:rtant." (Jefferson, 1978), to launch an extended telling involving news (that she and her husband, Ula's father) discovered in the *Washingtonian* (line 3), which is a magazine that covers aspects of living in Washington, DC. Although Ula initially aligns as a cooperative story recipient with "Yeah" (line 2) and "Uh hu:h?" (line 4; ibid.; Schegloff, 1982), she subsequently interrupts Mom (after "#A#n'"; line 6) with a question: "But did you get Pla:yboy." (line 7).

Based on the thorough American cultural penetration of the *Playboy* brand, it is likely, via commonsense knowledge (Schutz, 1962), that Mom not only knows about the repeated item itself (i.e., that *Playboy* is a softcore pornographic men's magazine), but that Mom understands Ula's use of *Playboy* in her query at line 7 (i.e., that Ula is asking Mom if she bought a copy of *Playboy*). However, rather than relying on stipulated commonsense knowledge, there is data-internal evidence that Mom knows about *Playboy* and that Ula expects such knowledge. For example, without having *Playboy* explained (i.e., at line 12, where *Playboy* is subsequently referred to with the pronoun *it*), in response to Ula's bawdy revelation (at line 12) that nude photos of her friend were featured in the magazine, Mom relevantly enacts surprise with an "astonished" and laugh-infused: "Wh(h)a(h)(h)t," (line 14; Selting, 1996). Furthermore, Ula claims to have discussed *Playboy* with her mom during a previous call: "I to:ld you↓ about th#a:t.#" (lines 15–16). In response to Mom's partial questioning repeat, "Playbo:y?" (line 11), Ula answers by justifying (i.e., accounting for) the relevance of her question, "a girl in my class was in it." (line 12), and thus treats Mom's partial questioning repeat as implementing a [K+] action, that is, as challenging the relevance of Ula's question as it involves *Playboy*.

For the second example, see example 3, which is drawn from a call between two adult friends, Kim and Matt, who are "catching up" after not having spoken in a while.

(03) PICTURES

Mat: Well how thuh hell you doin'.
Kim: I'm gre:at.
(1.3)
Mat: You were at Michigan, I take it,
Kim: .h Yeah– (.) Do you ev– (like)– read my letters?
h=h=h=
Mat: =Ye:ah. (u)– I mean (.) I've only got thuh one from
you,
(0.2)
Kim: Oh you didn' get thuh second one with thuh pictures?
(1.1)
Mat: -> Pictures?
(0.5)
Kim: You didn't get it?
Mat: No:: I haven't got it.
(0.2)
Kim: I sent=it a lo::ng time ago.
Mat: Hm:.

Kim lightly (i.e., with unit-final laughter) accuses Matt of not reading her letters: "Do you ev- (like)- read my letters? h=h=h" (lines 5–6; Schegloff, 1988). Matt resists Kim's accusation by claiming that he *does* read her letters, "Ye:ah." (line 7), and then (perhaps defensively) accounts for his minimal knowledge about Kim's stay at Michigan by asserting the limited nature of her letters: "I mean (.) I've only got thuh one from you," (lines 7–8).[4] After a brief silence (line 9), Kim backs off from her accusation by producing "Oh" (line 10), which claims a change in state from uninformed to informed (Heritage, 1984a), and then requests (dis)confirmation of a situation that would account for Matt's minimal knowledge: "you didn' get thuh second one with thuh pictures?" (line 10). This unit of talk embodies cross-cutting preferences of grammar and action (Schegloff, 2007). In terms of grammar, Kim formats her unit (i.e., *you didn't get*) so as to prefer a *No*-type answer (Sacks, 1987). In terms of action, insofar as Kim is asking about something that "should have happened," her unit arguably prefers a *Yes*-type answer (Schegloff, 2007).

This extract was collected in 1997, and commonsense knowledge suggests that Matt not only knows about the repeated item itself (i.e., that *pictures* refers to hard-copy, developed photographs), but that Matt understands the meaning of Kim's use of *pictures* in her query at line 10 (i.e., that Kim is asking Matt if he received *pictures* in a mailed envelope). This stipulation is again supported by data-internal evidence. For instance, without having *pictures* explained (i.e., at lines 13–14), Matt is able to relevantly respond to Kim's inquiry at line 14. Rather than answering Matt's partial questioning repeat, "Pictures?" (line 12), Kim reissues a modified version of her question at line 10: "You didn't get it?" (line 14). Here, Kim anticipates Matt's production of, and thus treats his partial questioning repeat as being preliminary to, a *No*-type answer that disaligns with the *action* of her question at line 10 (Schegloff, 2007). Kim's anticipation is realized by Matt, who ultimately disaligns with her *action*: "No:: I haven't got it." (line 15). In this example, Kim treats Matt's partial questioning repeat as implementing a [K+] action, that is, as contesting the presence of *pictures* in a letter that he might have received from her.

The third and fourth examples in this sub-section involve partial questioning repeats that are positioned after tellings/informings. (These cases can be compared to examples 10–11 in the next sub-section, where partial questioning repeats are similarly sequentially positioned.) Example 4 is drawn from a call between two adult friends, Dee and May. As context, Dee recently returned home to the United States from an extended trip overseas. While overseas, Dee had a US-based boyfriend, who called her frequently and flew to visit her three times. Dee broke up with her boyfriend either at the very end of her trip or very soon upon returning to the US. The boyfriend recently sent her a letter wherein he requested that she pay part of the long-distance phone bill accrued during the relationship (see lines 9–11). Dee's reported request by her ex-boyfriend is initially, strongly rejected by May: "Forget tha::t↓" (line 15). However, it turns out that Dee *is* inclined to "help 'im pa:y it." (lines 19–20).

(04) LETTER

01 Dee: .hhhhhhhh So: an' he's just– an' I'm like listen
02 you know you never know we might get back
03 together wa:y in thuh future: but I just can't
04 think about that no:w (an')=I wanna be free an'
05 all this stuff so .hhhhh tha:t an'=I just got a
06 le:tter from hi:m, h[hh] ((laugh))
07 May: [Oh]: gre:at.
08 Dee: .mtch an' he:'s li:ke .hh you know I really miss
09 you still an' blah >bl'=blah< an' he's like ↑by
10 thuh way (this) big phone bill can you h(h)elp
11 m(h)e p(h)ay it,↓ huh huh=
12 May: =N[:o: Wa::]y.=
13 Dee: [.hhhhh]
14 Dee: =↑$Ye:ah$↓=
15 May: =.h[h ↑Forget tha]::t↓ hhh=[huh]
16 Dee: [.h An' uhm] [Wha]::[t?]
17 Mat: [.h]h $Forget
18 tha::t,$
19 Dee: Well (.) no=no. (th')=thing is though is like I
20 w:ould help 'im pa:y it. be[cau]se (.) h:e: (.)
21 May: [Yeh-]
22 Dee: pa:id for e:verything. >like< (.) >( )<
23 seriously this guy spent like twelve thousand
24 dollars (h)on (h)our r(h)el(h)atio(h)nsh(h)ip.
25 or some[thing. ( )]
26 May: –> [Twelve thousan]d?
27 Dee: .hh Like he w(h)ent tuh- he flew to see=me: (.)
28 three ti:mes,=
29 May: =R:i[:ght. ye]ah that's tru[e.]
30 Dee: [Was it?] [>An'='e]'s< paid
31 for all thuh phone bills, ...

At lines 20–22, Dee begins to explain why she is willing to help her ex-boyfriend pay the long-distance phone bill: "because (.) h:e: (.) pa:id for e:verything." Dee continues to unpack and support this explanation by asserting that her ex-boyfriend "spent like twelve thousand dollars" on the relationship (lines 23–24). Commonsense knowledge suggests that May knows about/ understands *twelve thousand* dollars at it applies to a dating relationship. This stipulation is partially supported by the fact that, in response to May's partial questioning repeat, "Twelve thousand?" (line 26), Dee justifies her previous assertion, "Like he w(h)ent tuh- he flew to see=me: (.) three ti:mes," (lines 27–28), and the sense of this justification relies on May's understanding of *twelve thousand* dollars. With her justification, Dee treats May's partial questioning repeat as implementing a [K+] action, that is, as a challenge to the accuracy of *twelve thousand* dollars as an amount spent by the ex-boyfriend on the relationship. This claim is further supported by the fact that May responds to Dee's justification with "R:i:ght." (line 29), which orients to May's epistemic authority on the matter (Gardner, 2007), and then agrees with, and concedes to the veracity of, Dee's assertion: "yeah that's true." (line 29).

For the fourth example, see example 5, which is drawn from a call between two adult sisters, Ivy and Pia. As context, both women have recently returned from separate vacations. While on vacation, Ivy mailed Pia a postcard that arrived in Pia's mailbox prior to Pia's return from vacation. At line 1, Ivy is telling Pia about her (i.e., Ivy's) vacation, which included visiting Ivy's and Pia's grandparents. However, Ivy cuts herself off (symbolized in the transcript by the hyphen), "We stopped by grandma-" (line 1), to ask if Pia received her (i.e., Ivy's) postcard, ">did yuh get< my postcard?" (lines 1–2), presumably to avoid violating the interactional norm of telling someone something that they already know (Terasaki, 2004):

(05) POSTCARD

Ivy: .hh We stopped by grandma– (.) >did yuh get< my
postcard?
Pia: .h Ye:ah I jus[t got it to]day in thuh mail.
Ivy: [Oh good.]
(0.2)
Ivy: –> Today?
Pia: .hh Uhm yeah=eh– well=
=[we (picked) it up today. so]
Ivy: [Well sometime while you w'=go]ne.
Pia: .hhh Yeah. coulda=been hh Saturday, or hh=
Ivy: =Okay.

In response to Ivy's question, ">did yuh get< my postcard?" (lines 1–2), Pia initially answers affirmatively, "Ye:ah" (line 2). However, Pia continues to qualify her answer, "I just got it today in thuh mail." (line 3), which turns out to be the trouble-source action. Although Pia's "intended" meaning of *got it* in "I just got it today" (line 3) appears to have been *picked it up* (i.e., "we (picked) it up today"; (line 8)), Pia can alternatively be understood as asserting that Ivy's letter physically arrived "today," where *got it* is understood in terms of the letter "being delivered today." Based on Sacks's (1989) observations about members' reference terms for days of the week (e.g., *yesterday, today, tomorrow*), it is arguable that Ivy knows about/understands the meaning of *today* (this speculation is further supported by data below).

Prior to beginning her turn in which she responds to Ivy's partial questioning repeat, "Today?" (line 6), Pia produces an inbreath, ".hh" (line 7), and "Uhm" (line 7), both of which project a dispreferred, disconfirming response (Schegloff, 2007). Pia goes on to produce a confirmation token that is cut off, "yeah=eh-" (line 7), which projects self-repair (Schegloff, 1979), and then corrects her trouble-source action by replacing "I just got it" with "we (picked) it up" (line 8). Pia's correction, as well as Ivy's interruptive and simultaneous orientation to the correction, "Well sometime while you w'=gone" (line 9), are evidence that both women knew about/understood the repeated item *today*. Pia's correction treats Ivy's partial questioning repeat as implementing a [K+] action, that is, as a challenge to the accuracy of Pia's claim that the letter physically arrived *today*.

In sum, in examples 2–5, there are grounds for asserting that recipients of partial questioning repeats expect producers to know about (i.e., understand the contextualized meaning of) the repeated item (i.e., *Playboy*, *pictures*, *twelve thousand*, and *today*). In each case, partial questioning repeats are (accurately) treated as implementing [K+] repair-initiation actions, or ones that index their producers' "disagreement" (see earlier definition) with the repeated item.

It is worth showing two cases where recipients of partial questioning repeats treat them as implementing [K+] repair-initiation actions *even when the repeated items, as trouble sources, might seem highly prone toward making relevant understanding trouble, and thus as implementing [K−] actions*. Example 6 involves a person reference (i.e., *Jen Stein*), and is drawn from a call between two friends who attended college together but now live in different parts of the country. At lines 1–2, Ida is telling Vic about her life, specifically about a trip she took with: "Dave Abrahms,<.hh Melanie Lasslin_ (0.2) a:::nd Jen Stein."

(06) THAT GIRL

Ida: >Anyways. Dave Abrahms,< .hh Melanie Lasslin_ (0.2)
a:::nd Jen Stein. we all went to Mill Farr.
Vic: -> Jen Ste:in?
(.)
Ida: (h)Y(h)e:ah.
(.)
Vic: W'=that– >What thuh hell< (did) that girl do with her
life. d'she graduate?
(0.2)
Ida: Y:es. she uhm (0.3) she's w(h)aiting <to get> (.) her
c(h)ertification.

When practices of other-initiation of repair identify locally initial, recognitional-reference names (Sacks and Schegloff, 1979) as trouble sources – as does Vic's partial questioning repeat, "Jen Ste:in?" (line 3) – one might suppose that recognition (i.e., a type of understanding) would become strongly relevant as a possible trouble type (see Sacks and Schegloff, 1979; Enfield and Stivers, 2007). However, in cases where producers of partial questioning repeats actually know about the person in question (and context), and where respondents expect producers to have such knowledge, partial questioning repeats are commonly understood as implementing [K+] repair-initiation actions. For example, in example 6 (above), *Jen Stein* was a mutual friend of both Ida's and Vic's in college. Evidence that Vic recognizes *Jen Stein* is found in the fact that, without having her identity clarified (i.e., at lines 4–6), he is able to ask a relevant (albeit disparaging) question about *that girl*: ">What thuh hell< (did) that girl do with her life. d' she graduate?" (lines 7–8). Ida's confirmation is infused with laughter, "(h)Y(h)e:ah." (line 5), which displays her stance toward *Jen Stein's* presence as being in some way accountable, and thus orients to Vic's partial questioning repeat as making such accountability relevant. In sum, Vic's partial questioning repeat implements a [K+] repair-initiation action, that is, an index of surprise at the presence of *Jen Stein*.

Example 7 involves a relatively technical term (i.e., *open bar*), and is drawn from a call between Bob and Dan, two friends who attend separate colleges, and who enjoy partying (data not shown). At lines 1–3, Bob is remorsefully telling Dan about how he declined to attend a party during final-exams week in order to study.

(07) OPEN BAR

```
Bob:        .h Uh:m (.) .hh but anyway she uh:– (.) she invited
            me to a party=i' was a three kegger an' there was
            open bar.=hhh[h        ]
Dan:  ->                 [.mtch] Open ba:r,
Bob:        <Open,> #ba:r.#=hhh ((tone of admiration))
Dan:        Why: (di)– oh you (hadda=duh) test. you got thuh
            test to study fo[r. ]
Bob:                        [ Y]:e:ah.
```

When practices of other-initiation of repair identify technical terms as trouble sources – as does Dan's partial questioning repeat, "Open ba:r," (line 4) – one might suppose that recognition (i.e., a type of understanding) would become strongly relevant as a possible trouble type, and thus that Dan's partial questioning repeat would implement a [K–] action (re. specialist terms, see Kitzinger and Mandelbaum, 2007).[5] However, in cases where producers of partial questioning repeats know about/understand the specialist term (in context), and where respondents expect producers to have such knowledge, partial questioning repeats are commonly understood as implementing [K+]

actions. An *open bar* refers to the provision of free alcohol (including hard liquor), and is the proverbial Holy Grail for many party-minded college students. Evidence that Dan understands *open bar* is found in the fact that, without having its nature clarified (i.e., at line 5), he proceeds to challenge Bob's decision to not attend the party, indirectly deriding Bob for not taking advantage of the *open bar*; that is, at line 6, Dan begins to solicit an account for Bob's decision, "Why: (di)-", which is a cut-off version of *Why didn't …*, and on its way to something like *Why didn't you go?* (re. soliciting accounts for human behavior and their challenging nature, see Bolden and Robinson, 2011). Bob confirms the partial questioning repeat with a different type of repeat, "<Open,> #ba:r.#=hhh" (line 5), which is used to confirm an allusion (Schegloff, 1996). Bob's confirmation is produced with a marked tone of admiration, and confirms an allusion embedded in Dan's partial questioning repeat that an *open bar* is an unusual object of wonder and esteem. In sum, Dan's partial questioning repeat implements a [K+] repair-initiation action, that is, an index of surprise at the presence of an *open bar*.

Within the admittedly gross category of [K+] repair-initiation actions, there is still the analytic problem of action formation (Schegloff, 2007). That is: What resources do participants use to design recognizable [K+] actions *in their particularity* (e.g., a claim of ritualized disbelief vs. a serious challenge of accuracy)? Space limitations preclude a sufficient answer to this question, but data suggest that epistemics are again a factor, now in terms of epistemic imbalances between interactants' epistemic status (Heritage, 2012b) regarding repeated items in context. For example, data suggest that, when recipients of partial questioning repeats figure that producers have *strong* knowledge (e.g., personal or first-hand knowledge; Pomerantz, 1980) of the repeated item *that potentially equals or exceeds that of recipients' knowledge*, partial questioning repeats are understood as indexing more serious "disagreement." For example, in example 5 (above), because Ivy sent the postcard, she has strong knowledge about when it should have normally arrived that at least equals that of Pia, and note that Pia treats the partial questioning repeat as challenging the accuracy of *today*. For another example, in example 3 (above), Matt, as the receiver of the letters, has strong knowledge about whether or not they contained *pictures* that arguably exceeds that of Kim, and Kim treats Matt's partial questioning repeat as embodying a disaligning "No"-response.

Alternatively, data suggest that, when recipients of questioning repeats figure that producers have *weak* knowledge (e.g., hearsay; Pomerantz, 1980) of the repeated item *that does not equal that of recipients' knowledge*, partial questioning repeats are understood as indexing more *pro-forma* "disagreement." For example, see example 8, which is drawn from a call from a pregnant mom to a home-birth help line (this call is drawn from Wilkinson and Kitzinger, 2006). At line 1, the call taker (Clt) announces that she has had five home births: "I've had five at home." Because the caller (Ros) has yet to have a home birth, she has weak knowledge of home births that does not equal that of the call taker.

[08] FIVE

01	Clt:		I've had five at home ((*i.e., five home births*))
02	Ros:	->	Fi::ve,hh
03	Clt:		mm
04	Ros:		Goodness!

As a response to the caller's partial questioning repeat, "Fi::ve," (line 2), the call-taker's "mm" (line 3) treats it as a mere request for confirmation. Furthermore, insofar as the caller subsequently claims to be surprised, "Goodness!" (line 4), participants orient to Ros's partial questioning repeat as having indexed ritualized surprise/disbelief (Heritage, 1984a; Wilkinson and Kitzinger, 2006), and thus as having indexed *pro-forma* "disagreement" with the amount-formulation *five*.

9.2.2 *When partial questioning repeats are understood as [K−] repair-initiation actions*

In this sub-section, six cases are examined in which it is argued that recipients of partial questioning repeats have grounds for inferring that producers do *not* have sufficient, adequate, and/or accurate knowledge of repeated items. In each case, recipients treat partial questioning repeats as implementing [K−] repair-initiation actions that raise the relevance of trouble involving either understanding the meaning of the repeated items or adequately hearing them.

The first four cases deal with understanding trouble. The first two cases are designed to be comparable to examples 2–3 in that the partial questioning repeat is positioned after a request for information (see again note 1). For the first case, return to example 1 (above), which is drawn from a call between two adult friends, Moe and Bob. An analytically important piece of context is that the call takes place during winter, and Moe has previously made reference to gathering wood for a "heater" (i.e., a wood-burning stove) in his home (data not shown). Here, the topic has now shifted to Volkswagen buses, which both Moe and Bob own. At line 1, Moe asks Bob to assess how his bus is "running."

After Moe and Bob bring the assessment sequence regarding Bob's Volkswagen bus (at lines 1–9) to a place of possible completion/closure (Schegloff, 2007), Bob asks Moe to assess his *heater*: "How's your heater been working these last few w:eeks." (line 11). In this case, there are grounds for asserting that the repeated item, *your heater*, is possibly referentially ambiguous for

Moe, and that this possibility is knowable by Bob. Specifically, earlier in this phone call, Moe had referred to gathering wood for a "heater," but was referring to a wood-burning stove in his home (data not shown). At line 11, the ambiguity surrounding Bob's initial reference to a different type of "heater" (i.e., a car heater) is exacerbated by the fact that Bob's inquiry is interactionally disjoined, by a 1.2-second lapse (line 10; Sacks, Schegloff, and Jefferson, 1974), from the prior, possibly completed sequence involving Volkswagen buses. With the second unit of Bob's response, "in your car." (line 13), Bob treats Moe's partial questioning repeat, "My heater?" (line 12), as implementing a [K−] action, specifically a request for clarification of the potentially ambiguous term *heater*.

The second case is example 9, which is drawn from a call between two adult British friends, Leslie and Robbie, who are both primary-school teachers, here discussing two students. At lines 4–6, Robbie produces a request for confirmation regarding a pedagogical exercise wherein individual students are given the opportunity to share/describe something with/to the rest of the class.

(09) NEWS

Les: Yes. he's a ↑sweet↓ little bo:y, (.) and
'e's beautiful with 'is brothe:r,
(.)
Rob: Don't ↑you↓ find that when you give them chance
t'=do new:s they– they're terribly selfish. an'
they– (.) go on too long.
(0.4)
Les: -> e–=New::s,=h=
Rob: =News. when you talk– [when you're [( )]
Les: [>.hh< [Oh] ye:s yes
yes that's ri:ght. especially tho:se uhm .tch=.hhhh
(u)– twi:n:s,

Although the exercise referred to by Robbie (at lines 4–5) is commonly known, at least by primary-school teachers, as *show and tell* or *sharing time* (Michaels, 1981), Robbie refers to it at line 5 in a non-vernacular, slang fashion as "doing news" (i.e., "when you give them chance t'=do new:s"). Thus, there are grounds for asserting that Leslie may not recognize the reference to "doing news," and that this is knowable by Robbie, who is also a teacher. In response to Leslie's partial questioning repeat, "New::s," (line 8), Robbie initially produces a repeat-based confirmation, "News." (line 9; Schegloff, 1996), and then immediately continues to explain what she meant by *news*, "when you talk- …" (line 9). Robbie's explanation treats Leslie's partial questioning repeat as implementing a [K−] action, that is, as an index of her non-understanding of the slang term "doing news."

The next two cases (Extracts 10–11) are designed to be comparable to examples 4–5 (above) in that partial questioning repeats are positioned after tellings/informings. The third case in this sub-section is example 10, which is drawn from a call between a college-aged woman, Ara (who is calling long distance), and her mom. Prior to line 1, Ara described what she had for dinner, and at lines 1–4, her mom does the same.

(10) COOKER

01	Mom:		I had soup be::ans, barbequed ri:bs, fried potatoes,
02			(1.2)
03	Ara:		.mtch=(Oh)=[h]
04	Mom:		[An'] corn bre:ad,
05			(1.1)
06	Ara:		('ell),
07			(0.4)
08	Ara:		.hh[h]
09	Mom:		[(T]ey:–) (ott)– my:– my: (.) crock pot thet– (.)
10			(t)=I showed you what du:h (.) .hh Wanda got me for
11			Christmas didn't I.
12			(.)
13	Ara:		N:o:,
14	Mom:		Know that crock pot that she got me for Chri:stmas
15			(.)
16	Ara:		I remember she got you one a couple years ag[o .]
17	Mom:		[W]ell
18			she got me a: .hhh a cooker.
19	Ara:	–>	.hh A cooke[r?]
20	Mom:		[.h]h A o:blo:ng cooker that sits
21			down on a hot plate.
22			(0.5)
23	Mom:		.h[hhh]
24	Ara:		[Mm hm,]
25	Mom:		An' I put my:=ri:bs in there an' barbequed them...

At line 9, Mom begins a telling about how she cooked her ribs in a *Crock Pot*: "(Tey:-) (ott)- my:- my: (.) crock pot thet-".[6] However, Mom cuts herself off to establish that Ara is familiar with her new *Crock Pot*: "I showed you what du:h (.).hh Wanda got me for Christmas didn't I." (lines 10–11). After Ara twice claims a lack of familiarity (at lines 13 and 16), Mom summarily asserts that her friend bought her a *cooker*: "Well she got me a:.hhh a cooker." (lines 17–18).

There are grounds for asserting that the trouble source, *cooker*, is possibly ambiguous to Ara, and that this is knowable by Mom. At line 9, Mom initially refers to a *Crock Pot*. The term *Crock Pot* is a trademark name that is commonly used generically to refer to a wide range of types of countertop, electrical, slow-cooking devices. However, when Mom re-refers to the same *Crock Pot*, she uses a new and different reference term: "a cooker" (line 18). The term *cooker* is a nonstandard and shortened (and thus slang) form of the term *slow cooker*, and thus arguably not a commonly understood synonym for *Crock Pot*. Furthermore, perhaps the most widely known version of a *Crock Pot* is a single unit that both holds and heats food. However, Mom is actually referring to a less-widely known version of a *Crock Pot*, which is also referred to as a *slow cooker*, which involves two units, including a pot (that holds food) that sits on a separate/detachable heating plate (that heats food). In response to Ara's partial questioning repeat, "A cooker?" (line 19), Mom answers by clarifying the term *cooker*, "A o:blo:ng cooker that sits down on a hot plate." (lines 20–21), and thus treats Ara's partial questioning repeat as implementing a [K−] action, that is, as indexing her trouble understanding the meaning of the term *cooker*.

The fourth case is example 11, which is drawn from a call between two adult friends, Kay and Rod. At line 1, Kay is telling Rod, for the first time in the conversation, about the acquisition of a new kitten by a mutually known relational couple, Susan and Will.

(11) KITTEN

Kat: .hhh S:usan an' Will: took one=a thuh kitten:s.
Rod: Uh huh,
Kay: So they have a (.) cat no:w.
Rod: Uh huh,
(.)
Kay: Ca:lled (0.4) Ay Ce:. ((*the initials 'A' and 'C'*))
(.)
Rod: -> Ay Cee?
Kay: Fer (.) a ca:t. –uhh[h (.) h [hh hh hh] hh hh .hh
Rod: [<A cat.> [oh my.]

When Kay tells Rod about the kittens/cat (i.e., at lines 1 and 3), she tacitly claims to have relatively more knowledge about the subject matter in question (Terasaki, 2004), and Rod tacitly endorses her epistemic authority by aligning as a story recipient with continuers (i.e., "Uh huh," at lines 2 and 4; Schegloff, 1982). At line 6, Kay informs Rod of the name of the kitten using only an abbreviation, "Ay Cee:." (i.e., the letters "A" and "C"), which, given Rod's apparent lack of knowledge about the subject matter, is arguably a non-recognitional reference term (Sacks and Schegloff, 1979). Thus, there are grounds for asserting that Rod does not know what "Ay Cee:." stands for, and that Rod's lack of knowledge is known about by Kay. In response to Rod's partial questioning repeat, "Ay Cee?" (line 8), Kay answers by clarifying her abbreviation, "Fer (.) a ca:t." (line 9), and thus treats Rod's partial questioning repeat as implementing a [K−] action, that is, as indexing his lack of recognition/understanding of the abbreviation.

In sum, in examples 1 and 9–11 above, it was argued that recipients of partial questioning repeats have grounds for inferring that producers do *not* sufficiently, adequately, and/or accurately know/understand repeated items in context (i.e., *your heater*, *news*, *a cooker*, and *A. C.*). In each case, recipients treat partial questioning repeats as implementing [K−] repair-initiation actions that specifically involve trouble *understanding* the meaning of the repeated item. The role of epistemics is highlighted when you compare these extracts to examples 2–5. Examples 1 and 9 are comparable to examples 2–3 in that partial questioning repeats are positioned after requests for information, and examples 10–11 are comparable to examples 4–5 in that partial questioning repeats are positioned after tellings/informings (see again note 1). Thus, within these comparison groups, the actions being implemented by trouble-source units, the sequential positioning of partial questioning repeats, and the formal composition of partial questioning repeats (i.e., as non-astonished, verbatim repeats that end with rising intonation) are similar. What differs is producers' degrees of knowledge of repeated items in context, and how, by virtue of accurately inferring such knowledge, recipients understand partial questioning repeats as implementing either [K+] or [K−] repair-initiation actions.

Although examples 1 and 9–11 involved understanding trouble, this is not the only type of [K−] trouble. Insofar as understanding is predicated on adequate hearing, another type of [K−] action is a claim to have possibly not adequately heard the repeated item. Because partial questioning repeats are, by definition, virtually identical repeats of trouble sources, they do not index a claim of "lack" of hearing, *per se*. It is for this reason that, relative to other practices of other-initiation of repair – such as *open-class* practices (e.g., *Huh?*, *What?*, or *Sorry?*) (Drew, 1997; Robinson, 2006), or [partial repeats + *What?*] (Schegloff, Jefferson, and Sacks, 1977) – partial questioning repeats very rarely address hearing trouble; when they do, they display that their speakers heard a correct version of the trouble source and index a claim of possible inadequate hearing. In these cases, the constraints of grammar and action placed by partial questioning repeats on next-turn responses can be simultaneously satisfied by a single (dis)confirmation response.[7]

One environment in which partial questioning repeats are consistently treated as addressing possible inadequate hearing is when trouble sources are "seriously" obscured by overlapping talk. The most illuminating cases for the present argument are ones in which producers of partial questioning repeats would otherwise *have* knowledge/understanding of repeated items, and thus cases where partial questioning repeats would otherwise be prone to being understood as implementing [K+] repair-initiation actions. For instance, see example 12, which is drawn from a call between two adults, Buc and Eve. As context, extended snowy weather has made local roads treacherous, which has prevented Buc and Eve from going grocery shopping. At lines 1–2, Buc reports his family's willingness to settle for available food, "we've decided we can live on.hhhh macaroni an' tu:na.", which embodies a stance that Eve affiliates when she claims a similar position (lines 3–5).

(12) FISH

Buc:		I think we've decided we can live on .hhhh
		macaroni an' tu:na.=
Eve:		=Well=I sa:id (.) I will have macaroni
		an' ch(h)eese f(h)or s(h)upper before
		(I'll [ )]
Buc:		[We had fish la]st ni:ght.=h
Eve:	->	Fish?
Buc:		Y:e:[s.]
Eve:		[H]:ow was it.
		(0.4)
Buc:		It was fi:sh.
		(0.3)
Eve:		Yeah, how'd you fi:x it.
		(0.2)
Buc:		.h Gri:lled it,

At line 6, Buc interrupts Eve to announce, "We had fish last ni:ght.", the majority of which is produced in overlap with Eve's prior turn. Eve's partial questioning repeat, "Fish?" (line 7), targets a component of Buc's turn (i.e., "fish"; line 6) that was entirely overlapped. In this case, the effect of overlap on hearing is so extreme that the transcriptionist was not able to even approximate the majority of Eve's talk at line 5. As such, there are interactional grounds for arguing that Eve may not have adequately heard the trouble source (i.e., *fish*), and that Buc knows this (re. interruption and hearing, see Schegloff, 2002). Note that example 12 can be compared to example 2, where the trouble source *Playboy* is also entirely overlapped, but with no effect on either transcription or comprehension. Thus, the issue for participants does not appear to be whether or not trouble sources are objectively overlapped, but the subjective degree to which such overlap affects comprehension.

By responding with a simple confirmation "Y:e:s." (line 8), Buc treats Eve's partial questioning repeat as a [K−] repair-initiation action, specifically a request for confirmation of a possibly inadequate hearing. Buc's confirmation is "simple" in that it is not designed, lexically or prosodically, to display additional stances, as do, for example, laugh-infused *Yeah*s or *Yes*s (as in example 6, above) and repeat-based confirmations (as in example 7, above). Buc designs his confirmation so as to project turn completion by stretching it (symbolized in the transcript by colons) and producing it with final-falling intonation (Local, 2007). Likewise, Eve treats Buc's confirmation as both complete and sufficient in two ways. First, she comes in to speak slightly early at line 9 (i.e., overlapping the "s" of Buc's *Yes* with the "h" of her *How*). Second, she comes in early to progress (re. progressivity, see Schegloff, 2007) Buc's fish-announcement by inquiring into its culinary outcome: "H:ow was it." (line 9). Although the following is a negative observation (*ibid.*), nowhere in the data do Buc or Eve orient to any other type of trouble other than hearing.[8]

9.2.3 A deviant case and a caveat to prior argument

This chapter has argued that, if the recipient of a partial questioning repeat figures that the producer *has* knowledge of (e.g., thoroughly, accurately, and/or authoritatively understands the contextualized meaning of) the repeated item, then the recipient will be more likely to recognize the partial questioning repeat as implementing a [K+] action. However, knowing about/understanding the repeated item may not be sufficient for the recipient to conclude that a partial questioning repeat is designed to implement a [K+] action. It may additionally be necessary for the recipient to infer that the producer has grounds for identifying a type of trouble that extends beyond that of hearing or understanding. This observation is highlighted in deviant cases (Silverman, 2001), where it can be demonstrated that a recipient's epistemic status leads them to "inaccurately" assess the producer as *not* having grounds for identifying such a trouble. In these cases (of which only two exist in the data), recipients treat partial questioning repeats as implementing [K−] actions, even though they were arguably designed to implement [K+] actions.

For one example, see example 13. Kay is calling her friend, who is not home, and thus reaches her friend's mom. At line 2, the act of Mom informing Kay about her friend's college schedule (i.e., "she went tuh thuh co:llege, an' then she goes to work today.") displays Mom's orientation to Kay *not* knowing about her friend's schedule (Terasaki, 2004). However, Mom is mistaken. Kay not only subsequently claims to have such knowledge, "I kno:w.↓ I go with her [to college]" (lines 14–15), but precisely demonstrates it by providing the exact time that her friend's last class ends: "Twelve thirty." (line 20).

(13) COLLEGE

Kay: This's Kay. is she at wo:rk?
Mom: Uh yes Ka:y. she went tuh thuh co:llege, an' then
she goes to work today.
.
.
Mom: You wan' her office pho:ne number she'll be there
after three:.
(.)
Kay: –> .mtch After three:,
Mom: Yeah.
Kay: Oh sh(e)– What she doin' in thuh meantime.
Mom: .h She hadda go duh college. she goes tuh school
in thuh morning. [(So::)]
Kay: [I ↑kno:w.↓ I go] with
her. hh[h]
Mom: [Y]e[:ah,]
Kay: [.hhh]h[hh]
Mom: [An' I] think then she was done:
(what) abou' eleven twelve o'clo[:ck?]
Kat: [Twel]ve thirty.
Mom: Yeah. an' she's s'pposed tuh stop in (Fa:ll Park)
for an' hour or two, an' then she hadda get tuh
thee office ([ ).]
Kay: [Oh she stopped] in Fa:ll Park.
Mom: Y:eah. ri:ght.

At lines 6–7, Mom informs Kay that her friend will be at work "after three:." However, Kay assumes that her friend went directly to work after class, which ended at twelve thirty, and thus that her friend is currently at work (see Kay's question at line 1: "is she at wo:rk?"). As such, Mom's time reference "after three:" (line 7) produces, for Kay, an anomalous two-and-a-half hour gap of time between twelve thirty and three o'clock, when Kay had expected her friend to already be at work (See Kay's question at line 11: "Oh sh(e)- What she doin' in thuh meantime."). This anomaly raises the possibility that Mom's estimation of when the friend will be at work is inaccurate, and presumably motivates Kay's initiation of repair: "After three:," (line 9). With vocal stress (symbolized in the transcript by underlining), Kay identifies the trouble source as being the preposition "After", which she then frames with "three:," (re. "framing" other-initiations of repair, see Jefferson, 1972).

On the one hand, there is not only evidence that Kay *does* know about the repeated item in context – that is, that Kay understands the meaning of the preposition "after" as it is used to modify "three:"– *but also that Kay does have grounds for identifying trouble that extends beyond that of hearing or understanding Mom.* Thus, there is evidence that Kay designs her partial questioning repeat so as to implement a [K+] action that involves questioning the accuracy of Mom's time formulation. This claim is supported by the fact that Kay goes on, after Mom's simple confirmation, "Yeah." (line 10), to solicit an account for the anomalous gap of time: "What she doin' in thuh meantime." (line 11).

On the other hand, although it is likely that Mom assumes that Kay knows about the repeated item in context (i.e., that Kay understands the meaning of the preposition "after" as it is used to modify "three:"), from Mom's perspective, Kay does *not* have grounds for identifying trouble that extends beyond that of hearing or understanding. That is, if Kay does not know about her friend's schedule, then it is unlikely that Kay has (reasonable) grounds for challenging Mom's assertion (at lines 6–7). Arguably, Mom's "incorrect" knowledge about Kay's knowledge prevents Mom from being able to (reasonably) "rule in" the implementation of a [K+] action. If Mom orients to Kay (as a competent, native English speaker) as understanding the meaning of the preposition "after" as it is used to modify "three:", then this will also prevent Mom from being able to "rule in" the implementation of a [K−] action involving understanding trouble. In this scenario, from Mom's perspective, a remaining and viable type of trouble is Kay's possible inadequate hearing of "after." Along these lines, Mom responds with a simple confirmation, "Yeah." (line 10), which treats Kay's partial questioning repeat as implementing a [K−] action involving hearing trouble.[9]

9.3 Discussion

This chapter examined one practice of other-initiation of repair, the partial questioning repeat (Jefferson, 1972), and attempted to answer the question of how its recipient understands the particular repair-related action it was designed to implement. This chapter argued that, at least in the case of partial questioning repeats, *epistemics* (Heritage and Raymond, 2005; Raymond and Heritage, 2006; Stivers, Mondada, and Steensig, 2011; Heritage, forthcoming-a, forthcoming-b) is a necessary resource for *action formation* (Schegloff, 2007), and thus action recognition. This general idea was addressed over thirty years ago by Goffman:

> At the very center of interaction life is the *cognitive relation* we have with those present before us, without which relationship our activity, behavioral and verbal, could not be meaningfully organized. And although this *cognitive relationship* can be modified during a social contact, and typically is, the relationship itself is extrasituational, *consisting of the information a pair of persons have about the information each other has of the world, and the information they have (or haven't) concerning the possession of this information*". (Goffman, 1983: 4–5, emphasis added)[10]

Specifically, this chapter argued that, in order for a recipient to understand the *particular* repair-related action being accomplished by a partial questioning repeat, the recipient must determine how much the producer knows about the repeated item in context, that is, how thoroughly, accurately, and/or authoritatively the producer understands the meaning of the repeated item in the context of the unit of talk that contains the putative trouble. On the one hand, if the recipient figures that the producer *has* knowledge of the repeated item, then the recipient will be more likely to recognize the partial questioning repeat as implementing a [K+] repair-initiation action. [K+] actions index their producers' "disagreement" with the repeated item (see again note 2), where "disagreement" can range from *pro forma* disagreement, which can result in actions that constitute claims of ritualized disbelief or surprise concerning the repeated item (Heritage, 1984a), to "serious" disagreement, which can result in actions that constitute challenges to the relevance, appropriateness, accuracy, and so on of the repeated item (Sacks, Schegloff, and Jefferson, 1974). [K+] actions involve repair-related troubles that are predicated on producers hearing and understanding repeated items (i.e., trouble sources) in context. On the other hand, if the recipient figures that the producer of the partial questioning repeat does *not* have knowledge of the repeated item, then the recipient will be more likely to recognize it as implementing a [K−] action, or one that indexes either the producer's lack of understanding of the repeated item, or a lack of adequate hearing of the repeated item.

This chapter's findings mesh with those of previous research on repeat-based practices of other-initiation of repair. For example, Robinson and Kevoe-Feldman (2010) examined full (vs. partial), virtually identical, final-rising-intoned repeats of sentential questions, and found that:

> one frequent explanation for why the full repeats … are treated as addressing understanding trouble is that the format of the trouble-source question *cum prior context* provides for the relevance of possible understanding trouble (e.g., the question is sequentially/topically incoherent with prior talk). (p. 251, emphasis original)

In these cases, recipients of full repeats are able to determine that producers likely do *not* have (accurate) knowledge of the repeated item, and thus recipients treat full repeats as implementing [K−] actions (i.e., as requests for clarification). In other work, Robinson (2009) examined questioning repeats that target a particular type of *counterinforming* (Heritage, 1984a), or a turn in which one "speaker responds to another in a way that publicly exposes that the two speakers hold an incompatible position (e.g., knowledge or belief) on a same matter" (Robinson, 2009: 581). In these cases, recipients of questioning repeats are able to determine that producers *do* know (or at least claim to know) about the repeated item, and thus recipients treat questioning repeats as implementing [K+] actions (i.e., as various types of challenges).

One additional resource (beyond epistemics) that participants likely use to understand partial questioning repeats as implementing [K+] or [K−] actions, but a resource that this chapter did not specifically attend to, involves the prosodic nuances of a partial questioning repeat – such as its pacing/stretching, pitch, and amplitude, and whether its unit-final-rising intonation is large/strong or small/weak – as well as the relationship between the prosody of a partial questioning repeat and that of the original production of the repeated item (i.e., the trouble source). Although prosody certainly matters for what Selting (1996) termed "astonished" productions of other-initiation of repair, which tend to implement [K+] actions, the data for the present chapter did not include such cases, precisely in an attempt to "control" for prosodic variation.

This chapter provides yet another set of parameters, grounded in epistemics, that shape how participants *understand* action, and thus produce recognizable action. A central form (but not the only form) of evidence for participants' understandings of prior turns is how they *treat* them in next turn, and this type of evidence was heavily (although not exclusively) utilized in the present chapter. However, it is critical to note that people can *understand* practices of other-initiation of repair in one way yet "intentionally" *treat* them in another way (although this tends to be accountable in interaction, as seen in note 8). All sorts of actions/stances – such as "acting coy," "being modest," "being cautious," "being defensive," "being overly-sensitive," "playing dumb," and so on – can be accomplished by treating recognizable [K+] actions as [K−] actions, or vice versa (Robinson, 2009). Instances of intentional mis-treatment do not invalidate this chapter's claims about *understanding*. Finally, insofar as intersubjectivity is managed interactionally (for review, see Heritage, 1984b; Schegloff, 1992), there are also bound to be cases of unintentional mis-treatment due to participants' miscalculations of each others' knowledge.

The differences between how interactants understand and treat action highlight a topic for further research, which involves the possible existence of co-operating social orders that independently affect how participants *treat* practices of other-initiation of repair. Based on an early observation by Pomerantz (1984), one candidate is a preference, *at least in certain circumstances* (see below), for *treating* partial questioning repeats as implementing [K−] (vs. [K+]) actions (re. preference, see Schegloff, 2007). There are at least three grounds for this preference. First, Pomerantz observed that interactants tend to avoid interpersonal conflict (for review and confirmation of this line of argument, see Clayman, 2002), and speculated that what is referred to in the present chapter as [K+] actions are potentially more relationally/interpersonally conflictual than [K−] actions. Second, Pomerantz speculated that interpersonally conflictual practices of other-initiation of repair have the potential to further delay the normative progression of interaction (above and beyond the initiation of repair and the resolution of a trouble; re. progressivity, see Schegloff, 2007) by making relevant what Jefferson (1987) called "attendant activities," such as blaming, apologizing, accounting, etc. Third, insofar as people produce and understand talk in interaction primarily in terms of the social action it accomplishes (Schegloff, 1995), and insofar as interactants' recognition of talk's action is predicated on their hearing and understanding talk, the resolution of repair-related trouble involving hearing and understanding talk (i.e., the type of trouble indexed by [K−] repair-initiation actions) is arguably more critical to the fundamental operation of interaction as a social system (Sacks, Schegloff, and Jefferson, 1974) than is the resolution of repair-related trouble that is predicated on hearing and understanding what was said, such as someone saying something outlandish, untrue, inappropriate, or hurtful (i.e., the type of trouble indexed by [K+] repair-initiation actions).

At least in cases where partial questioning repeats are possibly (or accountably) ambiguous in terms of implementing [K+] or [K−] repair-initiation actions (re. possibles, see Schegloff, 2006), data offer some support for a preference for *treating* partial questioning repeats as implementing [K−] (vs. [K+]) actions.[11] For example, when recipients respond with turns that contain multiple units, and when one unit treats the partial questioning repeat as implementing a [K+] action and the other a [K−] action, [K−] treatments tend to *precede* [K+] treatments. For instance, see example 14, which is drawn from a living-room conversation between five friends. At lines 1–2, Ron continues a telling about being sick.

[14] ZINC

Ron:	So:: (0.8) >I was like< (0.2) s:o sick. (.) all week.
	an' I'm like >I gotta get< better before Friday.
	(.)
???:	hh=heh heh heh heh heh ((1.0))
Ron:	So: uh::m (0.7) I w's:=like popping zi:nc, a:n' (0.8)
	([ )]
Tom:	[Zinc?]
Ron:	Zinc pills:,
	(.)
Ron:	('Cause) they (.) help you recover faster.
Tom:	Do th[ey (really,)]
Ron:	[I believe] that,
	(.)
Ron:	I([ ),]
Zev:	[Supposedly.],

At line 5, Ron announces an attempt to remedy his sickness: "So: uh::m (0.7) I w's:=like popping zi:nc,". Ron's reference to *zinc* is to a mineral supplement, in tablet form, that some (but only some) people consider to be an effective alternative therapy for colds. On the one hand, *zinc* is a relatively technical term, and it was a relatively uncommon therapy in the United States in 1995, when this extract was collected. In this case, Tom's trouble might involve a lack of understanding of *zinc*, in which case his partial questioning repeat would implement a [K−] action. On the other hand, as a naturopathic (vs. more biomedically conventional) therapy, it is possible that Tom orients to *zinc* as having questionable benefits. In this case, Tom's trouble might involve his "disagreement" with the efficacy of *zinc*, in which case his partial questioning repeat would implement a [K+] action. In response, Ron initially produces "Zinc pills:," (line 8), which clarifies his previous use of "zi:nc" (line 5) by adding the modifier "pills:" (line 8), and thus treats Tom's partial questioning repeat as implementing a [K−] action. Note that Ron designs "Zinc pills:," to be possibly complete, that is, with slightly rising final intonation and a final-sound stretch (Local, 2007). After a micropause (line 9), which is arguably Tom's silence, Ron produces "('Cause) they (.) help you recover faster." (line 10), which is a justification of *zinc* as a cold remedy that now treats Tom's partial questioning repeat as implementing a [K+] action. At least the data used for this chapter *reject* an *unqualified* preference for *treating* partial questioning repeats as implementing [K−] (vs. [K+]) actions (cf. Pomerantz, 1984; Svennevig, 2008). For example, in cases where partial questioning repeats are "unambiguously" produced and understood as implementing [K+] actions, recipients frequently and unaccountably treat them as such in their responsive turns, as in examples 2–5 (above).

Precisely because interactants' "cognitive relationship" tends to be, as Goffman (1983) noted, "extrasituational," the task of demonstrating the relevance and procedural consequentiality (Schegloff, 1992) of participants' knowledge in the details of their conduct – versus merely stipulating it – is difficult, to say the least. Much more work is needed to validate this chapter's hypotheses and, if warranted, explore their implications for other-initiation of repair specifically, and for action formation more generally.

REFERENCES

Bolden, G. (2009). Beyond answering: repeat-prefaced responses in conversation. *Communication Monographs* 76: 121–143.

Bolden, G. and Robinson, J. D. (2011). Soliciting accounts with Why-interrogatives in conversation. *Journal of Communication* 61: 94–119.

Clayman, S. (2002). Sequence and solidarity. In E. J. Lawler and S. R. Thye, eds., *Advances in Group Processes: Group Cohesion, Trust, and Solidarity*, pp. 229–253. New York: Elsevier Science.

Drew, P. (1997). "Open" class repair initiators in response to sequential sources of troubles in conversation. *Journal of Pragmatics*, 28: 69–101.
Enfield, N. J. and Stivers, T. (2007). *Person Reference in Interaction: Linguistic, Cultural, and Social Perspectives*. Cambridge University Press.
Gardner, R. (2007). The "right" connections: acknowledging epistemic progression in talk. *Language in Society* 36: 319–341.
Garfinkel, H. (1967). *Studies in Ethnomethodology*. Englewood Cliffs, NJ: Prentice-Hall.
Goffman, E. (1983). The interaction order. *American Sociological Review* 48: 1–17.
Heritage, J. (1984a). A change of state token and aspects of its sequential placement. In J. M. Atkinson and J. Heritage, eds., *Structures of Social Action*, pp. 28–52. Cambridge University Press.
(1984b). *Garfinkel and Ethnomethodology*. Cambridge: Polity.
(2012a). Epistemics in action: action formation and territories of knowledge. *Research on Language and Social Interaction* 45: 1–29.
(2012b). The epistemic engine: sequence organization and territories of knowledge. *Research on Language and Social Interaction* 45: 30–52.
Heritage, J. and Raymond, G. (2005). The terms of agreement: Indexing epistemic authority and subordination in assessment sequences. *Social Psychology Quarterly*, 68, 15–38.
Jefferson, G. (1972). Side sequences. In D. Sudnow, ed., *Studies in Social Interaction*, pp. 294–338. New York: Free Press.
(1978). Sequential aspects of storytelling in conversation. In J. Schenkein, ed., *Studies in the Organization of Conversational Interaction*, pp. 219–248. New York: Academic Press
(1987). On exposed and embedded correction in conversation. In G. Button and J. R. E. Lee, eds., *Talk and Social Organization*, pp. 86–100. Clevedon: Multilingual Matters.
Kim, H. (2002). The form and function of next-turn repetition in English conversation. *Language Research* 38: 51–81.
(2003). Functions of single full NP turns with rising intonation in English conversation. *Discourse and Cognition* 10: 49–77.
Kitzinger, C. and Mandelbaum, J. (2007). Words and Worlds: "Specialist Terms" and Word Selection in Talk-in-interaction. Paper presented at the International Pragmatics Association, Gothenburg, Sweden, July 10.
Koshik, I. (2005). *Beyond Rhetorical Questions: Assertive Questions in Everyday Interaction*. Amsterdam: John Benjamins.
Levinson, S. C. (2000). *Presumptive Meanings: The Theory of Generalized Conversational Implicature*. Cambridge, MA: MIT Press.
Local, J. (2007). *Phonetic Detail and the Organisation of Talk-in-interaction*. Proceedings from the 16th International Congress of Phonetic Sciences. Saarbruecken, Germany.
Michaels, S. (1981). "Sharing time": children's narrative styles and differential access to literacy. *Language in Society* 10: 423–442.
Pomerantz, A. (1980). Telling my side: "limited access" as a "fishing" device. *Sociological Inquiry* 50: 186–198.

(1984). Agreeing and disagreeing with assessments: some features of preferred/ dispreferred turn shapes. In J. M. Atkinson and J. Heritage, eds., *Structures of Social Action: Studies in Conversation Analysis*, pp. 57–101. New York: Cambridge University Press.

Pomerantz, A. and Mandelbaum, J. (2005). A conversation analytic approach to relationships: their relevance for interactional conduct. In K. Fitch and R. Sanders, eds., *Handbook of Language and Social Interaction* (pp. 149–171). Mahwah, NJ: Lawrence Erlbaum Associates.

Quirk, R., Greenbaum, S., Leech, G., and Svartvik, J. (1985). *A Comprehensive Grammar of the English Language*. London: Longman.

Raymond, G. and Heritage, J. (2006). The epistemics of social relationships: owning grandchildren. *Language in Society* 35: 677–705.

Robinson, J. D. (2006). Managing trouble responsibility and relationships during conversational repair. *Communication Monographs*, 73: 137–161.

(2009). Managing counterinformings: an interactional practice for soliciting information that facilitates reconciliation of speakers' incompatible positions. *Human Communication Research* 35: 561–587.

Robinson, J. D. and Kevoe-Feldman, H. (2010). Using full repeats to initiate repair on others' questions. *Research on Language and Social Interaction* 43: 232–259.

Sacks, H. (1987). On the preferences for agreement and contiguity in sequences in conversation. In G. Button and J. R. E. Lee, eds., *Talk and Social Organization*, pp. 54–69. Philadelphia, PA: Multilingual Matters.

(1989). On members' measurement systems. *Research on Language and Social Interaction* 22: 45–60.

Sacks, H. and Schegloff, E. A. (1979). Two preferences in the organization of reference to persons in conversation and their interaction. In G. Psathas, ed., *Everyday Language: Studies in Ethnomethodology*, pp. 15–21. New York: Irvington Publishers.

Sacks, H., Schegloff, E. and Jefferson, G. (1974). A simplest systematics for the organization of turn-taking for conversation. *Language* 50: 696–735.

Sacks, H. and Shelf, E. A. (1979). Two preferences in the organization of reference to persons in conversation and their interaction. In G. Psathas, ed., *Everyday Language: Studies in Ethnomethodology*, pp. 15–21. New York: Irvington Publishers.

Schegloff, E. A. (1968). Sequencing in conversational openings. *American Anthropologist* 70: 1075–1095.

(1979). The relevance of repair to syntax-for-conversation. In T. Givon, ed., *Syntax and Semantics*, Volume XII: *Discourse and Syntax*, pp. 261–286. New York: Academic Press.

(1982). Discourse as an interactional achievement: some uses of "uh-huh" and other things that come between sentences. In D. Tanned, ed., *Analyzing Discourse: Text and Talk*, pp. 71–93. Washington, DC: Georgetown University Press.

(1987). Between micro and macro: contexts and other connections. In J. Alexander, B. Giesen, R. Munch, and N. Smelser, eds., *The Micro-macro Link*, pp. 207–234. Los Angeles: University of California Press.

(1988). Goffman and the analysis of conversation. In P. Drew and A. J. Wootton, eds., *Erving Goffman: Exploring the Interaction Order*, pp. 89–135. Cambridge: Polity Press.

(1992). Repair after next turn: the last structurally provided defense of intersubjectivity in conversation. *American Journal of Sociology* 97: 1295–1345.

(1995). Discourse as an interactional achievement III: the omnirelevance of action. *Research on Language and Social Interaction* 28: 185–211.

(1996). Confirming allusions: toward an empirical account of action. *American Journal of Sociology* 102: 161–216.

(1997). Practices and actions: boundary cases of other-initiated repair. *Discourse Processes* 23: 499–545.

(2000). When "others" initiate repair. *Applied Linguistics* 21: 205–243.

(2002). Accounts of conduct in interaction: interruption, overlap and turn-taking. In J. H. Turner, ed., *Handbook of Sociological Theory*, pp. 287–321. New York: Plenum.

(2006). On possibles. *Discourse Studies* 8: 141–157.

(2007). *Sequence Organization in Interaction: a Primer in Conversation Analysis.* Cambridge University Press.

Schegloff, E. A., Jefferson, G., and Sacks, H. (1977). The preference for self-correction in the organization of repair in conversation. *Language* 53: 361–382.

Schegloff, E. A. and Sacks, H. (1973). Opening up closings. *Semiotica* 8: 289–327.

Schutz, A. (1962). *Collected Papers, vol. 1: The Problem of Social Reality.* The Hague: Martinus Nijhoff.

Selting, M. (1996). Prosody as an activity-type distinctive cue in conversation: The case of so-called "astonished" questions in repair initiation. In E. Couper-Kuhlen and M. Selting, eds., *Prosody in Conversation*, pp. 231–270. Cambridge University Press.

Seo, M. and Koshik, I. (2010). A conversation analytic study of gestures that engender repair in ESL conversational tutoring. *Journal of Pragmatics* 42: 2219–2239.

Silverman, D. (2001). *Interpreting Qualitative Data: Methods for Analyzing Talk, Text, and Interaction* (2nd edn). Thousand Oaks, CA: Sage.

Sorjonen, M. (1996). On repeats and responses in Finnish conversations. In E. Ochs, E. A. Schegloff, and S. A. Thompson, eds., *Interaction and Grammar*, pp. 277–327. Cambridge University Press.

Steensig, J. and Drew, P. (2008). Introduction: questioning and affiliation/disaffiliation in interaction. *Discourse Studies* 10: 5–15.

Stivers, T. (2005). Modified repeats: one method for asserting primary rights from second position. *Research on Language and Social Interaction* 38: 131–158.

Stivers, T., Mondada, L., and Steensig, J. (2011). *The Morality of Knowledge in Conversation.* Cambridge University Press.

Svennevig, J. (2008). Trying the easiest solution first in other-initiation of repair. *Journal of Pragmatics* 40: 333–348.

Terasaki, A. K. (2004). Pre-announcement sequences in conversation. In G. Lerner, ed., *Conversation Analysis: Studies from the First Generation*, pp. 171–223. Amsterdam: John Benjamins.

Wilkinson, S. and Kitzinger, C. (2006). Surprise as an interactional achievement: reaction tokens in conversation. *Social Psychology Quarterly* 69: 150–182.

Wu, R. J. (2006). Initiating repair and beyond: the use of two repeat-formatted repair initiations in Mandarin conversation. *Discourse Processes* 41: 67–109.

NOTES

1 In this sentence, the descriptor "similar" does not mean "the same as." Even slight differences can matter for action formation, and these implications need to be examined in future research. For example, nouns (e.g., *Playboy*) are different from noun phrases (e.g., *My heater*), and proper nouns (e.g., *Playboy*) are different from non-proper nouns (e.g., *heater*). For another example, to say that trouble-source-units implement requests for information or tellings/informings does not exclude the fact that they may also be implementing other actions (see Steensig and Drew, 2008). For instance, in example 2, Ula's "But did you get Pla:yboy." (line 7) may also be teasing or "baiting."

2 The term "disagreement" is admittedly gross, and is not limited to its vernacular sense of "to disagree with." The term "pre-disagreement" was used, in reference to other initiation of repair, by Schegloff, Jefferson, and Sacks (1977: see p. 380 and footnote 28), and was re-used in this fashion by Pomerantz (1984). Based on some of Schegloff's more recent work (e.g., Schegloff, 2007), Svennevig (2008) has argued for the replacement of the term "disagreement" with that of "non-acceptability" (see pp. 336–337). In more recent work dealing with participants' stances toward each other's actions, the term "disaffiliation" might also apply (Stivers, Mondada, and Steensig, 2011).

3 The labels "[K+]" and "[K−]" – as in "[K]nowledge 'plus'" and "[K]nowledge 'minus'" – are borrowed from Heritage and Raymond (2005). In the conversation-analytic literature on epistemics, prior usages of [K+] and [K−] have tended to refer to one interactant having more, less, or equal knowledge *relative to another interactant*, and thus researchers have focused on "territories of knowledge" *between interactants*, interactants' *relative* "epistemic status," and "epistemic imbalance" *between interactants* (Heritage, 2012b). Note that the present chapter is concerned less with these concepts, and more with what recipients of partial questioning repeats know about their producers' knowledge *of repeated items* in context. Thus, [K+] and [K−] are intended to refer to whether producers of partial questioning repeats have, or do not have, knowledge *of repeated items*, and *not about whether producers have more or less such knowledge relative to recipients* (although this can also be the case, and does matter, and is discussed in the analysis regarding examples 3, 5, and 8).

4 Matt had previously indexed his minimal knowledge with "I take it," (line 4).

5 For example, at line 1 in the following example, Moe refers to a technical feature of a camera (i.e., *a self timer*, which is a device on a camera that gives a delay between pressing the shutter release and the shutter's firing). In response to Liz's partial questioning repeat, "A self timer?" (line 3), Moe provides a clarification, "With you right next to it?" (line 4; i.e., The *self timer* would allow Liz to release the camera and take a picture of herself), and thus treats Liz's partial questioning repeat as implementing a [K−] action.

[SELF TIMER]

01	Moe:		You can do like a self ti:mer.
02			(0.5)
03	Liz:	->	A self timer?
04	Moe:		With you right next to it?

6 For additional evidence that Mom is beginning a telling, note that she continues it at line 25.

7 This is not always the case when the trouble involves understanding or speaking because (dis)confirmation responses alone frequently do not adequately resolve the trouble (See examples 1–5 and 9–11, and example [Self Timer] in note 5).

8 Data suggest that, when partial questioning repeats make relevant speaking or understanding trouble, responding with simple confirmations is accountable (Garfinkel, 1967), evidenced at least by the fact that, in these situations, producers of partial questioning repeats tend to pursue trouble resolution, frequently immediately. For example, in the following example (PARTIES), Guy's partial questioning repeat, "Sti:ll?" (line 3) is designed to make relevant speaking trouble, and in the wake of Matt's simple confirmation, "Yeah." (line 4), Guy pursues trouble resolution: "It shoulda gotten out yesterday." (line 5).

[PARTIES]

Mat: Our highschoo:l's (.) still in (0.2) schoo:l.
(1.3)
Guy: -> Sti:ll?
MAT: .hh Yeah.
Guy: ->> It shoulda gotten out yesterday.
(1.2)
Mat: 'Ell I think toda:y.

For another example, in this next extract (PROFESSOR), Rob's partial questioning repeat, "David Sy:kes?" (line 3) is designed to make relevant understanding trouble, and in the wake of Tom's simple confirmation, "Yeah." (line 5), Rob pursues trouble resolution: "Who is David Sy:kes." (line 6)

[PROFESSOR]

Tom: We:ll n]ext time yuh come down you need duh (m/b)eet
uh:: (.) David Sy:kes. .hhhh
Rob: -> Davi[d Sy]:kes?=h
Tom: [(So: uh)–]
Tom: Yeah.
Rob: ->> .hhhh Who is David Sy:kes.
Tom: Oh: he speaks abo:ut uh:: (.) s:even languages...
((continues))

9 An alternative interpretation is that Mom does, in fact, understand Kay's partial questioning repeat as implementing a [K+] action, but that Mom "intentionally" avoids treating it as such, for example by providing an account similar to the one she ultimately provides at lines 21–22: "she's s'pposed tuh stop in (Fa:ll Park) for an' hour or two,." However, this interpretation makes the assumption that Mom's response (at line 10) to Kay's partial questioning repeat is non-cooperative (Levinson, 2000). Alone these lines, see again note 8.

10 I was reminded of this quote when reading Heritage (forthcoming a), who used the quote.

11 It is possible that one systematically accountable source of such ambiguity is overlapping talk, which raises the relevance of possible inadequate hearing (Schegloff, 2002), and does so concurrently with whatever (other) type of trouble possibly generated by the overlapped trouble source. This observation may extend beyond overlapping talk to any social/public phenomena – such as a jet engine, or being far away from one's interlocutor – that physically obstructs hearing.

10 Proffering insertable elements: a study of other-initiated repair in Japanese

Makoto Hayashi and Kaoru Hayano

10.1 Introduction

In every language for which we have adequate description, speakers have available a relatively stable set of turn-constructional practices that can be used to initiate repair on an utterance produced by a prior speaker. These practices for other-initiated repair (OIR) are "techniques for locating the trouble source" in a prior speaker's talk (Schegloff, Jefferson and Sacks 1977: 377). As such, various features of their composition are designed to indicate (or index) what aspect of prior talk has caused a problem for the repair-initiating speaker (e.g., Jefferson, 1972; Selting, 1988, 1996; Sacks, 1992; Egbert, 1996; Drew, 1997; Schegloff, 1997; Robinson, 2006; Svennevig, 2008; Sidnell, 2010). While much research on these "initiator techniques" has focused on English-language material, there is now a growing body of studies that explore commonalities and differences in OIR practices across languages (Egbert, 1996; Kim, 1999; Wu, 2006, 2009; Sidnell, 2008; Egbert, Golato, and Robinson, 2009). One important point raised in this body of work is that the formatting of initiator techniques is sensitive to the grammatical inventory of the language in which they are produced. Thus, Sidnell (2008: 498) argues:

> Other-initiated repair harnesses the available grammatical resources of a particular language. To the extent that those grammatical resources differ, we can expect to find systematic differences in the organization and operation of this otherwise generic organization of practice. This suggests that we might be able to explain just how a generic organization like other-initiated repair is "torqued," or adapted to local circumstances.

The present study pursues this line of inquiry and investigates one particular turn-constructional format used for OIR in Japanese that may be seen as an

Earlier versions of this paper were presented at the International Conference on Conversation Analysis (ICCA-2010) in Mannheim, Germany, and at the University of Wisconsin-Madison Interaction Interest Group lecture series. We are grateful for the helpful feedback we received from the audience at these meetings. We would also like to thank Jack Sidnell and Trevor Benjamin for their comments on a prepublication draft of this paper.

adaptation to the local (i.e., grammatical) organization of the language. The target practice to be examined takes the form of proffering an element that is "insertable" into the grammatical structure of the trouble-source turn, as illustrated by the following example. (Note that the element enclosed in double parentheses in the English translation for line 1 is left unexpressed in the Japanese original.)

(01) BB (A conversation between a barber and his customer. 'Backward shampoo' in line 2 refers to the method of shampooing with the customer reclining backwards into a sink while facing up.)

01	Bar:		yappari: (.) nenpaisha no hito iyagaru (yo)ne,
			after.all elderly LK person dislike FP
			After all (.) elderly people dislike ((it)).
02	Cst:	->	bakkushanpuu o:?,
			backward.shampoo O
			Backward shampoo:?,
03	Bar:		n:.
			Yeah.
04			(0.2)
05	Cst:		soo ka na:.
			that Q FP
			I wonder if it's that ((bad)).

While a fuller account of the structural details of this practice will be provided in the next section, let us note for the moment that, in line 2, the customer proffers a candidate understanding of an element that was left unexpressed in the barber's prior turn, i.e., the direct object of the verb *iyagaru* "dislike" in line 1. What is crucial here is that the formulation of this candidate understanding – a noun (*bakkushanpuu* "backward shampoo") followed by the direct object particle *o* – makes it syntactically dependent or "parasitic" on the structure of the trouble-source turn, rather than standing on its own. To be more precise, the customer's utterance is formatted in such a way as to be structurally *insertable* into the barber's turn in line 1, as in *yappari nenpaisha no hito* ***bakkushanpuu o*** *iyagaru yone* ("After all, elderly people dislike **backward shampoo**"). As Japanese is a predicate-final language where, canonically, a direct object is placed *before* the final predicate (e.g., a verb), the direct object noun phrase *bakkushanpuu o* ("backward shampoo") can be understood as an element insertable between the subject noun phrase (*nenpaisha no hito* "elderly people") and the verb complex (*iyagaru yone* "dislike"). Our aim in this chapter, then, is to examine this type of OIR format in Japanese, which we term a "proffer of insertable elements" (PIE), and explore the interactional import of its deployment in different sequential environments.

This chapter is organized as follows. In the next section, we will first discuss the design feature of the target practice by situating it within the typology of OIR formats. We will argue that, among the various forms used for OIR, PIEs serve as a way for the repair-initiating party to display a high degree of understanding of the trouble-source turn by voicing a part of it – a part that could (or perhaps should) have been produced by the trouble-source speaker him/herself. We will also consider the relevance of typological features of Japanese grammar to the way in which PIEs are configured. Section 10.3 then identifies three sequential environments in which PIEs are commonly employed, and explores to what interactional ends they are put to use in each environment. We will show that, while there is a range of interactional work accomplished by PIEs across different sequential environments, they are essentially used to align with the prior speaker's course of action in one way or another. Section 10.4 discusses a somewhat different usage of PIEs. We will examine cases where PIEs are used not so much to ensure correct understanding of the prior turn as to display a certain interactional stance. It will be shown that the use of a PIE in contexts where ensuring correct understanding of the prior is not at issue often embodies a disaffiliative move. Section 10.5 then concludes the chapter with a brief summary and discussion of our findings.

Our analysis is based on a total of thirty-eight instances of PIEs drawn from approximately twenty hours of naturally occurring recorded interaction among adult native speakers of Japanese. Some of the data come from the authors' personal collections, while others are taken from the *CallFriend* corpus available at www.talkbank.org.

10.2 Some notes on the format of the target practice

10.2.1 Situating PIEs within the typology of OIR formats

Our target practice, "proffering insertable items" is a type of "understanding check" (Schegloff et al., 1977), a practice whereby the repair-initiating party presents a candidate understanding of the trouble-source turn and seeks confirmation of that understanding from the trouble-source speaker. In this sub-section, we first discuss some general features of understanding checks within the typology of OIR formats. We then examine features specific to PIEs as compared to other forms of understanding checks.

Schegloff et al. (1977: 369) propose a typology of the major formats for OIR based on their relative strength in terms of their capacity to locate the trouble source. Thus, the so-called "open-class" repair initiators

(Drew, 1997), such as *Huh?* and *What?*, constitute the "weakest" of other-initiations in the sense that they display the least grasp of the turn they are targeting and therefore provide the least help to their recipient in locating what the trouble source is and what type of trouble their speakers have encountered (see also Enfield et al., this volume). On the other end of the scale are understanding checks. Understanding checks are considered the "strongest" of other-initiations because they not only locate the trouble source for their recipient, but also display (or *claim* to display) a high degree of understanding of the trouble-source turn – to such a degree as to be able to offer a possible *solution* to the trouble. Other major formats for OIR that fall between open-class repair initiators and understanding checks are, in the order of increasing strength to locate the trouble source, stand-alone uses of class-specific question words (*Who?, Where?*, etc.), partial repeat of the trouble-source turn plus a question word (*They're what?, Met whom?*, etc.), and partial or full repeat of the trouble-source turn (*Twelve minutes?*).[1]

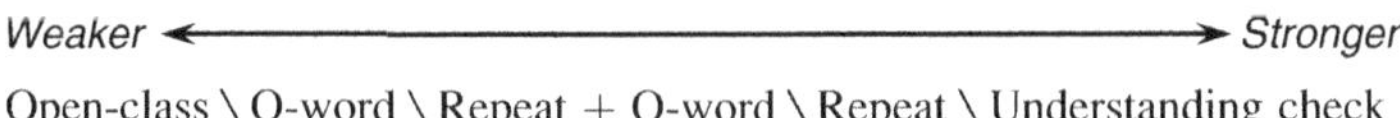

Open-class \ Q-word \ Repeat + Q-word \ Repeat \ Understanding check

Note that, other than understanding checks, none of the other forms offer a possible solution for the trouble targeted. Understanding checks thus convey the highest degree of grasp of the trouble-source turn on the part of the repair-initiating party.

Now, understanding checks can be performed with a range of different turn formats. One prominent type of format used for understanding checks is to reformulate what the prior speaker said and present the repair-initiating party's understanding *in their own words*. Such a turn is often framed with *you mean/y'mean* in English and *tte yuu koto/tte koto?* in Japanese. For example:

(02) NB: Goldbridge

Emm:	[A : ' RIGHT]
Lot:	[Ah'll ride m]y bike down
Emm:	A::lright. Yih gotcher li'l ba:sket °onnit°
Lot:	Ye:ah •hh uh↓::b (0.2) ü didju puudjer=
	=traini[ng wheels]
Emm:	[Y E : AH,]
	(0.2)
Lot:	Ev yih trie:d u[m?
EMM: ->	[YE:AH? 'n I still have a liddle
	pro:blem I'm scared tih dea:th b't ah'll do it ah'll

11 get out there with yuh
12 Lot: –>> You mean yih still to:pple over wih the training
13 wheels↑
14 Emm: We::ll you gotta ↓balance that front whee:l too:↓
15 (0.2)
16 Emm: But ah:'ll do it (.) ah'll do it ah'll show yuh,

(03) JAPN1684: 24 (Mayumi has told Kyoko that she is going to move to a friend's apartment.)

01 Kyo: eh jaa! .hh mayumi san soko DEru no:?
RC then Mayumi TL there move.out FP
Well then .hh are you moving out of there, Mayumi?
02 May: –> .hhh Un. >toriaezu< nikagetsu kan wa.
yeah for.the.time.being 2.months for TP
.hhh Yeah. For two months, for the time being.
03 (0.7)
04 Kyo: –>> dete mata kaeru tte koto:?
move.out again return QT thing
Y'mean you'll move out and come back again?
05 May: wakannai.=sono ato doo naru ka.
not.know that after how become Q
I don't know.=what will happen after that.

The understanding checks in these fragments are designed to "unpack" the prior speaker's formulation by articulating its meaning in the repair-initiating party's own words. That is, with these turns, the repair-initiating party proffers his/her understanding in the form of *an alternative formulation* of the prior turn and seeks confirmation of that formulation from the trouble-source speaker. Thus, in line 12 of example 2, Lottie proffers her understanding of "a little problem" that Emma mentions in line 9 by providing a reformulation of it and seeks confirmation from Emma. Similarly, in line 4 of example 3, Kyoko's understanding check articulates what she takes to be implied by Mayumi's formulation of her answer in line 2 and makes that understanding subject to Mayumi's confirmation/disconfirmation.

Compared to those observed in examples 2 and 3, understanding checks formatted as PIEs differ in the following respects. While the repair-initiating party in example 2 and 3 transforms/alters the formulation presented in the trouble-source turn and renders it in other words, with PIEs the repair-initiating party *accepts* and *uses* the prior turn's design as a basis for building an understanding check. In other words, rather than applying some transformative operation on the trouble-source turn, PIE-speakers build their understanding check as an "add-on" that is structurally dependent on the design of the prior speaker's turn.[2] Consider line 2 of example 4 below, in which Mika performs an understanding check by proffering an element (a postpositional locative phrase; *chiba ni* "in Chiba") insertable into the structure of the trouble-source turn (as in *donogurai* ***chiba ni*** *sundeta no?* "How long did you live **in Chiba**?"). The design of Mika's turn is such that it accepts and uses the prior turn's formulation as a basis for its intelligibility.

(04) DEM 9 (55:04)

01 Kum: -> eh (.) donogurai sundeta no:?
RC how.long were.living FP
How long did you stay/live?
02 Mik: ->> chiba ni?
Chiba in
In Chiba?
03 Kum: u[:n.
Yeah.
[
04 Tom: [u:n.
Yeah.
05 (0.3)
06 Mik: >atashi< ga chuu::gaku no ichinensee no
I SP junior.high.school LK 1st.year LK
We came there when I was in the first year...
07 to[ki ni kita kaRA:,]
time in came because
...of junior high school, so
[ ]
08 Tom: [a kekkoo nagai] janai.
oh pretty long TAG
Oh that's pretty long, isn't it?

In this practice, then, the proffered understanding is designed and presented in such a way as to show syntactic and semantic fittedness to the prior speaker's turn. As will be shown in subsequent sections, this feature of PIEs appears to make them an apt device to initiate repair while simultaneously aligning with the course of action being put forward by the prior speaker. That is, while initiating repair necessarily interferes with the forward progression of the prior speaker's course of action, and such disruption to progressivity is commonly regarded as indicative of incipient nonaffiliation with the prior speaker's project (Schegloff et al., 1977; Pomerantz, 1984a; Sacks, 1987; Schegloff, 1997, 2007; Stivers and Robinson, 2006), PIEs may be used as a way to keep disruption to progressivity to a minimum by articulating (and requesting confirmation of) an element that in effect "belongs" to the prior speaker's turn and thereby maintaining a high degree of fittedness to both the structure and action of the prior turn. We will show below that the types of sequential environments in which PIEs are recurrently employed are typically those where such "making disruption minimum while ensuring correct understanding of the just prior action" would be particularly suitable.[3]

10.2.2 Relevance of typological features of Japanese grammar

As noted above, performing understanding checks in the form of proffering an element that is dependent (or "parasitic") on the trouble-source turn's grammatical structure is not unique to Japanese. In English, for example, a repair-initiating party may produce an adjunct (typically – though not invariably – a prepositional phrase) that is grammatically continuous with the trouble-source turn as a way to present a candidate understanding. This practice, which Sacks (1992: I: 652, 660–663) termed an "appendor question," is illustrated in the following example:

(05) SN–4:12

She:		He collected a fo:rtune fer that.
	->	He claimed all k(h)i:nds of damages.
		(1.1)
Rth:		huh huh–huh=
Kar:	->>	=From Lama:ncha:?
She:		Yeah.

In line 5, Karen performs an understanding check targeted at Sherry's utterance in line 2. Here Karen designs her turn in such a way as to make it grammatically continuous with the trouble-source turn.

What is common between PIEs and appendor questions is that they both exploit the format of "incrementing" as a way to perform an understanding check. Increments are those turn extensions that are designed as grammatically dependent elements added on to a previously completed turn-constructional unit (TCU) and which extend the action performed by that prior TCU (Schegloff, 1996a; Lerner, 2004; Couper-Kuhlen and Ono, 2007; Sidnell, 2012).[4] As Lerner (2004: 155) points out, increments are "systematically used to elaborate, clarify, and amplify, that is, modify the TCU they extend – and they can do so in a relatively unmarked fashion because they lay claim to being part of the same TCU by the same speaker." While PIEs and appendor questions are not increments per se in that they do not extend the same action as that performed by the prior TCU (see Lerner, 2004: 160–161), they nonetheless take advantage of this format of providing grammatically dependent TCU extension in seeking to elaborate and clarify the prior TCU that they ostensibly extend.

There are differences between PIEs and appendor questions as well, however. From a structural standpoint, appendor questions are grammatically fitted to the *end* of the "host" TCU ("Glue-ons" in Couper-Kuhlen and Ono's [2007] terms), whereas PIEs do not properly fit the end of the host TCU but belong somewhere within it ("Insertables" in Couper-Kuhlen and Ono's [2007] terms). This difference stems from the presence/absence of strong syntactic closure in clause structure in the two languages. English does not mark the end of a syntactic unit as strongly as some other languages do, and elements can be tacked on indefinitely (at least in principle) to recomplete the preceding unit. Therefore, clausal TCUs in English can easily be prolonged by the addition of adjuncts and post-modifiers to the end of the preceding unit. In Japanese, on the other hand, due to its predicate-final structure, closure of a clausal TCU is strongly marked with the clause-final predicate (which is optionally followed by such utterance-final elements as final particles; Tanaka, 1999). Thus, additional elements tacked on to the end of a preceding clausal TCU are "out of place" in most cases because their "canonical" position is before the clause-final predicate.[5] This structural difference between appendor questions (Glue-ons) and PIEs (Insertables) in fact corresponds to the difference in the most common type of self-initiated, self-completed increments (i.e., those increments that are produced by the same speaker as that of the host TCU) between the two languages. Couper-Kuhlen and Ono (2007) report that the most frequent type of self-initiated, self-completed increments in English is Glue-ons, while that in Japanese is Insertables. We can say, therefore, that both appendor questions and PIEs exploit the most common format of incrementing in each language.

Another difference between appendor questions and PIEs is that, while the grammatical forms that appendor questions take appear to be limited to grammatically "optional" adjuncts (most typically, prepositional phrases), those that PIEs take include not only adjuncts, but also so-called "core arguments" of the clause, such as the subject and the direct object. In example 1 above, for instance, the PIE takes the form of providing the direct object insertable into the structure of the trouble-source turn. This difference stems from the fact that clauses in Japanese can be syntactically complete with unarticulated but contextually recoverable core arguments (i.e., so-called ellipsis or zero-anaphora), whereas in English core arguments are typically expressed overtly and, in fact, this may be required if the turn is to be heard as syntactically complete. Thus, PIEs appear to be more diverse in terms of the grammatical categories they take than appendor questions.

It is not clear at this point whether these structural similarities and differences between appendor questions and PIEs are interactionally relevant, i.e., whether they are consequential for the ways in which participants accomplish action in interaction. For now, we simply note the possibility that, given the functional similarity between the two – proffering a candidate understanding in the form of the most common type of turn extension available in the language and seeking clarification/elaboration of the prior turn – these two formats may be put to use in similar environments for similar ends. Obviously, more research on both appendor questions and PIEs will be necessary to verify this possibility.

We now turn to examining several sequential environments in which PIEs are commonly used and discuss the interactional import of their deployment.

10.3 Sequential environments for PIEs and their interactional import

10.3.1 After a sequence-initiating action: making a prior "response ready"

The most common position in which PIEs are employed is after a sequence-initiating action (or "First"; e.g., a question, an assessment, etc.). A recipient of such an action is normatively expected to produce a relevant response in the next turn (e.g., an answer after a question, an agreement or a disagreement after an assessment, etc.). Under this sequential mandate to produce a response, the recipient is systematically motivated to inspect the adequacy of the prior turn and assess whether there is any need for clarification of the prior turn in order to formulate an appropriate response. A majority of instances of PIEs in our collection (26 out of 38; 68%) are used in this "post-First" position to seek such clarification/specification. By producing a PIE in that position and thereby initiating an insert sequence (Schegloff, 2007), the recipient of a sequence-initiating action indicates that s/he is not ready to provide a sequentially relevant response yet and that some ambiguous or underspecified element of the prior turn must be confirmed first.

Example 6, which is an extended version of example 4, illustrates the use of a PIE after a quintessential sequence-initiating action, i.e., a question. This fragment is taken from a conversation among three women in their late twenties to early thirties, and prior to the segment below, Mika told the other two participants that she had received a phone call from her parents the day before and had been told that they were going to move from Chiba (near Tokyo) to their hometown in rural Kyushu. In the course of this telling, Mika mentioned that she was born and spent her childhood years in Kyushu before her family moved to Chiba. Lines 1 through 8 in the following fragment are the final part of Mika's telling about her parents' move.

(06) DEM 9

01 Mik: >(sonna)< itsudemo kaeru tte yutteta kara::,
such whenever return QT saying because
They'd been saying they might go back there anytime, so...

02 Kum: [u: : : [: n.]
Mmhm.
[[ ]

03 Tom: [u : : :[: : :]: : : n]
Mmhm
[ ]

04 Mik: [son]na:,] odor(h)ok(h)u k(h)oto d(h)e
such be.surprised thing CP
... it doesn't surprise me...

05 wa [nai n da ke[do. .hhh
TP not N CP but
...so much, but. .hhh
[[

06 Kum: [u : : n u [: : n
Right right
[

07 Tom: [u::::::n.
Yeah

08 Mik: °chotto, u::n.°
°*Just a little bit, yeah::.*°

09 (1.5)

10 ?: (° [°)
[

11 Kum: [( )kka.
I see.

12 Kum: -> eh (.) donogurai sundeta no:?
RC how.long were.living FP
How long did you stay/live?

13 Mik: ->> chiba ni?
Chiba in
In Chiba?

14 Kum: u[:n.
Yeah.
[
15 Tom: [u:n.
Yeah.
16 (0.3)
17 Mik: >atashi< ga chuu::gaku no ichinensee no
I SP junior.high.school LK 1st.year LK
We came there when I was in the first year ...
18 to[ki ni kita kaRA:,]
time in came because
...of junior high school, so
[ ]
19 Tom: [a kekkoo nagai] janai.
oh pretty long TAG
Oh that's pretty long, isn't it?

Kumi's question in line 12 is produced at a juncture where Mika's telling has come to possible completion. It is formulated as a follow-up question directly prompted by the preceding telling by Mika and inquiring about an as-of-yet unmentioned aspect of Mika's family's past. The formulation of this question, however, is deemed ambiguous given that Mika has mentioned in the prior telling that her family lived in two different places, Chiba and Kyushu, yet Kumi does not specify which location she is asking about. To resolve this ambiguity Mika proffers a candidate understanding in the form of a PIE in line 13 and seeks confirmation before answering (lines 17–8). A PIE is thus used in post-First position to make the prior question "response-ready."

In example 7, a PIE is used after another type of sequence-initiating action: an assessment. This fragment is taken from a phone conversation between Ken and Megumi, and, prior to the segment below, Ken complained that, because of his status as an international student at an American university, he is not legally permitted to obtain off-campus jobs. In response to this, Megumi draws his attention to the fact that there are many job opportunities on campus (line 1). While Ken acknowledges this (line 2), he goes on to counter this suggestion by stating that wages for on-campus jobs are low (line 4).

(07) JAPN 6149

01 Meg: da ip<u>pai</u> ↑<u>aru</u> ja nai.=gakkoo [no–
so a.lot exist CP not school LK
See, there're a lot ((of jobs)), right?=School((–related))
[

02 Ken: [u::::n.
Yeah::.

03 Meg: [( )
[

04 Ken: [ga– gakkoo demo n:anka yasui n da mo:n.=
school but like cheap N CP FP
But at sch– school, ((the pay)) is pretty low.=

05 –> =yon hyaku– yo– yo:nju– yo– y– a:: yon doru
four hundr– forty oh four dollar
=Four hundre– Fo– Forty– Fo– F– Oh:: Four dollars and

06 –> gosen– gojussento.=
5.cen– 50.cents
five cen– fifty cents.

07 Meg: –>> =ichijikan?
1.hour
=An hour?

08 Ken: n ichiji[kan
yeah 1.hour
Yeah an hour.
[

09 Meg: [yatte rann(h)ai y(h)o n(h)e(h):(h)heheheheh
do can't FP FP
That's ridiculous heheheheh

10 [s(h)onn(h)a sh(h)ig(h)ot(h)o.hh .hhhh hehhehhehh .hhh
such job
Such a job .hh .hhhh hehehhehh .hhh
[

11 Ken: [yas::u::
cheap
So low.

After making a negative assessment about wages for on-campus jobs, Ken goes on to present a typical wage for such a job to substantiate his assessment (lines 5 and 6). Ken's assessment and subsequent illustration of a low wage make relevant the addressee's agreement/disagreement in the next turn. Instead of such a sequentially relevant response, however, Mika performs an understanding check in the form of a PIE (*ichijikan* "an hour," which is insertable into the Ken's prior turn, as in ***ichijikan*** *yon doru gojussento* "four dollars and fifty cents **an hour**") and thereby indicates that this as-of-yet unarticulated element needs to be confirmed first before she formulates a relevant response. Indeed, after receiving confirmation from Ken (line 8), Megumi provides a strong agreement with Ken's prior assessment in the form of an upgraded negative assessment (lines 9–10). Just as in the previous fragment, then, a PIE is used here to make a prior sequence-initiating action "response-ready."

In both examples 6 and 7, a PIE displaces a sequentially relevant response by initiating repair on the prior turn and thereby disrupts the progressivity of the ongoing course of action. Previous studies have shown that initiating repair on prior talk often conveys incipient nonalignment with the action implemented by that prior talk (Schegloff et al., 1977; Schegloff, 1997, 2007). Thus, Schegloff (2007: 151) writes:

> A variety of features of other-initiated repair sequences makes them apt and suitable instruments for addressing disagreement-implicated talk. For example, by not quite "getting" what was said, they raise the possibility that it was "not quite right," often leaving the respects in which it was not quite right unexplicated. More to the point for the actual working out of the "problem," they provide a place in the very next turn in which the prior speaker can make some adjustment in what was said – to make it more accessible, and perhaps more "acceptable."

Looking at the workings of PIEs from this perspective, we observe the following divergences from the features of disagreement-implicated OIRs described above. First, rather than conveying the sense that one did not get what was said and/or leaving problematic aspects of the prior turn unexplicated, PIEs display the repair-initiating party's *high degree of understanding* of the prior turn. This is so because PIEs are built as a structural extension of the prior turn where the prior turn's design is understood and used by the repair-initiating party as a basis for proffering a candidate understanding of what was inferable, yet unarticulated in that turn. Second, rather than providing the prior speaker with a place to make adjustment in what was said so as to make it more acceptable, PIEs make relevant simple confirmation from the prior speaker. Indeed, in 21 out of the 26 cases of PIEs used in post-First position (81%) in our collection, the prior speaker only produces a minimal acknowledgment, such as *un* (examples 6 and 7) and a repeat (example 7), without any other adjustment or elaboration. Third, after receiving confirmation from the prior speaker, the PIE-speaker immediately moves on to resume the temporarily halted course of action by producing a response made relevant by the trouble-source turn. Thus, the trajectory of the OIR sequences introduced by PIEs suggests that PIEs provide a way for participants to initiate repair in a maximally aligning manner (i.e., "maximally aligning" within the constraints of having to take measures to achieve correct understanding). By keeping the disruption to the progressivity of the ongoing course of action to a minimum while ensuring correct understanding of the prior turn, the repair-initiating party aligns with the addressee by endorsing and cooperating with the project implemented by his/her talk.

10.3.2 After a topic-initial turn: making topical connections explicit

A second sequential position in which PIEs are commonly employed is after a topic-initial turn. Several studies have noted regular occurrences of OIRs in topic-initial position (Schegloff, 1979; Drew, 1997; Kim, 2001). One potential source of trouble faced by a recipient of a topic-initial turn is the opaqueness of topical connection between that turn and what precedes it. This becomes problematic when a new topic (or a new topical focus within the same overall topic) is introduced disjunctively without an explicit marker of topical continuity (e.g., a lexical repetition) or discontinuity (e.g., "anyway," "by the way," etc.). Conversation operates under the general assumption that, unless otherwise indicated, an utterance produced after some prior is to be understood as produced in response to or in relation to that prior (Schegloff and Sacks, 1973; Sacks et al., 1974; Heritage, 1984; Schegloff, 2007). Given this, the opaqueness in the current turn's relationship to the prior introduced by a disjunctive topic shift may result in a puzzle on the part of its recipient, for which repair may be initiated.

In this context repair is often initiated with an open-class initiator, such as *Huh?*, *Sorry?*, which may convey the sense that their producers have little clue as to how the just produced turn is topically and sequentially connected to what has transpired prior to that point (Drew, 1997). PIEs used in this environment operate differently. They are used as a way for the repair-initiating party to display their candidate understanding about how the topically disjunctive prior turn should be heard and understood in relation to what preceded it. In other words, PIEs are produced as the repair-initiating party's attempt to tie their understanding of the newly introduced topic talk to something in the prior sequence of talk. As will be shown below, what is proffered in the PIE turn is a key element that makes topical connections explicit between the just prior turn and what was produced before it. In other words, it is the key step in a stepwise topic transition (Sacks, 1992; Jefferson, 1984) that is articulated in the PIE turn.[6] Out of the 38 instances of PIEs in our collection, 12 cases (32%) are found in this environment.[7]

Example 8 provides an example. Here, two men (Seiji and Akira) and a woman (Haru) are talking about their experiences in public bathhouses. Prior to the segment below, Seiji mentioned that he would feel embarrassed to run into someone he knows in a public bathhouse. In response to this, Akira asked Seiji whether he felt embarrassed when he and Akira took a hot-spring bath together during a group trip in the past, to which Seiji said no. Seiji then adds that whether or not he feels self-conscious and embarrassed depends on whom he runs into (line 1).

(08) RKK 18

01 Sei: =hito ni yoru kedo <u>ne</u>
person PT depend but FP
=It depends on who it is, though.
02 Aki: [a::::::::.]
Oh::::::::.
[ ]
03 Sei: [nant(h)e(h)]
Just kidding!
04 .hhh [.hhhh n::nan ga hazukashii n de]shoo ka [ne:::
what SP embarrassing N CP Q FP
.hhh .hhhh Wha:::t makes me so embarrassed, I wonder.
[ ] [
05 Har: [n:::::::::::::::::::::::::::::::.] [ehehh
Hmm::::::::::::::::::::::::::::: *ehehh*
06 [hehh hehh hehh hehh]
[ ]
07 Aki: [hehh i(h)y(h)a ore mo omot]ta.=
well I also thought
hehh Well I wondered ((about that)), too.
08 =a:::: toka [ii nagara dare daroo t(h)o] omotte:
oh etc. say while who CP QT though
=While I was saying, "Oh::::", I wondered who it would be ((that makes you feel embarrassed)).
[ ]
09 Sei: [heh heh heh heh heh]
10 Har: ahah hah [hah hah hah]
[ ]
11 Aki: [hehh dooyuu] otoko no hito dattara
what.kind man LK person CP:if
hehh What kind of men would make...
12 hazukashii n [daroo ( )] .hhhh hehh=
embarrassed N CP
... you feel embarrassed ( ) .hhh hehh=
[ ]
13 Har: [ahh hahh hahh hahh]
14 Sei: =.hhhhhh
15 (1.2)

16 Sei: u::::::::::::::::n
Hmm:::::::::::::
17 (3.5)
18 Sei: .hhhhhhh mae:::::: kawagoe ni sundeta toki ni:[:,]
before Kawagoe in lived time at
.hhhhhhh When I lived in Kawagoe before,
[ ]
19 Har: [u:]:n.
Mmhm
20 (2.2)
21 Sei: -> nanka daigaku no sensee ni atteshimatte:,
like college LK professor PT met
I met a college professor,
22 (.)
23 Aki : ->> sentoo toka de?=
public.bathhouse etc. in
In like a public bathhouse?=
24 Sei: =u:n.
=Yeah.
25 Sei: .hhhhh iya kono hen ni jitsu wa kenkyuusho
well this vicinity in actually research.lab
.hhhhh ((he said)) "Well, actually, my research lab is...
26 ga arimashite ne::::,
SP exist FP
... in this neighborhood, and," ((Story continues ...))

Seiji's comment in line 1 engenders a round of playful teasing by both himself and Akira about what/who makes Seiji so self-conscious and embarrassed in a public bathhouse (lines 3–12), which is accompanied by laughter (and in-speech laugh tokens) by all the three participants. This is then followed by Seiji's extended in-breath (line 14), minimal vocalization (line 16), and long silences (lines 15 and 17). These may serve as a possible indication that the topic talk so far has come to the "state of attrition" (Jefferson, 1993) at this juncture. It is in this environment, then, that Seiji produces bits of talk that appear to bring up something new (lines 18 and 21). Recipients of this utterance are faced with the task of understanding not only what was said in a literal sense, but also why it was brought up here and now in this interaction. In this juncture, then, Akira initiates repair in the form of a PIE (line 23), in which he proffers a candidate understanding of an element that was inferable, yet undelivered in Seiji's turn – *sentoo toka de?* ("In like a public bathhouse?"). The word *sentoo* ("public bathhouse") clearly connects what

Seiji is bringing up now to the topic in the previous sequences of talk. Here, then, a recipient of a topic-initial turn employs a PIE as an instrument to make a topical connection explicit between the just prior turn and what came before it.

Initiating repair when another has just initiated what appears to be an extended telling interferes with the progressivity of that course of action. That said, a PIE works to voice a part of that telling – a part that was necessary to establish an explicit topical connection, yet unarticulated by the prior speaker – and thereby supports the action that the prior speaker is pursuing. Also, a PIE only makes relevant simple confirmation rather than extended elaboration or clarification from the prior speaker, and, therefore, it keeps disruption to the progressivity of the ongoing telling to a minimum. Indeed, Seiji only minimally confirms Akira's candidate understanding (line 24) and immediately resumes his story about running into a college professor in a public bathhouse (lines 25–26). From these observations, we argue that, as in post-First position, PIEs are used in topic-initial position as a way to initiate repair in a maximally aligning manner, i.e., to ensure correct understanding of topical connections while cooperating with the project implemented by the prior speaker.

10.3.3 After receipting an informing: reopening a once-completed course of action

In 10.3.1, we discussed cases where PIEs are used *before* a response made relevant by the prior turn is produced. In this sub-section, we show that, though they occur much less frequently (5 out of 38; 13%), PIEs are also used *after* a sequentially relevant response has been provided. In all of the five cases in our collection, the turns targeted by the PIEs produced in this position are those that perform some sort of informing. Thus, the sequential environment for this usage of PIEs can be characterized as follows:

A: informing
B: receipt of A's informing
B: PIE targeted at A's informing turn

As we saw in 10.3.1, when PIEs are produced *before* a sequentially relevant response, they serve as a way to resolve ambiguity/unclearness with the prior turn as a prerequisite for formulating an appropriate response. This clearly does not hold for the PIEs discussed in this sub-section because a relevant response has already been provided when PIEs are produced. Also, in 10.3.1, we saw that PIEs are used to voice a part of the prior speaker's turn that was projected but "missing" from his/her turn. In other words, the proffered element is presented as something that could (or perhaps should) have been said by the prior speaker. PIEs discussed in this sub-section work rather differently. As will be shown below, they are used not so much to voice what could/should have been said by the prior speaker as to add the PIE-speaker's own contribution to the prior informing that may not necessarily have been projected by the prior speaker's talk. In this usage, then, the format of "proffering an insertable element" is used strategically as a resource to connect something new to the addressee's already-complete action.

Example 9 illustrates the post-receipt deployment of a PIE. Here, two men (Masato and Yuta) are talking about the relationship between two companies, Asahi Broadcasting Corporation (a local broadcasting company in Osaka for which Yuta works) and the Asahi Shimbun (the second-largest national newspaper company in Japan). This topic talk is launched by Masato's question in lines 1 and 3.

(09) FH 22

```
01  Mas:  >tokorode< [ asa   ]hi hoosoo       [ te  no wa] asahi=
           by.the.way Asahi    Broadcasting  QT  N  TP   Asahi
          >By the way< is there any relationship between Asahi…
                      [      ]                [         ]
02  Yut:              [h a i .  ]             [ hai.     ]
                       Mmhm.                   Mmhm.
03  Mas:  =shimbun   to   nanka    kankee    [an   no.    ]
           Newspaper and something relationship exist FP
          ... Broadcasting Corporation and the Asahi Shimbun?
                                             [             ]
04  Yut:                                     [kankee     a]rimasu.
                                              relationship exist
                                              There is.
05        kankee     arimasu.
          relationship exist
          There is.
06  Mas:  ho: [ ::::::::::::::::::::::. ]
          Hu::h::
              [                         ]
07  Yut:      [ichioo      ano: (0.4)]    ano: (0.4)
              more.or.less uhm            uhm
              Like uh:m  (0.4) uh:m (0.4)
```

08 nan te yuu n desu ka? (1.5) KAbu o motten no ka na.
what QT say N CP Q share O hold N Q FP
What do you call it? (1.5) *They are one of our shareholders, I guess*
09 Mas: m:: [::::::::::::::::::::::m.]
Mm::::::::::::::::::::::::.
[ ]
10 Yut: [iya tteyuuka nanka tori]shimariyaku ni asahi
no rather like board.of.directors in Asahi
No, rather, it's like one of our board members ...
11 shimbun no (.) yakuin ga haittemasu ne.
Shimbun LK board.member SP joined FP
... comes from the Asahi Shimbun.
12 Mas: hmm.
Hmm.
13 Yut: maa teekee mitaina mon ya to omoimasu kedo.
well partnership like thing CP QT think but
Well it's like a partnership, I think.
14 [JOohoo no.]
information LK
In terms of ((sharing)) information.
[ ]
15 Mas: [hm. hm.]
Mmhm. Mmhm.
16 (1.2)
17 Mas: m::[::m.]
Hm:::::.
[ ]
18 Yut: -> [ano:] uchi de asahi shimbun nyuusu o yatteru yoona
uhm we at Asahi Shimbun News O doing like
Uhm, it's like ((a partnership where)) we air
19 -> mono ya to omoimasu ne:.
thing CP QT think FP
... Asahi Shimbun News.
20 Mas: -> a:: naruhodo ne h[mmm.]
oh I.see FP
Oh I see. hmmm.
[ ]
21 Yut: [( )]
22 Mas: ->> sono: i– shinya toka ni?
uhm midnight like at
Uhm like at midnight?
23 Yut: a: soo desu yo.=
oh so CP FP
Oh that's right.=
24 Mas: =a:::::::.
=Oh::::::.

Having confirmed that there is a relationship between the two companies (lines 4–5), Yuta offers several characterizations of that relationship, the last one of which is a "partnership in terms of sharing information" (lines 13–14). He then provides a concrete example of such a partnership, i.e., that Asahi Broadcasting Corporation airs a news program called "Asahi Shimbun News" (lines 18–19). This informing is receipted by Masato with *a:: naruhodo ne hmmm.* ("Oh I see. Hmmm.") in line 20. This is an upgraded response as compared to minimal acknowledgments he has been producing in response to earlier parts of Yuta's informing (lines 9, 12, 15). As such, it may indicate that Masato treats Yuta's informing as effectively complete at this point.

Following this receipt, however, Masato deploys a PIE (line 22) that syntactically ties with Yuta's last utterance. What he proffers in this turn – *sono: i- shinya toka ni?* ("Uhm like at midnight?") – is not necessarily an element that was projected in Yuta's prior informing; after all, Yuta's point in lines 18–19 was to give an example of a "partnership in terms of sharing information," for which the time of the day when the news program is broadcast is irrelevant. Rather, the PIE in line 22 brings up something Masato independently (albeit tentatively) knows about the news program. By requesting confirmation about that independently known matter, Masato reflexively locates a once-completed prior telling as in need of further expansion and reopens that prior course of action. He thus exploits the format of proffering an element that "belongs" to the prior speaker's turn as a resource to make his own contribution to the prior speaker's action and thereby display his independent knowledge of the matter being discussed. Yuta's response in line 23 corroborates this; it contains elements that acknowledge a more substantive contribution than a simple confirmation would, i.e., the turn-initial *a* ("oh") and the use of the confirmation token *soo*, which, according to Kushida (2011), indicates that the prior speaker has made an independent contribution.

In this section, we discussed three sequential environments in which PIEs are commonly employed, and explored the interactional import of their deployment. While there are divergent interactional ends served by PIEs in these different environments, there are also commonalities in their workings across different environments. One obvious commonality is that, as a form of understanding check, PIEs work to ensure correct understanding of something in one way or another, i.e., whether it is about an ambiguous/underspecified reference in the prior turn, an inexplicit topical connection with the prior talk, or a new element added to the prior speaker's talk. Another commonality is that PIEs implement an essentially affiliative move in that their producers endorse and cooperate with the prior speaker's course of action, whether in the form of keeping disruption to progressivity to a minimum or providing a further expansion of the prior speaker's action. In the next section, we will discuss a quite different usage of PIEs – those that are used in an environment where "ensuring correct understanding" is *not* an issue. We will show that, unlike those discussed in this section, PIEs used in such an environment implement a disaffiliative move.

10.4 When "understanding" is not an issue

All the cases of PIEs we have examined so far were used in the service of securing understanding without insinuating disaffiliation. However, this is not to say that PIEs never index incipient disaffiliation. In this section, we show how interactional contingencies and paralinguistic features provide a context in which a PIE is hearable as a harbinger of disaffiliation.

Let us first examine example 10. This is a telephone conversation between Yori, an older man, and Megu, a younger woman. They are talking about a movie that they watched together, *New Cinema Paradise*. After discussing who else was there to watch the movie with them, Yori makes a statement that it was a movie that *kodomo* ("kid") would not understand (lines 1–2). Though he leaves it unspecified whom he refers to by a "kid," we can see that Megu hears this as a tease directed at her: her response at line 4 is produced in a tone of voice that makes it sound like a brush-off conveying her irritation, and she does not join Yori in laughing at lines 5–6. Overlapping with what looks like the beginning of a counter criticism by Megu (line 8), Yori backs up his earlier statement by reporting that this unspecified person (the "kid") said that s/he was not touched by the movie (lines 7, 9). Here again, Yori does not articulate who it is that he is quoting ("you" that is supplied in the English translation is not expressed in Japanese), though it is almost certainly Megu. It is in this environment that Megu produces a PIE (line 10).

(10) JAPN1841

01	Yor:	.hhh are wa mada chotto kodomo ni wa wakan nai
		that TP still a.little kid to TP know not
		.hhh That was like a movie that
02		eega tte yuu kanji datta yona:.
		movie TP say like CP FP
		a kid would not understand.
03		(0.3)
04	Meg:	a: soo desu ka.
		oh that CP Q
		Oh is that right.

05 Yor : ehhh heh ehhehh
06 (0.5)
07 Yor : -> .hhh[h .hhhh [nanka anmari kandoo] shi nakatta=
like much touched do not
.hhhh .hhhh ((You)) said things like=
[[ ]
08 Meg: [.hhhh [mata:: soo yatte–]
again that do
.hhhh Again you are like–
09 Yor: -> =yoona koto yutteta ja:n.
like thing was.saying TAG
=((you)) were not really touched ((by the movie)), right.
10 Meg: ->> .hhh mata s– atashi::↑?
again th– I
.hhh Again y– I:: ((did))?
11 Yor: n:n.
Yeah:.
12 (.)
13 Yor: .hh chotto ne: toka itte sa:.
a.litte IP etc say IP
.hh ((You were)) saying "It's a bit, you know?" or something.
14 (0.2)
15 Meg: #n:::#::::::::::n soo ne.
that FP
Hm::::::::::::: that's true.

At line 10, Megu restarts her earlier utterance (*mata s-* "again th-"; cf. line 8) and then abandons it to produce a PIE: *atashi::?* ("I:: ((did))?"). This PIE cannot be heard to be addressing a problem in understanding, given that Megu correctly understood Yori's initial statement (lines 1–2) as a tease directed at her and disaffiliation has already emerged between them. It is more plausible to consider this PIE as a display of disbelief and challenge; by questioning the obvious referent, Megu indicates that she cannot believe she said she had not been moved by the movie.

Also relevant is the paralinguistic feature with which this PIE is produced: Megu puts a stress on the beginning of the word *atashi* ("I") and raises the pitch remarkably high towards its end as indicated with the underline on the colon and an upward arrow. According to Selting (1996), these features mark an OIR as a display of astonishment or surprise instead of a display of trouble in hearing or understanding, which makes it hearable as an indication of incipient disaffiliation. Thus, both (i) interactional contingencies under which a PIE is produced – the likelihood that understanding is not an issue and the fact that the speaker has already produced disaffiliative moves – and (ii) marked paralinguistic features contribute to the hearing of a PIE as a sign of disaffiliation.

We see these two factors play their roles in the next example as well. The following exchange transpires at the beginning of a dinner, where Kazu is hosting Masa and Yuki. While serving a portion of chicken onto her plate, Masa voiced her concern about her false teeth, saying she wonders if she can masticate the pieces of chicken. In response, Kazu said that she would get Masa a knife if necessary (chopsticks are provided to eat with, suggesting that Kazu considers that nothing on the table needs cutting). A while later, Masa displays a struggle in masticating; she awkwardly uses chopsticks to split a piece of chicken into smaller pieces. Having noticed this, Kazu grabs a pair of scissors on the table. As she picks it up, she says, *nakayama san sa:, ichiban rakuna no ga ne:, kore na no* ("Miss Nakayama, the easiest thing is this"; lines 3, 5 and 7), to Masa. Masa produces a PIE in the exchange that follows (line 13).

(11) TD

01 Mas: nank[ka–s:a::?, *((to Yuki))*
like IP
It's like,
[
02 Kaz: [n:
Uhm
03 Kaz: nakayama san [sa:,
Nakayama HT IP
Miss Nakayama,
[
04 Mas: [nanp[uraa toka (aji–) *((To Yuki))*
namplaa etc. taste
Namplaa or something
[
05 Kaz: [ichiban rakuna no ga ne:, *((picks up scissors))*
most easy N SP FP
The easiest thing is...
06 Mas: n:,= *((To Kazu))*
Mmhm
07 Kaz: =kore na no. *((raises scissors to mutual line of gaze*
this CP FP *with Masa))*
... this.

08 (0.2)
09 Mas: ↑n:,
↑*Mmhm,*
10 Kaz: -> ng–kore de –koo= *((snipping gesture with scissors))*
this with this
If you do like this (=snipping) with this (=scissors)...
11 -> =suru to ichiban rakuna [no. *((Masa opens mouth,*
do then most easy FP *raises eyebrows))*
... it's the easiest.
[
12 Yuk: [uhuhuhu
[
13 Mas: ->> [kore o?= *((points at*
this O *chicken))*
This?
14 Kaz: =nandemo taberu toki mo[shi.demo sore ga=
anything eat time if but that SP
Anything, when eating, if ((you'd like)).
But if you don't like that,
[
15 Mas: [^uwa::: honto?
wow really
Wow, really?
16 Kaz: =iya da ^ttara [naifu o age[ru.
dislike CP if knife O give
I'll give you a knife.
[[
17 Mas: [nn. [nn.nn.
Yeah. *Yeah.Yeah.*

Given that Kazu had earlier offered to get Masa a knife if necessary, and that Masa has displayed difficulty in eating the chicken, Kazu's turn at lines 5 and 7 is hearable as a suggestion of the scissors as an alternative to a knife, making an acceptance or a rejection relevant. However, Masa neither accepts nor rejects the suggestion in the next turn; after a short delay (line 8), she provides a minimal acknowledgment token (line 9). This lack of a relevant response raises a possibility that a rejection is incipient (Pomerantz, 1984a; Sacks, 1987). At this point, Kazu attends to this lack of response not as a sign of an incipient rejection but as a lack of understanding (Pomerantz, 1984b); she redoes her suggestion, this time making it clearer by adding what to do with the scissors with an accompanying snipping gesture (lines 10–11). In the midst of this turn, Masa opens her mouth and raises her eyebrows (line 11), visibly displaying surprise or shock.[8] She then produces something other than an acceptance or a rejection of Kazu's suggestion: an utterance formatted as a

PIE (line 13). With this, she proffers a candidate object for which to use the scissors, i.e., the chicken, referring to it with the demonstrative *kore* ("this one") marked with the object particle *o*, while pointing at the chicken on her plate. This noun phrase is designed to be structurally insertable into the preceding turn, as in *kore de* ***kore o*** *koo suru to ichiban rakuna no* ("if you do like this [=snipping] **to this** [=chicken] with these [=scissors], that's the easiest.").

Now, under the interactional circumstance where (i) Masa has already failed to respond to a suggestion once (line 9); (ii) Kazu has redone the suggestion with some clarification; and (iii) Masa has facially displayed surprise, it is difficult to hear this PIE as an "innocent" understanding check. Rather, it is more likely to be a display of surprise or shock, which then serves as a harbinger of a rejection of the suggestion. The heavy stress also contributes to the hearing of this PIE as a display of disaffiliation (Selting, 1996). Indeed, that is how Kazu understands this utterance. She first answers the question that the PIE raises, saying that the scissors can be used to cut anything to eat. She then makes concessions, a move often observed after a sign of an upcoming dispreferred response; she appends *moshi* ("if") to the first unit of line 14, which we take to be the beginning of or a highly truncated way of saying *moshi yokattara* ("if you'd like"). She then adds that she would get Masa a knife if she does not want to use the scissors. These two concessions are evidence that Kazu heard Masa's PIE as indicative of disaffiliation.

Overlapping with these concessions, Masa produces a newsmark (line 15; Jefferson, 1981) prefaced by an interjection that displays the speaker's astonishment, *uwaa* ("wow"). This utterance again displaces a relevant response to Kazu's suggestion. It is only after Kazu started to offer an alternative solution (i.e., giving Masa a knife) that Masa provides rather emphatic affirmative responses (line 17).[9]

In sum, although PIEs are generally used to initiate repair while aligning with the prior speaker's course of action, the two cases examined in this section suggest that particular interactional contingencies and distinctive paralinguistic features employed for their production may make PIEs serve as a sign of disaffiliation. This in turn reinforces our argument that PIEs are a class of OIR that is distinct from other forms of OIR; generally speaking, OIRs insinuate disaffiliation by virtue of conveying that their producers did not quite "get" the trouble source turn and delaying a due response. In contrast, it takes interactional contingencies and/or paralinguistic markings for a PIE to be heard as a harbinger of disaffiliation.

10.5 Conclusion

Other-initiated repair is a generic organization of practice, presumably available to speakers of any language. Yet, the specific ways in which OIR turns are formatted may vary across languages, and specific jobs that get done through different OIR formats within a language may vary as well. This study examined one particular OIR format observed in Japanese – proffers of insertable elements – and explored the "fit" between that turn format and the interactional work accomplished through it (cf. Schegloff, 1996b: 199–203). We noted that the format of the PIE as an "add-on" element structurally dependent on the design of the prior speaker's turn allows its users to display a high degree of understanding of the prior turn. We argued then that, by using the format of voicing a part of the prior turn and requesting only a minimal confirmation from the prior speaker, the PIE-speaker is able to keep disruption to the progressivity of the ongoing course of action to a minimum while ensuring correct understanding of the prior speaker's turn. In other words, the PIE provides an apt solution to the dilemma between achieving intersubjectivity while at the same time minimizing the disruption to progressivity (Heritage, 2007). As it is a minimally disruptive form of repair-initiation that exhibits a high degree of fittedness to the structure and action of the prior speaker's turn, the PIE is typically used in contexts where the repair-initiating party aligns with the course of action pursued by the prior speaker. We also showed, however, that, under certain interactional contingencies, the PIE can be used to convey a possibly disaffiliative stance.

The findings of this study suggest a number of directions for future research. Among them is a comparison with OIR formats used in other languages that exploit the format of "incrementing." As noted in section 10.2.2, English speakers utilize such a turn format for OIR when they carry out understanding checks with appendor questions. Do speakers of other languages also employ the format of incrementing for OIR? If they do, are there grammatical constraints on how those turns are formatted (e.g., "Insertables" vs. "Glue-ons")? What are the sequential/interactional environments in which such turn formats are typically employed, and are there cross-linguistic similarities and differences in their workings?

Another direction for future research is to explore the fit between OIR formats and their interactional workings *within* a language. So, for example, what motivates Japanese speakers to choose between presenting a candidate understanding in the form of the PIE and doing so by constructing a grammatically independent turn? Are these different turn formats used for demonstrably distinct interactional purposes? What about OIR turns constructed as a grammatically dependent unit with a WH-word in it (e.g., A: *kinoo itta?* "Did you go yesterday?" – B: *doko ni?* "To where?"). Do these work differently from PIEs? If so, how? Further investigation of the workings of different OIR turn formats may allow us to discover selection principles underlying their use in interaction (cf. Egbert, forthcoming).

REFERENCES

Couper-Kuhlen, E. and Ono, T. (2007). "Incrementing" in conversation: a comparison of practices in English, German and Japanese. *Pragmatics* 17: 513–552.

Drew, P. (1997). "Open" class repair initiators in response to sequential sources of troubles in conversation. *Journal of Pragmatics* 28: 69–101.

Egbert, M. (1996). Context-sensitivity in conversation: eye gaze and the German repair initiator "bitte?" *Language in Society* 25: 587–612.

(forthcoming). Selection principles for other-initiated repair turn formats. In J. Heritage, G. Lerner, and G. Raymond, eds., *Finding the Universal in the Particular: A Festschrift for Emanuel A. Schegloff on his 70th Birthday*. Boston: Blackwell.

Egbert, M., Golato, A., and Robinson, J. (2009). Repairing reference. In J. Sidnell, ed., *Conversation Analysis: Comparative Perspectives*, pp. 104–132. Cambridge University Press.

Heritage, J. (1984). *Garfinkel and Ethnomethodology*. Cambridge: Polity Press.

(2007). Intersubjectivity and progressivity in person (and place) reference. In N. J. Enfield and T. Stivers, eds., *Person Reference in Interaction: Linguistic, Cultural and Social Perpsectives*, pp. 255–280. Cambridge University Press.

Jefferson, G. (1972). Side sequences. In D. N. Sudnow, ed., *Studies in Social Interaction*, pp. 294–33. New York: Free Press.

(1981). The abominable "ne?": an exploration of post-response pursuit of response. In P. Schröder and H. Steger, eds., *Dialogforschung*, pp. 53–88. Düsseldorf: Pädagogischer Verlag Schwann.

(1984). On stepwise transition from talk about a trouble to inappropriately next-positioned matters. In J. M. Atkinson and J. C. Heritage, eds., *Structures of Social Action: Studies in Conversation Analysis*, pp. 191–222. Cambridge University Press.

(1993). Caveat speaker: preliminary notes on recipient topic-shift implicature. *Research on Language and Social Interaction* 26: 1–30.

Kim, K.-H. (1999). Other-initiated repair sequences in Korean conversation: types and functions. *Discourse and Cognition* 6: 141–168.

(2001). Confirming intersubjectivity through retroactive elaboration: organization of phrasal units in other-initiated repair sequences in Korean conversation. In M. Selting and E. Couper-Kuhlen, eds., *Studies in Interactional Linguistics*, pp. 345–372. Amsterdam/Philadelphia: John Benjamins.

Kushida, S. (2011). Confirming understanding and acknowledging assistance: managing trouble responsibility in response to understanding check in Japanese talk-in-interaction. *Journal of Pragmatics* 43: 2716–2739.

Lerner, G. (2004). On the place of linguistic resources in the organization of talk-in-interaction: grammar as action in prompting a speaker to elaborate. *Research on Language and Social Interaction* 37: 151–184.

Pomerantz, A. (1984a). Agreeing and disagreeing with assessments: some features of preferred/dispreferred turn shapes. In J. M. Atkinson and J. Heritage, eds., *Structures of Social Action: Studies in Conversation Analysis*, pp. 57–101. Cambridge University Press.

(1984b). Pursuing a response. In J. M. Atkinson and J. Heritage, eds., *Structures of Social Action: Studies in Conversation Analysis*, pp. 152–163. Cambridge University Press.

Robinson, J. (2006). Managing trouble responsibility and relationships during conversational repair. *Communication Monographs* 73: 137–161.
Sacks, H. (1987). On the preference for agreement and contiguity in sequences in conversation. In G. Button and J. Lee, eds., *Talk and Social Organisation*, pp. 54–69. Clevedon: Multilingual Matters.
(1992). *Lectures on Conversation*, volumes I and II. Ed. G. Jefferson, with an introduction by E. A. Schegloff. Oxford: Blackwell.
Sacks, H., Schegloff, E. A., and Jefferson, G. (1974). A simplest systematics for the organization of turn-taking for conversation. *Language* 50: 696–735.
Schegloff, E. A. (1979). The relevance of repair to a syntax-for-conversation. In T. Givon, ed., *Syntax and Semantics*, vol. XII, pp. 261–286. New York: Academic Press.
(1996a). Turn organization: one intersection of grammar and interaction. In E. Ochs, E. A. Schegloff, and S. A. Thompson, eds., *Interaction and Grammar*, pp. 52–133. Cambridge University Press.
(1996b). Confirming allusions: toward an empirical account of action. *American Journal of Sociology* 104: 161–216.
(1997). Practices and actions: boundary cases of other-initiated repair. *Discourse Processes* 23: 499–545.
(2007). *Sequence Organization in Interaction: A Primer in Conversation Analysis*. Cambridge University Press.
Schegloff, E. A. and Sacks, H. (1973). Opening up closings. *Semiotica* 8: 289–327.
Schegloff, E. A., Jefferson, G., and Sacks, H. (1977). The preference for self-correction in the organization of repair in conversation. *Language* 53: 361–382.
Selting, M. (1988). The role of intonation in the organization of repair and problem handling sequences in conversation. *Journal of Pragmatics* 15: 583–588.
(1996). Prosody as an activity-type distinctive cue in conversation: the case of so-called “astonished” questions in repair initiation. In E. Couper-Kuhlen and M. Selting, eds., *Prosody in Conversation: Interactional Studies*, pp. 231–270. Cambridge University Press.
Sidnell, J. (2008). Alternate and complementary perspectives on language and social life: the organization of repair in two Caribbean communities. *Journal of Sociolinguistics* 12: 477–503.
(2010). Questioning repeats in the talk of four-year old children. In H. Gardner and M. Forrester, eds., *Analysing Interactions in Childhood: Insights from Conversation Analysis*, pp. 102–127. Hoboken, NJ: Wiley.
(2012). Turn-continuation by self and by other. *Discourse Processes* 49: 314–337.
Stivers, T. and Robinson, J. (2006). A preference for progressivity in interaction. *Language in Society* 35: 367–392.
Suzuki, K. (2010). Other-initiated repair in Japanese: accomplishing mutual understanding in conversation. Unpublished doctoral dissertation. Kobe University.
Svennevig, J. (2008). Trying the easiest solution first in other-initiated repair. *Journal of Pragmatics* 40: 333–348.
Tanaka, H. (1999). *Turn-taking in Japanese Conversation: A Study in Grammar and Interaction*. Amsterdam/Philadelphia: John Benjamins.

Wu, R.-J. R. (2006). Initiating repair and beyond: the use of two repeat-formatted repair initiations in Mandarin conversation. *Discourse Processes* 4: 67–109.
(2009). Repetition in the initiation of repair. In J. Sidnell, ed., *Conversation Analysis: Comparative Perspectives*, pp. 31–59. Cambridge University Press.

NOTES

1 A preliminary observation of our data suggests that the major formats discussed in Schegloff et al.'s (1977) typology correspond more or less to those initiator techniques used for OIR in Japanese. See also Suzuki (2010).
2 There is a similar practice observed in English – what Sacks (1992) termed "appendor questions." See 10.2.2 for a discussion of similarities and differences between appendor questions and PIEs.
3 As we will show in section 10.4, there is an exception to this generalization.
4 An example of an increment in English is seen in the following (Lerner, 2004: 156):

R: We went straight to ah: visit Ted,
(1.0)
R: from the office.

5 It is not impossible to produce a Glue-on to extend a prior TCU in Japanese – see Couper-Kuhlen and Ono's (2007: 541–2) discussion of TCU extensions that start with the quotative particle *tte*. However, it appears to be limited to this one type of grammatical extension, and none of the cases of PIEs found in our data are of this type. (We should note, though, that it is theoretically possible to format an OIR in the form of a Glue-on, i.e., in the form of an appendor question, in Japanese.)
6 We owe this observation to Jack Sidnell (personal communication).
7 In 8 of these 12 cases, the topic-initial turn is formulated as a sequence-initiating action (e.g., a question; see example 6, for example). These cases are thus included in the post-First category discussed in 10.3.1 as well.
8 Note here that using scissors in place of a table knife is an out-of-norm behavior in the Japanese dining culture.
9 Masa provided the same affirmative token at line 9 after Kazu's initial suggestion. However, the affirmative token there cannot be heard as an acceptance of the suggestion since the suggestion was made indirectly in the form of a statement and to accept it as a suggestion would take a more substantive response than a minimal affirmation.

11 Alternative, subsequent descriptions

Jack Sidnell and Rebecca Barnes

"A barometric low hung over the Atlantic. It moved eastward toward a high-pressure area over Russia without as yet showing any inclination to bypass this high in a northerly direction. The isotherms and isotheres were functioning as they should. The air temperature was appropriate relative to the annual mean temperature and to the aperiodic monthly fluctuations of the temperature. The rising and the setting of the sun, the moon, the phases of the moon, of Venus, of the rings of Saturn, and many other significant phenomena were all in accordance with the forecasts in the astronomical yearbooks. The water vapour in the air was at its maximal state of tension, while the humidity was minimal. In a word that characterizes the facts fairly accurately, even if it is a bit old-fashioned: It was a fine day in August 1913." Musil, *The Man without Qualities*

11.1 Introduction

We start with a simple observation – one which we understand to have informed work in conversation analysis from its very inception: for anything that co-conversationalists talk about, there are multiple ways in which it can be described. Schegloff (1988) notes that two aspects of this have been examined in conversation analytic studies. First, and most commonly, conversation analysts since Sacks (1972a, 1972b) and Schegloff (1972) have described the ways in which speakers select from different *types* of forms in specific domains. For instance, in initial references to non-present persons, speakers can use either recognitional or non-recognitional reference forms (Sacks and Schegloff, 1979; Sacks, 1995; Schegloff, 1996; Enfield and Stivers, eds., 2007). Second, and less commonly, conversation analysts have considered the way in which next speakers may offer *alternative and*

Earlier versions of the analysis were presented at ICCA, July 2010 in Mannheim and at UCLA, February 2011. Thanks to the participants in those sessions – especially Steve Clayman, John Heritage, Tanya Stivers, Manny Schegloff – for many helpful comments and suggestions. For comments on an earlier written version we are very much indebted to Makoto Hayashi, Danielle Pillet-Shore, Jeffrey Robinson and Manny Schegloff.

competing descriptions, characterizations or formulations of the same state of affairs (Schegloff, 1988; Drew, 1992). Consider example 1 below. Here, in a conversation between friends, the same activity is described alternately as "drinking" and "having liquor."

(01) "After the movie" (FRAGMENT – From Schegloff, 1988: 6)

W: =D'people sit around eating in Nepal?
(0.2)
D: All the time that's all they d[o
C: [They never drink
without ('t) (0.2)
D: Yeah ya never have liquor without (1.0)
fried meat er

At line 74, Schegloff (1988) suggests that D is not selecting from an alternative *form* since while here "never drink" and "never have liquor" are treated as equivalent descriptions – they are not "canonical" or "standing" alternates.[1] Of course, despite the ever-present *possibility* that anything described might be described otherwise, participants typically treat descriptions given as adequate – they respond to the talk which contains the description and do not orient, overtly, to the other possible ways in which it might have been characterized. In the following we examine a set of cases in which participants *do* orient to the availability of alternative possible descriptions and further suggest that an initial description is in someway insufficient, inaccurate or otherwise problematic.

In what follows, then, we are concerned with the specific practices next speakers use to challenge or resist the describings, characterizings or referring formulations of a prior speaker. We suggest a basic distinction between, on the one hand, practices by which a next speaker merely *identifies* a possible description/formulation issue in prior talk and, on the other, practices by which a next speaker directly addresses the problem by offering a *replacement* description/formulation. We also suggest a second important distinction having to do with the domain of knowledge to which the matter talked about belongs. That is, there are cases in which the matter talked about falls squarely within the next speaker's domain of knowledge and there are cases in which the matter talked about is in the prior speaker's domain. Taking the perspective of the next speaker, we can think of this as a distinction between "MY domain" and "YOUR domain." These two distinctions combine to result in the following set of four possibilities: "my"-domain replacements, "my"-domain identifications, "your"-domain replacements, and "your"-domain identifications.

Our analysis suggests that participants orient to a basic, normative distribution of rights such that a subsequent speaker is entitled to *replace* (and possibly also correct) a first description with an alternative one if the talk describes something within her epistemic domain. On the other hand, a subsequent speaker is entitled only to identify a possible problem with an initial description (i.e., not replace it) where the talk describes something in the other's epistemic domain (this frequently being accomplished through the other-initiation of repair). This "rule" accounts for the majority of instances we have collected which are *either* my-domain replacements *or* your-domain identifications. In addition, the handful of exceptions which we have found share several features in common and can be analyzed in terms of what, in each case, is accomplished through the departure from the normatively sanctioned practice.

The practices we describe here overlap and intertwine with those typically understood as constituting the domain of "repair" in multiple ways (Schegloff, Jefferson, Sacks, 1977). Practices of replacing a prior description are often hearable as constituting a "correction," whereas those of identifying a possible problem often employ the vehicle of other-initiated repair. However, there are replacements that are designed to be heard as doing something other than correcting and there are cases in which identification is done by means other than repair initiation. We therefore suggest that the practices of identification and replacement we describe are ultimately distinct from the practices of repair initiation and correction whose form they sometimes take. Our analysis further intersects with research on the organization of repair by showing that, although there is ample evidence of the preference for self-correction, in the cases we consider that preference is modulated by epistemic issues (see also Haakana and Kurhila, 2009).

11.2 Methodological issues

The data for this chapter have been drawn from a range of naturally occurring recorded interactions from Canadian, American and British contexts. They include video- and audio-taped recordings of ordinary conversation, public inquiry, courtroom, radio interview and medical interaction. The data are drawn both from the authors' personal collections of recordings and from publicly available data.

This kind of study presents a number of methodological complications. Most crucially we are faced with something of a conundrum in terms of how to determine the "referential" or extensional equivalence of two descriptions or formulations. To describe two distinct items as alternative descriptions presupposes that they are referentially co-extensive/ equivalent, differing only in "sense" or what the philosopher Gottlob Frege (1948 [1892]) also described as "mode of presentation" (a classic example: "Venus" = "The morning star" = "the evening star," or "Clark Kent" = "Superman"). But obviously this requires our introducing a standard of THE SAME from outside the setting thus violating a basic methodological principle of conversation analysis. After all, we need some criteria of referential equivalence in order to distinguish cases such as example 2 from cases such as example 3.

(02) GTS:III: 42 (r) ST

```
Ken:      Hey (.) the first ti:me they stopped me from selling
          cigarettes was this morning.
          (1.0)
Lou:      From selling cigarettes?
Ken:      Or buying cigarettes.
```

(03) Sponsorship – 20401 qt 9:09

```
W:        I think when that happened it was out of the uhm:
          the sponsorship budget if I [recall correctly.
L:                                    [You– you stuck it
          in the sponsorship.
          (0.2)
L:        b[udget,
W: ->      [Pardon,
L:        You– you– you: deci:ded in '96 (.) to place these
          (.) purchases in thee sponsorship account correct?
W:        It's the only place I could place it.
```

Both examples involve the other-initiation of repair. However the repair in example 2 is a correction of "selling" by "buying," whereas the repair in example 3 is a reformulation of "stuck" by "decided to place." The distinction here thus hinges on our sense that "selling" and "buying" do not refer to the same action whereas "stuck" and "decided to place" (in this context) do. So in example 2 the trouble Lou locates is one of "mis-speaking" whereas in example 3 the witness reveals, by other-initiating repair, a problem with the way something has been described.

An added complication, from a conversation analytic perspective, is that participants in interaction can sometimes treat two expressions that *appear* to have quite different extensions as though they were equivalent. Consider, for instance, the following case in which Harry and Jean are talking about Jean's plans to renew the photo for her driving license.

(04) Dark glasses – Griffiths HE3 9:51

```
01   Jea:        oh no:. I'm not >gonna  wear< gla:sses. [(...)
02   Har:                                              [↑dark glasses.
03   Jea:        mm?
04   Har:        ↑dark ↓glasses,
05   Jea: ->     ↑different ↓glasses, [yes
06   Har:                             [no they're ↑dark >aren't they?<
07               ((lifts cup and drinks))
```

Notice that at line 05 Jean reformulates the reference "dark glasses" to "different glasses" while simultaneously treating what Harry has said as correct and thus what she is saying as equivalent. She does this by use of a turn format which Jefferson (1985) claims canonically takes the shape of [repeat]+"yeah" but which can alternately involve [replacement]+"yeah." "↑different ↓glasses, yes" conveys "I'm repeating and agreeing with what you've said." See example 5 below for a parallel case in which Sheila and Hank are discussing the James Bond series of spy films:

(05) Friedell: Alt:37 (From Jefferson, 1985: 32)

```
01   She:        WHICH ONE'S the one thet he marries the girl en she
02               die:s in the car wreck.
03   Han:        °ehho° That's : : : : : On'er (1.0) On Her Majesty's : : :
04               Service er : : :
05   She:  ->    On Her Majesty's Secret Service [°that's right° ]
06   Han:                                        [°Secret Se r v] ice=
07               =yeah.°
```

So here Sheila's talk at line 5 is not an exact repeat of Hank's talk at lines 3–4. Rather, it corrects what Hank has said by inserting the word "secret." However, by appending "that's right" (which Jefferson suggests is equivalent to "yeah" in this context) Sheila treats Hank's answer as adequate and agrees with it. We will show other examples in which a next speaker presents what appears to be a referentially quite different term as though it were equivalent (see also Jefferson, 1987).

So the methodological question, for us, is: how do we ground our sense of referential equivalence independently of how that is treated by the participants? This is a problem for which we have yet to find a definitive solution. Our analysis attempts to side-step it by considering only those cases in which there is some sense in which the participants are obviously engaged in reformulating, redescribing or rephrasing something in the prior talk.

11.3 Your-domain identifications

A first example in which a next speaker merely identifies a potentially problematic description in the prior speaker's talk is shown in example 6 below. The example is taken from *The Current*, a Canadian current affairs radio program in which E. Hunter Harrison, a railroader who worked his way up to serve as the president and chief executive officer of the Canadian National Railway, is being interviewed. Here the interviewer's repetition of Harrison's "some knack for it" is followed by the comment "I think some would say that's an understatement":

(06) Hunter Harrison – The Current 2:23

```
01   I:          So when didja fall in love with it.
02               (0.4)
03   HH:         Early on. uh once I learned thet uh oil
04               'n bearings wondn't the thing I wantid
05               tuh do (.) .hhhh as I started lookin'
06               'round an' seein' other opportunities
07               uh (.) uh all o' sudden fell in love
08               with the buisness .hh I'm not a buff or
09               a foamer as I call'em bu' I have enjoyed
10          ->   this business an' I developed some knack
11               for it. and uh .h I've stayed with it fer
12               a long time.
13   I:     ->   Some knack for it. I think some would say
14               that's an understatement.
15               (0.2)
16   HH:         Well thank you.
17   I:          heh.
```

So in this case the interviewer allows the description "some knack for it" to stand but characterizes it as an "understatement," thereby identifying what Harrison has said as "modest." This implicates a compliment which Harrison accepts in line 16 with "well thank you."

A similar case is shown as example 7. This is taken from an interview with Frank Iacobucci, who, after a distinguished career in law, had been appointed to the Supreme Court in Ottawa and, subsequently, became the interim president of the University of Toronto shortly before the interview was conducted. In this example, the interviewer's repeat of "to do things there" in line 8 is combined with laughter particles. Jefferson (1972) shows that such repeats typically appreciate something amusing or otherwise remarkable in the repeated talk but here Iacobucci treats it as a candidate hearing that other-initiates repair and confirms with "right" (he thus disattends the implication that what he has said is overly "modest"). After the interviewer (ironically) confirms the confirmation (line 10) she repeats the problematic description again at line 12 but inserts the word "big" to produce – "to do big things there", retroactively demonstrating the problem to be one of excessive modesty.

(07) Sounds Like Canada – Iacobucci 20/4/05

01	I:		[(it– di–) an this is a retur:n to you fer
02			the- to the University of Toronto.
03	FI:		That's right I: ah I was uh u–in the university
04			fer nearly twenty years then went to Ottawa,
05			(.)
06		–>	.h to do things there: an' [(turn)
07	I:		[hhh hah heh
08		–>	to do thi (h) ngs there.=
09	FI:		=right.
10	I:		ri[ght.
11	FI:		[(uh huh)=
12	I:	–>	to do ↑big things the[re.
13	FI:		[we:ll I- uhm I– I was:
14			Look.=I've been very fortunate. I: been very
15			very fortunate to have had the opportunities
16			to serve.

Mere identification of a potentially problematic description, as in these cases, establishes the relevance of a response from a first speaker. Such responses are obviously quite varied. In example 6, the implied compliment is accepted by Harrison, in example 7 the identification is first treated as a candidate understanding and is confirmed by Iacobucci. This leads to a modification and implied compliment "to do ↑big things there" that Iacobucci deflects. Another example, shown as example 8 below, comes from a fragment of ordinary conversation discussed by Schegloff (1988). This begins with Winnie asking her friends David and Cece whether people in Nepal "sit around eating." David has recently returned from a year in Nepal, Cece, his wife, has returned sometime earlier after having been in Nepal for eight months. After both David and Cece provide answers to the question (which we discuss below), Winnie targets "fried meat" with a questioning repeat. David initially treats this description as adequate, confirming in line 78. After Winnie pursues with a second repair initiation at line 80 (one which specifies more precisely the nature of the problem as she sees it – "generic fried meat," i.e., what kind of animal is being eaten), David offers "buff" as an alternative description.[2]

(08) "After the movie" (fragment – From Schegloff, 1988: 6)

69	W:	=D'people sit around eating in Nepal?
70		(0.2)
71	D:	All the time that's all they d[o
72	C:	[They never drink
73		without ('t) (0.2)

74 D: Yeah ya never have liquor without (1.0)
75 fried meat er
76 W: Fri:ed meat?
77 (hh hh)
78 D: Uh huh. [Fried]
79 ?: [(loin)]
80 W: [Y'mean j'st gen]eric frie[:d meat?
81 H: [*(hh hh)
82 D: (Mhm) usually buff.
83 H: (Oh y') [buff
84 W: [B(h)u:ff? (hh hh) *hh Buff as in "a–low"?=
85 H: =Buff burgers.
86 D: Mmyeh, (.) 's in "a–low".

As a final example of your-domain identification, consider the following case, in which an invitation is initially formulated as "to come over here and talk".

(09) JJ:1 (From Sacks, 1995: II: 370)

01 B: How ya doing? Say what are you doing?
02 C: Well we're going out, why?
03 B: Oh, I was just gonna say come out
04 and come over here and talk this evening,
05 but if you're going out [you can't very well do that
06 C: ['Talk'', you mean get drunk
07 don't you.
08 B: What?
09 C: It's Saturday.
10 B: What do you do. Go out and get drunk every Saturday?

So here B is describing the invitation s/he would have produced were the pre-invitation not "blocked" at line 2 with "Well we're going out," (see Schegloff, 2007). The invitation is described as having been to "come over here and talk," and in line 6 C identifies a problem with that by other-initiating repair with "Talk, you mean get drunk don't you." Although C here provides a candidate alternative description of what the invitation was for, s/he does this by first repeating the problematic talk and thus identifying it. The alternative description "get drunk" is offered for B's confirmation by formatting the turn which contains it as a candidate understanding.

Your-domain identifications respect the greater epistemic rights of the initial speaker – by merely identifying an issue the next speaker leaves it to the prior to provide a replacement or to respond in some other way. It is likely important that all these identifications come in (broadly conceived) third position and thus involve relatively minor progress interruptions – they topicalize some piece of a prior answer turn and thus invite elaborations of that answer (compare the identifications in my-domain, which we discuss below – all of which come in second position, and challenge the design of a question, their speakers refusing to answer the question as put and thus engendering significant interruptions to the progress of the sequence underway).

Before leaving these examples, let us note that, although all involve use of repetition in order to target some particular piece of prior talk, there are some differences in the formats used. For instance, in examples 6 and 7 the repeat is downwardly intoned whereas in example 8 it is "question" intoned. In example 7 the repeat is infiltrated by laughter. And finally, in example 9 the repeat is followed by a candidate alternative, which is framed as a question inviting first speaker's confirmation.

It can also be noted that it many cases, the initial formulation is produced with some hesitation or perturbation in the talk, suggesting that the speaker has encountered some problem or anticipates that the recipient will find the wording problematic (see also Lerner, this volume). So for instance in example 6, Harrison suggests "an' I developed some knack for it. and uh.h" and in example 7 there is some delay directly before the phrase "to do things there" is produced (at line 5 and 6). In example 8, "fried meat" is preceded by substantial delay (at line 74) and followed by what maybe the beginning of a self-repair ("er"). All of this is to suggest that the identification of some bit of talk as the target for eventual redoing may be an interactive accomplishment of a first and second speaker. The hitches that surround the phrases in examples 6 and 7 suggest that these speakers have already noted a possible modesty or understatement in their own talk.

11.4 My-domain replacements

My-domain replacements are those in which the matter talked about falls within the second speaker's epistemic domain and there is no prior identification of a possible problem attending the first description. A particularly clear case of this comes in our next example, taken from interaction among young children (seven years old). Here, the children are playing with blocks. When the structure falls, A screams and, at line 1, the supervising adult complains, "Guys too loud." This occasions an excuse from A, who assigns responsibility to C by saying "She po::ked it," in reference to the structure she is building. Notice then that the description concerns C's action and thus falls squarely within C's epistemic domain. In the next turn C replaces "po::ked" with "ta:pped."

(10) Kids_G2_T1_37:00

01	Ad:		Guys too loud.
02	A:	–>	She po: :ked it.
03	C:	–>	I ta:pped it.
04			(0.2)
05	A:		Well you knocked it over.
06	C:		No I didn't.
07	A:		Yes you did.
08	C:		Oh whatever.

In example 11, from an interview between reporter Andrea Canning and actor Charlie Sheen, the interviewer refers to Sheen's "anger" and "hate" at line 1–2. At line 3 Sheen replaces this with "passion."

(11) Charlie Sheen Interview – Anger/Hate vs. Passion

01	Int:	Your anger. an' your hate. I think is coming
02		off as erratic. Tuh peo [ple.
03	CS:	[passion. (.) My passion
04		(0.2)
05		It's all [passion
06	Int:	[okay your passion,=
07	CS:	=yes.=
08	Int:	=is coming off as erratic

Notice that the interviewer accepts the replacement in line 6 and uses it to reassert that Sheen is coming off as "erratic." In example 12, taken from a recording of ordinary conversation at a seniors' residence, Tom apparently means to pay Betty a compliment by referring to her belongings as "yer accomplishment." At line 19 Betty's well-prefaced turn replaces "accomplishment" with "stuff" (Schegloff and Lerner, 2009).

(12) IM030402-Coffee Chat

13	Tom:		We:ll thuh t– ih thuh time thuh lady came up ↓here
14			(0.6) when we were talkin about getning rid of all: :
15		–>	of yer (1.4) a (.) ccomplishment. [heh heh]=
16	Bet:		[–Yes?]=
17	Ric:		=Y:e : : ah
18	Tom:		Heh [heh
19	Bet:	–>	[Well all my ↑stuff?
20	Tom:		↓Y[eah:,
21	Bet:		[↑Y'know.
22			(0.5)
23	Bet:		An I'm getting rid of it.=an' jus keeping a few little
24			things<an then *Igh* (.) if I have to git new: whoever
25			gets (me) is when I have to buy it a:ll.

Example 13 comes from a primary care consultation between a family doctor and a patient. Earlier, the patient revealed that she has not been taking her blood pressure tablets as they made her feel "giddy." The doctor remarks that her blood pressure is "quite high" and the patient responds that 'things are a bit tense again.' The patient's replacement (from "up and down" to "dreadful") at line 3 occurs interruptively in overlap, eventually halting the ongoing talk by the doctor, which was moving towards a further recommendation to retry the tablets (lines 1 and 2). The patient's replacement reaches back into prior talk, pre-framing the replacement with "I've had a …" The replacement is a significant upgrade and treats the doctor's initial formulation as trivializing. In response it is met by a repair initiation "Sorry?" from the doctor (line 5), which occasions a repeat of the replacement, "dreadful," at line 7 and an extended unpacking of the assessment in lines 9–23.

(13) Byng: Up and down/dreadful

```
DR:   We:ll you've ↑had quite e:r (.) up and down ye:ar. An
      that prob'ly doesn't help your [blood pressure. But,
PT:                                  [>I've had a< dread↑ful yea:r
      (0.8)
DR:   Sorry?
      (0.5)
PT:   Dread↑ful,
DR:   Yeah.
PT:   I lost ↓my (0.5) the man I w's gonna marry? .Hh=
      =[I lost (.) ~my~ (0.5) aunt? Who was like more than
DR:    [Mm,
PT:   my mother [to me?
DR:             [M:m.
PT:   .Hh I lost my stepdaughter?
      (0.4)
DR:   Mm_
PT:   Even the cat die:d
      (0.4)
DR:   Mm_
      (1.2)
DR:   Yeah.
      (0.7)
PT:   It wun't my cat. It was somebody else's but_
      (0.3)
DR:   Mm_
      (1.1)
DR:   .Hh ↑okay.
```

Examples 10–13 begin to look very much like corrections precisely because the next, reformulating speaker makes no effort to acknowledge the, at least, partial adequacy of the prior speaker's formulation. Moreover, by accepting the replacement (the interviewer in example 11, line 6, with "okay your passion,"; Tom in example 12, line 20, "yeah"; the doctor in example 13, line 8, "yeah."), the prior speaker acknowledges the problematic character of the initial formulation as well as the entitlement of the other to produce the subsequent version as a correction. So in these cases both participants orient to the greater rights of a subsequent speaker to describe matters in their own domain. Even in example 10, where the participants are disputing who is responsible for the damage done to A's structure, A's "well you knocked it over" accepts the subsequent description of C's action even while simultaneously suggesting that the difference between "poking" and "tapping" is irrelevant given the result.[3]

So far we have considered cases in which the description falls squarely – indeed almost exclusively – in the second speaker's epistemic domain. This can be seen by considering the replacing formulation:

(10)	She poked it	vs. **I** tapped it
(11)	**Your** anger. an' your hate.	vs. **My** passion
(12)	All of **your** accomplishment	vs. All **my** stuff
(13)	**you**'ve had quite an up and down year.	vs. **I**'ve had a dreadful year

It can be observed that, while the initial descriptions are predominantly about the recipient, the subsequent descriptions are predominantly about the speaker. The exception is that in example 10 the initial description, although about a co-present person, is addressed to a third party. In all these cases we can observe a steep epistemic gradient between the initial speaker and the subsequent speaker in so far as the initial speaker is describing something unequivocally within the second speaker's epistemic domain.[4] In example 10 it is the second speaker's action that is being described; in example 11 it is the second speaker's "disposition" or "character"; in example 12 the second speaker's belongings; and in example 13 the second speaker's experience. In the cases considered so far, a second speaker employs the technology of framing, described for cases of same-turn, self-repair (Schegloff, this volume) in order to isolate a particular bit of the prior talk and operate on it (here to replace it). It is this that allows the replacement to be heard as "correcting" the initial description. And it is worth noting that in at least some of the cases so far considered the initial description/formulation is marked by perturbations in the talk. This is especially clear in examples 12 and 13, where the speaker arrives at the initial description (of the other's circumstances) after apparently searching for just the right way to put it.

In other cases the matters being described fall within the second speaker's epistemic domain but the gradient between the two participants is not as steep. For instance, in the following case, taken from the same conversation as example 12, the participants are talking about crooked people in business and government. Where the transcript begins, Tom suggests that these crooked people are not interested in the "common man" and Rich suggests that "their int'rest is in p-uppets:_." Tom appears to disattend Rich's contribution and produces his own continuation of the talk at line 14 saying, "THEY're int'rested in big busi↓ness." After a substantial delay Rich remarks "<Big (.) Co-ops::,>" apparently intending this to be heard as an elaboration of what Tom has said in line 21. Tom then replaces Rich's "Big Co-ops" with "Big Corporations."

(14) IM030402-Coffee Chat [P.4 Puppets/Big Business]

14 Tom: .t an' they're n[ot int'rested in the com↓mon ↓man.
15 [((bang in kitchen))
16 (1.4)
17 Tom: .t ((takes cup to sip coffee)) (2.5)
18 (0.9)
19 Ric: Yeah, their int'rest is in p–uppets:_
20 (0.9)
21 Tom: .t=.t THEY're int'rested in big busi↓ness.
22 (0.3)
23 Rich: Yeah,
24 (.)
25 Tom: .TCH
26 (1.0)
27 Tom: .t °.hh=.hh°
28 Ric: <Big (.) Co-ops::,>
29 Tom: Yep? (1.2) <Big (.6) ↓corporations,> (0.5) .tck (0.4) and
30 uh°m° (0.4) money people.
31 (1.2)
32 Tom: .TCH
33 (1.4)
34 Ric: °Yea:h that['s true.°]

Now although Tom has been acknowledged as the expert on money matters, his expertise is relative – this is not his domain exclusively and Rich's attempts to contribute to the discussion obviously presuppose that he is to some degree informed about these matters.[5] So while this, given his expertise, is within his domain, the epistemic gradient between the one who produces the initial description and the one who produces the subsequent description is not as steep as in the cases we have so far considered. Notice then that Tom prefaces the replacement "Big Corporations" with an agreement "yep?" and thereby marks what he is saying as amounting to the same thing as what Rich has said.

A similar example is given as example 15, which is taken from the same conversation as example 9. Here, both David and Cece are knowledgeable about the behavior of people in Nepal (David has recently returned from a year there, Cece has returned sometime earlier after having spent eight months). After Cece remarks, "They never drink without it," David replaces "drink" with "have liquor" (Schegloff, 1988, also discusses the substitution of "they" by "ya"). Notice that just as Tom prefaced "Big Corporations" with "Yep?", so David prefaces his talk here with "yeah" thereby marking it as standing in agreement with what Cece has said.

(15) "After the movie" (FRAGMENT – From Schegloff, 1988: 6)

W: =D'people sit around eating in Nepal?
(0.2)
D: All the time that's all they d[o
C: [They never drink
without ('t) (0.2)
D: Yeah ya never have liquor without (1.0)
fried meat er

Thus in examples 14 and 15 we see my-domain replacements in which the epistemic gradient is not as steep as it is in examples 10–13. Participants orient to that relatively flatter epistemic gradient by marking the replacement as essentially equivalent to the prior description. They do this by prefacing the turn with a marker of agreement. In modulating their replacement in this way, a second, subsequent speaker orients to the epistemic rights of the prior speaker even while claiming – via the act of replacing the description – greater epistemic authority. Crucially, this results in replacements, which are not obviously "corrective" – indeed by embedding these replacements within turns that are otherwise agreeing with the prior talk the second speaker is able to block an inference that what is being done here is "correcting" the prior.

11.5 My-domain identifications

We now turn to cases in which a next speaker merely identifies a problematic formulation that describes something that is clearly in his or her epistemic domain. In reference to these cases we can ask: why would a next speaker merely identify a problematic description where the matter discussed falls within his or her own domain, and where presumably he or she would be within his or her rights to simply replace that description? A clue to this is found in the fact that our only examples come from high-stakes contexts and specifically from courtroom cross-examination. In this context witnesses often identify problematic descriptions rather than replace/correct them.[6]

We begin with an example taken from the cross-examination of a woman who claimed she was sexually assaulted by former Green Bay Packers player Mark Chmura.[7]

(16) Chmura trial

LC: Mike Cleber comes up an asks you what went on in the
bathroom.
W: He didn' ask me.
LC: He didn' ask–-tell [yo–
W: [well that's sort of a nice way to
put it I think.
LC: well what did he do. he yelled at chu=
W: =he screamed at me.
LC: screamed at you.
W: in my face.

Although the witness here does not replace/correct the description of what Mike Cleber did, neither does she simply answer the question. As such, the fact that the witness does not immediately replace/correct the description (with for instance, "he screamed at me.") at line 3 should not be explained by reference to the fact that witnesses are normatively required to "answer the lawyer's question" (see Sidnell, 2009, 2010). Notice then that an initial identification can *lead* to the provision of a replacement. In example 16 the lawyer describes Mike Cleber as asking the witness "what went on in the bathroom" in line 1. The witness first indicates that this is incorrect ("He didn' ask me."), but after the lawyer initiates repair, she suggests that "that's sort of a nice way to put it I think." thereby indicating that "ask" may be referentially adequate but nevertheless problematic in terms of its "sense" or what it conveys (or doesn't convey, i.e., aggression). The lawyer eventually offers "yelled" as replacement and the witness subsequently replaces *this* with "screamed." So a few observations on this first case are the following:

(1) An identification can lead to a significant break in the progress of the sequence.
(2) An identification can expose a word-selection or word-choice, marking it as both not the only option and as in some sense inadequate.
(3) An identification can lead to a replacement of the item identified.

Consider now examples 17 and 18, both taken from cross-examination:

(17) Sponsorship – 20401 qt 9:09

W: I think when that happened it was out of the uhm:
the sponsorship budget if I [recall correctly.
L: [You– you stuck it
in the sponsorship.
(0.2)
b[udget,
W: -> [Pardon,
L: You– you– you: deci:ded in '96 (.) to place these
(.) purchases in thee sponsorship account correct?
W: It's the only place I could place it.

(18) Chmura trial

LC: and (.) when he was on the grou::nd. with you.
and he got up, he made no noise and you made no
noise.
W: no noise.
LC: correct?
W: yes.
LC: So thet if somebody was standin' right outside
the door listenin to you two move, (0.2) you
were doing it so quietly they wouldna heard
it right?
(2.5)
W: we were doin' it so quietly we wouldn'av heard
I– I'm not sure –I'm following you [here
LC: [didju get up
fast?

Across each of these instances, the key feature of My-domain identifications appears to be that they do not allow the prior speaker's initial formulation to stand as is. Identification by the next speaker implicitly (as in example 17) or explicitly marks the original description as problematic and invites the prior speaker either to replace it or withdraw it. In studies of repair, mere initiation (as opposed to the commission of repair or correction) is understood to preserve a preference for self-correction. In cases such as 16–18, however, the identification, relative to a replacement, has the added impact of encouraging/forcing the prior speaker to *withdraw or modify* what they have said and thus to acknowledge its inadequacy. In the legal context the practice of My-domain identification therefore makes it possible to have a prior speaker (in this case the lawyer) replace what they have said and thus go on record as having ultimately said something else.

11.6 Your-domain replacements

In our original collection we had no clear cases of your-domain replacements.[8] This seemed to fit with the basic organization in which second speakers have limited rights to replace a description which falls in the first speaker's epistemic domain. However, although we did not find any cases of your-domain replacement in our own data sets, we did find some discussion of them in the literature. Specifically, Rae (2008) describes a small set of instances of your-domain replacements in psychotherapy. For instance:

(19) little/lot (From Rae, 2008)

Patient: I am surviving and I am
Therap: But it feels (.) doesn't feel right
Patient: It feels a little uncomfortable
Therap: Or a lot uncomfortable.
Patient: It feels a l(hoh)ot unc(huh)omfortable actually

Table 11.1 Situational distribution of different practices

Your-domain identifications	**My-domain identifications**
>> Conversation and other	>> Court
Your-domain replacements	**My-domain replacements**
>> Psychotherapy	>> Conversation and other

(20) do/pretend (From Rae, 2008)

Patient: tis the season to be jolly and y'know
I can play I can do jo– I can do jolly
Therap: Pretend jolly
Patient: I can pretend jolly I can just be out there

The idea that an individual has privileged access to his or her own thoughts and experiences is clearly a basic presupposition of everyday life (see Heritage, 2012). Indeed, a whole range of rights and obligations in interaction, including those discussed in this chapter, flow from this one fundamental assumption. However, in psychotherapy, the therapist is in a certain sense professionally entitled to know the mind of the other better than the other knows it herself: reversing the ordinary assumptions of everyday life. Here, in replacing the client's descriptions (rather than merely identifying them as problematic), the therapist claims greater authority to talk about the other's thoughts and experiences – a claim that, in these cases at least, is completely uncontested.

With Rae's examples from psychotherapy we can see that the available data pattern is as in Table 11.1.

11.7 Conclusion

The general pattern we have identified in this chapter may be summarized as follows: where a description concerns matters in the initial speaker's domain the second speaker merely identifies the problem; where the description concerns matters in the second speaker's domain the second speaker replaces the problematic description. This finding supports the basic claim of the chapter that the preference for self-correction is modulated by epistemic relations such that a participant is entitled to produce a replacement/correction where the matter described falls within his/her epistemic domain.

Thus, with the exception of the cases shown from psychotherapy, we have found no clear examples of your-domain replacement whereas my-domain replacements are, relatively, common. Moreover, within the collection of my-domain replacements there is evidence that participants design their replacement-turns in relation to an epistemic gradient. Where the matter discussed is *wholly* within the replacing speaker's domain, straight-out replacement in the form of a correction is common. Where, on the other hand, the replacement speaker is only relatively more expert – where, that is, we find a flatter epistemic gradient – the replacement turn often includes some kind of "pro-forma" agreement and the two descriptions may be marked as essentially equivalent.

We have also seen that identifications in both "my" and "your" domains often, though not always, employ the vehicle of other-initiated repair. Thus we find subsequent speakers identifying an initial description as "problematic" through the use of open-class repair initiation ("pardon"), question-intoned repeats ("fried meat?") as well as other, possibly context-specific, forms of repair initiation (e.g., repeat + "I don't understand"). It seems important to note that, though OIR is frequently used to effect such identification, there are other practices available. For instance, laugh token repeats are used in example 7, and in example 16 the identification is done by rejecting the term used as appropriate ("He didn't ask me").

When we initially began to look at the data we assumed that identifications would be preferred over replacements in just the way that the other-initiation of self-repair is preferred in relation to other-repair and other-correction (Schegloff, Jefferson and Sacks, 1977). Like other-initiations, identifications merely locate a problem and leave the business of fixing it to the prior speaker. Replacements in comparison involve a next speaker fixing something in a prior speaker's talk. There is, as we have noted, some evidence to suggest that identifications are "preferred" in relation to replacements on just these grounds. However, there is another important factor that organizes the "preference" relation between these two alternative alternatives. Specifically, identifications can interrupt the progress of the official business of the talk (to differing degrees depending on their positioning). This is especially clear when, as in the examples from courtroom talk, the prior description is produced as part of a question and the identification, coming next, delays the production of an answer to it. Replacements, on the other hand, can be produced simultaneously with and as part and parcel of an answer – they can thereby be accomplished without interrupting the progress of the talk (see Drew, 1992, for examples).

This chapter has focused on the sequential and turn constructional organization of descriptions. These descriptions are implicated in a wide array of different action-types including complimenting, complaining, accusing, excusing and telling troubles. The analysis presented suggests that the activity of describing is organized by reference to sequential position, turn-composition and the distribution of epistemic rights and further that that organization is independent of whatever action is being accomplished. The interactional activity of describing thus appears to be underwritten by a robust normative structure specific to it.

REFERENCES

Dersley, Ian and Anthony Wootton (2000). Complaint sequences within antagonistic argument. *Research on Language and Social Interaction* 33: 375–406.

Drew, P. (1987). Po-faced receipts of teases. *Linguistics* 25: 219–253.

(1992). Contested evidence in courtroom cross-examination: the case of a trial for rape. In P. Drew and J. Heritage, eds., *Talk at Work: Interaction in Institutional Settings*. pp. 470–520. Cambridge University Press.

Enfield, N. J. and T. Stivers (2007). *Person Reference in Interaction*. Cambridge University Press.

Frege, G. (1948 [1892]). On sense and reference. *The Philosophical Review* 57(3): 209–230.

Haakana, M. and S. Kurhila (2009). Other-correction in everyday interaction: some comparative aspects. In M. Haakana, M. Laakso, and J. Lindström, eds., *Talk in Interaction: Comparative Dimensions*, pp. 152–179. Helsinki: Suomalaisen Kirjallisuuden Seura (Studia Fennica, Linguistica).

Heritage, J. (2012). Epistemics in action: action formation and territories of knowledge. *Research on Language and Social Interaction* 45: 1–29.

Heritage, J. and G. Raymond (2012). Navigating epistemic landscapes: acquiescence, agency and resistance in responses to polar questions. In J. P. de Ruiter, ed., *Questions: Formal, Functional and Interactional Perspectives*, pp. 179–192. Cambridge University Press.

Jefferson, G. (1972). Side sequences. In D. N. Sudnow, ed., *Studies in Social Interaction*, pp. 294–338. New York: Free Press.

(1985). An exercise in the transcription and analysis of laughter. In T. Van Dijk, ed., *Handbook of Discourse Analysis*, vol. III: Discourse and Dialogue, pp. 25–34. London: Academic Press.

(1987). On exposed and embedded correction in conversation. In G. Button and J. R. E. Lee, eds., *Talk and Social Organization*, pp. 86–100. Clevedon: Multilingual Matters.

Rae, J. P. (2008). Lexical substitution as a therapeutic resource. In C. Antaki, A. Perakyla, S. Vevilainen, and I. Leuder, eds., *Conversation Analysis and Psychotherapy*. Cambridge University Press.

Sacks, H. (1972a). An initial investigation of the usability of conversational data for doing sociology. In D. N. Sudnow, ed., *Studies in Social Interaction*, pp. 31–74. New York: Free Press.

(1972b). On the analyzability of stories by children. In J. J. Gumperz and D. Hymes, eds., *Directions in Sociolinguistics: The Ethnography of Communication*, pp. 325–345. New York: Holt, Rinehart & Winston.

(1995). *Lectures on Conversation*. 2 vols. Ed. G. Jefferson, with introduction by E. A. Schegloff. Oxford: Blackwell.

Sacks, H. and Schegloff, E. A. (1979). Two preferences in the organization of reference to persons and their interaction. In G. Psathas, ed., *Everyday Language: Studies in Ethnomethodology*, pp. 15–21. New York: Irvington Publishers.

Schegloff, E. A. (1972). Notes on a conversational practice: formulating place. In D. Sudnow, ed., *Studies in Social Interaction*, pp. 75–119. New York: The Free Press.

(1988). Description in the social sciences I: talk-in-interaction. *IPRA Papers in Pragmatics* 2(1): 1–24.

(1996). Some practices for referring to persons in talk-in-interaction: a partial sketch of a systematics. In B. A. Fox, ed., *Studies in Anaphora*, pp. 437–485. Amsterdam and Philadelphia: John Benjamins.

(2007). *Sequence Organization in Interaction: A Primer in Conversation Analysis I.* Cambridge University Press.

Schegloff, E. A. Jefferson, G. and Sacks, H. (1977). The preference for self-correction in the organization of repair in conversation. *Language* 53: 361–382.

Schegloff, E. A. and Lerner, G. H. (2009). Beginning to respond: well-prefaced responses to Wh-questions. *Research on Language and Social Interaction* 42(2): 91–115.

Sidnell, J. (2009) The design and positioning of questions in inquiry testimony. In A. F. Ehrlich and S. Freed, eds., *"Why Do You Ask?": The Function of Questions in Institutional Discourse.* Oxford University Press.

(2010) *Conversation Analysis: An Introduction.* Chichester: Blackwell.

Sudnow, D. (ed.) (1972). *Studies in Social Interaction*, pp. 75–119. New York: Free Press.

NOTES

1 The contrast here may be likened to an analogous one in linguistic analysis between paradigm alternatives within a closed grammatical set (e.g. pronouns, tenses) and choices among items in a relatively more open lexical field.

2 See the detailed analysis of this example in Schegloff 1988.

3 Dersley and Wootton (2000) consider a similar case in their analysis of complaints. Indeed, these authors note that one way of responding to a complaint is for the complainee to "take issue with the version of the complained-of action that is presented within the complaint. Implicitly, they agree that some relevant action or inaction on their part has taken place, but they dispute the characterization of that action offered by the complainer. Through providing an alternative characterization, they attempt to transform the complained-of action into one that is less at fault, even innocent."

4 On the notion of an epistemic gradient, see Heritage and Raymond (2012).

5 Earlier in the conversation Rich has joked to Betty that Tom is "gonnuh get me into um↓: (.) stocks." When Tom resists, Rich remarks "Well you're the expert on that?=" and asks "You can't->you can't guide me in any uh right derection."

6 Of course, as Drew (1992) shows, witnesses also often replace descriptions that fall in their own domain.

7 From Wikipedia: Chmura was accused of having sex on April 8, 2000 at a Waukesha Catholic Memorial High School party with the then 17-year-old babysitter of his children. Chmura was tried but found not guilty of all charges.

8 With one possible exception we found no cases of your-domain replacements. The exception is from a phone call between two friends:

[TG (p.1)]

Ava: [Yeah fuh like an hour enna ha:[lf.]
Bee: [·hh] Where
Bee: didju play ba:sk[etbaw.
Ava: [(The) gy]:m.
Bee: In the gy:m? [(hh)
Ava: [Yea:h. Like grou(h)p therapy.
(.)
Ava: Yuh know [half the grou]p thet we had la:s' term wz=
Bee: [O h : : : .]·hh
Ava: -> =there– <'n we [jus' playing arou:nd.
Bee: [·hh
Bee: -> Uh–fo[oling around.
Ava: [·hhh
Ava: Eh–yeah so, some a' the guys who were bedder y'know
wen' off by themselves so it wz two girls against this
one guy en he's ta:ll.Y'know? [·hh
Bee: [Mm hm?

Ava is telling Bee about an incident concerning a group of students, some of which are known to Bee. At line 10 Ava uses the descriptor "playing around" and Bee subsequently replaces that at line 12 with "fooling around." – a replacement that Ava then tentatively accepts with "Eh-yeah" (line 14). One interpretation of this is that Bee alludes to a possible sexual hearing of "playing around" and highlights this by offering a replacement "fooling around," or it may simply have been an attempt at co-telling from knowledge of what this group is like, but it seems this is essentially passed over by Ava in a bid to continue her story.

12 *Huh? What?* – a first survey in twenty-one languages

N. J. Enfield, Mark Dingemanse, Julija Baranova, Joe Blythe, Penelope Brown, Tyko Dirksmeyer, Paul Drew, Simeon Floyd, Sonja Gipper, Rósa S. Gísladóttir, Gertie Hoymann, Kobin H. Kendrick, Stephen C. Levinson, Lilla Magyari, Elizabeth Manrique, Giovanni Rossi, Lila San Roque, and Francisco Torreira

12.1 Introduction

A comparison of conversation in twenty-one languages from around the world reveals commonalities and differences in the way that people do open-class other-initiation of repair (Schegloff, Jefferson, and Sacks, 1977; Drew, 1997). We find that speakers of all of the spoken languages in the sample make use of a primary interjection strategy (in English it is *Huh?*), where the phonetic form of the interjection is strikingly similar across the languages: a monosyllable featuring an open non-back vowel [a, æ, ə, ʌ], often nasalized, usually with rising intonation and sometimes an [h-] onset. We also find that most of the languages have another strategy for open-class other-initiation of repair, namely the use of a question word (usually "what"). Here we find significantly more variation across the languages. The phonetic form of the question word involved is completely different from language to language: e.g., English [wɑt] versus Cha'palaa [ti] versus Duna [aki]. Furthermore, the grammatical structure in which the repair-initiating question word can or must be expressed varies within and across languages. In this chapter we present data on these two strategies – primary interjections like *Huh?* and question words like *What?* – with discussion of possible reasons for the similarities and differences across the languages. We explore some implications for the notion of repair as a system, in the context of research on the typology of language use.

The text was written by N. J. Enfield and Mark Dingemanse, and benefited from commentary on drafts from all authors. All authors contributed data, transcription and analysis on specific languages (as listed in Table 12.1), and all authors contributed conceptually to the study through participation in project meetings. We thank Paul Kockelman, Jack Sidnell, and Jeff Robinson for comments on earlier drafts, and Galina Bolden for providing Russian data at an early stage of the study. This research was supported by the European Research Council projects "Human Sociality and Systems of Language Use" and "INTERACT" and the Max Planck Institute for Psycholinguistics.

The general outline of this chapter is as follows. We first discuss repair as a system across languages and then introduce the focus of the chapter: open-class other-initiation of repair. A discussion of the main findings follows, where we identify two alternative strategies in the data: an interjection strategy (*Huh?*) and a question word strategy (*What?*). Formal features and possible motivations are discussed for the interjection strategy and the question word strategy in order. A final section discusses bodily behavior including posture, eyebrow movements and eye gaze, both in spoken languages and in a sign language.

12.2 Repair across languages

It is hard to imagine how people in a language-using social group could get by without a system for online repair of problems in speaking, hearing, and understanding. "If the organization of talk in interaction supplies the basic infrastructure through which the institutions and social organization of quotidian life are implemented, it had better be pretty reliable, and have ways of getting righted if beset by trouble." (Schegloff, 2006: 77; cf. Schegloff, 1992). Supposing that we do find a system of repair in all languages, many questions arise. In what sense can these be called systems? Are they conventionally linguistic in nature? Do they have emergent properties? Are there differences across human groups? If so, what sorts of factors can account for the differences – cognitive, cultural, communicative? How to determine whether repair is found in all cultural settings, and if it is found in the same form?

One way to approach these questions, following the tradition of systematic comparison of grammatical structure known as linguistic typology, is to build a case from systematic comparison of structures of talk in interaction across a maximally diverse sample. A problem is that, for the kind of data needed, there are no available secondary sources comparable to reference grammars of spoken languages. Grammarians do not describe structures of repair, partly because there is no tradition of such description in linguistics, and partly because linguists have tended not to work with the one kind of data in which these structures can be found: i.e., spontaneous talk in conversational interaction.[1] The only option is to collect primary data and start afresh. Here we present first findings from a comparative project based on video-recorded everyday conversation in twenty-one languages from around the world.[2] The broad aim is to make a contribution – in empirical, methodological, and theoretical terms – to the typology of systems of language use for human interaction.

12.2.1 Defining other-initiated repair

Here we focus on a type of other-initiation of repair,[3] defined as follows. A hearer of a turn at talk has the opportunity to initiate repair of what the prior speaker has just said, through a turn that, firstly, draws attention to a problem of speaking, hearing or understanding in the prior turn, and secondly, normatively requires the speaker of that problem-turn to fix the problem. This may be done for example by saying the turn again (for instance if it seemed that there had been a problem of hearing), or by rephrasing it (for instance if it seemed that there had been a problem not of hearing but of understanding). In examples 1a and 1b, the target line, highlighted by an arrow, points to a problem (in these cases, of person reference) in the other speaker's prior turn. The problem is addressed by the original speaker in the turn that follows the highlighted turn.

(1a) NBII:1:R:6 (English)

	01	Lot:	U[h:.
Trouble source	02	Emm:	[But PERcy goes with (.) Nixon I'd
	03		sure like tha:t.
Repair initiation	04	Lot: ->	Who:?
Repair	05	Emm:	Percy.
	06		(0.2)
	07	Emm:	That young fella thet uh (.) .hh his
	08		daughter wz m:urdered?
	09		(0.5)
	10	Lot:	.hhh [OH::: YE::AH:. YE:A[H. y–]
	11	Emm:	[They– [They:] said
	12		sup'n abou:t hi:s

(1b) Field XI:1:1:1:1 (English)

Trouble source	01	Les:	Ma:y is: ill too:. She's had eIther a
	02		heart attack or a, slight stro:ke,
Repair initiation	03	Mum: ->	Ma:ry?
	04		(.)
Repair	05	Les:	Ma:y.

We can schematize this kind of sequence as shown in Figure 12.1.

The critical turn in this three-part structure is "T0," the turn in which it first becomes publicly apparent that there is a problem. Speaker B's turn at T0 (e.g., "Huh?," "What?," "Who?") points back to a problem in Speaker A's prior turn (T−1), and points forward to a next turn in which Speaker A can repair the problem (T+1).

12.2.2 Questions

We are interested in two interlocking questions for research on other-initiated repair, the first being concerned with the relation between T0 and T−1, and the second being concerned with the relation between T−1 and T+1.

First: what are the ways in which a person can, at T0, initiate repair by the other speaker of the problem-turn at T−1? The defining turn at T0 can be

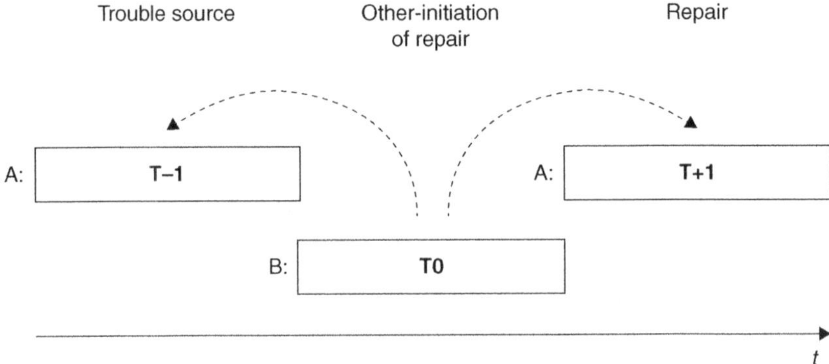

Figure 12.1: The anatomy of other-initiation of repair. Turn 0 points back to a problem in Turn −1 and points forward to a next turn Turn +1, where the problem can be repaired.

regarded as a structural slot in which a set of non-equivalent strategies can appear. These alternative strategies thus form a system paradigm, from a linguistic point of view; that is, something essentially akin to a paradigm of inflectional morphemes or words of a common form class. Examples 1a and 1b show different options for repair-initiation at T0 on a person-referring form in the prior turn: either by using a question word ("Who?" in (1a)), or by repeating one's understanding of what was said, for confirmation ("Mary?" in (1b)). One goal of research here is to describe the formal and functional resources for other-initiation of repair at T0 across languages and cultural settings; another is to look for constraints on that variation.

Second: what are the ways in which a speaker of a problem-turn at T−1 fixes the putative problem at T+1? One hypothesis is that the way in which speakers will redo T−1 (e.g., exact repeat versus rewording) is a function of the choice of repair initiator used at T0. Sidnell (2007), working on the Creole language of Bequia, pursues this idea with a focus on person reference, analyzing a set of alternatives for initiating repair (at T0) on a person reference (made in T−1). He argues that for three main types of trouble that can occur in person reference – problem of hearing, non-uniqueness of a name, and not knowing the person referred to – there are three distinct formats for repair-initiation at T0: "who," "who [NAME]," and "who is named so" (Sidnell, 2007: 307). The issue of how the problem is fixed goes beyond the scope of this chapter (see Section 2.4 below).

Note that there is a third critical question, connected to these two, which we do not systematically address in this chapter: What are the possible kinds of problem that can occur at T−1? The space of possibilities is usually defined as "problems of speaking, hearing and understanding" (Schegloff, Jefferson, and Sacks, 1977; Sidnell, 2010). Another way is to appeal to the logic of

Austin's nested layering of action in language use (Austin, 1962: 94–103); (Clark, 1996: 146). A speech act can be described on different levels simultaneously, and at each of these levels something can go wrong: a person produces noises or visual behavior for another to perceive (where problems will be of articulating and hearing); a person produces linguistic items for another to identify (where problems will be of word selection and recognition); a person has a communicative intention for another to infer (where problems will concern implicature and other "amplicative" interpretation); a person instigates an action for another to take up (where problems will concern appropriateness of response). While it is useful in principle to have this kind of breakdown of the nested layering of action components, when we look at data we find that it is often difficult or impossible to tell in a given instance what the problem actually was (or indeed whether there really was a problem of the kind being indicated), and it is not even in all cases possible to say unequivocally what the putative problem was *treated* as.

In examples 1a and 1b, the relevant practice of other-initiation of repair narrows in on just *part* of the prior turn. The speakers of the repair-initiating turns (T0, highlighted) are explicit about which part of the prior turn was the trouble source. In these cases, the problem had to do with a person-referring expression (though we note that in example 1 there are two person-referring expressions in T−1; *Percy* and *Nixon*). However, it is not necessarily clear to us precisely *what* the (claimed) problem was; e.g., whether it was a problem of hearing versus a problem of understanding or recognition. Example 1a illustrates that it is also not always clear to the participants, either. The speaker of the original trouble source repairs the utterance first by simply repeating the name she had used before ("Percy"), thus treating it as a hearing problem, only to find that this was insufficient; after a pause in which no uptake comes after the first attempt at repair, she then produces a recognitional reference (cf. Stivers, 2007) to the same person – "That young fella that uh . . . his daughter was murdered?" – where the new form also features "try-marking" (i.e., rising intonation as if checking for confirmation of recognition; Sacks and Schegloff, 1979: 18). This secures an explicit claim of recognition in the next turn ("Oh yeah") by the speaker who had initiated repair on the initial use of the referent's name.

12.2.3 This chapter's focus: open-class other-initiation of repair

Beyond these kinds of cases, in which a *part* of the trouble-source turn is focused on, there are practices for "open-class" other-initiation of repair (Drew, 1997).[4] In the open-class type of other-initiation of repair, the form used at T0 does not focus on any sub-part of the prior turn as being the source of trouble. Consider some examples (with the T0 turns highlighted with an arrow):

(02) NB IV:5:2 (English)

01 Gla: =An' now I've got (.) tuh wash my hair en get the
02 ↑goop out 'v it'n everything? .hh 'n ah have the
03 ↑paypuh here I thought chu might li:ke tih ↓have
04 it.↓.hhhh[h
05 Emm: [Th[a:nk yo]u.
06 Gla: [En then] you: could retuhrn it ub (.)
07 ↑Oh along about noo:n,
08 (0.2)
09 Emm: Yer goin up'n ge[tcher hair]: fixed t]ihda]↓: y .]
10 Gla: [befo : re]h e gets] ho]↓:me.]
11 (0.4)
12 Gla: -> What deah[r?
13 Emm: [Yer goin up tihday'n gitcher hai:r
14 ↓fi[xed.]
15 Gla: [Oh: n]:o. I'm gontuh wash it mah:self ↓heeuh.
16 Emm: ↑Oh:::.
17 Gla: I'm just goi[na sha]mpoo it,=
18 Emm: [↓Oh:.]
19 Gla: =en then I have some othuh things t'do arou:nd so I
20 won't be able to u– .hhh look et the paper=
21 (E): =[(M)
22 Gla: =['n ah know you li:ke tuh have it,=
23 =.hh[hh
24 Emm: [↑Well [th:a]:nk↑ you]=
25 Gla: [S o] u– e h]=
26 Emm: =dear ah'll be ↑o:↓v*er.
27 Gla: Al↓r*ight dear a:nd uh ↑front er b↓ack.h
28 (1.0)
29 Emm: -> Wu:t?
30 (.)
31 Emm: .h[huh]
32 Gla: [I s][ay f:–] [*u–
33 Emm: [OH::::]: AH [GUESS th'=
34 = FRO:nt. b[e be']er?]
35 Gla: [Alsah–].hh]h
36 I look like a wi:ld Indian [cuz] I'm] .hh
37 Emm: [Ye] a h]

(03) Holt 1:1:1 (English)

01 Les: m–[Jem's
02 Mum: [Are the family o:ff?
03 (0.5)
04 Les: -> SORRY?
05 Mum: 'Av your family gone o:ff?
06 (.)
07 Les: Ye:s,
08 Mum: Oh ↓goo:d,

(04) NB III.2.R*Rev (English)

01 (38.3)
02 Jim: Hello there.
03 (0.6)
04 Fra: Hello:.
05 Jim: Hello: hello.
06 (0.4)
07 Fra: W'ts goin o:n
08 Jim: Not mu:ch. Wuddi[yih know.
09 Fra: [Mh–
10 Fra: -> Huh?
11 Jim: Whuddiyih kno:w.
12 (0.3)

Examples (2–4) illustrate what we mean by *open-class* other-initiation of repair: namely, a practice for drawing attention to a problem in the other's prior turn, without restricting the scope of focus to any component of that turn as being the source of trouble, thereby initiating repair by the other.

12.2.4 Different strategies

As the English examples, (2–4) show, different kinds of linguistic formats can function as open-class other-initiators of repair. One basic kind of strategy is to use an interjection such as *Huh?*, as shown in example 4. Other possible forms of the interjection for this function in English include *hm?* and *mm?*

Interjections in language are of two types: primary versus secondary (see Bloomfield, 1933: 176). Defined broadly, an interjection is a word unit or equivalent unit that can stand as a complete utterance in itself (e.g., *Huh?*, *Yes*, *Wow!*, *No*, *Yuck*; see further discussion, below). A primary interjection is a form that has *only* this profile. In this way, *Huh?* can be distinguished from *What?*. While *What?* has morphosyntactic combinatoric potential in the language more broadly, *Huh?* does not. So, in identifying *Huh?* as the "interjection" strategy, we will always mean it in the sense of "primary interjection" as just defined.

The second basic strategy for open-class other-initiation of repair is to use a question-word form like *What?*, illustrated in example 2. This question-word form can also be used for other-initiation of repair in more syntactically elaborate structures such as *What's that?* and *What did you say?* By definition, these kinds of structures are distinct from the primary interjection type.

Beyond these two basic strategies – primary interjection and question-word – there are also further ways of doing open-class other-initiation of repair, including *Pardon (me)?*, *Excuse me?*, and *Sorry?* (see example 3). One way to think about the distinctions among these forms is in terms of a contrast of perceived formality or politeness (cf. *Huh?* versus *I beg your pardon?*). Another is that the options may differ in terms of specific action nuances. For example, it has been suggested that *Sorry?* portrays the problem as being the fault of the repair-initiator, not of the speaker of the trouble-source turn (Robinson, 2006).

The strategies in English for carrying the action of open-class other-initiation of repair in this position (immediately following another speaker's turn containing a trouble source) are *non-identical* alternatives. The existence of sets of alternatives that can each appear in a single slot is a hallmark of linguistic and other communicative systems. This is why we can speak of systems of language use in the domain of social interaction. Because *What?* and *Huh?* are alternatives for the same slot, it may be that there is a functional distinction between them. One possibility might be that the two formats indicate different types of problems in T−1. For instance, one form might be used when you didn't hear something and the other for when you didn't understand something (though this particular possibility appears not to be supported by data from English; Drew, 1997). Or maybe one form is just more polite than the other. Further research will provide answers to these questions (Drew, 1997: 73); (Robinson, 2006: 142).[5]

If the various alternatives – *Huh?*, *What?*, etc. – aren't merely interchangeable, then it is possible that one of them is *unmarked* relative to the other, in the sense of being a default choice for open-class other-initiation of repair. This would mean that among the possible forms for initiating repair, certain forms would be used for specific purposes (e.g., *Sorry?* for when you want to do other-initiation of repair *and* claim responsibility for the problem), and if none of those extra, specific purposes applied, then a default form would be used. This default would be semantically unmarked with reference to the alternatives (i.e., it would have fewer semantic specifications), but it would not necessarily be less frequent. If *Huh?* were pragmatically unmarked relative to *What?*, then *Huh?* would be the default way of doing other-initiation of repair. The choice of *What?* would then be less expected, thus signaling, by contrast within a system of alternatives, that something special were meant by its selection. Its core semantic meaning would contribute to understanding *just what* is specially meant by it. This kind of default/marked relation is seen in a whole range of linguistic pragmatic systems, such as systems for person reference (e.g., in English, "first name only" is unmarked relative to "description'; e.g., *Where's John?* versus *Where's His Majesty?*; Enfield and Stivers, 2007) or systems for responding to polar questions (e.g., the English system for answering with "type-conforming" interjections like *yes* versus marked alternatives such as a partial repeat of the question; e.g., A: *Is he going?* B: *He's going*; see Raymond, 2003).

To figure out the structure and dynamics of any one language's system for other-initiation of repair would be a major research project in itself, and we do not attempt that here. The aim of this first foray into the comparison of systems for open-class other-initiation of repair is, given that all languages from a broad sample appear to show the same sequential pattern of other-initiation of repair (Figure 12.1, above), to ask whether there is evidence of a basic system-level split between a primary interjection strategy and a question word strategy in the T0 slot. We demonstrate below that a basic *Huh?/What?* distinction will be found in most if not all languages, though it remains an open question as to what the functional distinction is (e.g., whether the use of "Huh?" versus "What?" can be found to correlate with different repair operations on T−1 that are performed at T+1).

12.3 Findings

Each researcher consulted a corpus of recorded interaction, and collected instances of open-class other-initiation of repair, to find out whether the two general types of strategy – primary interjection versus question word – were used.[6]

Since we are working with a large number of languages – twenty-one languages from six continents; see Table 12.1 – our scope is necessarily restricted. We ask: do all languages show a formal contrast between a primary interjection strategy and a question word strategy for other-initiation of repair? The answer to this question is "almost all languages in our broad sample." Two of the languages examined (Yélî Dnye and Tzeltal) did not yield clear evidence from the available corpora that a question word strategy is used for open-class other-initiation of repair.

A first finding – perhaps trivial but nevertheless deserving of explicit mention here – is that (open-class) other-initiation of repair is observed in all of the languages in our sample, with the sequential organization shown in

Table 12.1: Approximate phonetic forms used for open-class other-initiation of repair in "T0" in twenty-one languages.

Language	Affiliation	Location	Research by	Interjection[7]	Question word
ǂĀkhoe Hai‖om	Khoisan	Namibia	Hoymann	hɛ	mati
Cha'palaa	Barbacoan	Ecuador	Floyd	a:	ti
Chintang	Kiranti	Nepal	Dirksmeyer	hã	tʰɛm
Duna	Duna-Bogaia	PNG	San Roque	ɛ̃:/hm	aki
Dutch	Germanic	Netherlands	Dingemanse	hɜ	wat
English	Germanic	UK	Drew	hã:/hm	wɑt
French	Romance	France	Torreira	ɛ̃	kʰwa
Hungarian	Uralic	Hungary	Magyari	hm (ha)	mi
Icelandic	Germanic	Iceland	Gísladóttir	ha:	kʰva:θ
Italian	Romance	Italy	Rossi	ɛ:	kʰɔza
Kri	Vietic	Laos	Enfield	ha:	tuˈʔɪ̤:
Lao	Tai	Laos	Enfield	hã:	iˈɲaŋ
Mandarin Chn.	Sinitic	Taiwan	Kendrick	hã:	ʂəmə
Murrinh-Patha	Southern Daly	Australia	Blythe	a:	ṯaŋgu
Russian	Slavic	Russia	Baranova	ha:	ʃtɔ
Siwu	Kwa	Ghana	Dingemanse	hã	be:
Spanish	Romance	Spain	Torreira	e	ke
Tzeltal	Mayan	Mexico	Brown	hai	(binti)
Yélî Dnye	isolate	PNG	Levinson	ɛ̃	(lukwe)
Yurakaré	isolate	Bolivia	Gipper	æ/a	tæpʃæ
LSA[8]	Deaf sign language	Argentina	Manrique	NA	NA

Figure 12.1. In each language, we observe sequences in which people use other-initiation of repair to draw attention to problems, thus eliciting repair of an earlier trouble-source turn. Our main interest here is to examine the kinds of resources used across the languages in T0 position. The results are presented in Table 12.1.

12.3.1 Primary interjection strategy

The primary interjection strategy shows remarkable cross-linguistic similarity in phonetic form (see Table 12.1). It is always a monosyllable, typically involving an open front vowel or similar (e.g., [a, æ, ə, ʌ]), sometimes with a voiceless *h-* onset (English *huh?* [hã:] being a prime example), sometimes with nasalization, and typically done with rising, "questioning" pitch. In addition, it is always a primary interjection, in the sense of Bloomfield (Bloomfield, 1933; Goffman, 1978; Ameka, 1992; Kockelman, 2003). Goffman classified interjections as "non-word vocalizations" (1978: 809), stating that "non-words can't quite be called part of a language" (1978: 810).[9] Others have likewise suggested that interjections are "nonverbal" (Burling, 1993: 29) and "nonlexical" (Ward, 2006: 129). Contrary to this view, we do not want to call these expressions non-words. They are conventionalized signs that function as items within a linguistic system. They are subject to well-formedness constraints and they need to be learned. Matisoff (1994: 117, 127n8) relates how long it took him to learn that Lahu *hai*^{51} [hãî] is functionally equivalent to American English *huh* [hã:], because the Lahu form is intonationally different (cf. our discussion of Icelandic and Cha'palaa, below).

Now we present some examples to illustrate the interjection in situ. In an example from Tzeltal (a Mayan language of Mexico), the use of *jai* [hai] as an other-initiator of repair in line 2 elicits a near-exact repeat of the trouble-source turn:

(05) Tzeltal (EX1 T012017 BOT50, 12:14:4)

01 A: ya x'obol ba a'pas tatik?
You will do it please sir?
((perform a curing ceremony for patient))
02 B: -> jai? [hai]
-> *Huh?*
03 A: ya bal x'obol ba a'pas tatik?
Will you do it please sir?
04 B: yakuk
Okay.

In an example from Siwu (a Kwa language of Ghana), Speaker C wonders aloud why a batch of gunpowder is being made, suggesting (by means of a polar question in line 1) that it may be for a funeral. D asks where this supposed funeral is to take place (line 2) – this is followed by over a second of silence before C produces the open-class repair-initiator *hã* (in line 4). This elicits an exact repeat of the trouble-source turn (line 6).

(06) Siwu (GUNPOWDER_1452175)

01 C: ìɖe kàku kere tá–màbara kpòkpòkpò–ò?
S.I–be funeral just PROG–3PL–do IDPH.pounding–Q
isn't it for a funeral that the kpòkpòkpò [pounding] is being done?
02 D: Ilɛ̀ isɛ–ɛ?
place S.I–sit–Q
where is it?
03 (1.3)

04 C: –> hã? [hãː]
repair
huh?
05 (0.3)
06 D: Ilɛ̃ isɛ–ɛ?
place S.I–sit–Q
where is it?
07 (3.0)
08 C: i Mempeasem ngbe!
loc PSN here
in Mempeasem here!

In an example from Lao (a Tai language of Laos, Thailand, and Cambodia), three women are talking while they prepare to do a recording for the researcher. R wonders (in line 1) how long the recording will need to be. Either because her way of asking this is vague (not specifying that it is "time" she is asking about), or perhaps because it is a topical discontinuity (Drew, 1997), it results in other-initiation of repair by L (line 3), which in turn results in R's more specific rewording in line 5 of the trouble-source (line 1).

(07) Lao (LNEPVDP15AUG0503_000304)

01 R: qaw3 thòò1–daj3 naø
want extent–indef tpc
How much is required?
02 (0.6)
03 L: –> haa2? [hãː]
Huh?
04 (0.2)
05 R: cak2 naathii2
how.many minute
How many minutes?
06 (2.0)
07 R: kheng1 sua1–moong2 vaa3
half hour qplr.infer
Half an hour?
08 L: han5-dêê4 san4 laaw2 vaa1 kheng1 sua1–moong2
that's-right thus 3sg say half hour
That's right, he said half an hour...
09 laaw2 vaa1
3sg say
... he said.

In an example from Murrinh-Patha (a Southern Daly language of Australia), two elderly women are reminiscing. Line 2 is vaguely expressed by Mary, with ellipsis of the thing being spoken about ("trees"); Lily's interjection *aa* in line 5 elicits specification of this ellipsed material by Mary in line 6, which in turn elicits Lily's demonstration of understanding at line 7.

(08) Murrinh-Patha (Little Trees, 20091121JBVID03_1043611)

01 (0.2)
02 Mary: manandji dangathangadhawa kununginggi
ma– nandji dangatha –ngadha –wa kununginggi
not– residue still/yet –still/yet –Emph little
[They were] not [big] then, still little...
03 dangatha na.↓
dangatha na
still/yet Tag
... weren't they?'
04 (.)
05 Lily: -> aa¿ [a:]
Huh?
06 Mary: nandji thay kanyi mambinyerl
nandji thay kanyi mam –winyerl
residue tree prox 3sS.8 say/do.nFut –block the way
These trees all around
07 Lily: Yu kanyika manandji dangathanga°dha°.
yu kanyi –ka ma– nandji dangatha–ngadha
yes prox –Top not– residue yet –yet
Yeah, these [big trees were]n't here then.

In an example from Yurakaré (a language isolate of Bolivia), M and A are talking about a laptop computer that is being used in field work. M asks A in line 1 whether it does not have enough power at the moment. In line 3, A initiates repair with the interjection *ë*, after which M repeats her utterance in line 4.

(9) Yurakaré (270807_conv)

01 M: tishi nij da lacha?
tishilë nij da lacha
now NEG give.SP too
It doesn't have enough energy now either?
02 (.)
03 A: -> ë?=æ
INTJ
Huh?
04 M: =nij da layj tishilë
nij da lacha tishilë
NEG give.SP too now
It doesn't have enough energy right now either?

05 (0.7)
06 A: nijta
NEG
It doesn't.

In an example from Dutch (a Germanic language spoken in the Netherlands), B initiates repair with the interjection *hɜ*? (line 3). This elicits a near-identical repeat of the trouble source turn in line 4, leaving off only "dispensable" material that tied it to the larger sequence (Schegloff, 2004).

(10) Dutch (Femmie-Richard_566791)

01 A: ja hier [voor het spoor nog hè, hier-?
yes here before the tracks still TAG here
yeah here before the tracks actually right? Here–
02 B: [oh ja.]
oh yes
oh yes. ((shifts gaza to A))

03 -> he? [hɜ]
INTJ.OIR
huh?
04 A: hier voor het spoor nog.
here before the tracks still
here before the tracks.

And finally, in this case from Yélî Dnye (a language isolate spoken on Rossel Island in Papua New Guinea), two men are making arrangements concerning various debts. The interjection in line 2 elicits an exact repeat (in line 3) of the problem turn (line 1).

(11) Yélî Dnye (R03_v19_s2 13:56)

01 I: n:uu ye ngmepe?
Who 3Pl.DAT repay
Who is repaying them?
02 K: -> :êê [ɛ̃]
Huh?
03 I: n:uu ye ngmepe
Who 3Pl.DAT repay
Who is repaying them?
04 K: kî pini dy:eemi knî
That man.Spec with.brother.inlaw dual
That man with brothers in law

We also observed a non-open-mouth variant of the primary interjection in a number of the languages. In an example from Duna (a Trans New Guinea language spoken in Papua New Guinea), four women (Julinda, Keti, Weselin, and Weli) and two boys (Kelo and Kelson) are sitting preparing food. Julinda is relating who attended a social event at her house earlier in the week (lines 2–3). Apparently prompted by Kelo's interjection at line 5, she partially repeats her problem-turn as line 6.

(12) Duna (2010-08-07 DV17.2)

01			(0.5)
02	Jul:		Mindipi–ne apoko#o::#> Wili–ne kheno
			Mindipi–PR whatsit Wili-PR 3d
			Mindipi and what's-his-name, and Wili...
03			hutia–na<
			come.PFV.VIS.P-SPEC
			... *came* (*I saw*).
04			(0.6)
05	Klo:	–>	hmm?
			hmm?
06	Jul:		(Mindipi Wi[li-ne ((inaud.)))?]
			Mindipe Wili-PR
			Mindipi and Wili ((*inaudible*))
07	Wel:		sondopa-ne-[ngi, sondopa-ne-(ngi)]
			four–ORD–TIME four–ORD–TIME
			On Thursday, on Thursday.
08	Kls:		[Asde yupela (wa]ts) ( ) *a*?
			(Tok Pisin) yesterday 2p (?watch) ? TAG
			Did you guys (watch a movie) yesterday?
09	Klo:		((*looks away from Jul, possibly in direction of M/W's house*))
10			((*returns gaze to Julinda*))
11			(1.1)
12	Jul:		Mindipi Wili–ne kheno ko–na.
			Mindipi Wili-PR 3d be/stand/make.PFV–SPEC
			I said Mindipi and Wili!
13	Klo:		((*eyebrow flash to Julinda*))
14	Jul:		((*?nods*))
15	Wel:		sondopa-ne-ngi ra–ngi=pe.
			four–ORD–TIME SHRD–TIME=Q
			On Thursday, was it then?
16	Jul:		((*turns head away from Kelo, to her front*))
17			(1.5)

In an example from Hungarian, two university students are having a conversation by means of a telephone-like setup with headphones when one of them (Beáta) hears a knock through her headphones. She reacts with surprise (in line 8), wondering aloud what it was. Andrea initiates repair in line 10.

(13) Hungarian (ANDREA–BEÁTA 364.63S)

01 And: tehát érdekes volt legalább valakinek
thus interesting was "at least" someone–Dat
thus it was interesting at least someone ...
02 tetszett=
like-Past
... liked it=
03 Beá: =ja igen=
yeah yes
yeah yes
04 And: =[((laugh))] .h ja
yeah
((laugh)) .h yeah
05 Beá: [((laugh))]
06 ((knocks))
07 (0.46)
08 Beá: jaj mi ez
oh what this
oh what is this
09 (1.3)
10 And: –> hmm?=
PART
huh?=
11 Beá: =ja, csak hallottam valami kopogást
yeah, just hear–Past1s something knock–Acc
oh, I just heard some knocks

12.3.2 Possible motivations for form of interjection

Why are the interjection forms listed in Table 12.1 so close to each other in form despite the unrelatedness of these languages?[10] Why do we not see an interjection for open-class other-initiation of repair that features high vowels like [i] or [u]? Or with segmental onsets like [b], [t] or [j]? We can only presume that there is some kind of indexical-iconic motivation that makes the sound [ha: + RISING PITCH] appropriate for this function. While human language is unique in many ways, it is not exempt from the forces of ritualization that can shape form-function relations in any form of animal communication.

Darwin (1872) proposed three principles by which expressive behavior in animals can come to have meaning: (1) a principle of function (behavior associated with some function comes to stand for that function); (2) a principle of antithesis (behavior that maximally contrasts in form with a "functional" signal comes to stand for the opposite function); (3) a principle of direct response (behavior that is a direct response of the nervous system to some kind of input) (Darwin, 1872: 166).[11] While Darwin was mostly referring to visible behaviors of the body such as posture and facial expression, his principles are more broadly applicable. We now discuss some ways in which Darwin's principles could go some way to explaining what we find in the case of the other-repair-initiating interjections.

12.3.2.1 Motivation for form of the interjection by a principle of function? In illustrating his first principle of ritualization of expression, Darwin hypothesized, for example, that feelings of disgust are linked with "serviceable" (i.e., functional) gestures of revulsion, such as blowing air out of the mouth or nostrils, with the tongue protruding. He noted that the wide-open mouth and guttural sounds commonly found in interjections of disgust fit these gestures (Darwin, 1872; Wierzbicka, 1991: 313–316). Could interjections with conversational functions such as the ones considered here be approached using a similar logic? One argument might be that the form of *huh?* [ha:] is connected to a common bodily behavior we observe accompanying other-initiated repair in our sample: an accelerated leaning forward of the torso toward the speaker of the trouble-source turn, as illustrated in Figure 12.2.

One result of this behavior of bringing oneself physically closer to someone is to be better able to hear and see what the person is saying. If this visual signal were to be accompanied by a vocal signal, perhaps a least-effort form would be [hã], as initiation of articulatory airflow is assisted by the leaning forward (which compresses the lungs) and phonation is simply frication at the narrowest place in the vocal tract followed by voicing, all articulators are in neutral position. Nasalization of the interjection, also found in many of the languages, may be connected to the fact that, for reasons of articulatory ease, syllables with initial *h-* are commonly nasalized (Matisoff, 1975; Blevins and Garrett, 1992). While this hypothesis for a natural motivation for the form of *huh?* is not inconceivable, it is hard to imagine how it could be tested.

We can also apply Darwin's principle of function in motivating the common (though not universal) rising of pitch in these repair-initiating interjections. Gussenhoven (2004) describes the "frequency code" (Ohala 1983; 1984), a semiotic principle based on the size of the articulatory apparatus, "and by extension, on the size of the creature that possesses it" (Gussenhoven, 2004: 94). This principle is "widely used for the expression of affective meanings," where low pitch is associated with a physically larger signer and therefore with "masculinity, dominance/assertiveness, confidence, and protectiveness"; correspondingly, high pitch is associated with "femininity, submissiveness/friendliness, insecurity, and vulnerability." The connection between high pitch and uncertainty is widely regarded as a motivating factor for the association of rising pitch with "questioning."

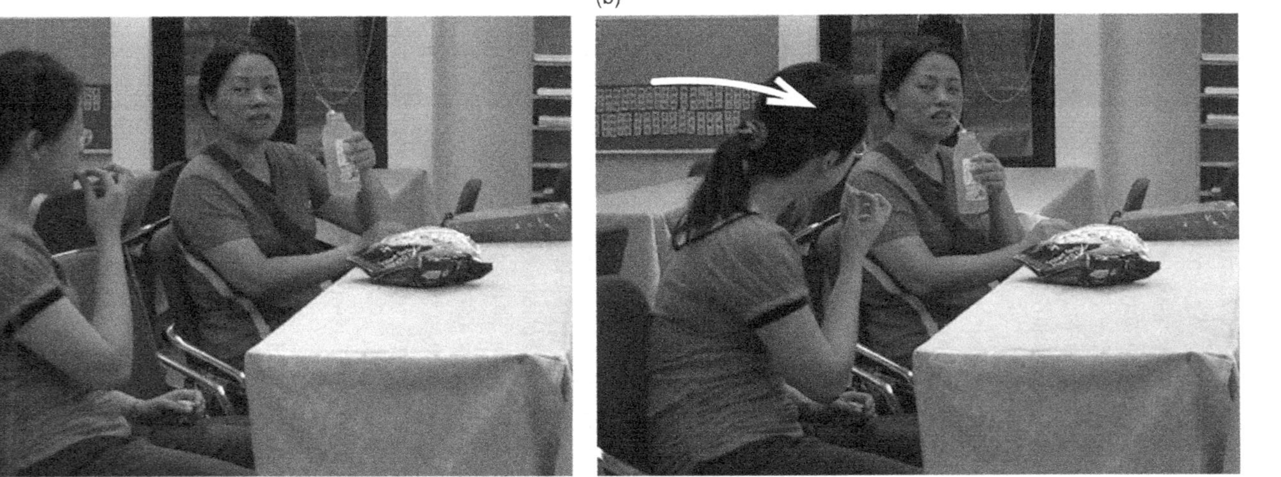

Figure 12.2: Mandarin speakers (Taiwan): the speaker on the right utters a problem-source turn at T−1 (left frame); then the speaker on the left initiates repair with *hm?* as she moves her body sharply forward, also tilting her head toward the speaker of T−1 (right frame) (TPE 15).

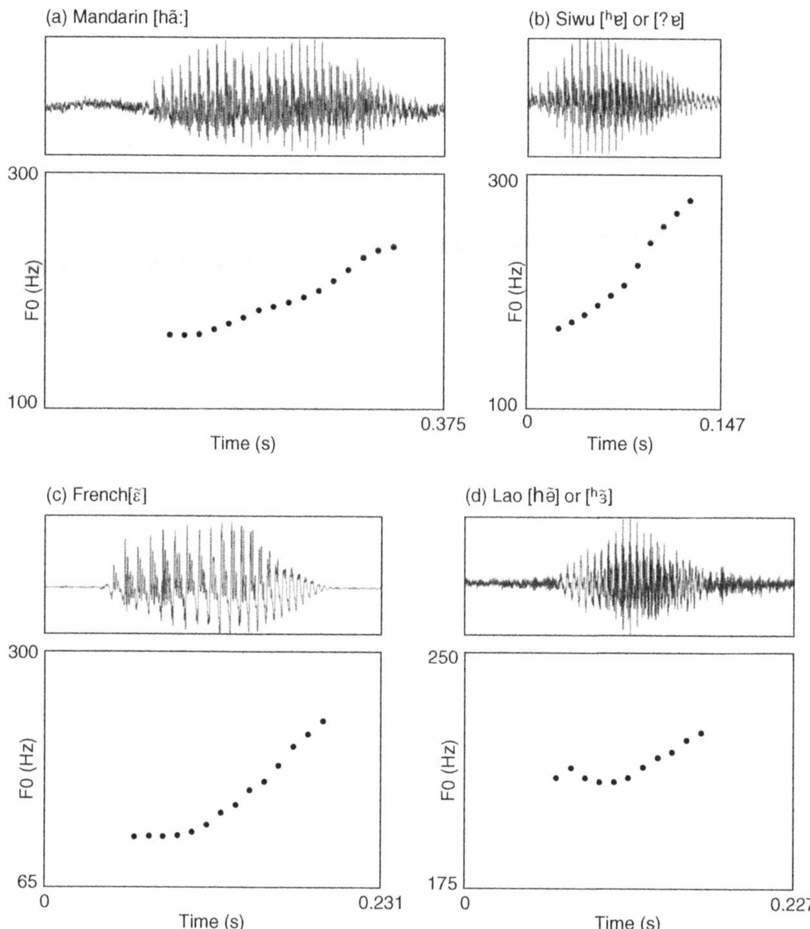

Figure 12.3: Pitch contours for typical tokens of the interjection strategy for other-initiation of repair in four languages: Mandarin, Siwu, French, and Lao.

Accordingly, the *huh*-interjection is generally rising in pitch in the languages in our sample, as illustrated by the examples given in Figure 12.3.

Two languages in our sample are exceptions to the tendency for *huh?* to have rising pitch: Icelandic and Cha'palaa. Let us take the Icelandic case as an example. In Icelandic, the open-class other-initiator of repair *ha* is pronounced with falling tone. A typical example is the OIR sequence in (14).

(14) Icelandic (ÍS-TAL: 04 ... 07 (11:56))

01	A:		( ) ræður þá hver því bara hvað hann gerir decides then each it just what he does *( ) then just each decides what to do ...*
02			við sinn hluta (0.5) with his share *... with his share*
03	H:	->	ha=[ha:] ((falling intonation; see Figure 12.4)) *huh*
04	A:		=ég segi það ræður þá bara hver því I say there. EXPL decides then just each it *I say then each just decides*
05			[hvað hann gerir við ( ) what he does with *what to do with ( )*
06	H:		[Já akkúrat yes precisely *yes precisely*

A falling intonation on the interjection for other-initiation of repair may sound counter-intuitive to many non-native ears, but it is consistent with the internal organization of the Icelandic system of pitch in questioning. Although there is considerable variation in question intonation in Icelandic, the preferred nuclear question contour in WH-questions and yes/no-questions is a falling bitonal pitch accent followed by a low boundary tone, H*L L% (Dehé, 2009). The low boundary tone is typically used at the end of utterances (both declaratives and questions) to mark finality (Árnason, 1998; Dehé, 2009).[12] It is therefore not surprising that one can request information in Icelandic using the interjection *ha* with falling intonation.

In all of the Icelandic cases we examined, the pitch of *ha* was falling in this way. We observed the same in the data from Cha'palaa, where the pitch of *ha* is also falling (though we have less certainty about the conventional use of pitch in the questioning system more generally). Figure 12.4 shows pitch contours for typical tokens of the interjections in Icelandic and Cha'palaa. Aside from these two languages in our sample, we have found one similar case reported in the literature: in Lahu, a Tibeto-Burman language of mainland Southeast Asia, the *Huh?* word has falling pitch (Matisoff 1994). So, while we see in our sample a common natural motivation for the rising pitch contour, we also find exceptions, illustrating how conventionalization and interaction with other subsystems – such as question prosody – can attenuate the forces of iconic-indexical motivation in a linguistic system. Further work will establish the nature of the connections between prosodic conventions and the other-initiation of repair.

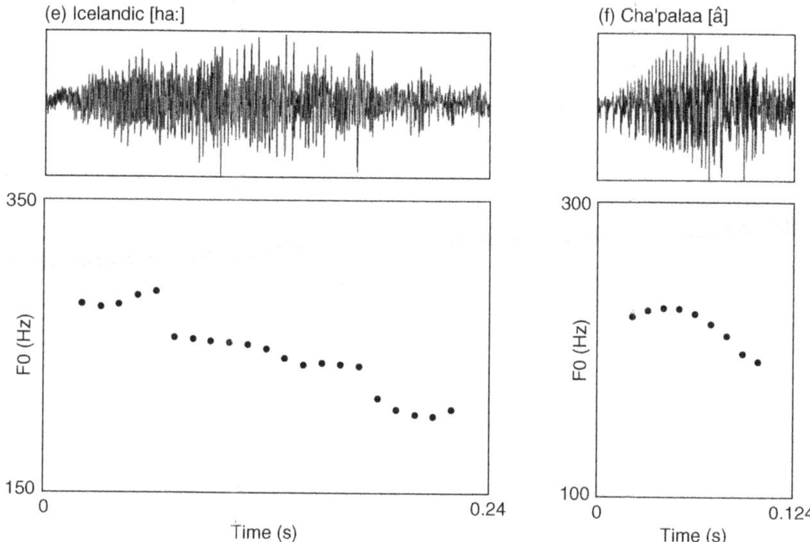

Figure 12.4: Pitch contours for typical tokens of the interjection strategy for other-initiation of repair in two languages: Icelandic and Cha'palaa.

12.3.2.2 Motivation for form of the interjection by a principle of antithesis?
Darwin's second principle by which expressions of emotion and related inner states may become fixed is a principle of antithesis: a bodily behavior can be a natural sign based not on what it *is*, but on what it *contrasts* with. Darwin (1872: 14–15) gives the example of how a dog signals affection. Darwin firstly notes the visible features of a dog in a "hostile frame of mind" – upright, stiff posture, head forward, tail erect and rigid, bristling hairs, ears forward, fixed stare – suggesting that these behaviors are intelligible by his first principle of function, that is, in that they "follow from the dog's intention to attack." With these behaviors positively associated with the aggressive meaning, he argues, the dog may exploit this to express the opposite of aggression by simply "reversing his whole bearing," that is, doing the opposite of what one would do when aggressive. Thus, when approaching his master in an "affectionate" attitude, visible behaviors include: body down, "flexuous movements," head up, lowered wagging tail, smooth hair, ears loosely back, loose hanging lips, eyes relaxed. Darwin wrote:

> None of [these] movements so clearly expressive of affection, is of the least direct service to the animal. They are explicable, as far as I can see, solely from being in complete opposition to the attitude and movements which are assumed when a dog intends to fight, and which consequently are expressive of anger. (Darwin 1872: 15–16).

Table 12.2: Some formal and functional contrasts between Huh? *and* Oh!

	Huh?	**Oh!**
vowel	low front	high back
rounding	unrounded	rounded
pitch contour	rising	falling
sequential position	initiating	responsive/closing
epistemic value	not-knowing	now-knowing

What, then, might *Huh?* maximally contrast with in form (and function)? A possibility is another common primary interjection with interactional function: *Oh!* (Heritage 1984; 1998; 2002; Wierzbicka 1991: 325). Supposing that *Oh!* is as cross-linguistically common as *Huh?*, could it be that these two simple conversationally procedural interjections get their meaning through a diagrammatic iconicity by which a maximal formal contrast in phonetic form (vowel quality, lip rounding) stands for a maximal functional contrast in interactional function (sequential position, epistemic value)? Consider Table 12.2.

If an opposition between *Huh?* and *Oh!* were to be motivated by Darwin's principle of antithesis *alone*, then it would explain the maximal distinction in form for these two functions, but it would not explain why the other-initiation of repair function would always map onto a [ha:]-like form rather than an [o:]-like form. But even somewhat weak functional motivations for those forms to have just those functions, in combination with the principle of antithesis, would presumably suffice to result in the form-meaning mappings that we observe.

12.3.2.3 Summary Naturally any ritualization arguments for form-meaning mappings like those just presented must remain tentative. Nevertheless, we submit that factors like effort, articulatory phonetics, bodily gestures, and systemic contrast should play a role in explaining phonetic similarities of interjection forms across languages, as in the striking case of *Huh?* across languages. For linguistic items like the interjections discussed here, these natural factors are overlaid by language-specific conventions. Sapir recognized this when he proposed that interjections, though linked historically to "instinctive cries," are fully conventional and "differ widely in various languages in accordance with the specific phonetic genius of each of these" (1921: 4).[13] As this chapter shows, the forms may differ less than widely. But in line with Sapir we would expect to see in interjection systems not *pure* natural meaning, but some attenuation of those forces due to the "specific phonetic genius" of individual language systems, and in general, the socially mediated nature of conventionalized interjections.

12.3.3 Question word strategy

The question word strategy for open-class other-initiation of repair shows much more variation across the languages not only in the phonetic form of the key lexical item (as is readily seen in the rightmost column of Table 12.1). Variation is also observable in whether the word may be used alone (as in the case of English *What?*), whether it may be phonetically reduced (English *Wha'?*), whether it is necessarily or more usually embedded in a more complex structure (such as in the Chintang form *themkha* "what + EMPHATIC PARTICLE" or the Icelandic form *hvað segirðu/sagðirðu* "What do/did you say?"), which question word is used (e.g., "what" versus "how"), or indeed whether the language does not seem to make this strategy available at all. We now discuss these different patterns of question word use in open-class other-initiated repair.

12.3.3.1 Bare question word "what" In some languages, the question word "what" can be used all by itself as an open-class other-initiator of repair (e.g., *What?* in English, as we saw in example 3). This question word tends to be the one also used for "things." In an excerpt from Cha'palaa (a Barbacoan language of Ecuador), a man tells his daughter (walking from off camera into the shot) not to walk in such a way that the floor vibrates, because it might cause the camera on the tripod to move. The daughter answers with the word *ti* ("what"), which then elicits a full repetition of the negative imperative form (with the addition of a reason for the admonition).[14] After the repetition H goes on to elaborate his negative imperative with a declarative clarification "It could fall."

(15) Cha'palaa (CHSF2011–01011S2 1:34–1:38)

01	H:		pikish –ne –tyu mama tremble–walk–neg mama Don't walk vibrating "mama" *Don't make the floor vibrate, daughter.*
02			(.)
03	N:	–>	ti *what*
04	H:		pikish –ne –tyu (.) tya'pu-mi tremble–walk–neg (.) fall.over–decl Don't walk vibrating (.) it falls. *Don't make the floor vibrate (.) the camera could fall.*

Here is a case from Mandarin (drawn from a recording of Beijing Mandarin). Friends are discussing each other's email addresses to determine whose is the coolest.

(16) Mandarin (CMC01)

01 Wan: haishi wo de zui ku.
or 1SG PRT most cool
then mine's the coolest.
02 Zha: ni de jiao sha?
2SG PRT call what
what's yours?
03 Wan: in my eyes. ((in English))
in my eyes.
04 Zha: -> shenme?
what
what?
05 Wan: in my eyes a. heh
PRT
in my eyes. heh
06 Nin: duo ku a. shi bijiao ku.
much cool PRT COP relatively cool
Very cool. It's cooler.

And here is an example from French:

(17) French (Torreira 27–11–07_2_F13R_2298)

01 A: Je pense pas qu'elle avait dit que les carreaux
I think not that.she had said that the tiles
I don't think she said that the tiles
02 allaient mieux
went better
looked better.'
03 B: -> Quoi?
What?
04 A: Je pense pas qu'elle avait dit que les carreaux
I think not that.she had said that the tiles
I don't think she said that the tiles
05 allaient mieux
went better
looked better.'

12.3.3.2 Abbreviated forms Some of the languages show a shortening or abbreviation of the "what" word in the function of other-initiation of repair. In an example from Kri (a Vietic language spoken in Laos), the usual word for "what" *tuqềề*, is shortened to *qềề*.

(18) Kri (050719D; 26.58)

01 M: khanờờ qôông côlq nờờ
still Mr. C qplr.agree
There's still Mr. Côlq, right?
02 L: -> **qềề?**
What? ((short for tuqềề))
03 M: coo–qiin qơr qôông côlq nờờ
really–say still Mr. C qplr.agree
(I) said there's still Mr. Côlq, right?

In an example from Russian, *shto* "what" occurs as *chio*:

(19) Russian (20110813_School_Friends_b_180010)

01 C: a ty setki ( ) ni pakupala?
PCL you-SG net-PL ( ) NEG bought-IMPFV-SG-F
You didn't buy the fly screens ( )?
02 (1.0)
03 A: -> **chio?**
what-Q ((short for *shto*))
What?
04 (0.2)
05 C: se:tki ni pakup[ala.
net-PL NEG bought-IMPFV-SG-F
didn't buy the fly screens.
06 A: [p'chimu.
whyQ
Why
07 (.)
08 A: vo:t setka
PCL net-F-SG
Here (is) a fly screen.

12.3.3.3 More complex forms In other languages, the question word occurs together with further material (either optionally or obligatorily).

In Icelandic, *hvað* "what" (neuter, singular, nominative/accusative form of *hver* "who") is used in open-class other-initiated repair as an element of the expression *hvað segirðu*, "What do you say" (often articulatorily reduced, as [kʰvasɛjɪrʏ]), or *hvað sagðirðu* "What did you say." *Hvað* cannot appear on its own as an open-class repair initiator (which may be partly explained by the fact that *hvað* usually only refers to neuter singular referents in nominative or accusative case).[15] The following example shows *hvað segirðu* combined with the open-class repair initiator *ha*. In the example, Halldóra is telling her friend Anna about a man who invited a woman she knows to a confirmation celebration at very short notice. Halldóra's speech becomes unclear due to laughter, which triggers Anna's repair initiation at line 5.

(20) Icelandic (ÍS–TAL:04…07 (00:05:40))

01 H: …þá um kvöldið sko
then in evening–the well
… then in the evening …
02 fermingardagskvöldið þá hafði hann
confirmation–day-evening–the then had he
… the evening of confirmation then he had …
03 hringt í þau (0.5) og ((laughs)) og boðið þeim
called to them and and invited them
… called them and, and invited them
04 ((laughs (1.2)))
05 A: -> ((laughs)) ha hvað segirðu
huh what say you
huh what do you say?
06 H: þegar hún Ragnheiður fermdist
when she Ragnheiður was confirmed
when Ragnheiður was confirmed
07 A: já
yes
08 H: þá hringdi hann (0.9) sem sagt (0.5) að kvöldi
then called he as said at evening
he called in the evening …
09 fermingardagsins
confirmation–day–the.GEN
… of the confirmation

In Italian, we see two distinct forms for "what" – *che* and *cosa* – occurring as an idiomatic combination. In example 22, Amerigo is talking to Giacinta about his friendship with Elisabetta (who is also present). The repair initiation is due to the fact that Giacinta doesn't catch Amerigo's word play with Elisabetta's name in line 2. In line 3 Giacinta seems to be using a continuer (from off-camera) to invite Amerigo to go ahead with his telling, and without showing any reaction to Amerigo's joking speech. Amerigo tries to resume his telling in lines 5 and 7. However, both Elisabetta's laughter in line 4 and Amerigo's smile-voice in 5 possibly make Giacinta realize that something happened in the prior turn which she didn't get, and she initiates repair in line 6. Her repetition of the pun in line 11 displays her appreciation of it, following Elisabetta's repair in line 8.

(21) Italian (Amerigo1:00.56.14)

01 Ame: da quando:: il nos– il rapporto fra
from when the our the relationship between
since:: ou– the relationship between …
02 me:: e l'ebilasetta: è cresciuto:?
me and the ebilasetta is grown
… me:: and Ebilasetta: has grow:n?

03 (Gia): [(eh)
(uh huh)
04 Eli: [ebilase(hh)tta ((laughs))
05 Ame: £(hh)e::h£, .hhh
06 Gia: –> [che cosa?
what?
07 Ame: [allo–
PCL
so–
08 Eli: hhh [ebilasetta
09 Ame: [da quando: il nostro =
from when the our
since: our ...
10 =rap[porto è-
relationship is–
... relationship has–
11 Gia: [ebila↑se(hh)t[ta
12 Ame: [((laughs))

In Chintang (a Tibeto-Burman language of Nepal), *them* "what" often occurs in combination with a special "emphasis" marker, *=kha*. In example 22, a group of villagers have been talking, when BSR – who has been silent for a long time – poses a question that is completely unrelated to the current sequence. This is received with an open-class other-initiation of repair from KBR (line 3), after which BSR asks the same question again, in reordered form (line 4).

(22) Chintang (PORCH_POSTMAN (00:32:07 – 00:32:13)

01 BSR: [moba sa]lo chace yuŋno ?
mo –ba sa –lo cha –ce yuŋ–no
DEM.DOWN–LOC who–NOM child–NSG sit–NPST
down who children is?
Up there, is that the children there?
((points upwards, with hold on *yuŋno*; after *salo*, KBR turns his head to face BSR))[16]
02 (0.3)
03 KBR: –> them(k)ha
them=kha
what=EMPH
what?
What?
04 BSR: chace uyuŋno , mo[ba]
cha –ce u –yuŋ –no mo –ba
child–NSG 3ns–sit –NPST DEM.DOWN–LOC
(the) children are, down?
Are the children there, up there?
((repeats point))
05 KBR: [ee] chace
ee cha –ce
INTERJ child–NSG
yes children
Yes, the children.

In many of the languages the "what" word can optionally occur as one element of more substantial expressions: examples are Siwu *fɔ sɔ be* "you said what?" and English *What's that?* or *What did you say?* The existence of these more complex forms suggests a derivational relation between the single word strategy ("what?") and the more complex phrase ("What did you say?").

12.3.3.4 Question words other than "what" While the question word that is used for open-class other-initiation of repair tends to be the one also used for "things," we note that in some languages a question word meaning "how" can also be used (cf. English *How do you mean?*). Here is an example from Spanish.

(23) Spanish (Torreira 23_23LM_461)

01 A: que él no estaba nunca porque la policía no
that he not is never because the police not
that he's never there because the police don't
02 deja
let
allow that.
03 B: -> ¿cómo?
how
what?
04 A: que la policía no deja
that the police not let
that the police don't allow that

Here is an example from ǂĀkhoe Hai||om (a Khoisan language of Namibia):

(24) ǂĀkhoe Hai||om GA_BEADS_2 (H002257, H002258)

01 Ma: ǂgona tsî–si nî ā ||î tē –e.
beg CONJ–3sf FUT drink DISC tea–3sn
she will beg for and drink it the tea
02 Ap: -> mâti,
how,
03 (1.0)
04 Ma: nē |gôa –te hā tsū tē ǂgona.
DEM child–3pf.A come only tea beg
These children come just to beg for tea.

In the languages in our sample, if a "how" word is available for the function of open-class other-initiation of repair, then the "what" word will also be available for that function.

12.3.3.5 Languages with no question word strategy? For two languages in our sample, the available data do not yield examples in which the question word strategy is used for open-class other-initiation of repair. These are Tzeltal, spoken in Mexico, and Yélî Dnye, spoken in island Papua New Guinea. This is not to say that the languages lack a question word for "what" (see Brown, 2010; Levinson, 2010 on the question systems of these languages). Rather, when the relevant "what" word is used in other-initiation of repair, it is to initiate restricted-focus repair, that is, it asks "what thing (did you mean)?" It remains to be seen whether further data collection may turn up cases of a question word functioning to initiate open-class repair in these languages. Our impression for many of the languages sampled here is that the question word strategy for "open-class" repair is less frequent than the interjection strategy.[17]

12.3.3.6 Summary We have seen in this section that there is considerable variation in the ways in which a question word can be used for "open-class" other-initiation of repair. One issue for us was whether a question word can be used for this function at all. We found that the answer seems usually to be "yes," but that this question word strategy appears to be less frequently used for this function than the interjection equivalent. For two languages in the sample we found no occurrences at all of a content word for open-class other-initiation of repair. A second question was the identity of the relevant question word: in most cases, it is "what?'; that is, the word for questioning "things." In a few cases, another question word may also be used, such as "how?', but this seems to be an additional option when "what?" is also available. A third question was whether the question word could be used all on its own, or whether it is embedded in a larger structure, for instance with certain morphosyntactic marking, or in a complete sentence. We found languages in which some morphosyntactic marking is obligatory (as in Icelandic) and also languages in which the question word may appear on its own but also optionally in more complex morphosyntactic structures (as in English: *What did you say?*).

12.3.4 Visible behavior in sign language and spoken language

The relevance of visible behaviors for the management of intersubjectivity in conversation is well established (Kendon, 1967; Goodwin, 1981; Rossano, Brown, and Levinson, 2008, inter alia). Goodwin has described how speakers can use *self*-repair to secure a recipient's gaze. The converse, the use of visible behaviors in *other*-initiation of repair, has been less commonly considered (but see Seo and Koshik, 2010). In our data, common visible behaviors associated with other-initiation of repair are (1) eyebrow movements (raising and/or bringing together), (2) gaze towards the speaker of T–1, and (3) head or body movement toward the speaker of T–1, as discussed above (Figure 12.2). Each of these behaviors is relevant to other-initiation of repair in its own way. Eyebrow movements commonly occur with questions in spoken as well as signed languages (Ekman, 1979; de Vos, van der Kooij, and Crasborn, 2009), recipient gaze is often used as a display of attention, and body movement toward the speaker improves perceptual access.

There is one language in our sample – Argentine Sign Language or LSA – that relies on the manual-visual channel entirely. As a sign language, LSA does not feature vocal forms as listed in Table 12.1, but its strategies for other-initiation of repair are nevertheless similar to what we find in the spoken languages in our sample. Firstly, we observe in LSA the same sequential structure for other-initiation of repair (both open-class and restricted-focus) as outlined in Figure 12.1. The strategies for open-class other-initiation of repair at T0 in LSA involve conventionalized eyebrow movements, hand signs such as "what," and movements of the head and/or body toward the signer of the problem turn.

In example 25, illustrated in Figures 12.5 and 12.6, two friends are chatting over dinner about places to live in Buenos Aires Province. Signer A (left), after multiple checks for signer B's attention, resumes a previous sequence in line 4 by asking a question (line 4 and Figure 12.5). However, B is looking down during the production of this turn. In the next turn, B initiates repair by raising his eyebrows (Figure 12.6, glossed as "ER" in line 5), then bringing them together and making the sign "wait" (Figure 12.7, glossed as "ET + wait" in line 5). As is evident from Figure 12.5, the problem is one of seeing, and accordingly, A treats it as such at line 6, when he fixes the problem by repeating the utterance and filling in the ellipsis.

(25) LSA (PIZZA 1.12)

01 A: ((looks at B while B is eating))
02 (0.3)
03 A: ((looks at B while B is looking in other direction))
q q
04 A: PRO1 SAY–NOT PRO3 PRO1 [PUs+ER::
I am not going to tell them, right?
05 B: -> [ER ET+WAIT::=
Ah wait, huh?
06 A: =PRO1 SAY-NO [PRO3 PALM-UP TAKE-CARE THIEVES
I am not going to tell them, you take care there are thieves (in the neighborhood where his friend is going to move)
07 B: [PU
Sure.

In the spoken languages in our sample, we also observed that certain visible behaviors were associated with other-initiation of repair. These behaviors are similar to the strategies used in LSA: leaning forward toward the speaker of

Figure 12.5: At line 4, A requests B's confirmation (see example 25).

Figure 12.6: At the start of line 5, B initiates repair on A's prior turn by raising his eyebrows as a first indication of a problem (see example 25).

Figure 12.7: Immediately after this, B initiates open-class repair by bringing his eyebrows together and signing "WAIT" (see example 25).

the problem turn in order to get physically and thus perceptually closer (illustrated by a case from Mandarin in Figure 12.2, p. 360 above); using certain facial expressions including marked positioning of the eyebrows (raised in some cases, drawn together in others).

The visible behaviors that we find to be associated with other-initiation of repair are arguably fitted to the role of repair in fixing problems in perceiving and understanding. For instance, leaning forward makes it more likely you will better perceive what is said. Also, eyebrow movements are associated with thinking and "wanting to know" (Ekman and Friesen, 1975; Wierzbicka, 1999: 4).

12.4 Conclusions

We have presented the first findings of a cross-linguistic study of open-class other-initiation of repair. The findings are consistent with the view that other-initiation of repair is a system, linked into other systems of language such as a system of interjections, a system for formulating questions, and a system of visible behavior. We hope that our findings will be treated as suggestive hypotheses to be tested more systematically in subsequent research.

In open-class other-initiation of repair, all spoken languages in our sample make use of a primary interjection strategy, in which a *huh*-like interjection is used to initiate repair. A notable finding was that the phonetic form of this interjection is strikingly similar across languages, suggesting that indexical-iconic motivation is one of the forces that shapes it. While we have considered possible motivations for this particular form-meaning mapping, further work is required to determine the extent to which the interjection takes a conventional form that fits the phonemic and prosodic system of a given language (as is known to be the case with interjections more generally). We would expect that natural motivation and conventionalization work together to shape the phonetic form of these items.

Most, but possibly not all, spoken languages, as well as the sign language in our sample, also have a question word strategy for open-class other-initiation of repair. This may involve a word that means "what" all by itself, or it might (in addition) involve a more complex phrase, or a different question word, such as "how." The specifics of the question word strategy are, again, in part determined by the wider linguistic system. Here the constraints of the wider system are not just phonological, as with the interjection strategy, but also grammatical. The existence of more complex forms like "What's that?" and "What did you say?" in many of the languages that can use the question word on its own suggests a derivational relation between the single word strategy ("What?") and the more complex phrase ("What did you say?").

We hope here to have made a contribution to research on repair by putting the issue of linguistic diversity front and center. The field of research on language in social interaction is only just beginning to become truly comparative, as we broaden our scope to include not only the world's larger, better-known languages, but also the much more numerous, and arguably more representative, languages spoken by smaller populations in widely ranging cultural environments.

REFERENCES

Ameka, Felix K. (1992). Interjections: the universal yet neglected part of speech. *Journal of Pragmatics* 18(2–3): 101–118.

Árnason, Kristján (1998). Toward an analysis of Icelandic intonation. In Stefan Werner, ed., *Nordic Prosody VII: Proceedings of the VIIth Conference, Joensuu 1996*, pp. 49–62. Frankfurt am Main: Peter Lang.

Austin, J. L. (1962). *How to Do Things with Words*. Oxford: Clarendon Press.

Blevins, Juliette and Garrett, Andrew (1992). Ponapaean nasal substitution: new evidence for rhinoglottophilia. In *Proceedings of the 18th Annual Meeting of the Berkeley Linguistics Society*, pp. 2–21. Berkeley: Berkeley Linguistics Society.

Bloomfield, Leonard (1933). *Language*. New York: Holt.
Boyd, Robert, and Richerson, Peter J. (1985). *Culture and the Evolutionary Process*. University of Chicago Press.
Brown, Penelope (2010). Questions and their responses in Tzeltal. *Journal of Pragmatics* 42(10): 2627–2648. doi:16/j.pragma.2010.04.003.
Burling, Robbins (1993). Primate calls, human language, and nonverbal communication. *Current Anthropology* 34(1): 25–53.
Chafe, W. (1980). *The Pear Stories: Cognitive, Cultural, and Linguistic Aspects of Narrative Production*. Norwood, NJ: Ablex.
Clark, Herbert H. (1996). *Using Language*. Cambridge University Press.
Darwin, Charles (1872). *The Expression of the Emotions in Man and Animals*. London: J. Murray.
Dehé, Nicole (2009). An intonational grammar for Icelandic. *Nordic Journal of Linguistics* 32 (01): 5–34. doi:10.1017/S0332586509002029.
Drew, Paul (1997). "Open" class repair initiators in response to sequential sources of trouble in conversation. *Journal of Pragmatics* 28: 69–101.
Durham, William H. (1991). *Coevolution: Genes, Culture, and Human Diversity*. Stanford: Stanford University Press.
Egbert, Maria (1997). Some interactional achievements of other-initiated repair in multiperson conversation. *Journal of Pragmatics* 27: 611–634.
Egbert, Maria, Golato, Andrea, and Robinson, Jeffrey D. (2009). Repairing reference. In *Conversation Analysis: Comparative Perspectives*, ed. Jack Sidnell, pp. 104–132. Cambridge: Cambridge University Press.
Ekman, Paul (1979). About brow: emotional and conversational signals. In *Human Ethology: Claims and Limits of a New Discipline*, eds. Mario von Cranach, Klaus Foppa, Wolf Lepenies, and Detlev Ploog, pp. 169–202. Cambridge: Cambridge University Press.
Ekman, Paul, and Friesen, Wallace V. (1975). *Unmasking the Face; a Guide to Recognizing Emotions from Facial Clues*. Englewood Cliffs, N.J: Prentice-Hall.
Enfield, N. J., and Stivers, Tanya, eds. (2007). *Person Reference in Interaction: Linguistic, Cultural, and Social Perspectives*. Cambridge University Press.
Goffman, Erving (1978). Response cries. *Language* 54(4): 787–815.
Goodwin, Charles (1981). *Conversational Organization: Interaction Between Speakers and Hearers*. New York: Academic Press.
Gussenhoven, Carlos (2004). *The Phonology of Tone and Intonation*. Cambridge University Press.
Halliday, M. A. K., McIntosh, A., and Strevens, P., eds. (1964). *The Linguistic Sciences and Language Teaching*. London: Longman.
Heritage, John (1984). A change of state token and aspects of its sequential placement. In J. Maxwell Atkinson and John Heritage, eds., *Structures of Social Action: Studies in Conversation Analysis*, pp. 299–345. Cambridge University Press.
(1998). Oh-prefaced responses to inquiry. *Language in Society* 27(3): 291–334.
(2002). Oh-prefaced responses to assessments: a method of modifying agreement/disagreement. In Cecilia E. Ford, Barbara A. Fox, and Sandra A. Thompson, eds., *The Language of Turn and Sequence*, pp. 196–224. Oxford/New York: Oxford University Press.

Kendon, Adam (1967). Some functions of gaze-direction in social interaction. *Acta Psychologica* 26: 22–63.
Kim, Kyu-hyun (2001). Confirming intersubjectivity through retroactive elaboration: organization of phrasal units in other-initiated repair sequences in Korean conversation. In Margret Selting and Elizabeth Couper-Kuhlen, eds., *Studies in Interactional Linguistics*, pp. 345–372. Amsterdam: John Benjamins.
Kockelman, Paul (2003). The meanings of interjections in Q'eqchi' Maya: from emotive reaction to social and discursive action. *Current Anthropology* 44(4): 467–497.
Lambrecht, Knud (1994). *Information Structure and Sentence Form: Topic, Focus, and the Mental Representations of Discourse Referents*. Cambridge University Press.
Levelt, Willem J. M. (1983). Monitoring and self-repair in speech. *Cognition* 14: 41–104.
Levinson, Stephen C. (2010). Questions and responses in Yélî Dnye, the Papuan language of Rossel Island. *Journal of Pragmatics* 2010(42): 2741–2755. doi:10.1016/j.pragma.2010.04.009.
Lyons, John (1968). *Introduction to Theoretical Linguistics*. Cambridge University Press.
Manrique, Elizabeth. 2011. Other-repair initiators in Argentine Sign Language: handling seeing and understanding difficulties in face-to-face interaction. MA thesis, Radboud University Nijmegen, August 2011.
Matisoff, James A. (1975). Rhinoglottophilia: the mysterious connection between nasality and glottality. In Charles A. Ferguson, Larry M. Hyman, and John J. Ohala, eds., *Nasálfest: Papers from a Symposium on Nasals and Nasalization*, pp. 265–287. Stanford University.
(1994). Tone, intonation, and sound symbolism in Lahu: loading the syllable canon. In Leanne Hinton, Johanna Nichols, and John J. Ohala, eds., *Sound Symbolism*, pp. 115–129. Cambridge University Press.
Moerman, Michael (1977). The preference for self-correction in a Tai conversational corpus. *Language* 53(4): 872–882.
Ohala, John J. (1983). Cross-language use of pitch: an ethological view. *Phonetica* 40(1): 1–18.
(1984). An ethological perspective on common cross-language utilization of F0 of voice. *Phonetica* 41(1): 1–16.
Raymond, Geoffrey (2003). Grammar and social organization: yes/no interrogatives and the structure of responding. *American Sociological Review* 68(6): 939–967.
Richerson, Peter J., and Boyd, Robert (2005). *Not by Genes Alone: How Culture Transformed Human Evolution*. Chicago/London: University of Chicago Press.
Robinson, Jeffrey (2006). Managing trouble responsibility and relationships during conversational repair. *Communication Monographs* 73: 137–161. doi:10.1080/03637750600581206.
Rossano, Federico, Penelope Brown, and Stephen C. Levinson (2008). Gaze, questioning, and culture. In Jack Sidnell, ed., *Conversation Analysis: Comparative Perspectives*, pp. 187–249. Cambridge University Press.
Sacks, Harvey, and Schegloff, Emanuel A. (1979). Two preferences in the organization of reference to persons in conversation and their interaction.

In George Psathas, ed., *Everyday Language: Studies in Ethnomethodology*, pp. 15–21. New York: Irvington Publishers.
Sapir, Edward (1921). *Language*. New York: Harcourt, Brace.
Schegloff, Emanuel A. (1992). Repair after next turn: the last structurally provided defense of intersubjectivity in conversation. *The American Journal of Sociology* 97(5): 1295–1345.
(2004). On dispensability. *Research on Language and Social Interaction* 37(2): 95–149.
(2006). Interaction: the infrastructure for social institutions, the natural ecological niche for language, and the arena in which culture is enacted. In Nick J. Enfield and Stephen C. Levinson, eds., *Roots of Human Sociality: Culture, Cognition and Interaction*, pp. 70–96. Oxford: Berg.
Schegloff, Emanuel A., Jefferson, Gail, and Sacks, Harvey (1977). the preference for self-correction in the organization of repair in conversation. *Language* 53(2): 361–382.
Seo, Mi-Suk and Irene Koshik (2010). A conversation analytic study of gestures that engender repair in ESL conversational tutoring. *Journal of Pragmatics* 42(8): 2219–2239. doi:16/j.pragma.2010.01.021.
Sidnell, Jack (2007). Repairing person reference in a small Caribbean community. In N. J. Enfield and Tanya Stivers, eds., *Person Reference in Interaction: Linguistic, Cultural and Social Perspectives*, pp. 281–308. Cambridge University Press.
(2010). *Conversation Analysis: An Introduction*. Chichester: Wiley-Blackwell.
Stivers, Tanya (2007). Alternative recognitionals in initial references to persons. In N. J. Enfield and Tanya Stivers, eds., *Person Reference in Interaction: Linguistic, Cultural, and Social Perspectives*, pp. 73–96. Cambridge University Press.
Talmy, Leonard (2000). *Toward a Cognitive Semantics*, vol. I: *Concept Structuring Systems*. Cambridge, MA: MIT Press.
de Vos, Connie, van der Kooij, Els, and Crasborn, Onno (2009). Mixed signals: combining linguistic and affective functions of eyebrows in questions in sign language of the Netherlands. *Language and Speech* 52(2–3): 315–339. doi:10.1177/0023830909103177.
Ward, Nigel (2006). Non-lexical conversational sounds in American English. *Pragmatics and Cognition* 14: 129–182. doi:10.1075/pc.14.1.08war.
Wierzbicka, Anna (1991). *Cross-cultural Pragmatics: The Semantics of Human Interaction*. Berlin/New York: Mouton de Gruyter.
(1999). *Emotions Across Languages and Cultures: Diversity and Universals*. Cambridge University Press.
Zhang, Wei (1999). *Repair in Chinese Conversation*. University of Hong Kong.

NOTES

1 Spoken texts such as recorded narratives and other kinds of monologue are now standardly used as sources for grammatical description, and while these will indeed contain cases of repair, those cases tend not to be a focus in linguistics (though they are sometimes a focus in psycholinguistics, e.g., Levelt 1983a inter alia). But even if one were to describe the cases of repair found in recorded monologues, one would

not capture data on the kind of repair discussed in this chapter: other-initiated repair. A further reason why field linguists have overlooked the description of repair may be a kind of "invisibility" of repair in communication, due to its very ordinariness. When field linguists say *Huh?* and it works, this doesn't end up in their field notes. It is only when it doesn't work at first that it gets noted (as in Matisoff 1994: 117, 127n8).

2 The project is supported by funding from ERC project "Human Sociality and Systems of Language Use" and "Interactional Foundations of Language" Project, Language and Cognition Department, Max Planck Institute Nijmegen.

3 Previous work on other-initiation of repair has mostly been on English (Schegloff, Jefferson, and Sacks 1977; Drew 1997; Robinson 2006, inter alia; Egbert, Golato, and Robinson 2009; Robinson this volume), but has also featured work on a few other languages (Moerman 1977 on Tai; Egbert 1997 on German; Zhang 1999 on Mandarin Chinese; Kim 2001 on Korean; Sidnell 2007 on Caribbean English Creole, inter alia).

4 We use the term "open-class" here for consistency with the conversation analytic literature on repair (cf. Drew 1997; Sidnell 2010: 119ff), though we note a terminological clash. "Open-class" has long been in use as a technical term in linguistics, with a different meaning (Halliday, McIntosh, and Strevens 1964: 22; Lyons 1968: 436; Talmy 2000: I: 22). In the lexicon, an open-class item is a member of a set that is large and in principle not limited – e.g., nouns and verbs in English – by contrast with closed-class items such as grammatical morphemes that mark case, agreement, etc. By contrast, with reference to other-initiation of repair, "open-class" does not refer to a class, but to a certain scope of *focus* in information structure terms (cf. e.g., Chafe, 1980 and Lambrecht, 1994): an open-class repair initiator has something like "unrestricted focus" (Lambrecht 1994: 233ff), that is, focus on the whole of the prior utterance. This is in contrast with other kinds of other-initiators of repair that have restricted focus on some sub-part of the relevant turn or clause (e.g., "Who?", "Where?", "Which one?", "He did what?"). For other-initiation of repair, when we say "open-class" in this chapter, we do not mean this in the linguistics sense of the word, but rather in the technical sense of "unrestricted focus."

5 Jeff Robinson notes some differences between English *What?* and *Huh?* in personal communication (cf. Robinson 2006: 142). Based on impressions from a large collection of the two forms in English, Robinson suggests that *Huh?* may be more often dealing with problems of hearing and understanding, while *What?* may be more likely to extend into dealing with problems of alignment/agreement/affiliation. He notes that *What?* can show greater formal variation as well (e.g., greater variety of prosodic variants). See Robinson (2006) for discussion of other distinctions in the English system for open-class other-initiation of repair; also Egbert, Golato and Robinson (2009), Robinson (this volume).

6 The data are all recordings of maximally informal interaction, typically between people who know each other well (family, friends, neighbors). None of the data are from institutional contexts. This means that we do not have the range of data necessary for looking at distinctions in formality or politeness. In most cases, the data were video-recorded, except in the cases of Icelandic and Hungarian, which were audio-only. In most cases, the data were collected in fieldwork by the researcher (with funding from MPI Nijmegen and ERC HSSLU project). Data

collection for ǂĀkhoe Haiǁom and Yurakaré was funded by the DoBeS program of the Volkswagen Foundation. We thank the University of Iceland and the Árni Magnússon Institute for Icelandic Studies for access to conversations in ÍS-TAL, the Corpus of Spoken Icelandic (*Íslenskur Talmálsbanki*), and Monica Turk for giving us access to her Beijing Mandarin data.

7 The forms in this column are representative tokens observed in our data sample. There is no implication that these are the only forms found in the language. A closed-mouth version [hm] was observed in the data for some of the languages, and therefore included in the table. It is likely that it is available in more languages and would surface in larger data samples.

8 We list LSA (Argentine Sign Language) for completeness in this table but we cannot give entries for the rightmost two slots because this table lists only vocal sounds. See section 3.4 for discussion of the situation in LSA (see also Manrique, 2011).

9 He was, however, equivocal on the non-word status of these forms. In the same paragraph he stated that "the sound that covers any particular non-word can stand by itself, is standardized within a given language community, and varies from one language community to another, in each case like full-fledged words" (1978: 810).

10 It is not unimaginable that the forms are borrowed across the languages, but this seems highly unlikely. While it is true that interjections, being free-standing units, may be more likely than many other elements of language to be borrowed across languages, due to their salience and their lack of grammar-specific contextual constraints, this would not be enough to account for the uncanny similarity across languages of such extreme typological and geographical diversity as those in our sample.

11 Perhaps when Levelt (1983b) refers to *uh*/*um* as a "symptom" he means that it is motivated by Darwin's third principle, that is, these interjections are comparable to "a start from a sudden noise" (Darwin 1872: 9).

12 Árnason (1998) notes that questions ending in an L% tone are "simple requests for information" while questions ending in a H% tone (less frequent) involve "a friendly suggestion by speaker A" (p. 56).

13 Human communicative systems for interaction include the full gamut of our inherited resources. Humans have a unique system of dual inheritance (Durham 1991; Boyd and Richerson 1985; Richerson and Boyd 2005), which means that a child inherits both a set of natural affordances grounded in phylogenetic history and a set of cultural affordances grounded in cultural history. In human communicative interaction we see these two sources grafted together.

14 In the repeated version of T−1, the speaker omits the address form *mama* (*mama* and *papa* are commonly used to address children in Cha'palaa, although they are more literally words referring to parents).

15 It can, however, function as a restricted-focus repair initiator picking out a singular, nominally expressed referent in nominative or accusative case, usually neuter.

16 The apparent contrast between the verbal and gestural messages can be resolved in the following way: the room in which BSR's grandchildren spend most of their time is vertically above him (licensing the pointing gesture), but to his left, thus on his "downhill" side (justifying *moba*).

17 Jeff Robinson (personal communication) confirms this for English based on a large collection.

Index

Made in the USA
Las Vegas, NV
07 March 2023

68693706R00223